W9-BKM-088

Rick Steves'
GREAT BRITAIN
& IRELAND
1999

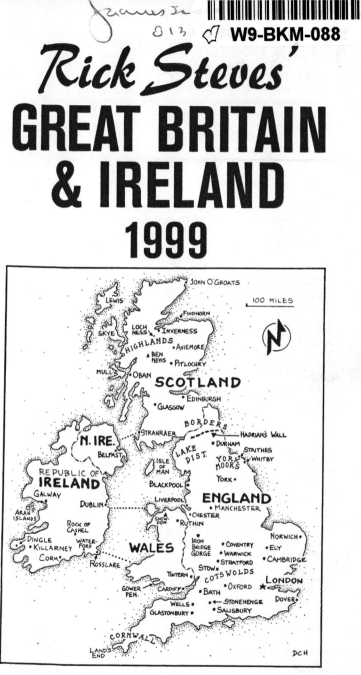

JOHN O'GROATS

100 MILES

LEWIS

FINDHORN

SKYE
LOCH NESS • INVERNESS

HIGHLANDS • AVIEMORE

BEN NEVIS • PITLOCHRY

MULL • OBAN

SCOTLAND

• EDINBURGH

• GLASGOW

BORDERS

STRANRAER HADRIAN'S WALL

N. IRE. • DURHAM

BELFAST LAKE DIST. STAITHES

YORK WHITBY
MOORS

ISLE OF MAN

REPUBLIC OF
IRELAND BLACKPOOL •

GALWAY LIVERPOOL • YORK

DUBLIN **ENGLAND**

ARAN ISLANDS • MANCHESTER

ROCK OF SNOW • CHESTER
CASHEL DON • RUTHIN

DINGLE WATER- NORWICH •
• KILLARNEY FORD IRON • COVENTRY • ELY
CORK BRIDGE • WARWICK • CAMBRIDGE
GORGE • STRATFORD
ROSSLARE **WALES** STOW
TINTERN COTSWOLDS
GOWER CARDIFF • OXFORD ★ LONDON
PEN. • BATH DOVER •
WELLS • • STONEHENGE
GLASTONBURY • SALISBURY

CORNWALL

LAND'S END DCH

John Muir Publications
Santa Fe, New Mexico

Other JMP travel guidebooks by Rick Steves

Europe 101: History and Art for the Traveler (with Gene Openshaw)
Rick Steves' Mona Winks: Self-Guided Tours of Europe's Top Museums
  (with Gene Openshaw)
Rick Steves' Postcards from Europe
Rick Steves' Best of Europe
Rick Steves' Europe Through the Back Door
Rick Steves' France, Belgium & the Netherlands (with Steve Smith)
Rick Steves' Germany, Austria & Switzerland
Rick Steves' Italy
Rick Steves' Russia & the Baltics (with Ian Watson)
Rick Steves' Scandinavia
Rick Steves' Spain & Portugal
Rick Steves' London (with Gene Openshaw)
Rick Steves' Paris (with Gene Openshaw and Steve Smith)
Rick Steves' Phrase Books for: German, Italian, French,
  Spanish/Portuguese, and French/German/Italian
Asia Through the Back Door (with Bob Effertz)

Thanks to my wife, Anne, for making "home" my favorite travel destination.
Thanks also to Roy and Jodi Nicholls for their research help, to our readers for
their input, and to local friends listed in this book who put the "Great" in Britain.

John Muir Publications, P.O. Box 613, Santa Fe, NM 87504
Copyright ©1999, 1998, 1997, 1996, 1995 by Rick Steves
Cover copyright ©1999, 1998 by John Muir Publications
All rights reserved.

Printed in the United States of America
First printing January 1999

For the latest on Rick's lectures, guidebooks, tours, and public television series,
contact Europe Through the Back Door, Box 2009, Edmonds, WA 98020,
tel. 425/771-8303, fax 425/771-0833, Web site: www.ricksteves.com.

ISSN 1090-6843
ISBN 1-56261-464-9

Europe Through the Back Door Editor Risa Laib
John Muir Publications Editors Krista Lyons-Gould, Jill Metzler
Research Assistant for London Tracy Turner
Research Assistant for Ireland Roy Nicholls
Production Rebecca Cook
Design Linda Braun
Cover Design Janine Lehmann
Maps David C. Hoerlein
Typesetting Melissa Tandysh
Printer Banta Company
Cover Photo Tower Bridge, London, England; Leo de Wys Inc./Steve Vidler

Distributed to the book trade by
Publishers Group West
Berkeley, California

The Best Destinations in Great Britain and Ireland

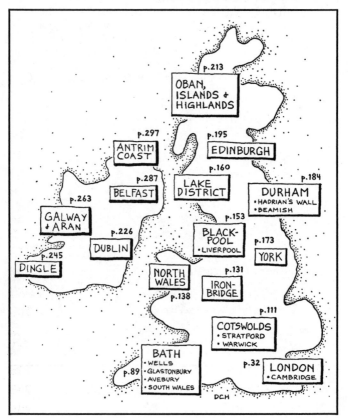

CONTENTS

Introduction 1

> Planning Your Trip 2 • Trip Costs 2 • Exchange Rates 4 • Prices, Times, and Discounts 4 • When to Go 5 • Sightseeing Priorities 5 • Itinerary Tips 6 • Red Tape and Taxes 6 • Banking 7 • Travel Smart 7 • Tourist Information 10 • Recommended Guidebooks 11 • Rick Steves' Books and Videos 11 • Maps 12 • Tours 12 • Transportation 13 • Telephones, Mail, and E-mail 20 • Sleeping 21 • Eating 27 • Stranger in a Strange Land 29 • Send Me a Postcard, Drop Me a Line 29 • Back Door Travel Philosophy 31

Great Britain

    London 32

    Bath 89

    The Cotswolds 111

    Ironbridge Gorge 131

    North Wales 138

    Blackpool 153

    Lake District 160

    York 173

    Durham and Northeast England 184

    Edinburgh 195

    Oban, Islands, and Highlands 213

Ireland

    Dublin 226

    Dingle Peninsula 245

    Galway, Aran Islands, and County Clare 263

    Northern Ireland 284

    Belfast 287

    Antrim Coast and Portrush 297

Appendix 305

> What's So Great About Britain? 305 • Basic British History for the Traveler 307 • Britain's Royal Families 308 • Architecture in Britain 309 • British TV 311 • Irish History 312 • The Irish Pub 315 • Traditional Irish Music 315 • Let's Talk Telephones 316 • London's Airports and Airlines 318 • Climate Chart 319 • Numbers and Stumblers 319 • Weights and Measures 319 • British–Yankee Vocabulary 320 • Road Scholar Feedback Form 323 • Jubilee 2000 324 • Hotel Reservation Form 325

Index 326

INTRODUCTION

This book breaks Britain and Ireland into its top big-city, small-town, and rural destinations. It gives you all the information and opinions necessary to wring the maximum value out of your limited time and money in each of these destinations. If you plan a month or less for Britain and Ireland, and have a normal appetite for information, this lean and mean little book is all you need. If you're a travel info fiend, this book sorts through all the superlatives and provides a handy rack upon which to hang your supplemental information.

Experiencing the British and Irish cultures, people, and natural wonders economically and hassle-free has been my goal for 25 years of traveling, tour guiding, and travel writing. With this new edition I pass on to you the lessons I've learned, updated for your 1999 trip.

Rick Steves' Great Britain & Ireland is a personal tour guide in your pocket. The places I cover are balanced to include a comfortable mix of exciting big cities and great-to-be-alive-in small towns. While including the predictable biggies (such as Big Ben, Stratford, bagpipes, and the Book of Kells), the book also mixes in a healthy dose of Back Door intimacy (nearly edible Cotswold villages, Gaelic folk pubs, angelic boys' choirs, and windswept Roman lookouts). I've been selective. On a short trip, visiting both Oxford and Cambridge is redundant; I cover just the best (Cambridge). There are plenty of great countryside palaces; again, I recommend just the best (Blenheim).

The best is, of course, only my opinion. But after more than two busy decades of travel writing, lecturing, and tour guiding, I've developed a sixth sense for what tickles the traveler's fancy. The places featured in this book will knock your spots off.

This Information Is Accurate and Up-to-Date

Most publishers of guidebooks that cover a country from top to bottom can afford an update only every two or three years, and then it's often by letter. Since this book is selective, covering only the top month of sightseeing, I'm able to update it each year. (Don't tell my publisher, but I'm so committed to this book, I'd do it for free.) Even with an annual update, things change. But if you're traveling with the current edition of this book, I guarantee you're using the most up-to-date information available. This book will help you have an inexpensive, hassle-free trip.

Use this year's edition. I tell you, you're crazy to save a few bucks by traveling on old information. If you're packing an old book, you'll learn the seriousness of your mistake . . . once you start your trip. To rescue those of you who will inevitably travel with a two-year-old edition of this book (and realize your mistake too late), I've sent the latest edition to my lead B&Bs in each town for you to transcribe over breakfast. Your trip costs about $10 per waking hour. Your time is valuable. This guidebook saves lots of time.

Planning Your Trip

This book is organized by destinations, each one a mini-vacation on its own, filled with exciting sights and homey, affordable places to stay. In each chapter, you'll find:

Planning Your Time, a suggested schedule with thoughts on how to best use your limited time.

Orientation, including tourist information, city transportation, and an easy-to-read map designed to make the text clear and your entry smooth.

Sights with ratings: ▲▲▲—Don't miss; ▲▲—Try hard to see; ▲—Worthwhile if you can make it; No rating—Worth knowing about.

Sleeping and **Eating** with addresses and phone numbers of my favorite budget hotels and restaurants.

Transportation Connections to nearby destinations by train and **Route Tips for Drivers**.

The Appendix is a traveler's toolkit with information on history, architecture, TV, climate, telephoning, and a British–Yankee vocabulary list.

Browse through this book, choose your favorite destinations, and link them up. Then have a great trip! You'll travel like a temporary local, getting the absolute most out of every mile, minute, and dollar. You won't waste time on mediocre sights because, unlike other guidebooks, this one covers only the best. Since your major financial pitfall is lousy, expensive hotels, I've worked hard to assemble the best accommodations values for each stop. And as you travel the route I know and love, I'm happy you'll be meeting some of my favorite British and Irish people.

Trip Costs

Five components make up your trip costs: airfare, surface transportation, room and board, sightseeing/entertainment, and shopping/miscellany.

Airfare: Don't try to sort through the mess. Find and use a good travel agent. A basic, round-trip, United States–to-London flight costs $500 to $1,000, depending on where you fly from and when. Always consider saving time and money in Europe by flying "open-jaws" (into one city and out of another; for instance, into London and out of Dublin).

Surface Transportation: For a three-week whirlwind trip of all my recommended British destinations, allow $450 per person for public transportation (train pass and key buses), or $500 per person (based on two people sharing) for a three-week car rental, gas, and insurance. About $150 more covers the ferry to Ireland and train and bus connections to its major sights. Car rental is cheapest if arranged from the United States. Train passes are normally available only outside of Europe. You may save money by simply buying tickets as you go (see Transportation, below).

Room and Board: You can thrive in Britain and Ireland on $60 a day per person for room and board. A $60-a-day budget allows $10 for lunch, $15 for dinner, and $35 for lodging (based on two people splitting the cost of a $70 double room that includes breakfast). That's doable. Students and tightwads do it on $40 ($15–20 per bed, $20 a day for meals and snacks). But budget sleeping and eating require the skills and information covered below (and in greater detail in my book *Rick Steves' Europe Through the Back Door*).

Sightseeing and Entertainment: In big cities, figure $5 to $10 per major sight (Imperial War Museum-$7.50, Edinburgh Castle-$9), $2 for minor ones (climbing church towers), $10 for guided walks, and $25 for bus tours and splurge experiences (Welsh and Scottish folk evenings). An overall average of $15 a day works for most. Don't skimp here. After all, this category directly powers most of the experiences all the other expenses are designed to make possible.

You will be tempted to buy the British Heritage Pass, which gets you into more than 500 British Heritage and National Trust properties (£28 for seven days, £39 for 15 days, £54 for 30 days; sold at airport information desks and the British Travel Centre on Regent Street in London). Of the 500 sights included (a list comes with the pass), here are the sights I describe and recommend for a three-week tour of Britain, along with their adult admission prices. A typical sightseer with three weeks will probably pay to see nearly all of these: Tower of London-£9 (London); Shakespeare's Birthplace and Anne Hathaway's Cottage-£7.50 (Stratford); Warwick Castle-£10 (near Stratford); Blenheim Palace-£8 (near the Cotswolds and Oxford); Roman and Medieval Baths-£6.30 (Bath); Stonehenge-£3.50 (near Bath); Caerphilly Castle-£2.40 and Tintern Abbey-£2.20 (South Wales); Caernarfon Castle-£4 (North Wales); Wordsworth's Dove Cottage-£4.40 (Lakes District); Housesteads Roman Fort-£2.70 (Hadrian's Wall); Edinburgh Castle-£6, Georgian House-£4.30, Gladstone's Land-£3, and Holyrood Palace-£5.30 (Edinburgh); Culloden Battlefield-£3 (near Inverness); and Urquhart Castle-£3.50 (near Loch Ness). Your pass also saves you £1 on all Guide Friday bus tours (you'll probably take four). This totals about £86 and takes the pain out of all these admissions with one big pill.

Shopping and Miscellany: Figure $1 per postcard, tea, or ice cream cone, and $2 per beer. Shopping can vary in cost from nearly nothing to a small fortune. Good budget travelers find that this category has little to do with assembling a trip full of lifelong and wonderful memories.

Exchange Rates

I list prices in pounds (£) throughout this book.

---

1 British pound (£1) = about $1.70
1 Irish pound (£1) = about $1.50

Britain: The British pound sterling (£), also called a "quid," is broken into 100 pence (p). Pence means "cents." You'll find coins ranging from 1p to £1 and bills from £5 to £50. To roughly convert pounds to dollars, multiply British prices by 2 and then subtract 10 percent: £6 is about $10.50, £3 is about $5, and 80p is about $1.40. Scotland and Northern Ireland issue their own currency in pounds, worth the same as an English pound. English, Scottish, and Northern Ireland's Ulster pounds are technically interchangeable in each region, although Scottish and Ulster pounds are "undesirable" in England. Banks in any of the three regions will convert your Scottish or Ulster pounds into English pounds at no charge.

Ireland: The Irish-English money relationship is like the Canadian-American one. The Irish call their pound a "punt." To convert punts into dollars, multiply Irish prices by 1.5: £6 is $9, £3 is $4.50, and 80p is $1.20. Use Irish, not English money on the Emerald Isle. Ireland is a different country—treat it that way.

Prices, Times, and Discounts

The prices in this book, as well as the hours and telephone numbers, are accurate as of late 1998. The economy is flat and inflation is low, so these prices should be pretty accurate in 1999. Britain and Ireland are always changing, and I know you'll understand that this guidebook, like any other, starts to yellow even before it's printed.

In Britain and Ireland you'll be using the 24-hour clock. After 12:00 noon, keep going—13:00, 14:00. . . . For anything over 12, subtract 12 and add p.m. (14:00 is 2 p.m.).

This book lists peak-season hours for sightseeing attractions (July and August). Off-season, roughly October through April, expect shorter hours, more lunchtime breaks, and fewer activities. Some places are open only on weekends or closed entirely in the winter. Confirm your sightseeing plans locally, especially when traveling between October and April.

While discounts (called "concessions" in Britain) are not

listed in this book, nearly all British and Irish sights are discounted for seniors (loosely defined as anyone retired or willing to call themselves a "senior"), youths (ages 8–18), students, groups of 10 or more, and families.

When to Go

July and August are peak season—my favorite time—with very long days, the best weather, and the busiest schedule of tourist fun. Prices and crowds don't go up as dramatically in Britain as they do in much of Europe. Still, travel during "shoulder season" (May, early June, September, and early October) is easier and a bit less expensive. Shoulder-season travelers get minimal crowds, decent weather, the full range of sights and tourist fun spots, and the joy of being able to just grab a room almost whenever and wherever they like—often at a flexible price. Winter travelers find absolutely no crowds and soft room prices, but shorter sightseeing hours. The weather can be cold and dreary, and nightfall draws the shades on sightseeing well before dinnertime. While England's rural charm falls with the leaves, city sightseeing is fine in the winter.

Plan for rain no matter when you go. Just keep going and take full advantage of "bright spells." In Ireland rainy weather is called "nice and soft." Conditions can change several times in a day, but rarely is the weather extreme. Daily averages throughout the year range between 42 and 70 degrees Fahrenheit. Temperatures below 32 or over 80 degrees are cause for headlines (see the climate chart in the Appendix). July and August are not much better than shoulder months. May and June can be lovely. While sunshine may be rare, summer days are very long. The summer sun is up from 6:30 until 22:30. It's not uncommon to have a gray day, eat dinner, and enjoy hours of sunshine afterward.

Sightseeing Priorities

Depending on the length of your trip, here are my recommended priorities:

Britain:

3 days:	London
5 days, add:	Bath, Cotswolds, Blenheim
7 days, add:	York
9 days, add:	Edinburgh
11 days, add:	Stratford, Warwick, Cambridge
14 days, add:	North Wales, Wells/Glastonbury/Avebury
17 days, add:	Lake District, Hadrian's Wall, Durham
21 days, add:	Ironbridge, Blackpool, Scottish Highlands
24 days, add:	South Wales

(The Whirlwind Tour map on page 9 and suggested three-week

itinerary on page 8 include everything in the above 24 days.
With 30 days you could slow down or add a five-day swing
through Ireland.)

Ireland:

3 days:	Not worth the trouble
5 days, add:	Dublin, Dingle Peninsula
7 days, add:	Galway and a day in Belfast
9 days, add:	County Clare/Burren
11 days, add:	Northern Ireland's Antrim Coast
15 days, add:	Aran Islands, Wicklow area

Itinerary Tips

Most people fly into London and remain there for a few days.
Instead, consider a gentler small-town start in Bath, and visit London at the end of your trip. You'll be more rested and ready to
tackle Britain's greatest city. Heathrow Airport has direct connections to Bath and other cities.

To give yourself a little rootedness, minimize one-night
stands. It's worth a long drive after dinner to be settled into a
town for two nights. B&Bs are also more likely to give a good
price to someone staying more than one night.

Many people save a couple of days and a lot of miles by
going directly from the Lake District to Edinburgh and skipping
the long joyride through Scotland. I consider a trip to Wales,
rather than Scotland or Ireland, the best quick look at Celtic
Britain.

Ireland, because of its nature and the expense and headaches
involved in getting there, is not worth a very quick visit. It
requires a minimum of five days. Don't overlook the handy ferry
connections from Belfast to Scotland and from southeast Ireland
to France. If you ask the Irish about ferries, they'll say, "I don't
believe in them. But they're there."

Red Tape and Taxes

You need a passport, but no visa or shots, to travel in Britain and
Ireland.

Sales Tax: Britain's and Ireland's sales tax—the "value added
tax," or VAT (17.5 percent)—is built into the price of nearly
everything you buy. Tourists can get this VAT refunded on souvenirs they take out of the country. But unless you buy something
worth at least $100, your refund won't be worth the trouble.
Before you make a substantial purchase of merchandise, ask the
store clerk if you will be able to get a VAT refund. You'll likely
get a "Tax-Free Shopping Cheque" which is redeemable for cash
or credit-card credit at virtually any European airport before you
fly home.

Banking

Credit or debit cards are widely accepted in Britain and Ireland (and are necessary for renting a car and handy for booking rooms and theater and transportation tickets over the phone). For cash advances you'll find that Barclays, National Westminster, and places displaying an Access or Eurocard sign accept MasterCard. Visa is accepted at Barclays and Midland banks. In general Visa is far more widely accepted than American Express.

Many travelers also carry an ATM card. They get you a better exchange rate than traveler's checks and are as commonplace in Britain and Ireland as they are in the United States. Be certain your PIN is only four numbers long.

Traveler's checks work fine in Britain and Ireland. Many people traveling exclusively in Great Britain buy traveler's checks in pounds sterling. On the road, save time and money by changing plenty of money at a time. Banks commonly charge a commission fee of £2 to £4 or even more. While policies vary, some British banks favor various traveler's checks by waiving the commission: Barclays and Visa checks at Barclays banks, American Express checks at Lloyds banks, and Thomas Cook checks at Midland banks or Cook offices. American Express exchange offices don't charge a commission on their checks or any others. This can save you around 2 percent. But don't let this cloud your assessment of their exchange rates.

On my last trip I bought all my pounds in cash from a good American foreign exchange service, stowed them safely in my money belt, and never needed a bank. Even in jolly old England and friendly Ireland you should use a money belt. Thieves target tourists. A money belt (call 425/771-8303 for our free newsletter/catalog) provides peace of mind. You can carry lots of cash safely in a money belt—and, given the high bank fees, you should.

Bank holidays bring most businesses to a grinding halt on Christmas, December 26, New Year's Day, Good Friday, Easter Monday, the first and last Monday in May, and the last Monday in August.

Travel Smart

Upon arrival in a new town, lay the groundwork for a smooth departure. Reread this book as you travel, and visit local tourist information offices. Buy a phone card and use it for reservations and confirmations. You speak the language; use it! Enjoy the friendliness of the local people. Ask questions. Most locals are eager to point you in their idea of the right direction. Pack along a pocket-size notebook to organize your thoughts, and practice the virtue of simplicity. Those who expect to travel smart, do. Plan ahead for banking, laundry, post office chores, and picnics. Mix intense and relaxed periods. Every trip (and

Best Three-Week Trip in Britain By Car

Day	Plan	Sleep in
1	Arrive in London, bus to Bath	Bath
2	Bath	Bath
3	Pick up car, Avebury, Wells, Glastonbury	Bath
4	South Wales, St. Fagans, Tintern	Stow
5	Explore the Cotswolds, Blenheim	Stow
6	Stratford, Warwick, Coventry	Ironbridge
7	Ironbridge Gorge, Ruthin banquet	Conwy
8	Highlights of North Wales	Conwy
9	Liverpool, Blackpool	Blackpool
10	Southern Lake District	Keswick area
11	Northern Lake District	Keswick area
12	Drive up west coast of Scotland	Oban
13	Highlands, Loch Ness, Scenic Drive	Highlands/Edinburgh
14	More Highlands or Edinburgh	Edinburgh
15	Edinburgh	Edinburgh
16	Hadrian's Wall, Beamish, Durham evensong	Durham
17	York Moors, York, turn in car	York
18	York	York
19	Early train to London	London
20	London	London
21	London	London
22	Side trip to Cambridge or Greenwich, London	Whew!

While this three-week itinerary is designed to be done by car, it can be done by train and bus or, better yet, with a rail 'n' drive pass (best car days: Cotswolds, North Wales, Lake District, Scottish Highlands, Hadrian's Wall). For three weeks without a car, I'd probably cut back on the recommended sights with the most frustrating public transportation (the Cotswolds, South and North Wales, Ironbridge Gorge, the Highlands). Lacing together the cities by train is very slick. With more time, everything is workable without a car.

Whirlwind Three-Week Tour of Great Britain

every traveler) needs at least a few slack days. Pace yourself. Assume you will return.

As you read this book, make note of festivals, colorful market days, and days when sights are closed. Sundays have pros and cons, as they do for travelers in the United States (special events, limited hours, closed shops and banks, limited public transportation, no rush hours). Saturdays are virtually weekdays. Popular places are even more popular on weekends—especially sunny weekends, which are sufficient cause for an impromptu holiday in this soggy corner of Europe.

Consider making the travel arrangements and reservations listed below before your trip or within a few days of arrival.

Before You Go
• Reserve a room for your first night.
• If you'll be traveling in late June, July, and August, and want to sleep in my lead listings, book the B&Bs on your route (and the Ruthin Medieval Banquet) as soon as you're ready to commit to a date.
• Confirm car rental and pick-up plans with your rental agency (picking up a car on Saturday afternoon or Sunday may be difficult).
• If you'll be attending the Edinburgh Festival (August 15–September 4 in 1999), call the festival office at 0131/473-2000 to book a ticket by credit card (Visa, MasterCard, Amex) after April 1. And while you're at it, book your Edinburgh room.
• If you want to attend the pageantry-filled changing of the keys in the Tower of London, write to Ceremony of Keys, H.M. Tower of London, London EC3 N4AB, at least five weeks in advance, with an international reply coupon (available at U.S. post offices), requesting an invitation to the "Ceremony of the Keys" (nightly at 21:30, small group of visitors allowed). Say which night or nights you can come (it's free). While they request five weeks' notice, you might try for an appointment near the end of your trip by sending a stamped envelope addressed to your London hotel once you arrive.

Within a Day or Two of Arrival
• If you'll be in London the last night of your trip, reserve a room and book tickets for a London play or concert.
• If the Royal Shakespeare Company will be performing at the Stratford Theater when you're in Stratford, book a ticket (tel. 01789/295-623).

Tourist Information
Virtually every town in Britain has a helpful tourist information center (abbreviated "TI" in this book) eager to make your visit as smooth and enjoyable as possible. Take full advantage of this service. Arrive (or telephone) with a list of questions and a proposed sightseeing plan. Pick up maps, brochures, and walking-tour information. In London you can pick up everything you'll need for Britain in one stop at the National Tourist Information Centre.

The TIs in Ireland have lost their government funding and are now little more than sales outlets for the various hotels and gimmicky new attractions. They have little of value to give you except flyers printed by whoever wants your money. Avoid the room-finding service offered by TIs throughout Britain and Ireland (bloated prices, fees, no opinions, and they take a cut from your host).

Each country's national tourist office in the United States is a wealth of information. Before your trip request any information you may want (such as city maps and schedules of upcoming festivals).

British Tourist Authority: 551 Fifth Avenue, seventh floor, New York, NY 10176, tel. 800/462-2748 or 212/986-2200, Web site: www.visitbritain.com. Meaty material, responsive to individual needs. Their free London and Britain maps are excellent (and the same maps are sold for £1.30 each at TIs in Britain).

Irish Tourist Board: 345 Park Avenue, 17th floor, New York, NY 10154, tel. 800/223-6470 or 212/418-0800, fax 212/371-9052, Web site: www.ireland.travel.ie.

Recommended Guidebooks

You may want some supplemental travel guidebooks, especially if you're traveling beyond my recommended destinations. I know it hurts to spend $25 or $35 on extra books and maps, but when you consider the money they'll save you and the improvements they'll make in your $3,000 vacation, not buying them would be penny-wise and pound-foolish.

While this book offers everything you'll need for the structure of your trip, each place you will visit has plenty of great little guidebooks to fill you in on local history. For cultural/sightseeing background in bigger chunks, Michelin and Cadogan guides to London, England, Britain, and Ireland are good. The best budget travel guides to Britain and Ireland are the Lonely Planet and Let's Go guidebooks. Lonely Planet's guidebook is more thorough and informative. Let's Go is youth-oriented with good coverage of nightlife, hosteling, and cheap transportation deals.

Rick Steves' Books and Videos

Rick Steves' Europe Through the Back Door 1999 (John Muir Publications) gives you budget-travel skills such as minimizing jet lag, packing light, planning your itinerary, traveling by car or train, finding beds without reservations, changing money, avoiding rip-offs, outsmarting thieves, hurdling the language barrier, staying healthy, taking great photographs, and much more. The book also includes chapters on 37 of my favorite "Back Doors," eight of which are in Great Britain and Ireland.

Rick Steves' Country Guides (John Muir Publications, 1999) are a series of eight guidebooks —including this book—covering Europe; France/Belgium/Netherlands; Italy; Spain/Portugal; Germany/Switzerland/Austria with Prague; Russia/Baltics; and Scandinavia. All but the last two are updated annually and come out in January.

My new **City Guides** cover Paris and London. With the sleek Eurostar train, London is now just three hours from Paris. Consider combining the two cities (and books) for a great visit.

Europe 101: History and Art for the Traveler (John Muir Publications, 1996, co-written with Gene Openshaw) gives you the story of Europe's people, history, and art. Written for smart people who were sleeping in their history and art classes before they knew they were going to Europe, *101* really helps Europe's sights come alive. However, this book is more applicable to travel on the European continent than to travel in Britain.

Rick Steves' Mona Winks (John Muir Publications, 1998, co-written with Gene Openshaw), provides fun, easy-to-follow, self-guided tours of Europe's top 20 museums. In London, *Mona* leads the way through the British Museum, British Library, National Gallery, Tate Gallery, Westminster Abbey, and the historic Westminster neighborhood.

My television series, *Travels in Europe with Rick Steves* (52 shows which air nationally on public television), includes eight half-hour shows on Britain and Ireland. A new series of 13 shows is planned for 2000, and earlier shows are still airing on both public television and the Travel Channel. These are also available in information-packed home videos, along with my two-hour slideshow lecture on Britain (call us at 425/771-8303 for our free newsletter/catalog).

Rick Steves' Postcards from Europe (John Muir Publications, 1999), my new autobiographical book, packs 25 years of travel anecdotes and insights into the ultimate 3,000-mile European adventure. Through my guidebooks, I share my favorite European discoveries with you. *Postcards* introduces you to my favorite European friends.

Maps

The maps in this book, designed and drawn by Dave Hoerlein, are concise and simple. Dave, who is well-traveled in Britain and Ireland, has designed the maps to help you locate recommended places and get to the tourist office, where you'll find more in-depth maps of the city or region (cheap or free).

Maps to buy in England: Train travelers can do fine with a simple rail map (such as the one that comes with your train pass) and city maps from the TI as you travel. If you're driving, get a road atlas (three miles to one inch) covering all of Britain. Ordnance Survey, AA, and Bartholomew editions are available for about £7 in TIs, gas stations, and bookstores. Drivers, hikers, and bikers may want much more detailed maps for the Cotswolds, North Wales, and Lake District (easy to buy locally).

Tours of Britain and Ireland

Your travel agent can tell you about all the normal Britain tours. But they won't tell you about ours. At ETBD we offer 20-day Britain tours and 14-day Ireland tours featuring the all-stars covered in this book (call us at 425/771-8303). And ETBD tour guide Roy Nicholls leads his own garden tours and south England tours in his spare time (call Roy in England at 44/1373-831-311, e-mail: brittours@online .rednet.co.uk).

Transportation in Britain and Ireland

By Car or Train?
Cars are best for three or more traveling together (especially families with small kids), those packing heavy, and those scouring the countryside. Trains and buses are best for solo travelers, blitz tourists, and city-to-city travelers.

Britain has a great train-and-bus system, and travelers who don't want (or can't afford) to drive a rental car can enjoy an excellent tour using public transportation. Britain's 100-mph train system is one of Europe's best. (For a free BritRail map and schedule, contact BritRail in the United States at 800/677-8585, 126 Westchester, White Plains, NY 10604.) Buses pick you up when the trains let you down.

My choice is to connect big cities by train and to explore rural areas (Cotswolds, North Wales, Lake District, and Highlands) footloose and fancy-free by rental car. You might consider a BritRail/Drive pass, which gives you various combinations of rail days and car days to use within a month's time.

Deals on Rails, Wheels, and Wings in Britain
Regular tickets on Britain's great train system (15,000 departures from 2,400 stations daily) are the most expensive per mile in all of Europe. Those who go round-trip (leaving after 9:30), buy in advance, or ride the bus save big.

Buying Train Tickets in Advance: Either go direct to any station, or call and book your ticket with a credit card. To book ahead, call 0345/484-950 (from the States call 011/44/345/484-950) to find out the schedule and best fare for your journey; then you'll be referred to the appropriate number to call—depending on the particular rail company—to book your ticket. Here are a few of the many deals. **Super Apex** fares offer the greatest savings, but must be booked at least 14 days in advance and apply only to journeys of about 250 miles (i.e., London–Edinburgh). **Apex** fares must be booked at least seven days in advance for journeys of about 100 miles (i.e., London–York) or longer. (You can book Apex and Super Apex tickets as early as six to eight weeks before your journey; be warned that cheap fares go fast in summer, tickets are non-refundable, and that you'll need to pin down dates and times.) To save a few pounds, get a **Super Advance** ticket (for any journey for any day) by buying your ticket before 14:00 on the day prior to

Cost of Public Transportation

1999 BRITRAIL CLASSIC PASS

	Adult first class	Adult standard	Senior (60+) first class	16-25 youth standard
8 consec. days	$400	$265	$340	$215
15 consec. days	600	400	510	280
22 consec. days	760	505	645	355
1 month	900	600	765	420

"Standard" is the polite British term for "second" class. No senior discounts for standard class. For each adult pass you buy, one child (5-15) gets a free pass of the same type (ask for the "Family Pass"). Additional kids pay the normal half-adult rate. Kids under 5: free. The "Family Pass" is available with all BritRail passes, except the SouthEast pass. These rules also apply to the Flexipasses listed below. "Party Pass" versions of Classic and Flexipasses are available, 1st-class only, for groups of up to four: the 3rd and 4th persons get 50% off.

1999 BRITRAIL FLEXIPASS

	Adult first class	Adult standard	Senior (60+) first class	16-25 youth standard
4 days in 2 months	$350	$235	$300	$185
8 days in 2 months	510	340	435	240
15 days in 2 months	770	515	655	360

1999 BRITRAIL PLUS CAR PASS

	First class	Senior (60+)	Standard class
Any 3 days by rail + 3 days by car in 1 month:	$442	$404	$358
Any 6 days by rail + 7 days by car in 1 month:	811	755	688

BritRail Plus Car gives you rail travel throughout England, Scotland and Wales and use of a Hertz car. Prices listed are per person for a manual shift 2-door economy car. An additional adult pays $250 (1st cl)/ $166 (2nd cl) for a 3+3 pass, or $364/$241 for a 6+7 pass. Add about $30 per person for a compact car, and another $45 for an intermediate car. Drivers must be 25 or older. No senior discounts for standard class.

Note: To order Classic and Flexipasses, call us at 425/771-8303; for Britrail Plus Car passes call your travel agent or Rail Europe at 800/438-7245.

Britain & Ireland:
The map shows approximate point-to-point one-way 2nd-class fares in $US by rail (solid line) and bus (dashed line). Add up fares for your itinerary to see whether a railpass will save you money.

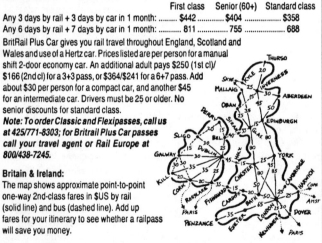

your journey. If you buy a ticket the same day you want to travel, leave after 9:30, and avoid traveling on Friday or summer Saturdays, you'll save a little with a **Super Saver** ticket. There can be up to 30 different prices for the same journey. A clerk at any station (or the helpful folks at tel. 0345/484-950, 24 hours daily) can figure out the cheapest fare for your trip. Savings can be significant. For a

London–Edinburgh round-trip, the regular fare is £73.50, Super Apex is £34, Apex is £48, Super Advance is £60, and Super Saver is £64. For a York–London round-trip, the regular fare is £59, Apex is £36, Super Advance is £43, and Super Saver is £49.

Railpasses: Consider getting a railpass. The BritRail pass comes in "consecutive day" and "flexi" versions, with price breaks for second class ("standard" class), youths, and seniors. BritRail passes cover England, Scotland, and Wales. There are now Scotland passes, England/Wales passes, and BritRail-Drive passes, which allow you to take a day of rail here and a day of car rental there. (Hertz seems to have more offices than Avis.) Any Brit pass or Eurailpass gives a discount on the Eurostar train that zips you to continental Europe under the English Channel. These passes are sold outside of Europe only. For specifics, contact your travel agent or Europe Through the Back Door (tel. 425/771-8303).

Buses: Although trains are twice as fast as buses, they're also 50 percent more expensive. Round-trip bus tickets usually cost little more than one-way fares (e.g. London–York one-way for £18, round-trip for £29). And buses go many places that trains don't. Budget travelers can save a wad with a bus pass. The National Express sells Tourist Trail bus passes (over the counter, tel. 0990-808-080, Web site: www.nationalexpress.co.uk): two days in three for £49, seven days within 21 for £120, 14 days within 30 for £187. Their U.S. sales agent offers passes as well as individual tickets for trips within Britain and into the Continent (tel. 540/298-1395). In Britain, bus stations are normally at or near train stations. The British distinguish between "buses" (for local runs with lots of stops) and "coaches" (long-distance express runs).

There are several **backpacker's bus circuits**. These hop-on-and-hop-off bus circuits take mostly youth hostelers around the country super cheap and easy with the assumption that they'll be sleeping in the hostels along the way. For instance, **Stray Travel** network does a six-day-or-more "tour" making a 1,600-kilometer circle connecting London, Bath, Stratford, the lakes, Edinburgh, York, Cambridge, and London hostels (£119 for six days, three buses weekly, commentary from driver, tel. 0171/373-7737). **Haggis Backpacker** offers a similar deal, with hop-on, hop-off buses circling Scotland (£75, 1,000 km: Edinburgh, Inverness, Skye, Fort William, Glencoe, Oban, Edinburgh, tel. 0131/557-9393, Web site: www.haggis-backpackers.com). The **Hairy Hog** does Wales for the same crowd (five-day trip for £140 with five nights in hostels, not hop-on, hop-off, tel. 01222/666-900, Web site: www.hairyhog.co.uk).

Flights: For reasonable flights, try **British Midland Airline**. If you've got more money than time, don't buy a ticket for a long train trip without considering a BM flight such as Heathrow–Dublin

BritRail Routes

KEY: * MAP NOT TO SCALE

LONDON STATIONS:

1 **VICTORIA** - S + SE ENG, CONN TO PARIS + BRUSSELS
2 **CHARING CROSS** - SE ENG
3 **WATERLOO** - S ENGLAND, PARIS + BRUSS (CHUNNEL)
4 **LIVERPOOL ST.** - EAST ANGLIA, AMSTERDAM
5 **KING'S CROSS** - MIDLANDS, N E ENG, E SCOTLAND
6 **ST. PANCRAS** - E MIDLANDS
7 **EUSTON** - MIDLANDS, N WALES, NW ENG, W SCOT
8 **PADDINGTON** - W ENG, S WALES

LONDON AIRPORTS:
A - HEATHROW   B - GATWICK

— RAIL --- BUS

···· FERRY WITH
(6H) CROSSING TIME

NOTE: FASTER ENGLISH
CHANNEL CROSSINGS WITH
HOVERCRAFT + HYDROFOIL
ON SOME RUNS CHECK!
THE CHUNNEL IS
FASTER STILL...

DCH

(10/day, 70 min, about £105 one-way, as little at £70 return for over a stay Saturday) and Heathrow–Edinburgh (8/day, 75 min, £110 one-way, £100 standby). BM also offers good £120 one-way fares on flights to Frankfurt, Amsterdam, Brussels, and Paris. For reservations and information, call 0345/554-554 or, in the United States, 800/788-0555 (the U.S. office sells Discover Europe air passes; flights out of London that are less than 500 miles—say, to Paris or Amsterdam—cost $109; flights over 500 miles cost $159). More cut-rate airlines are getting into the fray: Consider Easy Jet, Virgin Express, and Debonair.

Transportation within Ireland

Ireland's train system matches its sparse population. Trains work like spokes, connecting Dublin with each corner of the country (Rosslare in the southeast, Cork in the south, Limerick and Tralee in the southeast, Galway in the west, and Belfast in the north). Between the bus and train systems you can get around the Emerald Isle quite handily. Departures are not as frequent as the European norm.

Irish Explorer Passes make a public bus and train tour of Ireland inexpensive. All can be purchased easily and cheapest in Ireland at major stations (Dublin information tel. 01/836-6111, London office on Bond Street at tel. 0171/493-3201).

Rail only: in the Republic, any 5 days in 15 (£60); in all of Ireland, any 5 days in 15 (£75).

Bus only: in the Republic, 3 days in 8 (£28), 8 days in 15 (£68), and 15 days in 30 (£98).

Rail and bus: in the Republic, 8 days in 15 (£90); in all of Ireland, 8 days in 15 (£105) and 15 days in 30 (£180).

Car Rental

Car rental for this tour is cheapest if arranged in advance through your hometown travel agent. The best rates are weekly with unlimited mileage, or leasing (possible for "rentals" of over three weeks). You can pick up and drop off just about anywhere, any time. For a trip covering both Britain and Ireland you're better off with two separate car rentals. If you pick up the car in a smaller city, such as Bath, you'll more likely survive your first day on the British roads. If you drop it off early or keep it longer, you'll be credited or charged at a fair, prorated price. Big companies have offices in most cities. (Ask to be picked up at your hotel.) Small local rental companies can be cheaper but aren't as flexible.

The Ford 1.3-liter Escort-category car costs about $50 per week more than the smallest cars but feels better on the motorways and safer on the small roads. Remember, minibuses are a great budget way to go for five to nine people.

For peace of mind, spring for the CDW insurance (Collision

Public Transportation in Ireland

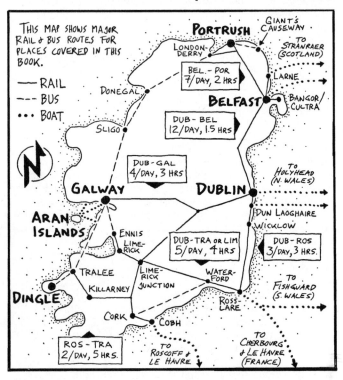

THIS MAP SHOWS MAJOR RAIL & BUS ROUTES FOR PLACES COVERED IN THIS BOOK.

—— RAIL
--- BUS
••• BOAT

GIANT'S CAUSEWAY
PORTRUSH
LONDON-DERRY
TO STRANRAER (SCOTLAND)
BEL.-POR 7/DAY, 2 HRS
LARNE
DONEGAL
BELFAST
BANGOR/CULTRA
DUB-BEL 12/DAY, 1.5 HRS
SLIGO
DUB-GAL 4/DAY, 3 HRS
TO HOLYHEAD (N. WALES)
GALWAY
DUBLIN
DUN LAOGHAIRE
ARAN ISLANDS
WICKLOW
ENNIS
LIMERICK
DUB-TRA OR LIM 5/DAY, 4 HRS
DUB-ROS 3/DAY, 3 HRS.
TRALEE
LIMERICK JUNCTION
WATERFORD
TO FISHGUARD (S. WALES)
KILLARNEY
DINGLE
CORK
COBH
ROSSLARE
ROS-TRA 2/DAY, 5 HRS.
TO ROSCOFF & LE HAVRE
TO CHERBOURG & LE HAVRE (FRANCE)

Damage Waiver, about $15 per day), which gives a zero (or low)-deductible rather than the standard value-of-the-car "deductible." A few "gold" credit cards cover CDW insurance; quiz your credit-card company on the worst-case senario. Or consider the $6/day policy offered by Travel Guard in the United States (tel. 800/826-1300).

Driving
Your U.S. license is all you need to drive in Britain and Ireland. Set your car up for a fun road trip. Establish a cardboard-box munchies pantry. Buy a rack of liter boxes of juice for the trunk. Buy some Windex and a roll of paper towels for cleaner sightseeing.

Britain: Driving in Britain is basically wonderful—once you remember to stay on the left and after you've mastered the "roundabouts." But be warned: Every year I get a few cards from traveling readers advising me that, for them, trying to drive British was a nerve-racking and regrettable mistake. To get a little slack on the roads, drop by an auto shop and buy the green

Standard European Road Signs

STOP	No Entry For Cars	All Vehicles Prohibited	No Entry	Speed Limit (in km)	Yield	No Passing	Danger	Parking
Duh				50		red	!	P

"L" (just passed the drivers test and still nervous) sign to put in your window.

A British Automobile Association membership comes with most rentals. Understand its towing and emergency road service benefits. Gas (petrol) costs over $4 per gallon and is self-serve. Green pumps are unleaded. Seat belts are required by law. Speed limits are 30 mph in town, 70 mph on the motorways, and 50 or 60 mph elsewhere. The national sign for 60 mph is a white circle with a black slash. Note that a new system of road surveillance cameras strictly enforces speeding limits. Any driver (including foreigners renting cars) photographed speeding will get a nasty bill in the mail. (Cameras—you'll see the foreboding gray boxes—flash on your rear license plate in order not to invade the privacy of anyone sharing the front seat with someone who they shouldn't be with.) Avoid driving in big cities whenever possible. Most have modern ring roads to skirt the congestion. The shortest distance between any two points is usually the motorway. Road signs can be confusing, too little, and too late. Study your map before taking off. Know the cities you'll be lacing together since road numbers are inconsistent. Miss a motorway exit and you can lose 30 minutes. A Britain road atlas (sold at gas stations and bookstores) is $10 very well spent.

Parking is confusing. One yellow line marked on the pavement means no parking Monday through Saturday during work hours. Double yellow lines mean no parking at any time. Broken yellow lines mean short stops are OK, but always look for explicit signs or ask a passerby. White lines are good news.

Even in small towns, rather than fight it, I just pull into the most central and handy "pay and display" car park I can find. Rates are reasonable by U.S. standards. Locals love to share "pay and display" stickers. If you stand by the machine, invariably someone on their way out with time left on their sticker will give it to you. I keep a bag of 10p and 20p coins in the ashtray for parking meters.

Ireland: In Ireland you'll be dealing with the same left-hand drives and roundabouts. Traffic and parking are rarely a problem. Ireland's roads, while getting much better with the financial help of the European Union, are still among the worst in Europe.

There simply aren't enough people to justify big, slick roads. Except for rush hour in the big cities, traffic is wonderfully sparse. But roads are so narrow, every car or truck that passes you comes with a slight adrenaline rush. Take things slowly. If you rush you'll wear yourself out, hit a pothole, and blow a tire—or worse.

In Ireland, a single yellow sign means parking is regulated (look for a street sign explaining the hours or limits on that street). A double yellow line means parking is not permitted at any time. Some towns require a disk which you can buy at the TI or newsstands. Parking lots are cheap and central. While theft is rare in Ireland, tourists' cars are likely targets. Don't tempt thieves needlessly.

Telephones, Mail, and E-mail

Use the telephone routinely. You can make long-distance calls directly, cheaply, and easily, and there's no language barrier. Call ahead to reserve or reconfirm rooms, check opening hours, confirm tour times, and reserve theater tickets.

To call long distance you'll need the correct area code. Britain and Ireland have about as many area codes as we have prefixes. For long distance you'll find area codes listed by city on phone booth walls, from directory assistance (free and happy to help, dial 192 in Britain), and throughout this book. Don't expect phone numbers or area codes to have a standard number of digits. For more information on telephoning, see the Appendix.

The British telephone system is great. Easy-to-find public phone booths are either coin- or card-operated. Phones take any coin from 10p to £1, and a display shows how your money supply's doing. Only completely unused coins will be returned, so put in biggies with caution. (If money's left over, rather than hang up, push the "make another call" button.) The more convenient phone-card booths are common only in cities. Buy a £2, £5, £10, or £20 phone card at newsstands, hotels, tourist offices, or post offices and use it for ease and economy. Some "credit-card phones" have a slot that will take—but not accept—your BT phone card. You need a "phone card" booth. Phone cards are your key to easy telephoning in Ireland as well. If you plan on expensive international calls (e.g., back home), save considerable money by purchasing the new cards which give you a pin number (sold where regular phone cards are sold).

The only tricky British phones you'll use are the expensive Mickey Mouse coin-op ones in bars and B&Bs. Some require money before you dial, while others wait until after you've connected. Many have a button you must push before you begin talking. But all have clear instructions. Long distance in Britain is most expensive from 8:00 to 13:00 and cheapest from 17:00 to 8:00. A short call across the country is quite inexpensive. Don't hesitate to call long distance.

Direct Dialing: When calling long distance within either Britain or Ireland, dial the area code (which starts with zero) first, then dial the local number. When dialing internationally, dial the international access code (of the country you're calling from), the country code (of the country you're calling to), the area code (without the initial zero), and the local number. For example, London's downtown area code is 0171. To call one of my listed London B&Bs from New York, I dial 011 (the U.S. international access code), 44 (Britain's country code), 171 (London's area code without the zero), then 727-7725 (the B&B's number). To call it from Britain's old York, dial 0171/727-7725.

To call my office from Britain, I dial 00 (Britain's international access code), 1 (the U.S. country code), 425 (Edmonds' area code), then 771-8303. For a listing of international access codes and country codes, see the Appendix.

USA Direct Services (with an AT&T, MCI, or Sprint calling card) are popular for calling the United States from any kind of phone. While these used to be a fine deal, direct-dial rates were recently cut in half, and now you can more cheaply call home using coins or a British or Irish phone card. For a list of calling-card operators, see the Appendix. Avoid using USA Direct for calls between European countries; it's far cheaper to call direct.

Mail: To arrange for mail delivery, reserve a few hotels along your route in advance and give their addresses to friends, or use American Express Company's mail services (available to anyone who has at least one Amex traveler's check). Allow 10 days for a letter to arrive. Phoning is so easy that I've dispensed with mail stops altogether.

E-mail: E-mail is gradually getting more common among hoteliers. I've listed e-mail addresses where possible. Cyber cafés are becoming popular in the bigger cities, giving you reasonably inexpensive and easy Internet access.

Sleeping

In the interest of smart use of your time, I favor accommodations (and restaurants) handy to your sightseeing activities. Rather than list hotels scattered throughout a city, I choose two or three favorite neighborhoods and recommend the best accommodations values in each, from $15 bunk beds to fancy-for-my-book $200 doubles. Outside of London you can expect to find good doubles, including full cooked breakfasts and tax, for $60 to $100.

I've described my recommended hotels and B&Bs with a standard code. Prices listed are for one-night stays in peak season, include a hearty breakfast, and assume you're going direct and not through a tourist information office. Prices may be soft for off-season and longer stays. While many places have larger rooms and

Sleep Code

To give maximum information with a minimum of space, I use this code to describe accommodations listed in this book. *Prices in this book are listed per room, not per person.* Breakfast is included.

S = Single room, or price for one person in a double.

D = Double or twin room. (I specify double- and twin-bed rooms only if they are priced differently, or if a place has only one or the other. When reserving, you should specify.)

T = Three-person room (often a double bed with a single).

Q = Four-person room (adding an extra child's bed to a T is usually cheaper).

b = Private bathroom with toilet and shower or tub.

t = Private toilet only. (The shower is down the hall.)

s = Private shower or tub only. (The toilet is down the hall.)

CC = Accepts credit cards (**V** = Visa, **M** = MasterCard, **A** = American Express). If CC isn't mentioned, assume you'll need to pay cash.

No smoking—With this edition, about 80 percent of my recommended B&Bs are smoke-free. While some places allow smoking in the sleeping rooms, breakfast rooms are nearly always smoke-free.

Family deal—Indicates that parents with young children can easily get a room with an extra child's bed or a discount for larger rooms. Call to negotiate the price. Teenage kids are generally charged as adults. Little kids sleep almost free.

According to this code, a couple staying at a "Db-£32, CC:VM" hotel would pay a total of £32 (about $55) per night for a room with a private toilet and shower (or tub). The hotel accepts Visa, MasterCard, or cash.

offer families special deals, Britain is peculiar in its insistence on charging per person rather than per room. Because of this, small groups often pay the same for a single and a double as they would for a triple. (Note: In this book, room prices are listed per room, not per person.)

Almost every place has three floors of rooms, steep stairs, and no elevator. Offhand, I can't think of a single elevator among my recommended places. If you're concerned about stairs, call and ask about ground-floor rooms.

All rooms have sinks. Any room without a bathroom has access to a free bath or shower on the corridor. In Britain and Ireland, rooms with private plumbing are called "en suite"; rooms that lack private plumbing are "standard." As more rooms go en suite, the hallway bathroom is shared with fewer standard rooms. If money's tight, ask for standard rooms.

British showers confuse (and scald) many tourists. A place built as a hotel has simple showers. But most B&Bs are retrofitted with showers, and rather than one central heating system, water is heated individually for each shower. While the switch is generally left on, in many rooms you'll have a hot-water switch to consider. Any cord hanging from the ceiling is for lights (not emergencies). Once in the shower you'll find a multitude of overly clever mechanisms designed to somehow get the right amount and temperature of water. Good luck.

Bed-and-Breakfasts (B&Bs)

Thank God Britain and Ireland have such lousy hotels, because the bed-and-breakfast alternative gives you double the cultural intimacy for half the price.

I'm assuming you have a reasonable but limited budget. Skip hotels. Go the B&B way. If you can use a telephone and speak English, you'll enjoy homey, friendly, clean rooms at a great price by sticking to my listings. Always call first.

If you're traveling beyond my recommended destinations, you'll find B&Bs where you need them. Any town with tourists has a tourist information office (TI) that books rooms or can give you a list and point you in the right direction. In the absence of a TI, ask people on the street for help.

B&Bs range from large guest houses with 15 to 20 rooms to small homes renting out a spare bedroom. The philosophy of the management determines the character of a place more than its size and facilities offered. Avoid places run as a business by absentee owners. My top listings are run by couples who enjoy welcoming the world to their breakfast table.

The B&Bs I've recommended are nearly all stocking-feet comfortable and very "homely," as they say in England. I look for a place that is friendly (enjoys Americans); located in a central, safe, quiet neighborhood; clean, with good beds, a sink in the room, and shower down the hall; a good value; not mentioned in other guidebooks (therefore, filled mostly by English or Irish travelers); and willing to hold a room until 16:00 or so without a deposit (though more and more places are requiring a deposit or credit-card number). In certain cases my recommendations don't meet all of these prerequisites. I'm more impressed by a handy location and a fun-loving philosophy than hairdryers and shoe-shine machines.

I promised the owners of the places I list that you will be reliable when you make a telephone reservation; please don't let them (or me) down. If you'll be delayed or won't make it, simply call in. Americans are notorious for "standing up" B&Bs. Being late is no problem if you are in telephone contact. Trusting travelers to show up is a huge, stressful issue and a financial risk for these small B&B owners.

A few tips: B&B proprietors are selective as to whom they invite in for the night. Risky-looking people (two or more single men are often assumed to be troublemakers) find many places suddenly full. If you'll be staying for more than one night you are a "desirable." Sometimes staying several nights earns you a better price—ask about it. If you book through a TI it takes a 10-percent commission. If you book direct the B&B gets it all (and you'll have a better chance of getting a discount). I have negotiated special prices with this book (often for cash). You should find prices quoted here good through 1999 (except for major holidays and festivals). In popular weekend getaway spots you're unlikely to find a place to take you for Saturday night only. If my listings are full, ask for guidance. (Mentioning this book can help.) Owners usually work together and can call up an ally to land you a bed.

B&Bs are not hotels. If you want to ruin your relationship with your hostess, treat her like a hotel clerk. Americans often assume they'll get new towels each day. The British and Irish don't, and neither will you. Hang them up to dry and reuse. You'll climb plenty of stairs. Expect good exercise and be happy you packed light.

In Britain and Ireland you'll pay £15 to £32 ($27–50) per person for a B&B in 1999. Small places (with a gross income of under £46,000) don't have to pay a 17-percent tax and can offer cheaper prices. Small places don't have hired help and can skimp on safety regulations, allowing them to operate cheaper yet. Prices include a big cooked breakfast. How much coziness, teddies, tea, and biscuits are tossed in varies tremendously.

"Twin" means two single beds, and "double" means one double bed. If you'll take either one, let them know or you might be needlessly turned away. "Standard" rooms come with just a sink. More and more are going en suite, meaning with a private shower/tub and a loo. Many better places have a basic room (with a shower down the hall) that they don't even advertise.

The British Tourist Board rates hotels and B&Bs with a crown system. B&Bs are rated as follows: no crowns (basic, clean, one bath per 12 people, safe); one crown (no nylon bed linen, a sink in the room, one bath per eight people); two crowns (tea and coffee in room on request, TV in room or lounge, luggage help); three crowns (hot evening meals, one-third of rooms with bathroom); four crowns (three-fourths of rooms with bathroom, nearly a hotel); five crowns (all with private bathroom, valet, porters, virtually a high-class hotel). Many idealistic proprietors are refusing to bow to the pressure to fill their B&Bs with all the gimmicks and extras. They continue to offer just a good bed with a shower down the hall, a traditional breakfast, and a warm welcome. So while unlisted by the tourist board, they are an excellent value.

Realizing that the facilities-based crown system was too impersonal, the tourist board added a rating measuring the cozy, personal, intangible touches (commended, highly commended, deluxe).

While many put great stock in the various tourist board ratings, most of my favorites have dropped out altogether and aren't even listed. Being "listed" is supposed to be a mark of quality. In practice it's a mark of paying your dues and playing by the materialistic rules that the tourist board sets and changes as it likes.

The Irish equivalent of the crown system is the posted tourist-board shamrock. This shamrock implies quality, but I find that it means only that the place sporting it is working with the tourist board. It really has nothing to do with value. Ignore shamrocks stuck on walls.

Making Reservations

It's possible to travel at any time of year without reservations, but given the high stakes, erratic accommodations values, number of people traveling with this book, and the quality of the gems I've listed, I highly recommend calling ahead for rooms at least a day or two in advance as you travel. When tourist crowds are down you might make a habit of calling your hotel between 9:00 and 10:00 on the day you plan to arrive, when the hotel knows who'll be checking out and just which rooms will be available. I've taken great pains to list telephone numbers with long-distance instructions (see Telephones and Mail, above; also see Appendix). Get a British or Irish phone card and use it to confirm and reconfirm as you travel. A hotel receptionist will trust you and hold a room until 16:00 without a deposit, though some will ask for a credit-card number. Honor (or cancel by phone) your reservations. Long distance is cheap and easy from public phone booths. Call and cancel if for some reason you won't be able to show up. Please don't let these people (or me) down.

While it's generally easy to find a room, a few national holidays jam things up (especially "bank holiday" Mondays) and merit reservations long in advance. Mark these dates in red on your travel calendar: Christmas, December 26, New Year's Day, Good Friday, Easter Monday, the first and last Monday in May, and the last Monday in August.

If you know exactly which dates you need and really want a particular place, reserve a room before you leave home. To reserve from home, call, fax, e-mail, or write the hotel. Phone and fax costs are reasonable. To fax, use the form in the Appendix. If you're writing, add the zip code and confirm the need and method for a deposit. A two-night stay in August would be "2 nights, 16/8/99 to 18/8/99"—European hotel jargon uses your day of departure. You'll often receive a letter back requesting one night's deposit. Your credit-card number and expiration date will usually be accepted as a deposit, though you may need to send a signed traveler's check or a bank draft in the local currency. If your credit card is the deposit, you can pay with your card or cash when you arrive; if you don't show up you'll be billed for one night. Reconfirm your reservations a day in advance for safety (or you may be bumped—really). Also, don't just assume you can extend. Take the time to consider in advance how long you'll stay.

Hostels

Britain and Ireland have more than 400 hostels of all shapes and sizes. They can be historic castles or depressing huts, serene and comfy or overrun by noisy children. Unfortunately, many of the international youth hostels have become overpriced and, in general, I no longer recommend them. The only time I do is if you're on a very tight budget, want to cook your own meals, or are traveling with a group that likes to sleep on bunk beds in big rooms. The informal private hostels are often more fun, easygoing, and cheaper. These alternatives to the IYHF hostels are more common than ever. If you're traveling alone, hosteling is the best way to conquer hotel loneliness. Hostels are also a tremendous source of local and budget travel information. If you hostel selectively you'll enjoy historical and interesting buildings.

You'll pay an average of £8 for a bed, £1 for sheets, and £2 for breakfast. Anyone of any age can hostel in Britain and Ireland. While there are no membership concerns for private hostels, IYHF hostels require membership. Those without cards simply buy one-night guest memberships for £1.50.

Forte Travelodge in Britain

The Forte Travelodge chain has 120 freeway-friendly motels throughout Britain. These are superconvenient, offering simple, clean, and comfortable rooms for up to four people for £34.50. Each room has a double bed, a single bed, a five-foot trundle bed, private shower, WC, and TV. Each hotel has an attached restaurant, good security, and a 24-hour staffed reception desk. You can reserve by credit card (CC:VMA, tel. 01384/78884 or toll-free tel. 0800/850-950 in Britain, Web site: www.travelodge.co.uk/index .htm) and pay when you check in (any time after 15:00, as late as you like). When you're ready to go (before noon), you just drop off the key, Lee. Of course they are as cozy as a Motel 6, but they're great for families, and many travelers love them. (If you call particular hotels direct, you're likely to discover some deep discounts.) The new Travel Inn chain is also opening up huge hotels with similarly tight and modern little £40 rooms for up to two adults and two kids (tel. 01582/414-341).

Eating

I don't mind English food. But then, I liked dorm food. True, England isn't famous for its cuisine and probably never will be, but we tourists have to eat. If there's any good place to cut corners to stretch your budget in Britain and Ireland, it's in eating. Here are a few tips on budget eating:

The traditional "fry" is famous as a hearty way to start the day. Also known as a "heart attack on a plate," the breakfast is especially feasty if you've just come from the land of the skimpy continental breakfast across the Channel. Your standard fry gets off to a healthy start with juice and cereal or porridge. (Try Weet-abix, a soggy English cousin of shredded wheat. Scotland serves great porridge.) Next, with tea or coffee, you get a heated plate with a fried egg, lean Canadian-style bacon, a bad sausage, a grilled tomato, and often a slice of delightfully greasy pan toast and sautéed mushrooms. Toast comes on a rack (to cool quickly and crisply) with butter and marmalade. Order kippers (herring filet smoked in an oak fire). This meal tides many travelers over until dinner. Order only what you'll eat. A B&B hostess, your temporary local mother, doesn't like to see food wasted. And there's nothing un-British about skipping the "fry"—few locals actually start their day with this heavy traditional breakfast.

These days, the best coffee is served in a *cafetiere* (also called a "French Press"). When your coffee has steeped as long as you like, plunge down the filter and pour. To revitalize your brew, pump the plunger again.

Many B&Bs don't serve breakfast until 8:00. If you need an early start, ask politely if it's possible. While they may not make you a cooked breakfast, they can usually put out cereal, toast, juice, and coffee.

Picnicking saves time and money. Try boxes of orange juice (pure by the liter), fresh bread (especially Irish soda bread), tasty English cheese, meat, a tube of Colman's English mustard, local eatin' apples, bananas, small tomatoes, a small tub of yogurt (they're drinkable), rice crackers, gorp or nuts, plain "Digestive Biscuits" (the chocolate-covered ones melt), and any local specialties. At open-air markets and supermarkets you can get food in small quantities. (Three tomatoes and two bananas cost me 50p.) Decent sandwiches (£2) are sold everywhere. I often munch a relaxed "meal on wheels" in a car, train, or bus to save 30 precious minutes.

British restaurants are fairly expensive, but cheap alternatives abound: fish-and-chips joints, Chinese and Indian take-outs, cafeterias, pubs (see below), B&Bs that serve evening meals, and your typical, good old greasy-spoon cafés. Bakeries have meat pies (and microwaves), pastries, yogurt, and cartons of "semi-skimmed" milk—ideal for fresh, fast, cheap lunches. Pasties (PASTE-eez) are "savory" (not sweet) meat pies that originated in mining country. They had big crust handles so miners with filthy hands could eat them and toss the crust. Today you'll find them in bakeries and cafés. They make a quick, cheap, hot meal.

People of leisure punctuate their day with a "cream tea." You'll get a pot of tea, two homemade scones, jam, and thick, creamy-as-honey clotted cream. For maximum pinky-waving taste per calorie, slice your scone thin like a miniature loaf of bread.

Pub Grub and Beer

Pubs are a basic part of the British and Irish social scene, and whether you're a teetotaler or a beer guzzler they should be a part of your travel here. Pub is short for "public house." It's an extended living room where, if you don't mind the stickiness, you can feel the pulse of Britain and Ireland. Most traditional atmospheric pubs are in the countryside and smaller towns. Unfortunately, many city pubs have been afflicted with an excess of brass, ferns, and video games. In any case, smart travelers use the pubs to eat, drink, get out of the rain, watch the latest sporting event, and make new friends.

Pub grub gets better each year. It's Britain's and Ireland's best eating value. For £5 you'll get a basic budget hot lunch or dinner in friendly surroundings. The *Good Pub Guide*, published annually by the British Consumers Union, is excellent. Pubs attached to restaurants often have fresher food and a chef who knows how to cook.

I recommend certain pubs, but food can spoil, and your B&B host is usually up-to-date on the best neighborhood pub grub. Ask for advice (but adjust for nepotism and cronyism, which run rampant). Locals will rarely recommend a rough pub that's a local hangout. If you want this experience (the food will be cheaper but not very good), ask for a "spit-and-sawdust" place. Big-city spit-and-sawdust places may not welcome tourists. Rural and village ones will. They are the most interesting.

Pubs generally serve assorted meat pies such as steak and kidney pie or shepherd's pie, curried dishes, fish, quiche, vegetables, and (invariably) chips and peas. Better pubs let you substitute a "jacket potato" (baked potato) for your fries. Servings are hearty, service is quick, and you'll rarely spend more than £4 to £6 ($6–9). Your beer or cider adds another pound or two. Free tap water is always available. In Britain a "ploughman's lunch" is a modern "traditional English meal" that nearly every tourist tries . . . once. Pubs that advertise their food and are crowded with locals are less likely to be the kind that serve only lousy microwaved snacks.

In a pub you order your beer at the bar. Part of the experience is standing before a line of "hand pulls" and wondering which on-tap beer you want. The British and Irish take great pride in their beer. They think that drinking beer cold and carbonated, as Americans do, ruins the taste. At pubs, long hand pulls are used to pull the traditional rich-flavored "real ales" up from the cellar. These are the connoisseur's favorites: They're fermented naturally, vary from sweet to bitter, and often include a hoppy or nutty flavor. Notice the fun names. Experiment with the obscure local microbrews. Short "hand pulls" at the bar mean colder, fizzier, mass-produced, and less interesting keg beers. Mild beers are sweeter with a creamy malt flavoring. Stout is dark and more bitter, like Guinness. For a cold, refreshing, basic American-style beer, ask for a "lager." Try the draft cider (sweet or dry) . . . carefully. Proper English ladies like a half-beer and half-lemonade "shandy." Teetotalers can order a soft drink. Drinks are served by the pint or the half-pint. (It's almost feminine for a man to order just a half; I order mine with quiche.) There's no table service. Order drinks and meals at the bar. Pay as you order, and don't tip.

Pub hours vary. The strictly limited wartime hours (designed to keep the wartime working force sober and productive) finally ended a few years ago, and now pubs can serve beer from 11:00 to 23:00, and Sunday from noon to 22:30. Children are served food and soft drinks in pubs, but you must be 18 to order a beer. A cup of darts is free for the asking. People go to a "public house" to be social. They want to talk. Get vocal with a local. Pubs are the next best thing to relatives in every town.

Stranger in a Strange Land

We travel all the way to Europe to enjoy differences—to become temporary locals. You'll experience frustrations. There are certain truths that we find God-given and self-evident, such as cold beer, ice in drinks, bottomless cups of coffee, easy shower faucets, and driving on the right side of the road. One of the benefits of travel is the eye-opening realization that there are logical, civil, and even better alternatives. A willingness to go local ensures that you'll enjoy a full dose of European hospitality.

Send Me a Postcard, Drop Me a Line

If you enjoy a successful trip with the help of this book and would like to share your discoveries, please fill out and send the survey at the end of this book to me at Europe Through the Back Door, Box 2009, Edmonds, WA 98020. I personally read and value all feedback. Thanks in advance—it helps a lot.

For our latest travel information, tap into our Web site:

www.ricksteves.com. My e-mail address is rick@ricksteves.com. Anyone can request a free issue of our newsletter.

Judging from the happy postcards I receive from travelers, it's safe to assume you're on your way to a great vacation—independent, inexpensive, and with the finesse of an experienced traveler. Thanks, and happy travels!

BACK DOOR TRAVEL PHILOSOPHY
As Taught in *Rick Steves' Europe Through the Back Door*

Travel is intensified living—maximum thrills per minute and one of the last great sources of legal adventure. Travel is freedom. It's recess, and we need it.

Experiencing the real Europe requires catching it by surprise, going casual . . . "Through the Back Door."

Affording travel is a matter of priorities. (Make do with the old car.) You can travel—simply, safely, and comfortably—anywhere in Europe for $60 a day plus transportation costs. In many ways, spending more money only builds a thicker wall between you and what you came to see. Europe is a cultural carnival and, time after time, you'll find that its best acts are free and the best seats are the cheap ones.

A tight budget forces you to travel close to the ground, meeting and communicating with the people, not relying on service with a purchased smile. Never sacrifice sleep, nutrition, safety, or cleanliness in the name of budget. Simply enjoy the local-style alternatives to expensive hotels and restaurants.

Extroverts have more fun. If your trip is low on magic moments, kick yourself and make things happen. If you don't enjoy a place, maybe you don't know enough about it. Seek the truth. Recognize tourist traps. Give a culture the benefit of your open mind. See things as different but not better or worse. Any culture has much to share.

Of course, travel, like the world, is a series of hills and valleys. Be fanatically positive and militantly optimistic. If something's not to your liking, change your liking. Travel is addicting. It can make you a happier American, as well as a citizen of the world. Our Earth is home to nearly 6 billion equally important people. It's humbling to travel and find that people don't envy Americans. They like us, but with all due respect, they wouldn't trade passports.

Globetrotting destroys ethnocentricity. It helps you understand and appreciate different cultures. Travel changes people. It broadens perspectives and teaches new ways to measure quality of life. Many travelers toss aside their hometown blinders. Their prized souvenirs are the strands of different cultures they decide to knit into their own character. The world is a cultural yarn shop. And Back Door Travelers are weaving the ultimate tapestry. Come on, join in!

LONDON

London is more than 600 square miles of urban jungle. With 9 million struggling people—many of whom speak English—it's a world in itself and a barrage on all the senses. On my first visit I felt very, very small. London is much more than its museums and famous landmarks. It's a living, breathing, thriving organism.

London has changed dramatically in recent years, and many visitors are surprised to find how "un-English" it is. Whites are now a minority in major parts of the city that once symbolized white imperialism. Arabs have nearly bought out the area north of Hyde Park. Chinese take-outs outnumber fish-and-chips shops. Many hotels are run by people with foreign accents (who hire English chambermaids), while outlying suburbs are home to huge communities of Indians and Pakistanis. London is learning—sometimes fitfully—to live as a microcosm of its formerly vast empire. With the English Channel Tunnel complete, many see more foreign threats to the Britishness of Britain.

With just a few days here, you'll get no more than a quick splash in this teeming human tidal pool. But, with a quick orientation, you'll get a good taste of its top sights, history, and cultural entertainment, as well as its ever-changing human face.

Have fun in London. Blow through the city on the open deck of a double-decker orientation tour bus, and take a pinch-me-I'm-in-Britain walk through downtown. Ogle the crown jewels at the Tower of London, hear the chimes of Big Ben, and see the Houses of Parliament in action. Hobnob with the tombstones in Westminster Abbey, duck WWII bombs in Churchill's underground Cabinet War Rooms, and brave the earth-shaking Imperial War Museum. Overfeed the pigeons at Trafalgar Square. Visit with Leonardo, Botticelli, and Rembrandt in the National Gallery.

Whisper across the dome of St. Paul's Cathedral and rummage through our civilization's attic at the British Museum. Cruise down the Thames River. You'll enjoy some of Europe's best people-watching at Covent Garden and snap to at Buckingham Palace's Changing of the Guard. Just sit in Victoria Station, at a major tube station, at Piccadilly Circus, or in Trafalgar Square, and observe. Spend one evening at a theater and the others catching your breath.

Planning Your Time

The sights of London alone could easily fill a trip to Britain. It's a great one-week getaway. On a three-week tour of Britain I'd give it three busy days. If you're flying in, consider starting your trip in Bath and make London your British finale. Especially if you hope to enjoy a play or concert, a night or two of jet lag is bad news.

Here's a suggested schedule:

Day 1: 9:00—Tower of London (Beefeater tour, crown jewels), 12:00—Munch a sandwich on the Thames while cruising from Tower to Westminster Bridge, 13:00—Follow the self-guided Westminster-Trafalgar walk (see below) with a quick visit to the Cabinet War Rooms, 15:30—Trafalgar Square and National Gallery, 17:30—Visit National Tourist Information Centre near Piccadilly, planning ahead for your trip, 18:30—Dinner in Soho. Take in a play or 19:30 concert at St. Martin-in-the-Fields.

Day 2: 9:00—If traveling around Britain, spend 30 minutes in a phone booth getting all essential elements of your trip nailed down. If you know where you'll be and when, call those B&Bs now. 9:30—Take the Round London bus tour (consider hopping off for the 11:30 Changing of the Guard at Buckingham Palace), 12:30—Covent Gardens for lunch and people-watching, 14:00—Tour British Museum. Have a pub dinner before a play, concert, or evening walking tour.

Days 3 and 4: Choose among these remaining London highlights: Tour Westminster Abbey, the British Library, Museum of the Moving Image, Imperial War Museum, Tate Gallery, St. Paul's Cathedral, or Museum of London; cruise to Greenwich or Kew; do some serious shopping at one of London's elegant department stores or open-air markets; or consider another historic walking tour.

After considering nearly all of London's tourist sights, I have pruned them down to just the most important (or fun) for a first visit of up to seven days. You won't be able to see all of these, so don't try. You'll keep coming back to London. After 25 visits myself, I still enjoy a healthy list of excuses to return.

Orientation

(downtown tel. code: 0171, suburban: 0181)

To grasp London comfortably, see it as the old town without the modern, congested sprawl. Most of the visitor's London lies between the Tower of London and Hyde Park—about a three-mile walk.

Tourist Information

London Tourist Information Centres are located at Heathrow Airport's Terminal 3 (daily 6:00–23:00, most convenient and least crowded); in the airport's Terminal 1, 2, and 3 tube stations; at Victoria Station (crowded and commercial, daily 8:00–18:00, shorter hours in winter); and at Waterloo International Terminal Arrivals Hall (daily 8:30–22:30). Like the LTICs, the handier British Tourist Info Centre (described below) covers London.

Bring your itinerary and a checklist of questions. Pick up these publications: *London Planner* (a great, free BTA monthly listing all the sights with latest hours and events), walking-tour schedule fliers, and a theater guide. Consider buying a Britain map (£1.30) and a London map (£1.30). The fine London map rivals the £4 maps sold at newsstands (free from BTA in the United States: tel. 800/462-2748 or 212/986-2200, 551 Fifth Avenue, seventh floor, New York, NY 10176, Web site: www.visitbritain .com). The TIs sell BT phone cards, passes for the tube (subway), long-distance bus tickets and passes, Great British Heritage Passes, and tickets to plays (steep booking fee). They also book rooms (avoid their £5 booking fee by calling direct). Smelling a new source of profit, London TIs are pushing a 50p-per-minute telephone information service. Avoid it.

The British Tourist Information Centre makes gathering information easy (Monday–Friday 9:00–18:30, Saturday–Sunday 10:00–16:00, just off Piccadilly Circus at 1-3 Lower Regent Street, tel. 0181/846-9000). Take advantage of its well-equipped London/ England desk, Wales desk (tel. 0171/409-0969), and Ireland desk (tel. 0171/839-8416 or 0171/493-3201). Gather whatever books, maps, and information you'll need for your entire trip at the center's extensive bookshop. Consider the *Michelin Green Guide* to London or Britain (£9). Train travelers can pick up *Let's Go: Britain and Ireland* (£15, 50 percent higher than the U.S. price) and hostelers may want the *Youth Hostel Association 1999 Guide* (£5). If traveling through the countryside, consider these maps (or their equivalents) to cover my recommended regions: Cotswolds Wyedean Official Tourist Map (Tintern to Coventry), the Lake District Touring Map (entire region or just the NW corner, Ordnance Survey), the Wales Tourist Map, and the Leisure Touring Map of Scotland. Drivers will need a *Britain Road Atlas* (£10). Stock up. You are your own guide. Be a good one.

The Scottish Tourist Centre (19 Cockspur Street, tel. 0171/ 930-8661) and the slick new French National Tourist office (Monday–Saturday 9:00–17:30, closed Sunday, 179 Piccadilly Street, tel. 0990-848-848) are nearby.

Helpful Hints

Theft Alert: Be on guard in London more than anywhere else in Britain for pickpockets and thieves, particularly on public transportation and in places crowded with tourists. Tourists, considered naive and rich, are targeted.

Changing Money: Standard transaction fees at banks are £2 to £4. American Express offices offer a good rate and change any brand of traveler's checks for no fee. There are several offices (Heathrow Terminal 4 tube station and at 6 Haymarket near Piccadilly, Monday–Friday 9:00–17:30, Saturday 9:00–17:00, Sunday 10:00–16:00, tel. 0171/930-4411). Avoid changing money at exchange bureaus. Their latest scam: They advertise very good rates with a same-as-the-banks fee of 2 percent. But the fine print explains that the fee of 2 percent is for *buying* pounds. The fee for *selling* pounds is 9.5 percent. Ouch!

Telephones: In London dial 999 for emergency help and 192 for directory assistance (free from public phone booths, otherwise 35p). The area code for any downtown London phone number is 0171; for suburban London, 0181. All numbers listed in this chapter with an area code of 0171 can be dialed directly (without the area code) within London. When dialing the suburbs (0181) from downtown (0171), you need to include the area code but it's a toll-free local call. Beware of area codes starting with 08. These are toll numbers with recorded information—usually slow moving and very expensive. Buy a handy BT phone card (£2, £3, £5, £10, or £20) at any newsstand, TI, or post office. It's a big city. If you call sights before heading out, you'll travel smoother and plan for special events or tours. While a few years ago the USA Direct services (AT&T, MCI, and Sprint) were a good value, now you can call the United States much cheaper by simply dialing direct from any phone booth (less than a dollar a minute). And new PIN phone cards (sold at exchange bureaus and in various kiosks) let you call the United States for about 12 pence a minute (that's more than five minutes for a dollar). The card (purchase for a minimum of £5) gives you an access number and a secret personal identification number. It works great from any push-button phone.

What's Up: For the best listing of what's happening (plays, movies, restaurants, concerts, exhibitions, protests, walking tours, shopping, and children's activities) and a look at the trendy London scene, pick up a current copy of *Time Out* (£1.80) at any newsstand. The TI's free monthly *London Planner* lists sights, plays, and events at least as well. For a fun Web site on London's entertainment, theater, restaurants, and news, go to www.thisislondon.com.

Children: *Time Out* has a fine listing of activities great for children and families.

Sunday Morning Activities: Plan your day carefully. Some sights don't open until 14:00 on Sunday. Some Sunday morning activities: a church service at St. Paul's or Westminster Abbey, Original London Sightseeing Bus Tour, a Thames cruise, a walking tour, or open-air markets at Petticoat Lane and Campden Market. "Speaker's Corner" in Hyde Park gets going at noon.

Free Sights: The British Museum, British Library, National Gallery, National Portrait Gallery, and Tate Gallery are always free. The Imperial War Museum, Museum of London, Natural History Museum, and Victoria and Albert Museums are free from 16:30 to closing (17:30 or 18:00), saving you £5 or so.

Travel Bookstores: Stanfords Travel Bookstore is good and stocks current editions of my guidebooks near Victoria Station (52 Grosvenor Gardens), at Covent Gardens (12 Long Acre, tel. 0171/240-3611), and at 156 Regent Street. Dillons Bookstore on the corner of Trafalgar Square is also handy with a fine travel selection.

Arrival in London

By Train: London has eight train stations, all connected by the tube and all with exchange offices and luggage storage. Enter the tube from any station and head to the stop nearest your hotel.

By Bus: The bus station is behind Victoria Station, which has a TI and tube entrance.

By Plane: For detailed information on getting from London's airports to downtown London, see Transportation Connections near the end of the chapter.

Getting Around London

London's taxis, buses, and subway system make a private car unnecessary. In a city this size you must get comfortable with public transportation. Don't be timid.

By Taxi: London is the best taxi town in Europe. Big, black, carefully regulated cabs are everywhere. I never met a crabby cabbie in London. They love to talk and know every nook and cranny in town. I ride one a day just to get my London questions answered. Rides start at £1.40 and cost about £1.50 per tube stop. Connecting downtown sights is quick and easy for about £4 (e.g., St. Paul's to the Tower). For a short ride, three people in a cab travel at tube prices. Groups of four or five should taxi everywhere. If a cab's top light is on, just wave it down. (Drivers flash lights when they see you.) Wave in either direction. They have a tiny turning radius. If waving doesn't work, ask for a taxi stand. Stick with metered cabs. While telephoning a cab gets one in minutes, it's generally not necessary and adds to the cost. London is such a great wave-'em-down taxi town that most cabs don't even have a radio phone.

By Bus: London's extensive bus system is easy to follow if you have a map listing the routes. Get a free map from a TI or tube station. Signs at stops list routes clearly. Conductors are terse

London

Approx. 1 Mile

N

LONDON STATIONS:
1 VICTORIA   5 KING'S CROSS
2 CHAR. CROSS   6 ST. PANCRAS
3 WATERLOO   7 EUSTON
4 LIVERPOOL ST.   8 PADDINGTON
* SEE BRITRAIL MAP FOR POINTS SERVED BY EACH STATION

SEE DETAIL MAP

Tower of London
St. Katherine's Dock
E. Smithfield
Tower Bridge
Tower
Barbican & Museum of London
Bishopsgate
Old St.
London Wall
Bank
Cannon
Cheapside
St. Paul's
London Wall
British Museum
Theobald's
High Holborn
Fleet St.
Covent Garden
Embankment
Strand
Russell Sq.
Euston Rd.
Shaftesbury
Theatre District & Leicester Sq.
Oxford St.
Piccadilly Circus
Piccadilly
Green Park
St. James's Park
The Mall
Bird Walk
Buck. Walk
Buck. Pal.
Whitehall
Victoria St.
Westminster Abbey
Houses of Parliament & Big Ben
Lambeth
Millbank
Tate
Vauxhall
Belgrave
Victoria West
Vict. Bus Stn.
Embankment
Chelsea
King's Road
Fulham Road
Marble Arch
Marylebone
Regent's Park
Zoo
Hyde Park
Bayswater Rd.
Kensington Gardens
Knightsbridge
Kens. Rd.
Albert Hall
Vict. & Albert Museum
Harrods
Brompton Road
Cromwell Road
Old Brompton Road
Kens. Pal.
Notting Hill Gate
Kensington High St.
Holland Park
Thames

TRAFALGAR Nat'l. Gallery, St. Martin's, Post Square

CENTRAL LONDON NEIGHBORHOODS
White-Chapel
City
Tower of London
Clerken-well
Hol-born
Old St.
Bloomsbury
Soho
South-wark
Marylebone
Mayfair
West-minster
Lambeth
Houses of Parliament
Thames
Regent's Park
Hyde Park
Kent. Gdns.
Knights-bridge
Belgravia
Pimlico
Chelsea
South Kens.
Paddington
Bayswater
Notting Hill
Notting Hill
Kens-ington
Earl's Court

DCH

London Underground

Copyright London Transport Executive

but helpful. Ask to be reminded when it's your stop. Just hop on, tell the driver where you're going, pay what he says, grab a ticket, take a seat, and relax. (The best views are upstairs.) Rides start at 90p. If the driver is not taking money, hop in, grab a seat, and the conductor will eventually sell you a ticket. If you have a transit pass, get in the habit of hopping buses for quick little straight shots (even just to get to a metro stop). During bump-and-grind rush hours (8:00–10:00 and 16:00–19:00) you'll go faster by tube.

By Tube: London's subway is one of this planet's great people-movers and the fastest (and cheapest) long-distance transport in town. Any ride in the Central Zone (on or within the Circle Line, including virtually all my recommended sights and hotels) costs £1.30. Avoid ticket-window lines in metro stations by buying tickets from coin-op machines; practice on the punchboard to see how the system works (hit "adult single" and your destination). Again, nearly every ride will be £1.30. (Note: These tickets are valid only on the day of purchase.)

Every city map includes a tube map with color-coded lines and names (free at any station window). Each line has a name (such as Circle, Northern, or Bakerloo) and two directions (indicated by end stop). In stations you'll have a choice of two platforms per line. Navigate by signs leading to the platforms (usually labeled north, south, east, or west) that clearly list the stops served by each line, or ask a local or an orange-vested staff person for help. Some tracks are shared by several lines, and electronic signboards announce which train is next and the minutes remaining until various arrivals. Each train has its final destination or line name above its windshield. Read the system notices clearly posted at the platform; they explain the tube's latest flood, construction, or bomb scare. Bring something to do to pass the waits productively. And always . . . mind the gap.

You can't leave the system without feeding your ticket to the turnstile. Save time by choosing the best street exit (look at the maps on the walls). Remember, "subway" means pedestrian underpass in "English." For tube and bus information, call 0171/222-1234.

London Tube and Bus Passes: These passes, valid on both the tube and buses, are worth considering. The "Travel Card," covering Zones 1 and 2, gives you unlimited travel for a day—starting after 9:30 and anytime on weekends—for £3.50. The all-zone version of this card costs £4.30 (includes Heathrow Airport). The "LT Card," a one-day, two-zone pass with no time restriction, costs £4.50. Families save with the one-day "Family Travel Card." The "Weekend Travel Card," for £5.20, costs 25 percent less than two one-day cards. The "7 Day Travel Card" costs £17, covers Zone 1, and requires a passport-type photo (cut one out of any snapshot and bring it from home). All passes are available for

Westminster Walk

more zones, and are purchased as easily as a normal ticket at any station. If you figure you'll take three rides in a day, get a day pass.

If you want to travel a little each day or if you're part of a group, consider buying a *carnet* for £10: you get 10 separate tickets for tube travel in Zone 1 (£1.00 each rather than £1.30).

Westminster Walk: From Big Ben to Trafalgar Square

Just about every visitor to London strolls the historic Whitehall boulevard from Big Ben to Trafalgar Square. This quick, nine-stop guided walk gives meaning to that touristy ramble. Under London's modern traffic and big city bustle lies 2,000 fascinating years of history. You'll get a whirlwind tour, as well as a practical orientation to the London. (Allow an hour for this leisurely ¾ mile walk.)

1. Start halfway across **Westminster Bridge**. Ding dong ding dong. Dong ding ding dong. Yes indeed, you are in London. **Big Ben** is actually "Not the clock, not the tower, but the bell that tolls the hour." However, since the 14-ton bell is not visible, everyone just calls the whole tower Big Ben. Although Ben (named for a fat bureaucrat) is scarcely older than my great-grandmother, it has quickly become the city's symbol.

Big Ben is the north tower of a long building, the **Houses of Parliament**, stretching along the Thames. Britain is ruled from this building. For centuries, it was the home of kings and queens. Then, as democracy was foisted on tyrants, a parliament of nobles was allowed to meet in some of the rooms. Soon, commoners were elected to office, the neighborhood was shot, and royalty moved down the road to Buckingham Palace. The current building, though it looks medieval, was built in the 1800s after a fire gutted old Westminster Palace.

Today, the House of Commons, which is more powerful than the Queen and Prime Minister combined, meets in the north half of the building. The rubberstamp House of Lords grumbles and snoozes in the south end of this 1,000-room complex.

2. Look upstream for **Westminster Pier** to the north of the bridge. Boats depart here for the Tower of London, Greenwich, and Kew (fine free public WC).

3. Walk to the edge of the bridge to the black statue of a lady on a chariot, **Boadicea**, the Queen of the Iceni. With her daughters by her side, this Celtic Xena leads her people against Roman invaders. Julius Caesar had been the first Roman to cross the Channel, but even he was weirded out by the island's strange inhabitants who worshipped trees, sacrificed virgins, and went to war painted blue. Later, Romans subdued and civilized them, building roads and making this spot on the Thames—"Londinium"—into a major urban center.

But Boadicea refused to be Romanized. In 60 A.D., after Roman soldiers raped her daughters, she rallied her people, liberated London and massacred 70,000 Romans. But the brief revolt was snuffed out, and she and her family took poison rather than surrender. (WC down stairs behind Boadicea). Cross the street and take the subway (underpass) to the busy intersection. You should be standing kitty-corner across from a big black statue of Winston Churchill.

4. Parliament Square, the small park between Westminster Abbey and Big Ben, is filled with statues of famous Brits. **Winston Churchill**, the man who saved Britain from Hitler, is shown wearing the military coat he wore as he stepped victoriously onto the beaches at Normandy after D-Day. According to tour guides, the statue has a current of electricity running through it to honor Churchill's wish that if a statue is made of him, his head shouldn't be soiled by pigeons.

Parliament Square is bordered by the Houses of Parliament and Westminster Abbey (with the two big towers). The cute little church, which snuggles under the Abbey "like a baby lamb under a ewe," is St. Margaret's Church. Since 1480 this has been *the* place for a high society wedding.

Turn right and walk away from the Houses of Parliament, down Parliament Street, which becomes Whitehall.

5. Today, **Whitehall** is the most important street in Britain, lined with the ministries of finance, treasury, and so on. Notice the ornamental arrowhead tops of the iron fences. Originally these were colorfully painted. When Prince Albert died in 1861, Queen Victoria ordered them all painted black. Probably the world's most determined mourner, when her beloved Albert died ("the only one who called her Vickie") she wore black for the standard two-and-a-half-year period of mourning for a Victorian widow—and added an extra 38 years.

Continue toward the tall square concrete monument in the middle of the road. On your right is a colorful pub, the Red Lion. Across the street, a 225-yard detour down King Charles Street leads to the Cabinet War Rooms, the underground bunker of 20 rooms that was the nerve center for Britain's campaign against Hitler (see Sights).

6. The **Cenotaph**, the big white stone monument in the middle of Parliament Street, honors those who died in two events that most shaped modern Britain—World Wars I and II. The monumental devastation of these wars helped turn a colonial superpower into a cultural colony of an American superpower.

The actual Cenotaph is the tomb-shaped slab that sits atop the obelisk. You'll notice no religious symbols on this memorial. The dead honored by this monument came from many creeds and all corners of Britain's empire.

It's hard for an American to understand the impact of the Great War on Europe. It's said that if all the WWI dead from the

Central London

British Empire were to march four abreast past the Cenotaph, the sad parade would last for seven days.

Continue up Parliament Street. Just past the Cenotaph, look across Whitehall at Downing Street, blocked off by an iron security gate.

7. #10 Downing Street is Britain's version of the White House, where the Prime Minister and his family live—a hundred yards down the blocked-off street on the right. It looks modest, but the entryway does open up into fairly impressive digs. There's not much to see here unless a V.I.P. happens to drive up. Then the bobbies check credentials, the gates open, the traffic barrier midway down the street drops into its bat-cave, the car drives in, and then . . . the bobbies go back to joking with the tourists again.

8. The Banqueting House, farther up Whitehall, is just about all that remains of what was once the biggest palace in Europe, stretching from here to the current Halls of Parliament. Henry VIII, Elizabeth I, Charles I and others lived here. The Banqueting House was the only part of the palace to survive a great fire in 1698 (see Sights).

Cross the street for a close look at the Horse Guards (11:00

inspection Monday–Saturday, at 10:00 on Sunday, and a dismounting ceremony daily at 16:00). Then continue up Whitehall.
Across the street behind the old Clarence Pub stood the original
Scotland Yard, headquarters of London's crack police force in the
days of Sherlock Holmes. Finally, Whitehall opens up into a
grand, noisy, traffic-filled square.

9. Trafalgar Square, London's "Times' Square," bustles
around the monumental column with Admiral Horatio Nelson
standing in the crow's nest. Nelson saved England at a time as
dark as World War II. After Nelson defeated the French at the
Battle of Trafalgar in 1805, Britannia ruled the waves. Napoleon's
once-invincible French army would be slowly worn down and
defeated at Waterloo.

Trafalgar is bordered by the National Gallery and St. Martin-
in-the-Fields (both described under Sights). Many Americans feel
at home with this church because its style—a church spire atop a
classical building—inspired many town churches in New England.
Its cool Cafe in the Crypt is an ideal place to end your walk and
enjoy a cup of tea.

Tours of London

▲▲▲**Original London Sightseeing Tour**—This two-hour, once-
over-lightly, double-decker bus tour drives by all the most famous
sights, providing a stressless way to get your bearings and at least
see the biggies. You "hop on and hop off" at any of the 26 stops and
catch a later bus (runs about every 10 minutes in summer, every 20
minutes in winter). The basic route comes with a fun, English-only,
live guide. (Live guided buses have only a Union Jack on the front
of the bus. If the front has many flags, it's a tape-recorded multilin-
gual tour—avoid it). It's an inexpensive form of transport as well as
an informative tour. There are daily departures from 9:00 (9:30 in
winter) until early evening from Victoria Street (one block north of
Victoria Station), Marble Arch, Piccadilly Circus, Trafalgar Square,
and so on (£12, £2 off with this book—limit two discounts per book,
they'll rip off the corner of this page, reservations unnecessary; buy
ticket from the driver, ticket good for 24 hours, tel. 0181/877-1722).
Bring a sweater and extra film. Note: If you start at Victoria at 9:30,
you can hop off near the end of the two-hour loop at the Buckingham Palace stop (Bressenden Place), a five-minute walk from the
palace and the Changing of the Guard at 11:30. The many copycat
tours offer about the same service and value.

▲▲**Walking Tours**—Several times every day top-notch local
guides lead small groups through specific slices of London's past.
Schedule fliers litter the desks of TIs, hotels, and pubs. (The
beefy, plain black-and-white *Original London Walks* newsletter lists
their extensive daily schedule.) *Time Out* lists many but not all
scheduled walks. Simply show up at the announced location, pay

£5, and enjoy two chatty hours of Dickens, the Plague, Shakespeare, Legal London, the Beatles, Jack the Ripper, or whatever is on the agenda. "Historic" pub crawls, with a fraction of the information, are a lesser value. "London Walks" is the dominant company (for recorded schedule, tel. 0171/624-3978, Web site: http://london.walks.com). They do private tours for £70.

Chris Salaman, a semiretired guide, loves to tailor walks for special and peculiar interests in London. He offers daylong private walking tours for just £30 per person including lunch, a tube travel card, and museum admissions (tel. 0181/871-9048).

▲▲**Cruise the Thames**—Boat tours with an entertaining commentary sail regularly between Westminster Pier (base of Westminster Bridge under Big Ben) and the Tower of London (£4.40, round-trip £5.60, 3/hrly, 10:20–21:00 in peak season, until 18:00 in winter, 30 min, tel. 0171/930-9033). Similar boats leave Westminster Pier for Greenwich (£5.80, round-trip £7, 2/hrly from 10:00–17:00, 50 min, tel. 0171/930-4097) and Kew Gardens (£6, round-trip £10, 7/day, 90 min, tel. 0171/930-2062). For pleasure and efficiency, consider combining a one-way cruise with a tube ride back.

Sights—Central London

Note: Summer hours are listed. Many sights have slightly shorter hours off-season. Students and seniors should ask for "concessions" (discounts). Since many places run sporadic tours, make a habit of telephoning first.

▲▲**Westminster Abbey**—England's historic coronation church is a crowded collection of famous tombs (including the tomb of the unknown soldier). Like a stony refugee camp waiting outside St. Peter's gates, this is an English hall of fame. Its tombstone history is thick with Richards, Annes, Henrys, Marys, Elizabeths, poets, and so on. The most Gothic-looking decor (like the fine choir in the center) is 19th-century neo-Gothic. Behind the high altar you'll see the historic coronation throne (£5, Monday 9:30–16:45, Tuesday–Friday 9:00–16:45, Saturday 9:00–14:45, also open for half-price on Wednesday 18:00–19:45—the only time photography is allowed, last admission one hour before closing, tube: Westminster, tel. 0171/222-5152). Praying is free—use separate marked entrance.

Well-produced and informative Walkman tours of the abbey cost £2 (offered until 15:00 weekdays, until 13:00 Saturdays). Vergers (the church equivalent of a bat boy) give more entertaining guided tours for £3 (up to 6/day, 90 min, tel. 0171/222-7110 to get times and make a reservation—generally not necessary). Tour themes are the historic church, the personalities buried here, and the great coronations. If you have 90 minutes to spare, either the Walkman or guided tour is worthwhile. Mornings are most crowded. 15:00 is less crowded. Come then and stay for the 17:00 evensong.

Evensong is on Monday, Tuesday, Thursday, and Friday at

Westminster Abbey

❶ NORTH TRANSEPT

❷ TOMB of EDWARD CONFESSOR

❸ TOMB of ELIZABETH

❹ CHAPEL of HENRY VII

❺ ROYAL AIR FORCE CHAPEL

❻ CORONATION CHAIR

❼ POET'S CORNER

❽ CORONATION SPOT

❾ CLOISTER + MUSEUM

❿ NAVE

17:00, Saturday and Sunday at 15:00. An organ recital is held Sunday at 17:45 (confirm times, tel. 0171/222-5152).

▲▲**Houses of Parliament**—While too tempting to terrorists to be opened wide to tourists, if Parliament is in session you can view debates in either the bickering House of Commons or the gentile House of Lords (Monday, Tuesday, and Thursday 14:30–22:00 with long waits until 18:00, Wednesday 9:30–22:00, Friday 9:30–15:00, use St. Stephen's entrance, tube: Westminster, tel. 0171/219-4272 for current situation).

While it's not worth a long wait and the actual action is generally extremely dull, it is a thrill to be inside and see the British government inaction. The House of Lords has more pageantry, shorter lines, and less-interesting debates (tel. 0171/219-3107 for schedule). If confronted with a too long House of Commons line, see the House of Lords first. Once you've seen the Lords you can often go directly to the Commons. If there's only one line, it's for the House of Commons. Go to the gate and tell the guard you want the Lords. You may slip right in. While other guidebooks tout the U.S. Embassy "entry cards" which get you directly in, they only give out four per day and trying to land one is most likely futile.

After passing security, slip to the left and study the big dark Westminster Hall, which survived the 1834 fire. The hall is 11th century, and its famous self-supporting hammer-beam roof was added in 1397. The Houses of Parliament are located in what was once the Palace of Westminster, long the palace of England's medieval kings before it was largely destroyed by fire in 1834. The palace was rebuilt in Victorian Gothic style after the fire (a move away from neoclassicism back to England's Christian and medieval heritage, true to the romantic period). Completed in 1860, only a few of its 1,000 rooms are open to the public. For more information about Parliament (or to get a look without actually going in), visit the **Jewel Tower** (across the street, 100 meters from the entry, weekdays 10:00–18:00 in summer) for a video presentation.

The clock tower (315 feet high) is named for its 13-ton bell, Ben. The light above the clock is lit when the House of Commons is sitting. For a hip HOP view, walk halfway over Westminster Bridge.

▲▲**Cabinet War Rooms**—This is a fascinating walk through the underground headquarters of the British government's fight against the Nazis in the darkest days of the Battle for Britain. The nerve center of the British war effort was used from 1939 through 1945. Churchill's room, the map room, and so on, are left just as they were in 1945. For all the blood, sweat, toil, and tears details, pick up the headsets at the entry and follow the included and excellent 45-minute Walkman tour (£4.60, daily 9:30–18:00, last admission 17:15, on King Charles Street just off Whitehall, follow the signs, tube: Westminster, tel. 0171/930-6961).

Horse Guards—The Horse Guards have an 11:00 inspection Monday through Saturday (at 10:00 on Sunday) and a colorful dismounting ceremony daily at 16:00. The rest of the day is terrible for camcorders (on Whitehall, between Trafalgar Square and #10 Downing Street, tube: Westminster). When the weather's bad, all pageantry is canceled.

▲**Banqueting House**—England's first Renaissance building (designed by Inigo Jones around 1620) and one of the few London landmarks spared by the 1666 fire, the House is the only surviving part of the original Palace of Whitehall. Don't miss its Rubens ceiling which, at Charles I's request, drove home the doctrine of the legitimacy of the divine right of kings. In 1649, divine right ignored, Charles I was beheaded on the balcony of this building by a Cromwellian parliament. Admission includes a restful 15-minute audiovisual history which shows the palace in banqueting action, a 30-minute tape-recorded tour that is interesting only to history buffs, and a look at a fancy banqueting hall (£3.50, Monday–Saturday 10:00–17:00, last entry at 16:00, subject to closure for government functions, aristocratic WC, immediately across

Whitehall from the Horse Guards, tube: Westminster, tel. 0171/930-4179).

▲▲**Trafalgar Square**—London's central square is a thrilling place to just hang out. Lord Nelson stands atop his 185-foot-tall fluted granite column, gazing out to Trafalgar where he lost his life but defeated the French fleet. Part of this 1842 memorial is made from the melted-down cannons of his victims at Trafalgar. He's surrounded by giant lions, hordes of people, and even more pigeons. Packets of bird-pleasing seed are on sale. (When bombed, resist the impulse to wipe immediately—it'll smear. Wait for it to dry then flake it off gently.) The square is the climax of most marches and demonstrations (tube: Charing Cross).

▲▲**National Gallery**—Wonderfully renovated, displaying Britain's top collection of European paintings from 1250 to 1900 (works by Leonardo, Botticelli, Velázquez, Rembrandt, Turner, van Gogh, and the Impressionists), this is one of Europe's classiest galleries. While the collection is huge, following the 33-stop route suggested on this map will give you my best quick tour. Don't miss the "Micro Gallery," a computer room even your dad could have fun in (closes 30 minutes earlier than museum). You can study any artist, style, or topic in the museum and even print out a tailor-made tour map. (Free, Monday–Saturday 10:00–18:00, Wednesday until 20:00, Sunday 12:00–18:00, free one-hour tours weekdays at 11:30 and 14:30 and Saturdays at 14:00 and 15:30, on Trafalgar Square, tube: Charing Cross or Leicester Square, tel. 0171/839-3321.) The CD Walkman tours, covering each room and each painting in the gallery at the push of a button, are the best I've used in Europe (£3 donation requested). With these, art lovers could spend four of the best hours of their lives wandering these halls.

National Portrait Gallery—Put off by halls of 19th-century characters who meant nothing to me, I used to call this "as interesting as someone else's yearbook." But a select walk through this five-centuries-long Who's Who of British history is quick, free, and puts a face on the story of England. An added bonus is the chance to admire some great art by painters such as Holbein, Van Dyck, Hogarth, Reynolds, and Gainsborough. The collection is well-described, not huge, and runs in historical sequence from the 16th century on the top floor to today's royal family on the bottom.

Highlights, in order, include: Henry VIII and wives (top floor landing); several fascinating portraits of the "Virgin Queen" Elizabeth I, Sir Francis Drake, Sir Walter Raleigh, and the only real-life portrait of Shakespeare (room 1); Charles I with his head on and Oliver Cromwell (room 2); self-portraits and other portraits by Gainsborough and Reynolds (room 9); the romantics (Blake, Byron, Wordsworth, and company, room 13); Queen Victoria and her era (rooms 17–21); and the present royal family including the late Princess Diana (first floor landing, rooms 16 and 28). For more

National Gallery Highlights

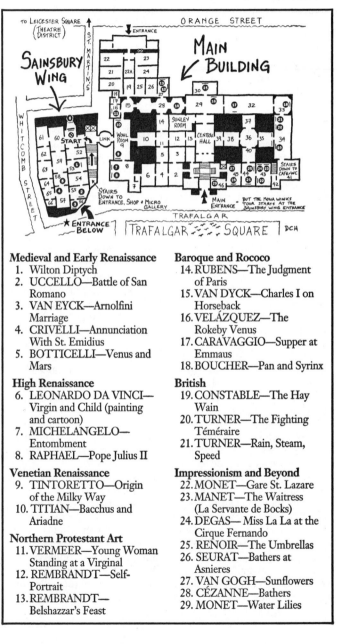

Medieval and Early Renaissance

1. Wilton Diptych
2. UCCELLO—Battle of San Romano
3. VAN EYCK—Arnolfini Marriage
4. CRIVELLI—Annunciation With St. Emidius
5. BOTTICELLI—Venus and Mars

High Renaissance

6. LEONARDO DA VINCI—Virgin and Child (painting and cartoon)
7. MICHELANGELO—Entombment
8. RAPHAEL—Pope Julius II

Venetian Renaissance

9. TINTORETTO—Origin of the Milky Way
10. TITIAN—Bacchus and Ariadne

Northern Protestant Art

11. VERMEER—Young Woman Standing at a Virginal
12. REMBRANDT—Self-Portrait
13. REMBRANDT—Belshazzar's Feast

Baroque and Rococo

14. RUBENS—The Judgment of Paris
15. VAN DYCK—Charles I on Horseback
16. VELÁZQUEZ—The Rokeby Venus
17. CARAVAGGIO—Supper at Emmaus
18. BOUCHER—Pan and Syrinx

British

19. CONSTABLE—The Hay Wain
20. TURNER—The Fighting Téméraire
21. TURNER—Rain, Steam, Speed

Impressionism and Beyond

22. MONET—Gare St. Lazare
23. MANET—The Waitress (La Servante de Bocks)
24. DEGAS— Miss La La at the Cirque Fernando
25. RENOIR—The Umbrellas
26. SEURAT—Bathers at Asnieres
27. VAN GOGH—Sunflowers
28. CÉZANNE—Bathers
29. MONET—Water Lilies

information follow the fine CD Walkman tours (donation requested, mostly history rather than art, actual interviews of 20th-century subjects) or the 50p quick overview guidebooklet. (Free, Monday–Saturday 10:00–18:00, Sunday 12:00–18:00, entry just off Trafalgar Square, around the corner from National Gallery and opposite Church of St. Martin-in-the-Fields, tel. 0171/306-0055.)

▲**St. Martin-in-the-Fields**—This church, built in the 1720s with a Gothic spire placed upon a Greek-type temple, is an oasis of peace on wild and noisy Trafalgar Square. St. Martin was a man who cared for the poor. "In the fields" was where the first church stood on this spot (in the 13th century), between Westminster and the city. Stepping inside you still feel a compassion for the needs of the people in this community. The church is famous for its great concerts. Consider a free lunchtime concert (most weekdays at 13:05) or an evening concert (Thursday–Saturday 19:30, £6–15, tel. 0171/930-0089). Downstairs you'll find a ticket office for concerts, a good shop, a brass-rubbing center, and a fine, budget, support-the-church cafeteria.

▲▲**Piccadilly Circus**—London's touristy "Town Square" is surrounded by fascinating streets and swimming with youth on the rampage. The Rock Circus offers a commercial but serious history of rock music with Madame Tussaud wax stars. It's an entertaining hour under radio earphones for rock-'n'-roll romantics (£8, daily 10:00–20:00, plenty of photo ops, many enter with a beer-buzz and sing happily off-key under their headphones—nearly as entertaining as the exhibit itself, tube: Picadilly Circus). For overstimulation, drop by the extremely trashy Pepsi Trocadero Center's "theme park of the future" for its Segaworld virtual reality games, nine-screen cinema, and thundering new IMAX theater (admission to Trocadero is free; individual attractions cost £2–8; find a discount ticket before paying full price for IMAX; between Coventry and Shaftesbury, just off Piccadilly). Chinatown, to the east, has swollen since Hong Kong lost its independence. Nearby Shaftesbury Avenue and Leicester Square teem with fun-seekers, theaters, Chinese restaurants, and street singers.

Soho—North of Piccadilly, seedy Soho is becoming trendy and is well worth a gawk. This is London's red-light district where "friendly models" wait in tiny rooms up dreary stairways and scantily-clad con artists sell strip shows. While venturing up a stairway to check out a model is interesting, anyone who goes into any one of the shows will be ripped off. Every time. Even a £3 show comes with a £100 cover or minimum (as it's printed on the drink menu) and a "security man." The door has no handle until you pay. By the way, telephone sex is hard to avoid these days in London. Phone booths are littered with racy fliers of busty ladies for sale. Some travelers gather six or eight phone booths worth of fliers and take them home for kinky wallpaper.

▲**Covent Garden**—This boutique-ish shopping district is a people-watcher's delight with cigarette-eaters, Punch 'n' Judy acts, food that's good for you (but not your wallet), trendy crafts, sweet whiffs of pot, two-tone hair (neither natural), and faces that could set off a metal detector. For the best lunch deals, walk a block or two away from the eye of this touristic tornado. Check out the places along Neal Street and Endell Street—each a block north of the tube station, and try the "Food is Fun" Dinner Crawl; see "Eating" below (tube: Covent Gardens).

▲▲▲**British Museum**—This is the greatest chronicle of our civilization anywhere. Visiting this immense museum is like hiking through Encyclopedia Britannica National Park. After an overview ramble, cover just two or three sections of your choice more thoroughly. The Egyptian, Mesopotamian (Assyrian), and Greek (Parthenon) sections are highlights.

The huge winged lions (which guarded Assyrian palaces 800 years before Christ) guard the museum's three great ancient galleries. For a brief tour, connect these ancient dots:

Start with the Egyptian. Wander from the Rosetta Stone past the many statues. At the end of the hall, climb the stairs to mummyland.

Back at the winged lions, wander through the dark, violent, and mysterious Assyrian rooms. The Nimrud Gallery is lined with royal propaganda reliefs and wounded lions.

The most modern of the ancient art fills the Greek section. Find room #1 behind the winged lions and start your walk through Greek art history with the simple and primitive Cycladian fertility figures. Later, painted vases show a culture really into partying. The finale is the Elgin Marbles. The much wrangled over bits of the Athenian Parthenon (from 450 B.C.) are even more impressive than they look. To best appreciate these ancient carvings, read through the orientation material in the tiny intro rooms between rooms 7 and 8. (Free but £2 donation requested, Monday–Saturday 10:00–17:00, Sunday 14:30–18:00, least crowded weekday mornings, guided 90-minute £6 tours offered daily—3/day on Sunday, 2/day in winter—call museum for times, tube: Tottenham Court Road, tel. 0171/636-1555.)

The British Museum is undergoing a major transformation for the millennium and for its 250th birthday in 2003. With more than 6 million visitors a year, Britain's most popular museum is due for an upgrade. The Great Court, unused until now, will become a two-acre glass-domed hub of a new cultural complex. From here you'll enter a reorganized (better-flowing) British museum, a restored and once-again-public Round Reading Room (Marx's hangout), new Ethnographic Galleries (collections on life

British Library

in Africa, Asia, and the Americas will fill what used to be the British Library quarters), and a bustling people zone of shops and restaurants. For the latest, see www.british-museum.ac.uk.

▲▲**British Library**—Wander through the manuscripts that have enlightened and brightened our lives for centuries in the new and impressive British Library. While containing 180 miles of bookshelves filling London's deepest basement, one beautiful room filled with state-of-the-art glass display cases shows you the treasures: ancient maps, early gospels on papyrus, illuminated manuscripts from the early Middle Ages, the Gütenberg Bible, the Magna Carta, pages from Leonardo's notebooks, and original writing by the titans of English literature, from Chaucer and Shakespeare to Dickens and Wordsworth. There's also a wall dedicated to music with manuscripts from Beethoven to the Beatles. To virtually flip through the pages of a few precious books, drop by the "Turning the Pages" room. (Free, Monday–Saturday 9:30–18:00, Sunday 11:00–17:00, tube to King's Cross/St. Pancras; leaving station, turn right and walk a block to 96 Euston Road, tel. 0171/412-7332, Web site: www.bl.uk.)

▲**Buckingham Palace**—In order to pay for the restoration of fire-damaged Windsor Castle, the royal family is opening its lavish home to the public until 2000 (£10 to see the state apartments and throne room, open August and September only, daily 9:30–16:30, limited to 8,000 visitors a day—come early to get an appointed visit time, tube: Victoria, tel. 0171/930-4832 to reserve a ticket with your credit card).

▲**Changing of the Guard at Buckingham Palace**—Overrated but almost required (daily April–July at 11:30, generally every even-numbered day August–March, no band when wet). Join the mob at the back side of the palace (the front faces a huge and extremely private park). The pageantry and parading are colorful and even stirring, but the actual changing of the guard is a non-event. It is interesting, however, to see nearly every tourist in London gathered in one place at the same time. Hop into a big black taxi and say, "To Buck House, please." For all the color with none of the crowds, see the Inspection of the Guard ceremony at 11:00 in front of the Wellington Barracks, east of the palace on Birdcage Walk. Afterward, stroll through nearby St. James's Park. For guards' schedule, call 0171/930-4832. (Tube: Victoria, St. James' Park, or Green Park.)

▲▲**Tate Gallery**—One of Europe's great arthouses, the Tate specializes in British painting (14th-century through contemporary), pre-Raphaelites, Impressionism, and modern art (Matisse, van Gogh, Monet, Picasso). Learn about the mystical watercolorist Blake and the romantic, nature-worship art of Turner (free, daily 10:00–18:00, fine £2 CD Walkman tours, free tours weekdays: 11:30—Turner, 14:30—British, and 15:30—Modern, confirm schedule by phone, tel. 0171/887-8000, tube: Pimlico). In 2000 the Tate's modern collection will be moving to the new Tate Modern Art Gallery (on the South Bank) and the current museum will become the Tate Gallery of British Art.

Sights—West London

▲**Hyde Park and Speakers' Corner**—London's "Central Park" has more than 600 acres of lush greenery, a huge man-made lake, the royal Kensington Palace (not worth touring), and the ornate neo-Gothic Albert Memorial across from the Royal Albert Hall. Early afternoons on Sunday, Speaker's Corner offers soapbox oratory at its best (tube: Marble Arch). "The grass roots of democracy" is actually a holdover from when the gallows stood here and the criminal was allowed to say just about anything he wanted to before he swung. I dare you to raise your voice and gather a crowd—it's easy to do.

▲▲**Victoria and Albert Museum**—The world's top collection of decorative arts is a gangly (150 rooms over 12 acres) but surprisingly interesting assortment of artistic stuff from the West as well as Asia and Islam. The V&A grew out of the Great Exhibition of 1851—that ultimate festival celebrating the Industrial Revolution and the greatness of Britain—and was originally for manufactured art. But after much support from Queen Victoria and Prince Albert, it was renamed after the royal couple and its present building was opened in 1909. The idealistic Victorian notion that anyone can be continually improved by education and example remains the driving force behind this museum.

While just wandering works well here, consider catching one of the regular one-hour orientation tours, buying the fine *Hundred Highlights* guidebook, or walking through these ground floor highlights: Medieval Treasury (room 43, well-described treasury of Middle Age European art), the finest collection of Indian decorative art outside India (room 41), the Dress Gallery (room 40, 400 years of English fashion corsetted into 40 display cases), the Raphael Gallery (room 48a, seven huge watercolor "cartoons" painted as designs for tapestries to hang in the Sistine Chapel; among the greatest art treasures in Britain and the best works of the High Renaissance), reliefs by the Renaissance sculptor Donatello (room 16), a close-up look at medieval stained glass (room 28, much more upstairs), the fascinating Cast Courts (46a and 46b, two giant rooms filled with plaster copies of the greatest art of our civilization—such as *Trajan's Column* and Michelangelo's *David*—made for the benefit of 19th-century art students who couldn't afford to travel), and a hall lined with "great" fakes and forgeries (room 46). Upstairs you can walk through the British Galleries for centuries of aristocratic living rooms. (£5, Monday 12:00–18:00, Tuesday–Sunday 10:00–18:00, and usually Wednesday evenings until 21:30 in summer, free after 16:30, pleasant garden café, tube: South Kensington, a long tunnel leads directly from the tube station to the museum, tel. 0171/938-8500.)

Natural History Museum—Across the street from the Victoria and Albert Museum, this mammoth museum is housed in a giant and wonderful Victorian neo-Romanesque building. Built in the 1870s specifically to house the huge collection (50 million specimens), it presents itself in two halves: the Life Galleries (creepy-crawlies, human biology, origin of the species, "our place in evolution," and awesome dinosaurs) and the Earth Galleries (meteors, volcanoes, earthquakes, and so on). Exhibits are wonderfully explained with lots of creative interactive displays (£6, families £16, free after 16:30 and after 17:00 on weekends, daily 10:00–18:00, Sunday 11:00–18:00, a long tunnel leads directly from the South Kensington tube station to the museum, tel. 0171/938-9123, Web site: www.nhm.ac.uk).

Sights—East London, "The City"

▲▲**The City of London**—When Londoners say "The City," they mean the one-square-mile business, banking, and journalism center that 2,000 years ago was Roman Londinium. The outline of the Roman city walls can still be seen in the arc of roads from

The City

Blackfriars Bridge to Tower Bridge. Within the City are 24 churches designed by Christopher Wren. It's a fascinating district to wander but, since nobody actually lives there, it's a ghost town on Saturday and Sunday. An hour in the City's Central Criminal Courts, known as "Old Bailey," is always interesting (Monday–Friday 10:30–13:00, 14:00–16:30, quiet in August, no cameras, no bags, no cloakroom, no kids under 14, at Old Bailey and Newgate Streets, tube: St. Paul's, tel. 0171/248-3277).

▲▲**St. Paul's Cathedral**—Wren's most famous church is the great St. Paul's, its elaborate interior capped by a 365-foot dome. St. Paul's was Britain's World War II symbol of resistance, as Nazi bombs failed to blow it up. (There's a memorial chapel to the heroic firefighters who kept watch over it with hoses cocked.) The crypt (free with admission) is a world of historic bones and memorials, including Admiral Nelson's tomb and interesting cathedral models. This was the wedding church of Prince Charles and the late Princess Diana. Climb the dome for a great city view and some fun in the whispering gallery. Whisper sweet nothings into the wall and your partner (and anyone else) on the far side can hear you. (£4 entry, free on Sunday but restricted viewing due to services, £3.50 extra to climb dome, allow an hour to climb up and down the dome, open daily 9:30–16:30, last entry 16:00, £3.50 for guided 90-minute cathedral and crypt tours offered at 11:00, 11:30, 13:30, and 14:00, or £3 for a Walkman tour anytime, Sunday services at 8:00, 8:45, 11:00, and 15:15, evensongs weekdays at 17:00, tube: St. Paul's, tel. 0171/236-4128.)

▲**Museum of London**—Stroll through London history—from

St. Paul's Cathedral

1 NAVE	**4** HIGH ALTAR & CHOIR	**7** JOHN DONNE
2 WELLINGTON MONUMENT	**5** AMERICAN MEM. CHURCH	**8** CLIMB THE DOME
3 THE DOME	**6** BLITZ PHOTOS	**9** CRYPT

pre-Roman times to the Blitz up through today (£4.30, free after 16:30, Monday–Saturday 10:00–18:00, Sunday 12:00–18:00, tube: Barbican or St. Paul's, tel. 0171/600-3699). This regular stop for the local schoolkids gives the best overview of London history in town.

▲▲**Tower of London**—William I, still getting used to his new title of "the Conqueror," built the stone "White Tower" (1077–1097) to keep the Londoners in line. The tower served as an effective lookout for invaders coming up the Thames. His successors enlarged it to its present 18-acre size. Because of the security it provided, it has served over the centuries as the Royal Mint, the Royal Jewel House, and a prison. You'll find more bloody history per square inch in this original tower of power than anywhere in Britain. Don't miss the entertaining 50-minute Beefeater tour (free, leaving regularly from inside the gate, last one usually at 15:30) of this historic fortress, palace, prison, and host to more than 3 million visitors a year. A rare and lovely Norman chapel (St. John's Chapel, 1080) is in the White Tower. At the execution site, Anne Boleyn, Thomas More, Lady Jane Grey, and many others lost their heads. The crown jewels, which date from the Restoration (Cromwell sold or melted down the earlier jewels), are the best on earth; the long midday summer lines are made almost enjoyable by museum videos along the way. Prisoners ranging from unlucky royal rugrats to Sir Walter Raleigh to Rudolph Hess once called the Bloody Tower home. The furnished Medieval Palace is near the entrance to the medieval

Tower of London

100 YARDS

MOAT

TO TOWER HILL TUBE

MOAT

ENTER

TOWER GREEN

WHITE TOWER

MOAT

MOAT

WC

MOAT

DCH

THAMES

RIVER

- **1** ENTRANCE GATE
- **2** TRAITOR'S GATE
- **3** WHITE TOWER
- **4** EXECUTION SITE
- **5** THE CROWN JEWELS
- **6** BLOODY TOWER
- **7** MEDIEVAL PALACE
- **8** WALK THE WALL

wall—worth a walk. To avoid the crowds arrive at 9:00 and go straight for the jewels, doing the tour and tower later—or do the jewels after 16:30. The crowd hits after the 9:30 cheap tube passes start. (£9, Monday–Saturday 9:00–18:00, Sunday 10:00–18:00, the long but fast-moving line is worst on Sunday, last entry at 17:00, tube: Tower Hill, tel. 0171/709-0765.) Visitors are welcome on the grounds to worship in the Royal Chapel on Sunday (free, 11:00 service with fine choral music).

Every night at 21:30, with pageantry-filled ceremony, the Tower of London is locked up (as it has been every night for the last 700 years). To attend this free event you need to request an invitation at least five weeks before your visit. Write to: Ceremony of Keys, H.M. Tower of London, London EC3N 4AB. Include your name, number of people (up to seven), requested date, alternative dates, and an international reply coupon (buy at a U.S. post office). Although five week's notice is requested, you might try for an appointment near the end of your trip by sending a stamped envelope addressed to your London hotel once you arrive.

Sights Next to the Tower—The best remaining bit of London's Roman Wall is just north of the tower (at the Tower Hill tube station). Freshly painted and restored, **Tower Bridge** has an 1894-to-1994 history exhibit (£5.70, daily 10:00–18:30, last entry at 17:15, good view, poor value, tel. 0171/403-3761). **St. Katherine Yacht Harbor,** chic and newly renovated, just east of the Tower Bridge, has mod shops and the classic old Dickens Inn, fun for a drink or pub lunch. If you cross the bridge, you'll find the trendy new Butler's Wharf area with happening restaurants and the Coffee and Tea Museum (see below). From here it's a pleasant riverside walk along the South Bank up to the Globe Theater. **The Docklands** is the latest rage in London's growth. Since the weather blows in from the west, London's bad air ended up in the east. Before pollution was conquered, gritty east London was home only to the poor and a huge harbor (the largest 19th-century port in the world). Newly cleaned up and enjoying fine air, the east end is now trendy.

Sights—South London

The South Bank is rapidly becoming gentrified and a thriving arts and cultural center. From Westminster Bridge to the Tower of London bridge, a slick Jubilee Promenade is a trendy jogging, yuppie pub-crawling walk.

▲▲**Globe Theater**—The original Globe Theater has been rebuilt—half-timbered and thatched—exactly as it was in Shakespeare's time. It's open as a museum and hosts authentic old-time performances of Shakespeare's plays. The theater and exhibit are open to tour when there are no plays (£5, daily 9:00–12:15, 14:00–16:00, includes guided 30-minute tour offered on the half hour; if a play is scheduled, the museum is open only 9:00–12:30; on the south bank directly across the Thames over Southwark Bridge from St. Paul's, tube: Mansion House, tel. 0171/902-1500, for details on seeing a play, see Entertainment, below).

▲▲**Imperial War Museum**—This impressive museum covers the wars of this century, from heavy weaponry to love notes and Varga Girls, from Monty's Africa campaign tank to Schwartzkopf's Desert Storm uniform. You can trace the development of the machine gun, watch footage of the first tank battles, hold your breath through the gruesome WWI trench experience, and buy WWII-era toys in the fun museum shop. Rather than glorify war, the museum does its best to shine a light on the powerful human side of one of mankind's most persistent traits (£5, daily 10:00–

18:00, free after 16:30, 90 minutes is enough time for most visitors, tube: Lambeth North, tel. 0171/416-5000).

▲▲**Museum of the Moving Image**—This high-tech, interactive, hands-on museum traces the story of moving images from a caveman's flickering fire to modern TV. There's great footage of the earliest movies and TV shows. Turn-of-the-century-clad staff speak as if silent films are the latest marvel. Don't miss Agit-Train (1919 propaganda film train that brought indoctrination to the far reaches of the early USSR) or the breathtaking 50-years-in-10-minutes montage of magic MGM moments (big screen above the Odeon marquee). Brit movie buffs will enjoy the montage of British cinematic highlights in the large theater. And children will enjoy making their own animated cartoon (£6.25, daily 10:00–18:00, last ticket sold at 17:00, from Embankment tube stop walk across the Thames pedestrian bridge and turn left; it's under the Waterloo bridge, tel. 0171/928-3535).

Bramah Tea and Coffee Museum—Aficionados of tea or coffee will find this small museum fascinating. It tells the story of each drink almost passionately. The owner, Mr. Bramah, comes from a big tea family and wants the world to know how the advent of commercial television with breaks not long enough to brew a proper pot of tea required a faster hot drink. In came the horrible English instant coffee. Tea countered with finely chopped leaves in tea bags, and it's gone downhill ever since. (£3.50, daily 10:00–18:00, in the Butlers Wharf complex just across the bridge from the Tower, tel. 0171/378 0222).

Honorable and Dishonorable Mention

Honorable—**Madame Tussaud's Waxworks** is expensive but dang good (£10, children £6.60, under age five free, combined ticket for Tussaud's and planetarium is £12 for adults, £8 for kids, daily from 9:30, last admission at 17:30, buy ticket at TI—no more than 24 hours in advance—to save a little money and get in with no wait, Marylebone Road, tube: Baker Street, tel. 0171/935-6861). At **Geffrye Decorative Arts Museum** you can walk through British front rooms from 1600 to 1930 (free, Tuesday–Saturday 10:00–17:00, Sunday 14:00–17:00, closed Monday, tube: Liverpool Street, then bus 149 or 242 north, tel. 0171/739-9893). Architects and fans of eclectic knickknacks love the quirky **Sir John Soane's Museum** (free, Tuesday–Saturday 10:00–17:00, 13 Lincoln's Inn Fields, tube: Holborn, tel. 0171/405-2107).

Dishonorable—The venerable BBC broadcasts from Broadcasting House: Of all its productions, its new "BBC Experience" tour for visitors is the worst. Avoid it. On the South Bank, the **London Dungeon**, a much-visited but amateurish attraction, is just a highly advertised, overpriced haunted house—certainly not worth the £10 admission, much less your valuable London time. Wait for

Halloween and see one in your hometown to support a better cause. The **Design Museum** (next to the Bramah Tea and Coffee Museum) and **"Winston Churchill's Britain at War Experience"** (next to the London Dungeon) are disappointments.

More Sights—Outer London

▲**Kew Gardens**—For a fine riverside park and a palatial greenhouse jungle, take the tube or the boat to every botanist's favorite escape, Kew Gardens. While to most visitors the Royal Botanic Gardens of Kew is simply a delightful opportunity to wander among 33,000 different types of plants, it is a hardworking organization committed to understanding and preserving the botanical diversity of our planet. The Kew tube station drops you in a herbal little business community a two-block walk to Victoria Gate (the main garden entry). Watch the five-minute orientation video and pick up a map brochure with a monthly listing of best blooms.

Garden lovers could easily spend all day exploring Kew's 300 acres. For a quick visit, spend a fragrant hour wandering through three buildings: the Palm House—a humid Victorian world of iron, glass, and tropical plants, built in 1844; a Waterlily House that Monet would swim for; and the Temperate House—a modern greenhouse with many different climate zones growing countless cacti, bug-munching carnivorous plants, and more (£4.50, Monday–Saturday 9:30–18:00, Sunday 9:30–19:00, until 16:30 in off-season, galleries and conservatories close 30 minutes earlier, entry discounted to £3 late in day, tube: Kew Gardens, tel. 0181/940-1171). For tea, consider the Maids of Honor (280 Kew Road, near garden entrance, tel. 0181/940-2752).

Hampton Court Palace—Fifteen miles up the Thames from downtown (£16 taxi ride from Kew Gardens) is the 500-year-old palace of Henry VIII. Actually, it was the palace of his minister, Cardinal Wolsey. When Wolsey, a clever man, realized Henry VIII was experiencing a little palace envy, he gave it to his king. The Tudor palace was also home to Elizabeth I and Charles I. Parts were updated by Christopher Wren for William and Mary. The stately palace stands overlooks the Thames with some impressive Tudor rooms including a Great Hall with its magnificent hammer-beam ceiling. The industrial-strength Tudor kitchen was capable of keeping 600 schmoozing courtesans thoroughly—if not well—fed. The sculpted garden features a rare Tudor tennis court and a popular maze. The palace, fully restored since its 1986 fire, tries very hard to please, but it falls flat to me. The costumed guides seem to be low on energy. The Walkman tours are slow and boring. From the information center in the main courtyard, visitors book times for guided tours or grab Walkmans for taped tours (all free). The Tudor Kitchens, Henry VIII's Apartments, and the King's Apartments are most interesting. The Georgian Rooms are pretty dull. The maze in the nearby garden is a curiosity some find fun. The train (2/hrly, 30 minutes) from London's Waterloo station drops you just across the river from the palace (£10, daily 10:15–18:00, until 16:30 November–March, tel. 0181/781-9500).

Thames Barrier—East of Greenwich, the world's largest movable flood barrier welcomes visitors with an informative and entertaining exhibition (£3.40, Monday–Friday 10:00–17:00, weekends 10:30–17:30; catch 70-minute boat from Westminster Pier, or take 30-minute boat from Greenwich Pier, or train from London's Charing Cross station to Charlton then walk 15 minutes, tel. 0181/305-4188).

Sights—Greenwich

The Tudor kings preferred Greenwich to their other palaces. Henry VIII was born here. Later kings commissioned Inigo Jones and Chris Wren to beautify the place. In spite of its architectural and royal treats, this is England's maritime capital, and visitors go for things salty. And now, as the millennium approaches, the home of the Zero Meridian will be more visited than ever.

Getting to Greenwich is a joy by boat or a snap by tube. You have good choices: Cruise down the Thames from central London's piers at Westminster, Charing Cross, or Tower of London; tube to Island Gardens in Zone 2, free with tube pass, then walk under pedestrian Thames tunnel; or catch the train from Charing Cross station.

Cruise from Westminster to Greenwich. Upon arrival, visit the two great ships and check out the Millennium Experience Visitors Centre. Then walk the shoreline promenade with a possible lunch or drink in the venerable Trafalgar Tavern before heading up to the National Maritime Museum and Old Royal Observatory. Finally, browse the town before catching the tube or train back to London (Greenwich TI tel. 0181/858-6376).

▲▲*Cutty Sark*—The Scottish-built *Cutty Sark* was the last of the great China tea clippers. Handsomely restored, she was the queen of the seas when first launched in 1869. With 32,000 square feet of sail, she could blow with the wind 300 miles in a day. Below deck you'll see the best collection of merchant ships' figureheads in Britain and exhibits giving a vivid peek into the lives of Victorian sailors back when Britain ruled the waves. Stand at the big wheel and look up at the still rigged main mast towering 150 feet above. During summer afternoons costumed storytellers tell tales of the high seas (£3.50, Monday–Saturday 10:00–18:00, Sunday 12:00–18:00; October–April Monday–Saturday 10:00-17:00, Sunday 12:00–17:00, tel. 0181/858-3445, Web site: www.cuttysark.org.uk).

▲*Gipsy Moth IV*—Tiny next to the *Cutty Sark*, the 53-foot *Gipsy Moth IV* is the boat Sir Francis Chichester used for the first solo circumnavigation of the world in 1966 and 1967. Climb through to see the clever and fascinating ways the boat was custom-designed for its historic voyage. Upon Chichester's return, Queen Elizabeth II knighted him in Greenwich using the same sword Elizabeth I had used to knight Francis Drake in 1582 (50p, open Easter–October Monday–Saturday 10:00–18:00, Sunday 12:00–18:00).

Millennium Experience Visitors Centre—The Millennium Experience will take place under a vast dome a mile downriver from Greenwich town. This dome—covering over 20 acres, is the biggest ever built. Throughout 2000, millions will gather here to celebrate British ideas and technology at the birth of the third millennium. Throughout 1999, the Millennium Experience Visitors Centre (next to the *Cutty Sark* in Greenwich) will give visitors a sneak preview of the grand festivities planned. There's plenty of futuristic hoopla as everyone wonders what exactly the Millennium Dome will be filled with (Visitors Centre free, weekdays 11:00–19:00, weekends 10:00–18:00, Web site: www.mx2000.co.uk).

Stroll the Thames to Trafalgar Tavern—From the *Cutty Sark* and *Gipsy Moth*, pass the pier and wander along the Thames on Five Foot Walk (the width of the path) for grand views in front of the Royal Naval College. Founded by William III as a naval hospital and designed by Wren, the college was split in two because Queen Mary didn't want the view from Queen's House blocked. The riverside view's good, too, with the twin-domed towers of the college (one giving the time; the other, the direction of the wind) framing Queen's House and the Old Royal Observatory crowning the hill beyond.

Continuing downstream, just past the college, you'll see the Trafalgar Tavern. Dickens knew the pub well, and even used it as the setting for the wedding breakfast in *Our Mutual Friend*. Built in 1837 in the Regency style to attract Londoners downriver, the tavern is still popular with Londoners for its fine lunches. And the upstairs Nelson Room is still used for weddings. Its formal moldings and elegant windows with balconies over the Thames are a step back in time (bar meals 10:00–20:00 except Sunday, restaurant meals 12:00–15:00).

In 1999 the Royal Naval College's buildings will no longer be a military training installation. Whether they'll be open to the public is still uncertain. From the Trafalgar Tavern, walk the two long blocks up Park Walk and turn right onto Ha Ha Walk, which borders the park.

▲**Queen's House**—This was the first Palladian-style villa in Britain. Designed in 1616 by Inigo Jones for James I's wife, Anne of Denmark, it's the architectural centerpiece of Greenwich. Exploring its Great Hall and Royal Apartments offers a sumptuous look at royal life in the 17th century—or lots of stairs if you're suffering from manor house fatigue (combo ticket to Queen's House,

Maritime Museum, and Observatory costs £5.50, daily 10:00–17:00, off-season 10:30–15:30, tours every 15 minutes).

▲▲▲**National Maritime Museum**—At the largest and most important maritime museum in the world, visitors can taste both the romance and harshness of life at sea. Experience 20th-century naval warfare on a WWII frigate or get to know Britain's greatest naval hero, Nelson, whose display covers both his public career and scandalous private life (don't miss the uniform coat in which he was fatally shot). The museum's ambitious Neptune Court development opens in June 1999; it will greatly increase the number of galleries and better profile the sweep of Empire and the role of the sea in British history (combo ticket to Queen's House, Maritime Museum, and Observatory costs £5.50, daily 10:00–17:00, tel. 0181/312-6565, Web site: www.nmm.ac.uk).

▲▲**Old Royal Observatory**—On December 31, 1999, the eyes of the world will be focused on Greenwich and its observatory. All time is measured from longitude zero degrees, the prime meridian line—the point from which the new millennium will actually begin. However, the observatory's early work had nothing to do with coordinating the world's clocks to GMT, Greenwich mean time. The observatory was founded in 1675 by Charles II to find a way to determine longitude at sea. Today the Greenwich time signal is linked with the BBC (which broadcasts the "pips" worldwide at the top of the hour). Straddle the prime meridian and set your wristwatch to the new digital clock showing GMT to a 10th of a second (and whizzing down the seconds to New Year 2000). See how your foot measures up to *the* foot where the public standards of length are cast in bronze. View historic astronomical instruments and watch the Time Ball, visible from the Thames, drop daily at 13:00.

Finally, enjoy the view: the symmetrical royal buildings, the Thames, the square-mile "City" of London with its skyscrapers and the dome of St. Paul's, the Docklands with its busy cranes, and the Millennium Dome itself (combo ticket to Queen's House, Maritime Museum, and Observatory costs £5.50, daily 10:00–17:00).

Greenwich town—Wander beyond the touristy Greenwich Church Street and Greenwich High Road to where flower stands spill into the side streets, and antique shops sell brass nautical knickknacks. King William Walk, College Approach, Nelson Road, and Turnpin Lane are all worth a look. Covered markets and outdoor stalls are popular year-round as are the covered flea markets. Don't miss the Arts & Crafts Market, an entertaining mini-Covent Garden between College Approach and Nelson Road (daily but busiest on weekends). Greenwich will throb with daytrippers on weekends as the millennium approaches. Visit on a weekday if you can. (TI, 46 Greenwich Church Street, tel. 0181/858-6376).

Shopping in London

▲**Harrods and Harvey Nichols (Big, Fancy English Department Stores)**—Harrods is London's most famous and touristed department store. Artfully mixing big and classy and filled with wonderful displays, Harrods has everything from elephants to toothbrushes. The food halls (with cafeterias) are sights to savor (10:00–18:00, until 19:00 on Wednesday, Thursday, and Friday, closed Sunday, Brompton Road, tube: Knightsbridge, tel. 0171/730-1234). Many readers report that Harrods is now over-priced (its £1 toilets are the most expensive in Europe), snooty, and teeming with American and Japanese tourists. The nearby Harvey Nichols store was Princess Diana's favorite and the department store du jour (tube: Knightsbridge).

For royal window-shopping, cruise nearby King's Road in Chelsea. Most stores close around 18:00, but many stay open until 20:00 on Wednesday or Thursday, depending on the neighborhood.

▲**Oxford Circus/Regent Street/Piccadilly Circus Shopping Walk**—From the Oxford Circus tube station, Regent Street leads past a fun array of diverse places to shop (all on the lefthand side of street). You'll find: Laura Ashley, Liberty (a big stately local favorite, 10:00–18:30, closed Sunday, 214 Regent Street), Hamleys (the biggest toy store in Britain, 10:00–20:00, Sunday 12:00–18:00), Warner Bros. Studio Store, Beatles Shop (a block behind Warner Bros., 8 Kingly Street, tel. 0171/434-0464), Waterford Wedgwood, British Air Travel Shops (9:30–18:00, Saturday 10:00–16:00, accessories, guidebooks, shots, travel agents, British Air agents, travelers' clinic, WC, and theater ticket agency), a Disney store, Garrard the Crown Jewelers (notice the three royal seals indicating that this shop is a favorite of the Queen, her mom, and Prince Charles), the Scotch House (knits, sweaters, wool stuff), and Piccadilly Circus.

From Piccadilly turn right and wander down Piccadilly Street. You'll pass Christopher Wren's St. James Church (tiny flea market and healthy café) and Fortnum & Mason, an extremely classy department store. Consider a traditional tea in its fourth-floor St. James Restaurant (£13.50, daily 15:00–17:15, closed Sunday, tel. 0171/734-8040). Relaxing under this plush and elegant tearoom's chandeliers, you'll get the standard three-tiered silver tea tray: finger sandwiches on the bottom, fresh scones with jam and clotted cream on the first floor, and decadent pastries and "tartlets" on the top floor with unlimited tea.

Just past Fortnum & Mason is the French Travel Center, across the street is the delightful Burlinton Arcade, and a block farther down is the original "Ritz" Hotel (where the tea is much fancier).

▲**Street Markets**—Antique buffs, people-watchers, and folks who break for garage sales love London's street markets. The tourist office has a complete, up-to-date list. The best are Portobello Road (Saturday 8:30–17:00, antique and flea market, near recommended B&Bs, tube: Notting Hill Gate) and Camden Market (Saturday and Sunday 10:00–17:00; a huge, trendy arts and crafts festival; tube: Camden Town). There's some good early morning market activity somewhere any day of the week. Warning: Street markets attract two kinds of people—tourists and pickpockets. **Famous Auctions**—London's famous auctioneers welcome the curious public. For schedules (most weekdays, closed midsummer), telephone Sotheby's (tel. 0171/493-8080, tube: Oxford Circus) or Christie's (tel. 0171/839-9060, tube: Green Park).

Entertainment and Theater in London

London bubbles with top-notch entertainment seven nights a week. Everything's listed in the monthly *Time Out* magazine, available at newsstands. You can choose from classical, jazz, rock, and far-out music, Gilbert and Sullivan, dance, comedy, Bahai meetings, poetry readings, spectator sports, film, and theater.

London's theater rivals Broadway's in quality and beats it in price. Choose from the Royal Shakespeare Company, top musicals, comedy, thrillers, sex farces, and more. Performances are nightly except Sunday, usually with one matinee a week. Matinees (Wednesday, Thursday, or Saturday) are cheaper and rarely sell out. Tickets range from about £8 to £35.

Most theaters, marked on tourist maps, are in the Piccadilly–Trafalgar area. Box offices, hotels, and TIs carry the handy *Theater Guide* brochure that lists what's playing.

To book a seat, simply call the theater box office directly, ask about seats and dates available, and buy one with your credit card. You can call from the United States as easily as from England (photocopy your hometown library's London newspaper theater section or visit the Web site: www.officiallondontheatre.co.uk). Pick up your ticket 15 minutes before the show.

Ticket agencies are scalpers with an address. Booking through a ticket agency (at most tourist offices or scattered throughout London) is quick and easy, but prices are inflated by a standard 25-percent booking fee. When buying from an agency, see the ticket, read it carefully (your price should be no more than 30 percent over the printed face value; the 17-percent VAT and all other taxes are included in the face value; if your view is restricted it will say on ticket), and understand where you're sitting according to the theater floorplan. Agencies are worthwhile only if a show you've got to see is sold out at the box office. They scarf up hot tickets, planning to make a killing after the show is sold out. U.S. booking agencies get their tickets from another agency, adding even more to your expense by involving yet another middleman. Many tickets sold on the streets are forgeries. With cheap international phone calls and credit cards, there's no reason not to book direct.

Theater lingo: stalls (ground floor), dress circle (first balony), upper circle (second balcony), balcony (sky-high third balcony).

Cheap theater tricks: Most theaters offer cheap returned tickets, standing room, matinee, and senior or student stand-by deals. These "concessions" are indicated with a "conc" or "s" in the listings. Picking up a late return can get you a great seat at a cheap-seat price. Standing room can be very cheap. If a show is "sold out," there's usually a way to get a seat. Call and ask how. The famous (but overrated) "half-price booth" in Leicester Square sells cheap tickets to shows on the push list the day of the show only (Monday–Saturday 14:30–18:30). I buy the second-cheapest tickets directly from the theater box office. Many theaters are so small that there's hardly a bad seat. After the lights go down, "scooting up" is less than a capital offense. Shakespeare did it.

Royal Shakespeare Company—If you'll ever enjoy Shakespeare, it'll be here. The RSC splits its season between the Royal Shakespeare Theatre in Stratford (tel. 01789/295-623) and the Barbican Centre in London (daily 9:00–20:00, credit-card booking, they mail out schedules, tel. 0171/638-8891 or, for recorded information, tel. 0171/628-9760). Tickets range in price from £7 (preview) to £40. The best way to book is direct, by telephone and credit card. You can pick up your ticket at the door. Stand-by tickets for £6 are sold to students and seniors at 9:00 the day of the show. For a complete schedule write to the Royal Shakespeare Theatre, Stratford-upon-Avon, CV37 6BB Warwickshire.

Shakespeare at the New Globe Theater—To see Shakespeare in an exact replica of the theater for which he wrote his plays, attend a play at the Globe. This thatch-roofed, open-air, round theater does the plays as Shakespeare intended (with no amplification). Curtain times from May through September are usually at 14:00 and 19:30, Sunday at 16:00 only, with no plays on Monday. You'll pay £5 to stand and £10 to £20 to sit (on a backless bench). The £5 "groundling" tickets, while the only ones open to rain, are most fun. You're a crude peasant. You can walk around, munch a picnic dinner, lean your elbows on the stage, and even interact with the actors. I've never enjoyed Shakespeare as much as here, performed as it was meant to be in the "wooden O." The theater is on the South Bank directly across the Thames over Southwark Bridge from St. Paul's (tube: Mansion House, tel. 0171/902-1500 to book a ticket with your credit card). Plays are long. Many groundlings leave before the end. If you like, hang out an hour before the finish and beg or buy a ticket off someone leaving early (groundlings are allowed to come and go). The Globe is far from public transport but the courtesy phone in the lobby gets a mini-cab in minutes. Confirm

London Area

the cost, but they seem to be much cheaper than the official black cabs (£5–6 to Victoria Station).

Music—For cheap or free and easy concerts in fine settings, check the listings for lunch concerts given in historic churches around town (listed at TI; especially Wren's St. Bride's Church, tel. 0171/353-1301; and St. Martin-in-the-Fields, most weekdays at 13:05, tel. 0171/930-1862). St. Martin-in-the-Fields also hosts fine evening concerts occasionally by candlelight (see above). For a fun classical event (June–September only), attend a "Prom Concert." This is an annual music festival with almost nightly concerts in the Royal Albert Hall at give-a-peasant-some-culture prices (£3 standing-room spots sold at the door, tel. 0171/589-8212).

Day Trips from London

You could fill a book with the many easy and exciting day trips from London (Earl Steinbicker did: *Daytrips in Britain by Rail, Bus or Car from London and Edinburgh*). Several tour companies take London-based travelers out and back every day. Original London Walks offers a variety of day trips using the train for about £10 plus transportation costs (see their walking-tour brochure). Some big bus tours can be used by those without a car as a "free" way to get to Bath or Stow-on-the-Wold (saving you, for instance, the £28.50 London–Bath train ticket). Evan Evans' tours leave from behind Victoria Station daily at 9:00 (with your bag stowed under the bus), include a full day of sightseeing with £5 to £10 worth of admissions, and leave you in Bath before returning to London

(£30 for Stonehenge and Bath; £46 for Salisbury Cathedral, Stonehenge, and Bath; tel. 0181/332-2222). Travelline does a tour of Bath and Stonehenge for £24 (tel. 0181/668-7261, office in Fountain Square directly south of Victoria Station).

The British rail system uses London as a hub and normally offers round-trip fares (after 9:30) that cost virtually the same as one-way fares. "Day return" tickets are best (and cheapest) for day trips. You can save a little money if you purchase Super Advance tickets before 14:00 on the day before your trip. But given the high cost of big-city living and the charm of small-town England, rather than side-tripping I'd see London and get out.

Sleeping in London
(£1 = about $1.70, tel. code: 0171)
Sleep Code: **S** = Single, **D** = Double/Twin, **T** = Triple, **Q** = Quad, **b** = bathroom, **t** = toilet only, **s** = shower only, **CC** = Credit Card (**V**isa, **M**asterCard, **A**mex). Unless otherwise noted, prices include a big English breakfast and all taxes.

London is expensive. For £50 ($80) you'll get a sleepable double with breakfast in a safe, clean, tiny, dreary place where the landlords are absent and service is minimal. (Hang up your towel to dry and reuse.) For £60 you'll get a basic, clean, reasonably cheery double in a usually cramped, cracked-plaster building, with a hearty English (as opposed to continental) breakfast. My London splurges, at £100 to £170, are spacious, thoughtfully appointed places you'd be happy to entertain or make love in. TVs are nearly standard in rooms.

Reserve your London room with a phone call or e-mail as soon as you can commit to a date. Many places will hold a room with no deposit if you promise to arrive by midday. Others want your credit-card number as security. Most have expensive cancellation policies. If you must send a deposit, ask if you can send a signed $100 traveler's check. (Leave the "pay to" line blank and include a note explaining that you'll be happy to pay cash upon arrival, so they can avoid bank charges, if they'll just hold your check until you arrive.)

Sleeping in Victoria Station Neighborhood, Belgravia
The streets behind Victoria Station teem with budget B&Bs. It's a safe, surprisingly tidy and decent area without a hint of the trashy touristy glitz of the streets in front of the station. This neighborhood is proud to be part of Belgravia. Even with Margaret Thatcher living around the corner (you'll see the policeman standing outside 73 Chester Square), this is a classy and peaceful place to call home in London. Decent eateries abound (see Eating, below). The cheaper listings are relatively dumpy. Don't expect £80 cheeriness in a £50 room. Those traveling on a shoestring off-season save a few

London, Victoria Station Neighborhood

❶ Tube, Tourist Info, Taxi + City Buses
❷ City Bus Tours
❸ Woodville
❹ Lime Tree
❺ Cherry Court
❻ Limegrove
❼ Eliz. Hotel
❽ Eliz. House
❾ Topham's Belgravia
❿ Starlight Express

pounds by arriving late without a reservation and checking around. Competition is fierce and prices are often soft, especially for multi-night stays. Particularly for Warwick Way hotels (and in the summer when you'll want the window open at night), request a quiet back room. All are within a five-minute walk of the Victoria tube, bus, and train stations. There's a £8-per-day garage and a nearby launderette (self-serve or full-serve, 3 Westmoreland Terrace, tel. 0171/821-8692).

In **Woodville House** the quarters are dollhouse tight, showers are down the hall, and several rooms are next to the noisy street (doubles are on the quiet backside, twins and singles on the street). But this well-run, well-worn place is a good value with lots of travel tips, and endless tea, coffee, and friendly chat (especially about the local rich and famous) from Rachel Joplin (S-£39, D-£58, bunky family deals—£75–100—for three, four, or five in a room; CC:VM, easy credit-card reservations, 107 Ebury Street, SW1W 9QU, tel. 0171/730-1048, fax 0171/730-2574).

Lime Tree Hotel is enthusiastically run by David and Marilyn Davies. The thoughtfully decorated public areas and rooms are spacious for this area and guests can relax in the peaceful garden off the fun-loving breakfast room. (Sb-£70, Db-£90–100, Tb-£120, family room-£140, David will deal in slow times and is good at helping travelers in a bind, CC:VMA, 135 Ebury Street, SW1W 9RA, tel. 0171/730-8191, fax 0171/730-7865). Each room comes with a TV, phone, hair dryer, safe, and teapot.

Cherry Court Hotel, run by the friendly Patel family, offers cramped rooms, tiny bathrooms, and a worthless shrink-wrapped breakfast at youth hostel prices. It's on a quiet street very close to the station. (S-£28, Sb-£35, Db-£45, Tb-£65, CC:VMA, no twins—only double beds, pleasant garden, 23 Hugh Street, SW1V 1QJ, tel. 0171/828-2840, fax 0171/828-0393, e-mail: cherryc @globalnet.co.uk).

Cedar Guest House, across the street, is a minimal place with eight rooms at youth-hostel prices. It's run by a Polish organization to help Poles afford London, but all are welcome (D-£38, T-£54, 30 Hugh Street, SW1V 1RP, tel. 0171/828-2625).

Limegrove Hotel, run by harried Joyce, is a little smoky but its nine rooms are a fine value and come with a full English breakfast (S-£26, small D-£36, D-£38, Db-£45, T-£45, Tb-£60, cheaper off-season or for stays of six days or more, 101 Warwick Way, SW1V 4HT, tel. 0171/828-0458). Back rooms are quieter.

Elizabeth House (not related to the Elizabeth Hotel, below) feels institutional and a bit bland—as you might expect from a former YMCA—but the rooms are clean and bright and the price is right (S-£30, D-£50, Db-£60, T-£75, Q-£85, CC:VMA, 118 Warwick Way, SW1 4JB, tel. 0171/630 0741, fax 0171/630 0740).

Tophams Belgravia Hotel packs the formality and service of a top-class hotel into a tight and tangled building beautifully situated on a quiet corner two blocks from Victoria station. Carefully attired rooms come with all the comforts and carefully attired maids serve breakfast with none of the chat common at funkier places (S-£85, Sb-£110, Db-£120–140, Tb-£155, CC:VMA, 28 Ebury Street, SW1W 0LU, tel. 0171/730 8147, fax 0171/823 5966, Web site: www.tophams.com, e-mail: tophams_belgravia.compuserve.com).

Lesser values near Victoria Station for travelers wanting more comforts: **Quality Hotel Eccleston** is big and modern (Db-£87–100, 82 Eccleston Square, SW1V 1PS, tel. 0171/834-8042, fax 0171/630-8942, e-mail: admin@gb614.u-net.com). Smaller, warmer, and farther from Victoria Station is **Windermere Hotel** (S-£59, Sb-£70, D-£70, Db-£85–100, CC:VMA, 142 Warwick Way, London SW1V 4JE, tel. 0171/834 5163, fax 0171/630 8831, e-mail: 100773.1171@compuserve.com).

Elizabeth Hotel, once a budget bargain, is currently under-going renovation into a four-star hotel. Its prices will be sky-high, though it will still have a great location and traditional feel, a large elegant lobby with an elevator, airy and pleasant rooms, and free access to the private park the hotel overlooks (call for prices and re-opening info, 37 Eccleston Square, SW1V 1PB, tel. 0171/828-6812, fax 0171/828-6814).

Big, Cheap, Modern Hotels

The Travel Inn chain runs three hotels in London, each of which offers 200-plus cookie-cutter rooms with all the necessary com-forts. With long soulless halls and cheesy restaurants and bars, you won't want to savor the ambience, but you can't beat the price for a no-nonsense hotel room (Db-£55 for two adults and up to two children, breakfast extra, book long in advance, no-show rooms are released at 16:00, elevator, some smoke-free and easy-access rooms, CC:VMA, tel. 01582/414-341, fax 01582/400-024 for all). Choose from **London Euston** near the British Library and Euston Station (141 Euston Road, NW1 2AU London) and the much more central **London County Hall**, just across Westmin-ster Bridge from Big Ben, built into the old County Hall building (Belvedere Road, SE1 7PB London). A third Travel Inn, **London Putney Bridge**, is farther away at London's Putney Bridge (tube: Putney Bridge).

"South Kensington," She Said, Loosening His Cummerbund

If you'd like to live on a quiet street so classy it doesn't allow hotel signs, surrounded by trendy shops and colorful restaurants, call "South Ken" your London home. Shoppers like being a short walk from Harrods and the designer shops of King's Road and Chelsea. Budget ethnic eateries line Old Brompton Road (each hotel has restaurant scrapbooks or wall charts). But this ultimate fairy-tale London home-away-from-home comes with a price. When I splurge, I splurge here. Sumner Place is 200 yards from the South Kensington tube station (on Circle Line, two stops from Victoria Station, direct Heathrow connection; at top of the stairs of South Ken tube stop, exit left, cross doubled street, go right two blocks down Old Brompton Road, and turn left onto Sumner Place).

Aster House Hotel has classy rooms, each with a TV, tele-phone, and fridge. Enjoy breakfast in the whisper-elegant Orangerie, a Victorian greenhouse and lounge in the tidy back garden (Sb-£60–80, third floor Db-£110, Db-£120, deluxe four-poster Db with bath and shower-£135, CC:VM, entirely non-smoking, 3 Sumner Place, SW7 3EE, tel. 0171/581-5888, fax 0171/584-4925, e-mail: asterhouse@btinternet.com, run by man-ager Simon Tan).

Five Sumner Place Hotel is informal but professional, "highly commended," and recently voted "the best small hotel in London." You'll talk softly but not feel like you should have dressed up as you wander under the chandeliers out to the Victorian-style conservatory—a greenhouse dressed in blue—for breakfast. Each room in this 150-year-old building is tastefully decorated with traditional period furnishings (Sb-£88, Db-£130–141, third bed is £24 extra, elevator, CC:VMA, easy CC reservations, nonsmoking, 5 Sumner Place, South Kensington, SW7 3EE, tel. 0171/584-7586, fax 0171/823-9962, e-mail: no.5@dial.pipex.com).

Nearby are lesser values for classier travelers: **16 Sumner Place** has over-the-top formality and class (Db-£155–185, CC:VMA, no breakfast room, 16 Sumner Place, London SW7 3EG, tel. 0171/589 5232, fax 0171/584 8615, U.S. tel. 800/592 5387). **Kensington Juries Hotel** is big and stately (Sb/Db/Tb-£99–145 depending upon "availability," breakfast extra, piano lounge, elevator, Queen's Gate, South Kensington, SW7 5LR, tel. 0171/589-6300, fax 0171/581-1492). **The Claverley**, just a couple of blocks from Harrods, is on a quiet street similar to Sumner Place. The rooms are warmly furnished with elegant drapery and all the comforts (S-£70, Sb-£75–115, Db-£110–140, sofa-bed Tb-£160–215, CC:VMA, some balconies, 13-14 Beaufort Gardens, SW3 1PS, tube: Knightsbridge, tel. 0171/589-8541, fax 0171/584-3410, from the United States tel. 800/747-0398).

Sleeping in Notting Hill Gate Neighborhood

Residential Notting Hill Gate has quick and easy bus or tube access to downtown, it's on the A2 Airbus line from Heathrow (second and third stops from airport, after Kensington Hilton), and, for London, is very "homely." Notting Hill Gate has a self-serve launderette, an artsy theater, a late-hours supermarket, and lots of fun budget eateries (see Eating, below). All recommended accommodations are near the Holland Park or Notting Hill Gate tube stations. (Notting Hill Gate is in the central zone and on the Circle Line, handier and 40p cheaper from anywhere in the center than the Holland Park station.)

Westland Hotel is comfortable, convenient, and hotelesque with a fine lounge and a friendly family-run feel. The spacious 1970s-style rooms come with a phone, video-player, hair dryer, and coffeemaker (Sb-£80, Db-£95, cavernous deluxe Db-£110, sprawling Tb-£120, gargantuan Qb-£135, elevator, free garage, CC:VMA, reserve with a credit card, midway between Notting Hill Gate and Queensway tube stations, 154 Bayswater Road, W2 4HP, tel. 0171/229-9191, fax 0171/727-1054). A block away, their **Westland Annex** offers plainer, quieter, cheaper rooms (Sb-£66, Db-£82, family deals also, same front desk and breakfast room as hotel).

London, Notting Hill Gate Neighborhood

1 WESTLAND HOTEL	**4** NORWEGIAN YWCA	**7** LADBROKE ARMS PUB
2 VICARAGE PRIVATE HOTEL & ABBEY HOUSE HOTEL	**5** MAGGIE JONES RESTAURANT	**8** GEALE'S FISH & CHIPS
3 RAVNA GORA HOTEL	**6** CHURCHILL ARMS PUB	**9** MODHUBON INDIAN REST.

Vicarage Private Hotel, understandably popular, is family-run and elegantly British in a quiet, classy neighborhood. It has 19 rooms furnished with taste and quality, lots of stairs, a TV lounge, and facilities on each floor. Mandy, Richard, and Tere maintain a homey and caring atmosphere. Reserve long in advance with a one-night deposit. There's no better room for the price (S-£40, D-£63, T-£80, Q-£88, a six-minute walk from the Notting Hill Gate and High Street Kensington tube stations, near Kensington Palace at 10 Vicarage Gate, Kensington, W8 4AG, tel. 0171/229-4030, fax 0171/792-5989, Web site: www.londonvicaragehotel.com). **Abbey House Hotel**, next door, is similar but has no lounge and is a bit less cozy (S-£40, D-£65, T-£78, Q-£90, Quint-£100, 11 Vicarage Gate, Kensington, W8 4AG, tel. 0171/727-2594).

Hotel Ravna Gora was formerly the mansion of 18th-century architect Henry Holland. Now it's a large Slavic-run B&B—eccentric and well-worn, but handy for the price. Wry

Manda and jocular Rijko offer a royal pre-Tito TV room and a good English breakfast. It has plain, tired rooms, musty shower stalls, a creaky spiral staircase, easy parking, and a Balkan ambience. With the right approach a stay here is a fun memory. With the wrong approach it's a big mistake (S-£30, D-£50, Db-£60, T-£60, Tb-£80, Q-£80, Qb-£88, CC:VM, 50 yards from Holland Park tube station, facing but set back from a busy road, 29 Holland Park Avenue, W11 3RW, tel. 0171/727-7725, fax 0171/221-4282).

Norwegian YWCA (Norsk K.F.U.K.) is for women under 30 only (and men with Norwegian passports). It's an incredible value. Located on a quiet, stately street, it offers smoke-free rooms, a study, TV room, piano lounge, and an open-face Norwegian ambience. All rooms (except singles) have private showers. They have mostly quads, so those willing to share with strangers are most likely to get a place (July–August: Ss-£27, bed in shared double-£25, shared triple-£21 apiece, shared quad-£18 apiece, with breakfast; September–June: same prices but with dinner included; CC:VM, 52 Holland Park, W11 3R5, tel. & fax 0171/727-9897). With each visit I wonder which is easier—getting a sex change or a Norwegian passport?

Sleeping in Other Neighborhoods

Near King's Cross: Methodist International House is a youthful Christian residence filled mostly with Asian and African students. It's great if you want a truly worldwide dorm experience at a price that will bolster your faith. The smoke-free rooms are studious, with a desk and reading lamp. The atmosphere is friendly, safe, clean, and controlled, with a silent study room, reading lounge, TV lounge, game room, and laundry facilities (S-£26, D-£46, a bed in a shared T-£21, includes breakfast and a cafeteria dinner, 81-103 Euston Street, W1 2EZ, reserve long in advance, tel. 0171/380-0001, fax 0171/387-5300. Rooms are most likely available during school breaks, including summer. The included evening "tea" (supper) is great for meeting other residents.

Bloomsbury, near the British Museum: Cambria House, a fine value, is run by the Salvation Army (a plus when it comes to cheap big-city hotels.) This smoke-free old building with a narrow maze of halls is all newly painted and super clean, if institutional. The rooms are large and perfectly good. You'll find ample showers and toilets on each floor, a TV lounge, and a warm welcome (S-£27, D-£43, Db-£53, T-£64, CC:VM, north of Russell Square, handy to British Museum at 37 Hunter Street, WC1N 1BJ, tel. 0171/837-1654, fax 0171/837-1229).

Downtown near Baker Street: For a homey alternative in the center, consider renting comfortable well-appointed rooms in this B&B (Db-£80, Tb-£120, strictly smoke-free, at 22 York Street between Baker Street and Oxford Street, tel. 0171/224-3990, fax 0171/224-1990, Liz and Michael).

Near St. Paul's: The **City of London Youth Hostel** is clean, modern, friendly, and well-run. You'll pay about £23 for a bed in two- to five-bed rooms, £25 in a single (CC:VM, cheap meals, 36 Carter Lane, EC4V 5AD, tube: St. Paul's, tel. 0171/236-4965, fax 0171/236-7681).

Near Sloane Square: Hotel Oakley is like a run-down B&B in a fine neighborhood (S-£32, D-£42, Db-£56, CC:VMA, 73 Oakley Street, just off King's Road, 10-minute walk from Sloane Square tube, tel. 0171/352-5599).

South of town: Mary Ward's Guest House is sleepable but very simple. On a quiet street in a well-worn neighborhood south of Victoria near Clapham Common, this beats the hostel. Friendly Mary Ward (Edith Bunker's English aunt) has been renting her five super-cheap rooms to budget travelers for 25 years (S-£12.50, D-£25 with English breakfast, 98 Hambalt Road, Clapham Common, SW4 9EJ London, tel. 0181/673-1077). It's 15 minutes by tube to Clapham Common, then a short bus ride or a 12-minute walk—exit left down Clapham South Road, left on Elms, right on Abbeville Road, left on Hambalt. Rooms in Mary's son's house are an equally good value.

Near Gatwick Airport: The peaceful **Crutchfield Farm B&B** offers three comfortable rooms in a 600-year-old renovated farmhouse. Gillian Blok includes a ride to the airport (Sb-£45, Db-£65, Tb-£75, Qb-£85, two miles from Gatwick Airport—£5 by taxi, 30 minutes by train from London, at Hookwood, Surrey, RH6 OHT, tel. 01293/863-110, fax 01293/863-233). **Barn Cottage**, a converted 17th-century barn in a large garden, has quiet rooms 10 minutes from Gatwick (S-£28, D-£45, Leigh/Reigate/Surrey RH2 8RF, tel. 01306/611-347, warmly run by Pat and Mike Comer). **Lynwood Guest House** (10 minutes by train to Gatwick, 30 minutes by train from London) offers a cozy alternative to big-city lodging in Redhill, a normal workaday English town. It's just a five-minute walk from the train station, but the gracious owner Shanta may pick you up if she's got the car. Ask for a quiet room off the street (Ss-£28, Ds-£42, Db-£45, Tb-£58, Qb-£65, cheaper off-season, 50 London Road, Redhill, Surrey RH1 1LN, tel. 01737/766-894, fax 0171/778-253).

Sleeping and Eating in Hampstead, the Small-Town Alternative

If you must "do" London but wish it was a small town, make Hampstead your homebase-on-the-hill. Just 15 to 30 minutes north of the center by tube (to Hampstead on the sometimes tardy Northern Line) and you're in the former resort of wealthy Londoners—drawn by spas in the 1700s and the brilliant views of London from the popular Hampstead Heath, an 800-acre park.

Hampstead today glows with Georgian village elegance—

narrow cobblestone lanes, gas lamps (now electrified), blue plaques noting where Keats, Freud, and other famous locals lived. Even McDonald's has a mock-Tudor facade.

The tube station marks the center of the town. From there, busy High Street cuts downhill though the center. Following it downhill takes you into a cheery business district with side streets flickering with gaslit charm. The hotel is a three-minute walk uphill. The B&B is a brisk 10-minute walk downhill. The Freemason's Arms pub (best for dinner) is a couple of blocks beyond the B&B. And all other pubs and restaurants are within five minutes of the tube station. Everything's near the park.

Make a point to explore the back lanes where you can pop into churches and peek into windows—drapes are left open so their elegant interiors can be envied.

Hampstead Village Guesthouse is run in a laissez-faire style by Anne Marie van der Meer, who rents nine rooms and raised her family in this Victorian house. The homey rooms, most named after her children, lack locks, but come with a phone, miniature fridge, TV, and even a hot-water bottle (S-£32, D-£55, Db-£65, breakfast-£6, CC:VMA only for reservation deposit, payment in cash, nonsmoking, extremely quiet, book well in advance, walk 10 minutes from tube: downhill on High Street, left on Pilgrims Lane to 2 Kemplay Road, Hampstead, London NW3 1SY, tel. 0171/435 8679, fax 0171/794-0254, e-mail: hvguesthouse@dial.pipex.com).

La Gaffe Hotel is a sweet Italian-run hotel and restaurant right on Heath Street. Rooms are small and well-worn but floral, comfy, and quiet (Sb-£55, Db-£80–115, includes breakfast, TV, phones, nonsmoking, walk uphill from the tube station three minutes to 107 Heath Street, Hampstead, London, NW3 6SS, 0171/435 8965, fax 1071/794-7592, e-mail: la-gaffe@msn.com).

Eating in Hampstead: Freemason's Arms is the place for classy pub grub. If the lighting doesn't make your partner look delicious, the Czech lager will. Set on the edge of the heath with a spacious interior and sprawling beer garden for summer outdoor seating, the Freemason's Arms serves great English food every day (£7 meals, skittles downstairs three nights a week—private but peeking permitted; down High Street, left on Downshire Hill Road to #32, tel. 0171/433-6811).

Down High Street from the tube stop you'll find Hampstead swinging at **The House on Rosslyn Hill** (international cuisine, modern brasserie, young, trendy, popular with locals; meals start at £10, 34 Rosslyn Hill, tel. 0171/435-8037).

French Hampstead cooks a block below the tube station. For a quick bite, **Maison Blanc** not only has the best croissants in town, but also makes great savories like Roquefort and walnut *fougasse* (focaccia pockets) or *tarte Provençal* (tomato, zucchini, and

Gruyère mini-quiche); all this plus lovely strong French coffee for £2 to £3, on Hampstead High Street. **Cafe des Arts** serves French food in a rustic candlelit English setting (nightly until 23:00, 82 Hampstead High Street). Next door there's even a little crepe cart in search of Paris.

There's a handy grocery store next to the tube station. But for real village atmosphere, shop at the **Hampstead Foodhall** on Fitzjohn Avenue. There's no place better for a dinner picnic with a view than Hampstead Heath (a 10-minute hike away).

For a laid-back crowd and a good fireplace to enjoy with your beer, visit the **Holly Bush** pub (no meals but toasted sandwiches, hidden on a quiet lane uphill from tube). For a livelier spit-and-sawdust pub, toss your darts with the locals at **The Flask** (on Flask walk, two blocks below the tube station).

Eating in London

If you want to dine (as opposed to eat), check out the extensive listings in *Time Out* (or the train schedule for Paris). The thought of a £25 meal in Britain generally ruins my appetite, so my London dining is limited mostly to unremarkable but inexpensive alternatives. I've listed places by neighborhood—handy to your sightseeing or hotel.

Your £5 budget choices are pub grub, a café, fish and chips, pizza, ethnic, or picnic. Pub grub is the most atmospheric budget option. Many of London's 7,000 pubs serve fresh, tasty buffets under ancient timbers, with hearty lunches and dinners priced around £5. Ethnic restaurants from all over the world more than make up for England's lackluster cuisine. Eating Indian is "going local" in London. It's also going cheap (cheaper if you order take-out). Chinese and Italian places are not quite the same value. Most large museums (and many churches) have reasonable and handy cafeterias. Of course, picnicking is the fastest and cheapest way to go. Good grocery stores and sandwich shops, fine park benches, and polite pigeons abound in Britain's most expensive city.

Eating near Trafalgar Square

For a tasty meal on a monk's budget in an ancient crypt sitting on somebody's tomb, descend into the **St. Martin-in-the-Fields Café in the Crypt** (Monday–Saturday 10:00–20:00, Sunday 12:00–20:30, £5–7 cafeteria plates, cheaper sandwich bar, profits go to the church; underneath St. Martin-in-the-Fields on Trafalgar Square, tel. 0171/839-4342). Down Whitehall (toward Big Ben), a block from Trafalgar Square, you'll find the touristy but atmospheric **Clarence Pub** (decent grub) and several cheaper cafeterias and pizza joints. For a classy lunch, treat your palate to the pricier **Brasserie** (open daily, on first floor of Sainsbury Wing of the National Gallery). **Simpson's in the Strand** serves a stuffy, aristocratic old-time carvery dinner (where the chef slices your favorite red meat from a fancy trolley at your table) in their elegant smoky old dining room (£20, daily 12:00–15:00 and 17:30–23:00, tel. 0171/836-9112).

Chandos Bar's Opera Room is amazingly apart from the tacky crush of tourism around Trafalgar Square. Look for the pub opposite the National Portrait Gallery (corner of William Street and St. Martin's Lane) and climb the stairs to the Opera Room. They serve pub lunches and dinners, and £5 cheese, salad, and cold plate deals all day long (tel. 0171/836-1401). This is my favorite rendezvous point around Trafalgar. It's a smoky but wonderfully London scene.

Gordon's Wine Bar is the place to go for a local crowd and atmosphere. A simple steep staircase leads into a cellar filled with candlelight, dusty old wine bottles, faded British memorabilia, and local nine-to-fivers (hot meals only for lunch, fine cheese and salad buffet all day until 21:00—one plate of each feeds two for £7). While Gordon's is usually crowded, you can normally corral two chairs and grab the corner of a table (11:00–23:00, Saturday 17:00–23:00, closed Sunday, two blocks from Trafalgar Square, bottom of Villiars Street at #47, between the Embankment and Charing Cross tube stations, tel. 0171/930-1408).

Eating near Piccadilly

Hungry and broke in the theater district? Head for Panton Street (just off Haymarket, two blocks southeast of Picadilly Circus) for a line of decent eateries. **Stockpot**, is a mushy-peas kind of place, famous and rightly popular for its edible, cheap meals (Monday–Saturday 8:00–23:00, Sunday 8:00–22:00, 40 Panton Street). The **West End Kitchen** (across the street at #5, same hours and menu, fine seating downstairs) is a direct competitor and just as good. The original **Stockpot**, a few blocks away, has better atmosphere (daily noon–23:00, a block north of Shaftesbury near Cambridge Circus at 18 Old Compton Street).

The palatial **Criterion Brasserie**, serving a two-course menu for £15 under gilded tiles and chandeliers (12:00–14:30 and 18:00–18:30 only) is right on Piccadilly Circus but a world away from the punk junk (tel. 0171/930-0488). The **Wren Café** at St. James Church is exclusively vegetarian, wonderfully green, and in a pleasant garden next to one of Wren's best churches—peek inside (Monday–Saturday 9:00–17:00, Sunday 10:00–16:00, two minutes southwest of Piccadilly Circus at 192 Piccadilly Street, tel. 0171/437-9419).

Near Covent Gardens, the area around Neal Yard is busy with fun eateries. One of the best is **Food for Thought** (serving until 20:15, closed Sunday, very good £4 vegetarian meals, smoke-free, two blocks north of Covent Garden tube stop, 31 Neal Street, tel. 0171/836-0239).

The Food-Is-Fun Dinner Crawl: From Convent Garden to Soho

London has a trendy, Generation X scene that most beefeater-seekers miss entirely. For a multicultural moveable feast and a chance to sample some of London's most popular eateries, consider sampling these. To avoid lines, to get in on early specials, and to find waiters happy to let you split a meal, start around 18:00. Prices, while reasonable by London standards, add up. Servings are large enough to share. All are open nightly.

Suggested nibbler's dinner crawl for two: Arrive before 18:00 at Belgo and split the early-bird dinner special: a kilo of mussels, fries with a dark Belgian beer; at Soho Spice Indian, split the "Tandoori selections"; at Yo Sushi, have beer or sake and a few dishes; slurp your last course at Wagamama; for dessert, people-watch at Leicester Square, where the serf's always up.

Belgo Centraal is a space station world overrun with Trappist monks serving hearty Belgian specialties. The classy restaurant section requires reservations, but just grabbing a bench in the boisterous beer hall is much more fun. Belgians eat as well as the French and as hearty as the Germans. Specialties include mussels, great fries, and a stunning array of dark, blond, and fruity Belgian beers. Belgo actually makes things Belgian trendy—a formidable feat (£12 meals, Monday–Friday 17:00–18:30, "beat-the-clock" meal specials cost only the time . . . £5–6.30 and you get mussels, fries, and beer; no meal-splitting after 18:30, £5 lunch special daily, one block north of Covent Garden tube station at intersection of Neal and Shelton Streets, 50 Earlham St, tel. 0171/813-2233).

Soho Spice Indian is where modern Britain meets Indian tradition—fine Indian cusine in a trendy jewel-tone ambience (£14 "Tandoori selections" meal is the best "variety" dish and big enough for two, nonsmoking section, five blocks due north of Piccadilly Circus at 124 Wardour Street, tel. 0171/434-0808).

Wagamama Noodle Bar is a mod, watch-it-boiled, pan-Asian slurpathon. As you enter, check out the kitchen and listen to the roar of the basement where a youthful crowd shares benches and waiters take orders with walkie-talkies. Everything's organic—stand against the wall to feel the energy of all this "positive eating" (daily 12:00–23:00, crowded after 20:00, just past the porno and prostitition core of Soho but entirely smoke-free, 10A Lexington Street, tel. 0171/292-0990).

Yo! Sushi is a futuristic Japanese food extravaganza experience. With thumping rock, Japanese cable TV, a 60-meter-long conveyor-belt sushi bar (the world's longest), automated sushi machines, and a robotic drink trolley, just sipping a sake on a barstool here is a trip. For £1 you get unlimited tea (request), water (from spigot at bar, with or without gas), or miso soup. Grab dishes as they rattle by and a drink off the robot (daily 12:00–24:00, two blocks south of Oxford Street, where Lexington Street becomes Poland Street, 52 Poland St., tel. 0171/287-0443).

Soho Soho French Bistro-Rotisserie is a chance to go French in a Matisse-esque setting. The ground floor is a trendy wine bar. Upstairs is an oasis of peace serving £17, three-course French "pre-theater specials"—order from 18:00 to 19:30 (near Cambridge Circus, two blocks east of Charing Cross Road at 11 Frith Street, tel. 0171/494-3491).

Andrew Edmunds Restaurant is a tiny, candlelit place where you'll want to hide your camera and guidebook and act as local as possible. The continental and traditional cooking is worth the splurge (three courses for £20, 46 Lexington Street, Soho, reservations are smart, tel. 0171/437-5708).

Eating near Recommended Victoria Station Neighborhood Accommodations

Here are some places a couple of blocks southeast of Victoria Station where I've enjoyed eating: **Jenny Lo's Tea House** is a simple, for-the-joy-of-good-food kind of place serving up £5 Cantonese meals to locals in the know (Monday–Saturday 12:00–15:00 and 18:00–22:00, 14 Eccleston Street, tel. 0171/259-0399). For pub grub with good local atmosphere, consider the **Plumbers Arms** (filling £5 hot meals and cheaper sandwiches, closed Saturday and Sunday nights, indoor/outdoor seating, 14 Lower Belgrave Street, tel. 0171/ 730-4067; ask about the murdered nanny—and the distraught wife who ran into the plumber's arms).

Next door, the small but classy **La Campagnola** is Belgravia's favorite budget Italian restaurant (£10 meals, closed Sunday, reservations wise on Thursday and Friday, 10 Lower Belgrave Street, tel. 0171/730-2057). Across the street, the **Maestro Bar** is the closest thing to an English tapas bar I've seen, with salads, sandwiches, and 10 bar stools (very cheap).

The **Ebury Wine Bar** offers a French, smoky ambience and pricey but delicious meals (£15, daily 12:00–15:00 and 18:00–22:30, 139 Ebury Street at intersection with Elizabeth Street, near the coach station, tel. 0171/730-5447). Several cheap places are around the corner on Elizabeth Street (#23 for take-out or eat-in fish and chips).

The **Duke of Wellington** pub is good, if smoky, for dinner (£5 meals, 12:00–15:00 and 18:00–21:30, closed Sunday evening, 63 Eaton Terrace). **Peter's Restaurant** is the cabbie's hangout— cheap food, smoke, and chatter (at intersection of Ebury and Pimlico). Nearby, the **Flamenco** has decent, if pricey, Spanish tapas (54 Pimlico).

For picnics, the nearest supermarket is **J. Sainsbury**, a five-minute walk from Victoria Station (Monday–Saturday 7:30–20:00, Sunday 10:00–16:00, on Victoria Street, just after the intersection with Palace Street). The late-hours **Whistle Stop** grocery at the station has decent sandwiches and a fine salad bar. The **Marche** is an easy cafeteria north of Victoria Station at Bressenden Place.

Eating near Recommended Notting Hill Gate B&Bs

Best classy English meal in London: The rustic and very English **Maggie Jones** serves my favorite £20 London dinner. You'll get solid English cuisine with huge plates of vegetables by candlelight (daily 18:30–23:00, CC:VMA, 6 Old Court Place, just east of Kensington Church Street, near the High Street Kensington tube stop, reservations recommended, tel. 0171/937-6462). If you eat well once in London, eat here (and do it quick, before it burns down).

Good pub grub: The **Churchill Arms** pub is a local hangout with good beer and old-English ambience in front and hearty £5 Thai plates in an enclosed patio in the back (Monday–Saturday 11:00–23:00, 119 Kensington Church Street, tel. 0171/727-4242). The **Windsor Castle Pub** is a great, smoky, and happy scene specializing in traditional sausages and oysters (114 Campden Hill, tel. 0171/243-9551). The smoky **Ladbroke Arms Pub** serves country-style meals that are one step above pub grub in quality and price (daily 12:00–14:30 and 19:00–22:00, great indoor/outdoor ambience, 54 Ladbroke Road, behind Holland Park tube station, tel. 0171/727-6648).

Top fish and chips: The almost-too-popular **Geale's** has long been considered one of London's best fish-and-chips joints (£8 meals, Tuesday–Saturday 12:00–15:00 and 18:00–23:00, 2 Farmer Street, just off Notting Hill Gate behind the Gate Cinema, tel. 0171/727-7969). Get there early for a place to sit (they take no reservations) and the best selection of fish.

Miscellaneous NHG eateries: Costas has eat-in or take-out fish and chips (£5 meals, Tuesday–Saturday 12:00–14:30 and 17:30-10:30, near the Coronet Theatre at 18 Hillgate Street). Next door, the **Hillgate Pub** has good food and famous hot saltbeef sandwiches (daily 11:00–23:00, indoor/outdoor seating, tel. 0171/727-8543). The **Modhubon** Indian restaurant is not too spicy, "vedy vedy nice," and has cheap lunch specials (Sunday–Friday 12:00–15:00 and 18:00–24:00, Saturday 12:00–24:00, 29 Pembridge Road, tel. 0171/727-3399). Next door is a cheap Chinese take-out (daily 17:30–24:00, 19 Pembridge Road) and the tiny **Prost Restaurant and Schnapps Bar** which busily keeps yuppie vegetarians as well as carnivores happy (£10 meals, Monday–Friday 17:30–23:00, weekends 10:30–23:00, 35 Pembridge Road, tel. 0171/727-9620). **Cafe Diana** is a healthy little sandwich shop where you eat surrounded by photos of Princess Diana (5 Wellington Terrace, on Bayswater Road, opposite Kensington Palace Garden Gates).

For a picnic dinner, shop at the **Europe Superstore** (Monday–Saturday 8:30–23:00, Sunday 12:00–18:00, 50 yards west of Notting Hill tube station on Notting Hill Gate).

Just a short tube ride away, you'll find Old Brompton Road and Thurloe Street (each starting at the South Kensington tube station), lined with popular little eateries. Case out the several places along Thurloe Street. At the end you'll find **Daquise**, a smoké-free, authentic-feeling Polish place, ideal if you're in the mood for kielbasa and kraut. It's fast, cheap, faded, family-run, and a part of the neighborhood (daily until 23:30, 20 Thurloe Street, tel. 0171/589-6117).

Transportation Connections—London

Flying into London's Heathrow Airport

Heathrow Airport is user-friendly. Read signs, ask questions. Most flights from the United States land at Terminal 3, but British Air's transatlantic flights land at Terminal 4 (same services as Terminal 3, but no TI).

In Terminal 3 you'll find: exchange bureaus (24 hours daily, OK rates, £3 fees), an airport terminal information desk (pick up a map and ask questions, but for the official TI, see below), car rental agencies (if you're renting a car, stop to confirm your plans), a £3-a-day baggage-check desk, and a TI. The American Express desk, with better rates than the banks, is in the "underground" at Terminal 4. For Heathrow's flight and transfers information call 0181/759-4321.

Heathrow's TI gives you all the help that London's Victoria Station does, with none of the crowds (daily 8:30–18:00, a five-minute walk from Terminal 3, TI next to tube station, follow signs to the "underground"). If you're riding the Airbus into London, have your partner stay with the bags at the terminal. At the TI, get a free simple map and brochures, and buy a subway pass if you're riding the tube into London.

Buses from Heathrow: The National Express Central Bus Station offers direct bus connections to **Cambridge** (hrly, 3.5 hrs, £16), **Cheltenham** (6/day, 2 hrs, £19), **York** (3/day, 6 hrs, £32), **Gatwick** (2/hrly, 1 hr), and **Bath** (9/day, starting at 8:35, 10:35, and so on, 2.5 hrs, £19, direct, tel. 0990-808-080). Or try the slick 2.5-hour Heathrow–Bath bus/train connection via Reading. Buy the £26 ticket at the desk in the terminal (credit cards accepted), then catch the twice-hourly shuttle bus to Reading (RED-ding) to hop on the express train to Bath.

Heathrow and the Four Terminals

Transportation to London from Heathrow Airport

By Tube (subway): For £3.20 ("free" with £4.30 all-zone, all-day-after-9:30 tube pass) the tube takes you 14 miles to Victoria Station in 45 minutes (6/hrly, one change).

By Airbus: All my recommended hotel neighborhoods are on one of the two airbus lines (serving each terminal, £6, 2/hrly, 5:00–20:00, buy ticket on bus, tel. 0181/400-6655). If you take A1, South Kensington is the third stop, and Victoria Station is the last stop. On A2, the second and third stops cover Notting Hill Gate. The tube works fine, but with baggage I prefer the airbus—no connections underground and a lovely view from the top of the double-decker bus. Ask the driver to remind you when to get off. If you're going to the airport, exact pick-up times are clearly posted at each bus stop.

By Taxi: Taxis from the airport cost about £35. For four traveling together this can be a deal. Hotels can often line up a cab back to the airport for £28.

By Heathrow Express Train: This new train service zips air travelers between Heathrow and the Paddington Station in town (£5, 4/hrly from 5:10–22:40, 30 min, tel. 0845/600-1515). Unfortunately, Paddington is far from the recommended B&Bs.

Flying into London's Gatwick Airport

More and more flights, especially charters, land at Gatwick Airport, halfway between London and the southern coast. Trains—clearly the best way into London from here—shuttle conveniently between Gatwick and London's Victoria Station (4/hrly, 30 min, £9). Those catching a train for York or Edinburgh can ride a Thameslink train from Gatwick directly to Thameslink King's Cross (100 yards from the King's Cross Station and trains to the north). Gatwick information tel. 01293/535-353.

Trains and Buses

For train schedules and fares for any journey in Britain, call 0345/484-950 from anywhere in Britain (or from the States: dial 011/44/345-484-950). Ask for the cheapest fare for your journey; if you want to book with a credit card you'll be referred to the appropriate rail company's phone number. You'll save money on point-to-point train tickets if you purchase in advance: To get Apex fares, buy seven days ahead (available for moderate-length or longer journeys); for Super Apex fares, buy 14 days in advance (for long journeys only). This is worth the expense and trouble only if you're willing to pin down dates for your longer trips. For more information, see Transportation in the Introduction.

London, Britain's major transportation hub, has a different train station for each region. The train station you arrive at (or leave from) depends on where you came from (or where you're going). King's Cross covers northeast England and Scotland (tel. 0171/278-2477). Paddington covers west and southwest England and South Wales (tel. 0171/262-6767). For the others, call 0171/928-5100.

National Express's excellent bus service is considerably cheaper than trains. (For a busy signal, call 0990-808-080; or visit the bus station a block south of Victoria train station.)

To Bath: Trains leave London's Paddington Station every hour (at a quarter after) for the £28.50, 75-minute ride to Bath. Consider taking a guided bus tour from London to Stonehenge and Bath, and simply leaving the tour in Bath. Both Evan Evans (tel. 0181/332-2222) and Travelline (tel. 0181/668-7261) offer Stonehenge/Bath day trips from London.

To points north: Trains run hourly from London's King's Cross Station and stop in York (2 hrs), Durham (3 hrs), and Edinburgh (5 hrs). For Cambridge connections, see below.

To Dublin, Ireland: The boat/rail journey takes 10 hours, all day or all night (£40–60). Consider a British Midland flight (Heathrow–Dublin, 10/day, 70 min, about £105 one-way, as little as £70 return for a stay over Saturday, tel. 0345/554-554 or, in the United States, 800/788-0555).

Flights

British Midland, the local discount airline, offers many flights cheaper than train connections. For £120 you can fly round-trip to Dublin, Paris, Amsterdam, or Frankfurt. For the latest, call 0345/554-554 or, in the United States, 800/788-0555.

Crossing the English Channel

By Eurostar Train: The fastest and most convenient way to get from Big Ben to the Eiffel Tower is now by rail. Eurostar is the speedy passenger train that zips you (and up to 800 others in 18 sleek, TGV-type cars) from downtown London to downtown Paris (12/day, 3 hrs) or Brussels (6/day, 3 hrs). The train goes 100 mph in England and 160 mph on the Continent. The actual tunnel crossing is a 20-minute black, silent, 100 mph nonevent. Your ears won't even pop. You can change at Lille to catch a TGV directly to Paris' De Gaulle Airport or Disneyland Paris. Yes!

Channel fares (essentially the same to Paris or Brussels) are reasonable but complicated. For the latest fares, call 800/EUROSTAR in the United States (or go to www.eurostar.com). The "Leisure" ticket is cheap ($109 second class, $179 first class, 50 percent refundable up to two days before departure). Fully refundable "Full-fare" first class costs $219 including a meal (a dinner departure nets you more grub than breakfast); second class ("standard") costs $149.

Discounts are available for travelers holding railpasses that include France, Belgium, or Britain (about $50 off "Full-fare"); youths under 26 ($70 off 2nd class "Full-fare"); and children under 12 (half the fare of your ticket). Cheaper seats can sell out. You can book your ticket from the United States. When you're ready to commit to a date and time, book a reservation through your travel agent. Prices do not include FedEx delivery. Note: Britian's time zone is one hour earlier than the Continent's (times listed on ticket are local times).

If you buy your Eurostar ticket in London, here are some sample fares for standard (second class) travel from London to Paris or Brussels: Those with a railpass pay £45 one-way, any day. Without a railpass, a same-day round-trip on a Saturday or Sunday costs £79. A Leisure ticket, if you stay at least three nights or over a Saturday night, is £119 round-trip. Excursion fares (purchased 7 days in advance for travel on Tuedsay, Wednesday, or Thursday, with a round-trip over a Saturday) are cheaper: round-trip for £109, and one-way for £79.

Sample first class and business class fares from London to Paris or Brussels: A regular first-class round-trip costs £319, one-way £179. A regular business-class round-trip is £220, one-way £120. A first-class Leisure ticket, if you stay at least three nights or over a Saturday night, costs £199 round-trip.

In Europe get your Eurostar ticket at any major train station or at any travel agency that handles train tickets (expect a booking fee). In Britain you can order your tickets over the phone with a credit card by calling 0345/303-030; pick up your tickets at London's Waterloo station an hour before the Eurostar departure.

By Train, Bus, and Boat: The old-fashioned way of crossing the Channel is very competitive and cheaper than Eurostar; it's also twice as romantic, twice as complicated, and twice as time-consuming. You'll get better prices arranging your trip in London than you would in the United States. Taking the bus is cheapest, and round-trips are a bargain. By bus to Paris or Amsterdam from Victoria Coach Station: £33 one-way, £49 round-trip, 10 hours, day or overnight, on Eurolines (tel. 0990-143-219) or CitySprint (tel. 0990-240-241). By train and ship: £42 one-way overnight, £59 by day, seven hours.

By Plane: Typical fares are £90 regular, £40 student stand-by. Call in London for the latest fares.

NEAR LONDON: CAMBRIDGE

Cambridge, 60 miles north of London, is world-famous for its prestigious university. Wordsworth, Isaac Newton, Tennyson, Darwin, and Prince Charles are a few of its illustrious alumni. This historic town of 100,000 people is more pleasant than its rival, Oxford. Cambridge is the epitome of a university town with busy bikers, stately residence halls, plenty of bookshops, and proud locals who can point out where electrons and DNA were discovered and where the first atom was split.

In medieval Europe, higher education was the domain of the Church and was limited to ecclesiastical schools. Scholars lived in "halls" on campus. This scholarly community of residential halls, chapels, and lecture halls connected by peaceful garden courtyards survives today in the colleges that make the universities at Cambridge and Oxford. By 1350 Cambridge had eight colleges (Oxford is roughly 100 years older), each with a monastic-type courtyard and lodgings. Today Cambridge has 31 colleges. While a student's life revolves around his or her independent college, the university organizes lectures, presents degrees, and promotes research.

The university dominates—and owns—most of Cambridge. The approximate term schedule is January 15 through March 15, April 15 through June 18, and October 8 through December 8. The colleges are closed to visitors during exams, from mid-April until late June. But the town is never sleepy.

Planning Your Time

Cambridge is worth most of a day, but not an overnight. While Cambridge can be visited on your way from London to York, the cheap day-return train plan makes Cambridge easiest and economical as a side trip from London (from London's King's Cross Station, £12.30, 2/hrly, one hour, fast trains depart at :15 and :45 past each hour each way; the budget ticket requires a departure after 9:30 except Saturday and Sunday). You can arrive in time for the 11:30 walking tour (an essential part of any visit) and spend the afternoon touring King's College and the Fitzwilliam Museum and simply enjoying the ambience of this stately old college town. Accommodations are frustrating in Cambridge.

Orientation (tel. code: 01223)

Cambridge is small but congested. There are two main streets separated from the river by the most interesting colleges. The town center has a TI, a colorful marketplace, and several parking lots. Everything is within a pleasant walk.

Tourist Information: The TI is on the town square (Monday–Saturday 10:00–18:00 or 18:30, summer Sundays 11:00–16:00, closed winter Sundays, tel. 01223/322-640).

Arrival in Cambridge: To get to downtown Cambridge from the train station, take a 20-minute walk, a £3.50 taxi ride, or bus #1 (90p, every eight minutes). For drivers, Cambridge's huge, central Short Stay Parking Lot is handy.

Tours of Cambridge

▲▲**Walking Tour of the Colleges**—A walking tour is the best way to understand Cambridge's mix of "town and gown." Walks give a good rundown on the historic and scenic highlights of the university, as well as some fun local gossip. (Walks are run by and leave from the tourist office. July and August tours start at 10:30, 11:30, 13:30, and 14:30; the rest of the year they generally start at 11:30 and 13:30). Tours cost £6.25 and include admission to King's College Chapel. Drop by the TI early to reserve a spot, or call to book a spot with your credit card (TI tel. 01223/322-640). Particularly if you're coming from London, try calling to at least confirm that a tour is scheduled and not full. Private guides are also available.

Bus Tours—Guide Friday hop-on, hop-off bus tours (£7.50, departing every 15 minutes) are informative and cover the outskirts, but walking tours go where the buses can't—right into the center.

Sights—Cambridge

▲▲**King's College Chapel**—Built from 1446 to 1515 by Henrys VI through VIII, England's best example of Perpendicular Gothic is the single most impressive building in town. Stand inside, look up, and marvel, as Christopher Wren did, at what was the largest single span of vaulted roof anywhere—2,000 tons of incredible fan vaulting. Wander through the Old Testament via the 25 16th-century stained-glass windows (the most Renaissance stained glass anywhere in one spot; it was taken out for safety during World War II, then painstakingly replaced). Walk to the altar and admire Rubens' masterful *Adoration of the Magi* (£3, erratic hours depending on school and events, but generally 9:30–16:30). During term you're welcome to enjoy a Cambridge-quality evensong service (Tuesday–Saturday at 17:30, Sunday at 15:30).

▲▲**Trinity College**—Half of Cambridge's 63 Nobel Prize winners came from this richest and biggest of the town's colleges, founded in 1546 by Henry VIII. Don't miss the Wren-designed library with its wonderful carving and fascinating original manuscripts (free, Monday–Friday 12:00–14:00, also Saturday 10:30–12:30 during term). Just outside the library entrance, Sir Isaac Newton, who spent 30 years at Trinity, clapped his hands and timed the echo to measure the speed of sound as it raced down the side of the cloister and back. In the library you can read Newton's handwritten account of this experiment, alongside the original, handwritten *Winnie the Pooh*.

▲▲**Fitzwilliam Museum**—Britain's best museum of antiquities and art outside of London is the Fitzwilliam. Enjoy its wonderful painting collection (Old Masters; an impressive English section featuring Gainsborough, Reynolds, Hogarth, and others; works by all the famous Impressionists), old manuscripts, and Greek, Egyptian, and Mesopotamian collections (free, Tuesday–Saturday 10:00–17:00, Sunday 14:15–17:00, closed Monday, tel. 01223/332-900).

Museum of Classical Archeology—While this museum contains no originals, it offers a unique chance to see accurate copies (from 19th-century casts of the originals) of virtually every famous ancient Greek and Roman statue (more than 600 statues, free, Monday–Friday 9:00–17:00, Sidgwick Avenue, tel. 01223/335-153).

▲**Punting on the Cam**—For a little levity and probably more exercise than you really want, try hiring one of the traditional (and inexpensive) flat-bottom punts from any of four places along the river (look for stalls at either bridge) and pole yourself up and down (around and around, more likely) the lazy Cam. Once you get the hang of it, it's a fine way to enjoy the scenic side of Cambridge. After 17:00 it's less crowded and less embarrassing.

Transportation Connections—Cambridge
By train to: London's King's Cross or Liverpool Station (departures at :15 and :45 past each hour, 1 hr, one-way £13.10, cheap day-return for £13.20), **York** (hrly, 2.5 hrs, transfer in Petersborough), **Birmingham** (6/day, 3 hrs), **Liverpool** (5/day, 5 hrs), **Heathrow** (hrly buses, 3.5 hrs). Train info tel. 0345/484-950.

Route Tips for Drivers
By car it's 60 high-speed miles (with no gas stations) on the M11 motorway to London. From Cambridge any major road going west or south will direct you to the M11 motorway leading to the London ring road. Catch the poorly marked M25 outer ring road (you'll see Heathrow and Gatwick signs) and circle around to the best position to start your central attack. (You can buy a good London map at the Cambridge TI for £1.) It's a four-hour drive to York (take the more interesting A1 instead of the more tempting M1 motorway).

BATH

Any tour of Britain that skips Bath stinks. Two hundred years ago this city of 80,000 was the trend-setting Hollywood of Britain. If ever a city enjoyed looking in the mirror, Bath's the one. It has more "government-listed" or protected historic buildings per capita than any other town in England. The entire city, built of the creamy warm-tone limestone called "Bath stone," beams in its cover-girl complexion. An architectural chorus line, it's a triumph of the Georgian style. Proud locals remind visitors that the town is routinely banned from the "Britain in Bloom" contest to give other towns a chance to win. Bath's narcissism is justified. Even with its mobs of tourists, it's a joy to visit.

Long before the Romans arrived in the first century, Bath was known for its hot springs. What became the Roman spa town of Aquae Sulis has always been fueled by the healing allure of its 116-degree mineral hot springs. The town's importance carried through Saxon times when it had a huge church on the site of the present-day Abbey and was considered the religious capital of Britain. Its influence peaked in 973 when England's first king, Edgar, was crowned in the Abbey. Bath prospered as a wool town.

Bath then declined until the mid-1600s, when it was just a huddle of huts around the Abbey and a hot springs with 3,000 residents oblivious to the Roman ruins 18 feet below their dirt floors. Then, in 1687, Queen Mary, fighting infertility, bathed here. Within 10 months she gave birth to a son . . . and a new age of popularity for Bath.

The town boomed as a spa resort. Ninety percent of the buildings you'll see today are from the 18th century. Local architect John Wood was inspired by the Italian architect Palladio to build a "new Rome." The town bloomed in the neoclassical style and streets were lined not with scrawny sidewalks but with wide "parades," upon which the women in their stylishly wide dresses could spread their fashionable tails.

Beau Nash (1673–1762) was Bath's "master of ceremonies." He organized both the daily regimen of the aristocratic visitors and the city—lighting and improving security on the streets, banning swords, and opening the Pump Room. Under his fashionable baton, Bath became a city of balls, gaming, concerts, and the place to see and be seen in England. This most civilized place became even more so with the great neoclassical building spree that followed.

Planning Your Time

Bath needs two nights even on a quick trip. There's plenty to do and it's a joy to do it. On a three-week British trip, spend three nights in Bath with one day for the city and one for a side trip to Wells, Glastonbury, and Avebury. Bath could easily fill another day. Ideally, use Bath as your jet-lag recovery pillow and do London at the end of your trip.

Consider starting a three-week British vacation this way:

Day 1: Land at Heathrow. Catch the National Express bus to Bath (9/day, 2.5-hr trip). While you don't need or want a car in Bath, and most rental companies have an office there, those who pick up their cars at the airport can visit Stonehenge on their way to Bath on this day.

Day 2: 9:00—Tour the Roman Baths, 10:30—Catch the free city walking tour, 12:30—Picnic on the open deck of a Guide Friday bus tour, 14:30—Free time in the shopping center of old Bath, 16:00—Tour the Costume Museum.

Day 3: Pick up your rental car and tour Avebury, Glastonbury (Abbey and Tower), and Wells (17:15 evensong at the cathedral). Without a car, consider a one-day Avebury/Stonehenge/cute towns "Mad Max" minibus tour from Bath.

Day 4: 9:00—Leave Bath for South Wales, 10:30—Tour Welsh Folk Museum, 15:00—Stop at Tintern Abbey, then drive to Cotswolds, 18:00—Set up in your Cotswold home base.

Orientation (tel. code: 01225)

Bath's town square, three blocks in front of the bus and train station, is a bouquet of tourist landmarks including the Abbey, Roman and medieval baths, and royal Pump Room.

Tourist Information: The TI is in the Abbey churchyard (walk two blocks up Manvers Street from the bus or train station and turn left, Monday–Saturday 9:30–18:00, Sunday 10:00–16:00, shorter hours off-season, tel. 01225/477-101). Pick up the 25p Bath map/mini-guide and the free, packed-with-info *This Month in Bath*, and browse through scads of flyers. There's an American

Express outlet in the TI (decent rates, no commission on any checks, open seven days a week).

Arrival in Bath: The Bath train station is a pleasure (small-town charm, an international tickets desk, and a Guide Friday office masquerading as a tourist information service). The bus station is immediately in front of the train station. My recommended B&Bs are all within a 10- or 15-minute walk or a £3.50 taxi ride. For Brock House and the B&Bs on Marlborough Lane, consider using the Guide Friday city bus tour (described below) as transportation (5/hrly, from Lane 1 of the bus station). Start the tour, jump out, check into your B&B, and hop back on to finish the circle.

Driving within Bath is a nightmare of one-way streets. Nearly everyone gets lost. Ask for advice and minimize driving in town. Streets with no lines allow free unlimited parking.

Car Rental: Avis (behind the station and over the river at Unit 4B Riverside Business Park, Lower Bristol Road, tel. 01225/446-680), Budget (Brassmill Lane, tel. 01225/482-211), and Hertz (at the train station, tel. 01225/442-911) are all trying harder (consider hotel delivery, usually £8). Most offices are a 10-minute walk from most recommended accommodations. Most offices close Saturday afternoon and all day Sunday, complicating weekend pick-ups. Ideally, pick up your car only on the way out and into the countryside. Take the train or bus from London to Bath and rent a car as you leave Bath rather than in London.

Tours of Bath

▲▲**City Bus Tours**—The Guide Friday green-and-cream open-top tour bus makes a 70-minute figure-eight circuit of Bath's main sights with an exhaustingly informative running commentary. For one £7.50 ticket (buy from driver), tourists can stop and go at will for a whole day. The buses cover the city center and the surrounding hills (14 signposted pick-up points, 5/hrly in summer, hrly in winter, about 9:25–18:00, tel. 01225/464-446). This is great in sunny weather and a feast for photographers. You can munch a sandwich, work on a tan, and sightsee at the same time. Several competing hop-on, hop-off tour bus companies offer basically the same tour but in 45 minutes and without the swing through the countryside for a couple pounds less. Generally, the Guide Friday guides are better.

▲▲▲**Walking Tours**—These two-hour tours, offered free by trained local volunteers who want to share their love of Bath with its many visitors, are a chatty, historical gossip-filled joy, essential for your understanding of this town's amazing Georgian social scene. How else will you learn that the old "chair ho" call for your sedan chair evolved into today's "cheerio" greeting? Tours leave from in front of the Pump Room daily at 10:30 (often at 14:00 and

Bath

19:00, May–October). For Ghost Walks and Bizarre Bath Comedy Walks, see Evening Entertainment, below. For a private walking tour from a local gentleman who's an excellent guide, contact Patrick Driscoll (2 hours for £40, tel. 01225/462-010).

Sights—Bath

▲▲▲**Roman and Medieval Baths**—Back in ancient Roman times, high society enjoyed the mineral springs at Bath. From Londinium, Romans traveled so often to Aquae Sulis, as the city was called, to "take a bath" that finally it became known simply as Bath. Today a fine Roman museum surrounds the ancient bath. The museum, with its well-documented displays, is a one-way system leading you past Roman artifacts, mosaics, a temple pediment, and the actual mouth of the spring piled high with Roman pennies. Enjoy some quality time looking into the eyes of Minerva, goddess of the hot springs. The included self-guided tour audio-wand makes the visit easy and plenty informative. In-depth 40-minute tours leave from the end of the museum at the edge of the actual bath for those with a big appetite for Roman history (included, on the hour, a poolside clock is set for the next

departure time). You can revisit the museum after the tour.
(£6.30, £8.40 combo ticket includes Costume Museum at a good
savings, a family combo costs £22, daily 9:00–18:00, in August
also 20:00–22:00, slightly shorter hours off-season, tel.
01225/477-000.)

▲**Pump Room**—After a centuries-long cold spell, Bath was
reheated when the previously barren Queen Mary bathed here and
in due course bore a male heir to the throne (1687). Once Bath was
back on the aristocratic map, high society soon turned the place into
one big pleasure palace. The Pump Room, an elegant Georgian hall
just above the Roman baths, offers the visitor's best chance to raise a
pinky in this Chippendale elegance. Drop by to sip coffee or tea to
the rhythm of a string trio (tea/coffee and pastry for £4, live music
all year 10:30–13:00, summers until 17:00, good place for a traditional high tea—after 14:30). Above the newspaper table and sedan
chairs a statue of Beau Nash himself sniffles down at you. Now's
your chance to have a famous (but forgettable) "Bath bun" and split
(and spit) a 45p drink of the awfully curative water. The Pump
Room's toilets are open to the discreet public.

A quarter of a million gallons of mineral water still bubble
through the spa daily. In 2001 a new spa facility will be opened for
the public to once again bathe in Bath.

▲**Abbey**—Bath town wasn't much in the Middle Ages. But an
important church has stood on this spot since Anglo-Saxon times.
In 973, Edgar, the first king of England, was crowned here. Domi-
nating the town center, the present church—the last great
medieval church of England—is 500 years old and a fine example
of Late Perpendicular Gothic, with breezy fan vaulting and
enough stained glass to earn it the nickname "Lantern of the
West" (Monday–Saturday 9:00–18:00, from 13:00 on Sunday, concert and evensong schedule posted on the door, worth the £1.50
donation, handy flier narrates a 19-stop tour). The Abbey's Heritage Vaults is a small but interesting exhibit telling the story of
Christianity in Bath since Roman times (£2, Monday–Saturday
10:00–16:00, closed Sunday). Take a moment to really appreciate
the Abbey's architecture from the Abbey Green square.

▲**Pulteney Bridge and Boats**—Bath is inclined to compare its
shop-lined bridge to Florence's Ponte Vecchio. That's pushing it.
But to best enjoy a sunny Bath kind of day, pay £1 to go into the
Parade Gardens below the bridge (free after 20:00). Across the
bridge at Pulteney Weir, tour boats run cruises from under the
bridge (£3.80, 50 minutes to Bathampton and back, one boat stops
there if you'd like to walk back, the other company has a sundeck
ideal for picnics).

▲▲**Royal Crescent and the Circus**—If Bath is an architectural
cancan, these are the kickers. These first elegant Georgian "condos"
by John Wood (the Elder and the Younger) are well-explained in

the city walking tours. "Georgian" is British for "neoclassical," or dating from the 1770s. Stroll the Crescent after dark. Pretend you're rich. Pretend you're poor. Notice the "ha ha fence," a drop in the front yard offering a barrier, invisible from the windows, to sheep and peasants.

▲▲**Georgian House at #1 Royal Crescent**—This museum (on the corner of Brock Street and the Royal Crescent) offers your best look into a period house. It's worth the £3.50 admission to get behind one of those classy exteriors. The volunteers in each room are determined to fill you in on all the fascinating details of Georgian life . . . like how high-class women shaved their eyebrows and pasted on carefully trimmed strips of furry mouse skin in their place (Tuesday–Sunday 10:30–17:00, closed Monday, "no stiletto heels, please," tel. 01225/428-126).

▲▲▲**Costume Museum**—One of Europe's great museums, displaying 400 years of fashion—from Anne Boleyn to Twiggy—one frilly decade at a time, is housed in Bath's elegant Assembly Rooms. Follow the included and excellent CD wand self-guided tour. Learn why Yankee Doodle "stuck a feather in his cap and called it macaroni," and much more (£3.80, cheaper on combo ticket with Roman Baths, daily 10:00–17:00, tel. 01225/477-789).

▲▲**Industrial Heritage Centre**—This is the grand title for Mr. Bowler's Business, a turn-of-the-century engineer's shop, brass foundry, and fizzy-drink factory with a Dickensian office. It's just a pile of meaningless old gadgets until a volunteer guide lovingly resurrects Mr. Bowler's creative genius. Fascinating hour-long tours go regularly; just join the one in session upon arrival. (£3.50, plus a few pence for a glass of genuine Victorian lemonade, daily 10:00–17:00, weekends only in winter, two blocks up Russell Street from the Assembly Rooms, call to be sure a volunteer is available to give a tour, tel. 01225/318-348.) There's a Bath stone exhibit downstairs and a café/shop upstairs.

The Building of Bath Museum—This offers a fascinating look behind the scenes at how the Georgian city was actually built. This is just one large room of exhibits but those interested in construction find it worth the £3 (Tuesday–Sunday 10:30–17:00, closed Monday, near the Circus on a street called "the Paragon," tel. 01225/333-895).

Royal Photographic Society—A hit with shutterbugs, this exhibits the earliest cameras, photos, and their development, along with temporary contemporary exhibits (£3, daily 9:30–17:30, on Milsom Street, tel. 01225/462-841).

▲**American Museum**—I know, you need this in Bath like you need a Big Mac. But this museum offers a fascinating look at colonial and early-American lifestyles. Each of 18 completely furnished rooms (from the 1600s to the 1800s) is hosted by an eager guide waiting to fill you in on the candles, maps, bedpans, and various religious sects that make domestic Yankee history surprisingly interesting. One room is a quilter's nirvana (£5, Tuesday–Sunday 14:00–17:00, closed Monday and November–March, at Claverton Manor, tel. 01225/460-503). The museum is outside of town and a headache to reach if you don't have a car (15-minute walk from the Guide Friday stop or a 10-minute walk from bus #18).

Walking, Biking, and Swimming—The TI has a brochure describing options. Consider the idyllic walk up the canal path to Bathampton (from downtown, walk over Pulteney Bridge, through Sydney Gardens, turn left on canal, and in 30 minutes you'll hit Bathampton with its much-loved Old George Pub). The Bath sky-line walk is a six-mile wander around the hills surrounding Bath (75p leaflet available at TI). Consider taking the river cruise up to Bathampton and walking back (see Pulteney Bridge and Boats, above). From Bathampton it's another two hours along the canal to the fine old town of Bradford-on-Avon, from which a train can zip you back to Bath. You could rent a bike from behind the Bath train station (£9/half day, £14/all day, tel. 01225/442-442) and bike this route. The scenic 12-mile bridle/biking/walking path along the old Bath–Bristol train tracks is also popular. The Bath Sports and Leisure Centre has a swimming pool and more (£2.40, just across the North Parade Bridge, 8:00–22:00, call for free swim times, tel. 01225/462-563).

Shopping—There's great browsing between the Abbey and the Assembly Rooms. Shops close at 17:30, later on Thursday. Interested in antiques? Explore the antique center on Bartlett Street just below the Assembly Rooms. You'll find the most stalls open on Wednesday. For the best deal, pick up the local paper (usually out on Friday) and shop with the dealers at estate sales and auctions listed in the "What's On" section.

Evening Entertainment

This Month in Bath (available at the TI and many B&Bs) lists events and evening entertainment.

Plays—The Theatre Royal, newly restored and one of England's loveliest, offers a busy schedule of London West End–type plays, including many "pre-London" dress rehearsal runs (£10–20, cheap standby tickets, tel. 01225/448-844). You can often get late cancellation seats for sold-out performances (drop by around 18:00).

Bizarre Bath Walks—For a walking comedy act—street theater at its best "with absolutely no history or culture"—follow JJ or Noel Britten on their creative and entertaining Bizarre Bath walk. Their 90-minute "tour," which plays off local passersby as well as tour members, is a kick (£3.50, 20:00 nightly April–September; heavy on magic, careful to insult all kinds of minorities and sensitivities, just racy enough but still good family fun; from the Huntsman pub near the Abbey, confirm time and starting place at TI or call 01225/335-124). Ghost Walks are another way to pass the after-dark hours (£3, 20:00, 2 hrs, unreliably Monday–Friday, tel. 01225/463-618). And for the scholarly types, there are almost nightly historical walks (19:00, 2 hrs, ask at TI).

Drinks—For a good spit-and-sawdust pub, drink real ale at the Star Pub (top of Paragon Street, Bass sold by the jug if you don't want to mess with pints). Or, for maximum entertainment, look up two particularly musical local residents, Van Morrison and Peter Gabriel.

Sleeping in Bath
(£1 = about $1.70, tel. code: 01225)
Sleep Code: **S** = Single, **D** = Double/Twin, **T** = Triple, **Q** = Quad, **b** = bathroom, **t** = toilet only, **s** = shower only, **CC** = Credit Card (**V**isa, **M**asterCard, **A**mex).

Bath is one of England's busiest tourist towns. To get a good B&B, make a telephone reservation in advance. Competition is stiff, and it's worth asking any of these places for a non-weekend, three-nights-in-a-row, or off-season deal. Friday and Saturday nights are tightest—especially if you're staying only one night, since B&Bs favor those staying longer. If staying only Saturday night, you're very bad news. There's a laundrette around the corner from Brock's Guest House on the cute pedestrian lane called Margaret's Buildings, and another, scruffier place on Upper Bristol Road (tel. 01225/429378).

Sleeping near the Royal Crescent
Brock's Guest House will put bubbles in your Bath experience. Marion Dodd and her husband Geoffrey have redone their Georgian townhouse (built by John Wood in 1765) in a way that would make the famous architect proud. This charming house is perfectly located between the prestigious Royal Crescent and the elegant Circus (Db-£58–68, Tb-£78–82, Qb-£90–95, reserve with a credit-card number far in advance, strictly nonsmoking, 32 Brock Street, BA1 2LN, tel. 01225/338-374, fax 01225/334-245, e-mail: marion@brocks.force9.net). If you can't find a sedan chair, Brock's is a 15-minute uphill walk, £3.50 taxi, or short bus ride (to Assembly Rooms and short walk) from the station. Guide Friday buses stop on Brock Street. If you're in a transportation jam, Marion can occasionally arrange a reasonable private car hire.

Woodville House is run by Anne and Tom Toalster. This grandmotherly little house has three charming rooms, one shared shower, and a TV lounge. Breakfast is a help-yourself buffet around a big, family-style table (D-£36, minimum two nights, anyone who smokes at all is not welcome, below the Royal Crescent at 4 Marlborough Lane, BA1 2NQ, tel. and fax 01225/319-335, e-mail: AnneToalster@compuserve.com).

Other recommended B&Bs on Marlborough Lane:
Elgin Villa is also a fine value (Ds-£36, Db-£40, minimum two nights, kids £10 extra, four rooms, parking, nonsmoking, 6 Marlborough Lane, BA1 2NQ Bath, tel. & fax 01225/424-557. They serve a big continental breakfast in your bedroom. **Athelney Guest House** (D-£38, three rooms, nonsmoking, parking, 5 Marlborough Lane, tel. & fax 01225/312-031, Sue and Colin Davies) also serves a continental breakfast. **Parkside Guest House** is more upscale, renting five classy Edwardian rooms (Db-£60, nonsmoking, 11 Marlborough Lane, tel. & fax 01225/429-444, Erica and Inge Lynall). The **Marlborough House** is a Victorian place renting five rooms (tel. 01225/318-175, fax 01225/466-127, run by Americans Laura and Charles). **Armstrong House B&B** is closer to town on a busier road, but it's behind double-paned windows and is cozy and well run (five rooms, Db-£50, continental breakfast in room, nonsmoking, 41 Crescent Gardens, Upper Bristol Road, tel. 01225/442-211, fax 01225/460-665, Tony Conradi).

Sleeping behind the Train Station

These pleasant hotels are in a residential neighborhood.

Holly Villa Guest House, with a cheery garden and a cozy TV lounge and an eight-minute walk from the station and center, is enthusiastically and thoughtfully run by Jill McGarrigle (Ds-£40, Db-£48, Tb-£63, prices with this book, seven rooms, strictly nonsmoking, easy parking, 14 Pulteney Gardens, BA2 4HG, tel. 01225/310-331, fax 01225/339-334). From the city center, walk over North Parade Bridge, take the first right, then take the second left. It's a block from a Guide Friday bus stop.

Muriel Guy's B&B is another fine value. It mixes Georgian elegance with homey warmth a 10-minute walk out of town with fine city views (Db-£45, nonsmoking, over the bridge on North Parade Road, left on Pulteney Road, right up Bathwick Hill, on left at 14 Raby Place, tel. 01225/465-120, fax 01225/465-283).

Sleeping in the Town Center

Henry Guest House is a clean and vertical little eight-room, family-run place two blocks in front of the train station on a quiet side street (S-£19, D-£38, T-£57, TVs in rooms, lots of narrow stairs, one shower and one bath for all, 6 Henry Street, BA1 1JT, tel. 01225/424-052). This kind of decency at this price, centrally located, is found nowhere else in Bath.

Harington's of Bath Hotel, with 13 newly renovated rooms on a quiet street in the town center, is run by Susan Pow (Db-£86, family-room deal, slow-time discounts, nonsmoking, lots of stairs, CC:VMA, extremely central at 10 Queen Street, tel. 01225/461-728, fax 01225/444-804).

Parade Park Hotel, with clean rooms and helpful owners, is centrally located (Sb-£45, Db-£55–65, special four-poster Db-£75, Tb-£90, Qb-£105, nonsmoking rooms available, 10 North Parade, BA2 4AL, tel. 01225/463-384, fax 01225/442-322, Nita and David Derrick).

Pratt's Hotel is as proper and old English as you'll find in Bath. Its creaks and frays are aristocratic. Its public places make you want to sip a brandy, and its 46 rooms are bright, spacious, and come with all the comforts (Sb-£65, Db-£95, prices promised with this book in 1999, dogs £2.95 but children free, CC:VMA, elevator, two blocks immediately in front of the station on South Parade, BA2 4AB, tel. 01225/460-441, fax 01225/448-807, e-mail: martin@prattshotel.demon.co.uk).

Sleeping near Pulteney Bridge

Kennard Hotel is a comfortable hotel with 14 charming Georgian rooms. Richard Ambler runs this place warmly, with careful attention to detail (S-£45, Db-£85–95 depending upon size, nonsmoking, CC:VMA, just over Pulteney Bridge at 11 Henrietta Street, BA2 6LL, tel. 01225/310-472, fax 01225/460-054, e-mail: kennard@dircon.co.uk).

Laura Place Hotel is another elegant Georgian place (eight rooms, two on the ground floor, Db-£60–90 from small and high up to huge and palatial, 10-percent discount with cash and this book, family suite, nonsmoking, easy parking, CC:VMA, 3 Laura Place, Great Pulteney Street, just over Pulteney Bridge, tel. 01225/463-815, fax 01225/310-222, Patricia Bull).

Henrietta Hotel is a very plain place in the same elegant neighborhood with nearly no character (10 rooms, Db-£45–65, cash discount when quiet, CC:VM, 32 Henrietta Street, tel. 01225/447-779, fax 01225/444-150).

Cheap Dorm Beds

The **YMCA**, institutional but friendly, and wonderfully central on a leafy square down a tiny alley off Broad Street, has industrial-strength rooms and scuff-proof halls (S-£14, D-£26, T-£39, Q-£52, beds in big dorms-£11, includes breakfast, surcharge for one night, families offered a day nursery for kids under five, cheap dinners, CC:VM, tel. 01225/460-471, fax 01225/462-065, e-mail: info@ymcabath.u-net.com).

Bath Backpackers Hostel (likely to close in 1999) bills itself as a totally fun-packed mad place to stay. It's an Aussie-run hostel three blocks up from the station renting bunk beds in 6- to 10-bed coed rooms (£12 per bed with continental breakfast, nonsmoking, no lockers, Internet café, 13 Pierrepont Street, tel. 01225/446-787, fax 01225/446-305).

The **Youth Hostel** is in a grand old building outside of town

(£10 per bed without breakfast in 2- to 14-bed rooms, bus #18 from the station, tel. 01225/465-674).

Eating in Bath

While not a great pub grub town, Bath is bursting with quaint eateries. There's something for every appetite and budget—just stroll around the center of town. A picnic dinner of take-out fish and chips in the Royal Crescent Park is ideal for aristocratic hoboes.

Eating between the Abbey and the Station

Four fine and popular places share North Parade Passage, a block behind the Abbey: **Tilley's Bistro** serves healthy French, English, and vegetarian meals at great prices with fine atmosphere (three-course meals for £15, smoke-free, nightly 18:30–23:00, North Parade Passage, tel. 01225/484-200). **Sally Lunn's House** is a cutesy, quasi-historic place for expensive doily meals, tea, pink pillows, and lots of lace (£12 meals, nightly, 4 North Parade Passage, tel. 01225/461-634). It's fine for tea and buns, and customers get a free peek at the basement museum (otherwise 30p). Next door, **Demuth's Vegetarian Restaurant** serves good three-course £10 meals (nightly, tel. 01225/446-059). **Crystal Palace Pub**, with hearty meals under rustic timbers or in the sunny courtyard, is a handy standby (meals under £5, daily 12:00–14:30 and 18:00–20:30, closed Sunday; children welcome on the patio, not indoors; 11 Abbey Green, tel. 01225/423-944).

Evans Self-Service Fish Restaurant is the best eat-in or take-out fish-and-chips deal in town (Monday–Wednesday 11:30–18:30, Thursday–Saturday 11:30–20:30, closed Sunday, student discounts, 7 Abbeygate, tel. 01225/463-981). For very cheap meals try **Spike's Fish and Chips** (open very late) and the neighboring café just behind the bus station.

Eating between the Abbey and the Circus

George Street is lined with cheery eateries (Thai, Italian, wine bars, and so on). **Guildhall Market**, across from Pulteney Bridge, is fun for browsing and picnic shopping, with a very cheap cafeteria if you'd like to sip tea surrounded by stacks of used books, bananas on the push list, and honest-to-goodness old-time locals.

Eastern Eye has tasty Indian food under the sumptuous domes of a Georgian auction hall (£15 meals, daily 12:00–14:30 and 18:00–23:00, 8a Quiet Street, tel. 01225/422-323).

The **Green Tree Pub** on Green Street is a rare pub with good grub and a nonsmoking room (lunch only, no children).

Pasta Galore is a bit scruffy but serves decent Italian food (daily 18:00–22:30, good homemade pasta, call to reserve a table— avoid the basement, 31 Barton Street, tel. 01225/463-861). Next door is a cheap and fast Mexican joint.

Devon Savouries serves greasy, delicious take-out pasties, sausage rolls, and vegetable pies (on the main walkway between New Bond Street and Upper Borough Walls). The **Waitrose supermarket**, at the Podium shopping center, is great for groceries (open until 19:00 or 20:00, across from the post office on High Street).

For a classy, intimate setting and "new English" cuisine worth the splurge, dine at **No. 5 Bistro** (main courses with vegetables £12–15, Monday and Tuesday are "bring your own bottle of wine" nights—no corkage charge, Monday–Saturday 18:30–22:00, closed Sunday, just over Pulteney Bridge at 5 Argyle Street, smart to reserve, tel. 01225/444-499).

The **Bathtub Restaurant**, on Grove Street just around the corner from No. 5, is cheaper (£8 meals) and funkier, serving international vegetarian cuisine (nightly 18:00–23:00, tel. 01225/460-593).

Eating near the Circus and Brock's Guest House
Circus Restaurant is intimate and a good value with Mozartian ambience and candlelight prices: £15 for a three-course dinner special including great vegetables and a selection of fine desserts (daily, 34 Brock Street, tel. 01225/318-918, Felix Rosenow).

Woods Restaurant serves modern English cuisine to well-dressed locals in a sprawling candlelit brasserie (£7 lunches, £16 three-course dinners, closed Sunday, 9-13 Alfred Street near Assembly Rooms, tel. 01225/314-812).

On the opposite end of the decency spectrum, the **Chequers Inn** (two blocks up the hill, 50 Rivers Street) is a smoky dive of a pub with cheap, finger-sticking, disgusting grub and darts.

Transportation Connections—Bath
To: London's Paddington station by train (hrly, 75 min, £28.50 one-way or round-trip), or cheaper by National Express bus (hrly, 3 hrs, £19 round-trip, £18 one-way, ask about £8 day returns). To get from London to Bath, consider using an all-day Stonehenge and Bath organized bus tour from London. For about the same cost as the train ticket, you can see Stonehenge, tour Bath, and leave the tour before it returns to London (they'll let you stow your bag underneath). Evan Evans (£29.50, tel. 0181/332-2222) and Travelline (£24, tel. 0181/668-7261) offer Stonehenge/Bath day trips from London. Train info tel. 0345/484-950.

London's airports: By National Express bus to **Heathrow Airport** (9/day, at 10:35, 12:35, 13:35, 14:35, 16:35, and so on, 2.5 hrs, £10, tel. 0990-808-080), and **Gatwick** (8/day, 4.5 hrs, change at Heathrow). Trains are faster but more expensive (hrly, 2.5 hrs, £22.50, see London Connections section for details). Coming from Heathrow you can also take the tube from the airport to London's Paddington station, then catch the Exeter train to Bath.

The Cotswolds: By train to **Moreton-in-Marsh** (2.5 hrs, transfers in Didcot Parkway and Oxford). By National Express bus (tel. 0990/808-080) to **Cheltenham** (4/day, 2 hrs), **Stratford** (2/day, 3 hrs), and **Oxford** (3/day, 2 hrs).

Birmingham, points north: By train to **Birmingham** (hrly, 2.5 hrs, transfer in Bristol). From Birmingham, a major transportation hub, trains depart for **Blackpool**, **York**, **Durham**, and **Scotland**. Use a train/bus combination to reach **Ironbridge Gorge**, **North Wales**, and the **Lake District**.

NEAR BATH: GLASTONBURY, WELLS, AVEBURY, STONEHENGE, AND SOUTH WALES

Oooo, mystery, history. Glastonbury is the ancient home of Avalon, King Arthur, and the Holy Grail. Nearby, medieval Wells gathers around its grand cathedral, where you can enjoy an evensong service. Then get neolithic at every Druid's favorite stone circles, Avebury and Stonehenge.

An hour east of Bath, at the Welsh Folk Museum, you'll find South Wales' traditional story vividly told in a park full of restored houses. Relish the romantic ruins and poetic wax of Tintern Abbey, the lush Wye River Valley, and the quirky Forest of Dean.

Planning Your Time

Avebury, Glastonbury, and Wells make a wonderful day out from Bath. Splicing in Stonehenge is possible but stretching it. Everybody needs to see Stonehenge. But I'll tell you now, it looks just like it looks. You'll know what I mean when you pay to get in and rub up against the barbed wire that keeps tourists at a distance. Avebury is the connoisseur's circle: more subtle and welcoming. Wells is simply a cute town, much smaller and more medieval than Bath, with a uniquely beautiful cathedral that's best experienced at the 17:15 evensong service. Glastonbury is normally done surgically, in two hours: See the abbey, climb the tower, ponder your hippie past (and where you are now), and scram.

Think of the South Wales sights as a different grouping. Ideally, they fill the day you leave Bath for the Cotswolds. Anyone interested in Welsh culture can spend four hours in the Welsh Folk Museum. Castle-lovers and romantics will want to consider the Caerphilly Castle, Tintern Abbey, and Forest of Dean (each a worthwhile quick stop). See beginning of this chapter for a day-by-day schedule.

Getting Around near Bath

Wells and Glastonbury are easily accessible by bus from Bath; the Badgerline offers a "Day Rambler" ticket (£5, £10 per family, tel.

Bath Area

01225/464-446) and several day tours from Bath. You can get to
South Wales by train via Bristol, connecting by bus from the
Welsh train station to the various sights.

Avebury and Stonehenge are trickier. The most convenient
and quickest way to see Avebury and Stonehenge if you don't have
a car is to take an all-day bus tour. Of those tours leaving from
Bath, "Mad Max" offers the cheapest and liveliest. Another way to
get from Bath to Stonehenge is to take the train to Salisbury (£10
round-trip) then catch the Guide Friday bus (£7.50) from the Salisbury train station to Stonehenge.

Maddy Brookes runs all-day **"Mad Max" minibus tours**
(£14, 6 to 14 people). Her thoughtfully organized, informative,
and inexpensive tours last from 8:45 to 16:40 and cover 110
miles with stops in Avebury, Stonehenge, and two cute villages—
Lacock and Castle Combe. Castle Combe, the southernmost
Cotswold village, is as cute as they come. The Mad Max bus
picks up passengers at 8:45 at the statue on Cheap Street (behind
Bath Abbey). Maddy, an authority on the region's rich history
and mystery, has taught her driver/guides well. To reserve a seat,
call the Bath youth hostel (tel. 01225/465-674, please honor or
cancel your seat reservation, e-mail: maddy@madmax.abel.co.uk).
Drivers can do a day loop from Bath to Avebury (25 miles) to
Glastonbury (56 miles) to Wells (6 miles) and back to Bath (20
miles). A loop trip from Bath to South Wales is 100 miles,
mostly on the 80-mph motorway. Each of the Welsh sights is
just off the motorway.

GLASTONBURY

Marked by its hill, or "tor," and located on England's most powerful line of prehistoric sights (called a "ley" line), the town of Glastonbury gurgles with history and mystery.

In A.D. 37, Joseph of Arimathea carried vessels containing the blood and sweat of Jesus to Glastonbury; and with them, Christianity came to England. While this is "proven" by fourth-century writings and accepted by the Church, the Holy Grail legend that sprang from this in the Middle Ages isn't. Many think the Grail trail ends at the bottom of the Chalice Well (described below), a natural spring at the base of the Glastonbury Tor.

In the 12th century, England needed a morale-boosting folk hero for inspiration during a war with France. The fifth-century Celtic fort at Glastonbury was considered proof enough of the greatness of the fifth-century warlord Arthur. His supposed remains (along with those of Queen Guinevere) were dug up from the abbey floor, and Glastonbury became woven into the Arthurian legends. Reburied in the abbey choir, their grave site is a shrine today.

The Glastonbury Abbey was England's most powerful in the 10th century. In the 16th century, English monasteries owned one-sixth of all English land and had four times the income of the crown. Henry VIII dissolved the abbeys in 1536. Recognizing Glastonbury as a bastion of the church he fought, he was particularly harsh. He destroyed the abbey and—for emphasis—hung and quartered the abbot, sending the parts of his body to four different towns.

But Glastonbury rebounded. In an 18th-century tourism campaign, thousands signed affidavits stating that water from the Chalice Well healed them, and once again Glastonbury was on the tourist map. Today Glastonbury and its tor are a center for searchers, too creepy for the mainstream church but just right for those looking for a place to recharge their crystals.

Orientation (tel. code: 01458)

The tourist information office (daily 10:00–17:00, until 16:00 in winter, tel. 01458/832-954) is on High Street—as are many of the dreadlocked folks who walk it. The Lake Village Museum in the TI is nothing special (£1.50). Tuesday is market day—a combo crafts, flea, and produce gathering behind the TI (9:00–15:00).

Glastonbury, quickly becoming "the windy city," has no shortage of healthy eateries. The vegetarian **Rainbow's End** is a fine café for beans, salads, and New Age people-watching (next to TI, 17 High Street, tel. 01458/833-896). If you're looking for a midwife or a male-bonding tribal meeting, check their notice board. If this all causes you to wonder if you need spiritual guidance or just an odd rune read, wander through the **Glastonbury Experience**, a New Age mall at the bottom of High Street.

The Tor Bus shuttles visitors from the town center and abbey to the base of the tor, stopping at the Rural Life Museum and the Chalice Well (50p, 6/hrly, 9:30–17:00 throughout the summer). Their brochure outlines a good tor-to-town walk (a brisk, 10-minute walk).

Sights—Glastonbury

▲▲**Glastonbury Abbey**—The evocative ruins of the first Christian sanctuary in the British Isles stand mysteriously alive in a lush, 36-acre park. Start your visit in the museum where a model shows the abbey in its pre–Henry VIII splendor and exhibits tell the story of a place "grandly constructed to entice even the dullest minds to prayer." Today the abbey attracts people who find God within. Tie-dyed starry-eyed pilgrims seem to float through the grounds naturally high. Others lie on the grave of King Arthur, whose burial site is marked off in the center of the abbey ruins. The only surviving building is the Abbot's conical kitchen, which often comes with a cheery singing monk demonstrating life in the abbey kitchen (£2.50, daily 9:00–18:00, 9:30–dusk during off-season, tel. 01458/832-267).

Somerset Rural Life Museum—The Abbey Farmhouse is now a collection of domestic and work mementos that illustrate the life of farmer John Hodges "from the cradle to the grave." Exhibits include peat digging, cider making, and cheese making. The fine 14th-century barn, with its beautifully preserved wooden ceiling, is filled with Victorian farm tools (£2.20, Tuesday–Friday 10:00–17:00, weekends 14:00–18:00, closed Monday, open Easter–October, free car park, tel. 01458/831-197).

Chalice Well—The well is surrounded by a peaceful garden. According to tradition, Joseph of Arimathea brought the chalice of the Lord's Supper to Glastonbury in A.D. 37. Even if the chalice is not in the bottom of the well and the water is red from rust and not Jesus' blood, the tranquil setting is one where nature's harmony is a joy to ponder. Have a drink (£1.50, daily 10:00–18:00, in winter 13:00–16:00).

Glastonbury Tor—Seen by many as a Mother Goddess symbol, the tor, a natural plug of sandstone on clay, has an undeniable geological charisma. The tower is the remains of a 14th-century church of St. Michael. A fine Somerset view rewards those who hike to its 520-foot summit.

Transportation Connections—Glastonbury

By bus to: Wells (2/hrly, 30 min, tel. 0117/955-3231) and **Bath** (hrly, 90 min). The nearest train station is in Bath.

WELLS

This wonderfully preserved little town has a cathedral, so it can be called a city. It's England's smallest cathedral city, with one of its most interesting cathedrals and more medieval buildings still doing what they were originally built to do than in any town you'll visit. Market day fills the town square on Wednesday and Saturday.

Tourist Information: The TI is on the main square (daily 9:30–17:30, in winter 10:00–16:00, tel. 01749/672-552).

Sights—Wells

▲▲**Wells Cathedral**—England's first completely Gothic cathedral (dating from about 1200) is the highlight of the city. The newly restored west front displays nearly 300 original 13th-century carvings (the Last Judgment, lots of kings, bottom row of niches empty—all too easily reached by Cromwell's men, who were hell-bent on destroying "graven images").

Inside you're immediately struck by the general lightness and the unique "scissors" or hourglass-shaped double arch (added in 1338 to transfer weight from the west—where the foundations were sinking under the tower's weight—to the east, where they were firm). You'll be warmly greeted, reminded how expensive it is to maintain the cathedral, and given a map of its highlights.

Don't miss the fine 14th-century stained glass (the "Golden Window" on the east wall). The medieval clock does a silly but much-loved joust on the quarter-hour (north transept, its face dates from 1390). The embroidery work in the choir (the central zone where the daily services are sung) is worth a close look. Walk the well-worn steps up to the grand fan-vaulted chapter house—an intimate place for the theological equivalent of a huddle among church officials. The cathedral library (14:00–16:00 only, 50p), with a few old manuscripts, offers a peek into a real 15th-century library. The requested £3 donation for the cathedral is not intended to keep you out (daily 7:30–19:00 or dusk, 45-minute-long tours at 10:15, 11:15, 12:15, 14:15, and 15:15, good shop and a handy restaurant, tel. 01749/674-483). See Evensong, below.

Lined with perfectly pickled 14th-century houses, the oldest complete street in Europe is **Vicar's Close** (just a block north of the cathedral). It was built to house the vicar's choir, and it still houses church officials. The mediocre city museum is next door to the cathedral. For a fine cathedral-and-town view from your own leafy hilltop bench, hike 10 minutes up Tor Hill.

▲▲**Cathedral Evensong Service**—Weekdays at 17:15 and Sunday at 15:00, the cathedral choir takes full advantage of heavenly acoustics with a 45-minute entirely sung evensong service (boys' and men's voices, great pipe organ, you'll sit right in the old "quire;" note: generally not sung when school is out in July and August unless a visiting choir is performing, tel. 01749/674-483 to check). At 17:05 the verger ushers visitors to their seats. There's generally plenty of room. Unfortunately, the last bus to Bath is at

17:50 (and you can't leave the service early), so on weekdays those without a car or a bed in Wells can't enjoy this experience.

Bishop's Palace—Next to the cathedral stands the moated Bishop's Palace. On the grounds are a fine garden with the idyllic springs that gave the city its name. The interior offers a look at elegant furniture and clothing (£3, daily in August 10:30–18:00; April–October Tuesday–Friday 11:00–18:00, Sunday 14:00–18:00, closed Monday; closed in winter, tel. 01749/678-691).

Cheddar Cheese—If you're in the mood for a picnic, drop by an aromatic cheese shop for a great selection of tasty Somerset cheeses. Real farmhouse cheddar puts "American" cheddar to Velveeta shame. The Laurelbank Dairy Company is a traditional cheese shop with all the local edibles (Monday–Saturday 9:00–17:30, closed Sunday, 14 Queen Street, tel. 01749/679-803). Ask for a pound's worth of the most interesting mix. The Cheddar Gorge (and the Cheddar Gorge Cheese Company, which welcomes and educates guests) is just down the road.

Sleeping and Eating in Wells
(£1 = about $1.70, tel. code: 01749)

Wells is a pleasant overnight stop. The first two guest houses and the Fountain Inn are all within a block of each other behind the cathedral. The last B&B has an idyllic setting in the next village.

The **Tor Guest House**, with eight rooms in a 17th-century building facing the east end of the cathedral, is a good value (D-£40–45, Db-£45–54, family deals, CC:VM, cozy lounge stocked with great regional coffee-table books, breakfast room, quiet, nonsmoking, car park, 20 Tor Street, BA5 2US, tel. & fax 01749/672-322, warmly run by Letitia Corray).

If that's too expensive, try **Mrs. Woods' Old Poor House**, a tidy but frumpy alternative in a 14th-century cottage next to the Fountain Inn (S-£19, D-£38, nonsmoking, park in the triangle across the street from the Fountain Inn, 7A St. Andrew Street, BA5 2UW, tel. 01749/675-052).

Manor Farm B&B in the village of Dulcote, a mile or so outside Wells, rents four fine rooms in a cozy 17th-century farmhouse (D-£37, Db-£40, huge Db suite-£50, smoke-free, BA5 3PZ, tel. 01749/672-125). The place comes complete with farm animals and the good care and cooking of Rosalind Bufton. It's a peaceful 20-minute walk through green farmland to the Wells Cathedral.

Fountain Inn is great for pub grub (£6–10 meals, creative vegetarian meals, real ales, and draft cider, CC:V, behind the cathedral on St. Thomas Street, tel. 01749/672-317). Their award-winning cheese plate lets you sample cheddar and its local cousins. For a good, traditional local dish, try their founders beef pie. In town, consider **Anton's Bistro** in the Crown Hotel. The **Cathedral**

Cloister Restaurant (in the Cathedral) and the **Good Earth** (just off High Street) each serve good healthy lunches.

Transportation Connections—Wells
By bus to: Bath (hrly, 75 min, Badgerline Buses, tel. 01749/673-084), **Glastonbury** (2/hrly, 20 min), **London** (£15, London Flyer departs daily except Sunday from Wells at 7:00 and from London at 18:00, 3 hrs, tel. 01934/616-000).

Sights—Near Wells
▲**Wookey Hole**—This lowbrow commercial venture, possibly worthwhile as family entertainment, is a real hodgepodge. It starts with a wookey-guided tour of some big but mediocre caves complete with history, geology lessons, and witch stories. Then you're free to wander through a traditional rag paper-making mill with a demonstration, and into a 19th-century amusements room—a riot of color, funny mirrors, and old penny-arcade machines that visitors can actually play for as long as their pennies (on sale there) last. They even have old girlie shows. (£6.70, daily May–September 9:30–19:00, October–April 10:30–18:00, tickets sold until two hours before closing, two miles east of Wells, tel. 01749/672-243.)

Scrumpy Farms—Scrumpy is the wonderfully dangerous local hard cider brewed in this part of England. You don't find it served in many pubs because of the unruly crowd it attracts. (The Beehive pub in Bath still serves its Scrumpy and seems to enjoy the consequences.) Scrumpy, 8 percent alcohol, will rot your socks. "Scrumpy Jack," carbonated mass-produced cider, is not real Scrumpy. The real stuff is "rough farmhouse cider." This is potent stuff. It's said some farmers throw a side of beef into the vat and when fermentation is done only the teeth remain. TIs list local cider farms open to the public, such as Mr. Wilkins Land's End Cider Farm—a great "back door" travel experience (Monday–Saturday 10:00–20:00, Sunday 10:00–13:00, in Mudgeley near Wells, two miles from Wedmore on the B3151 Glastonbury Road, tel. 01934/712-385). Glastonbury's Somerset Rural Life Museum has a cider exhibit. Apples are pressed from September through December. Hard cider, while not quite Scrumpy, is still Westcountry typical but more fashionable, decent, and accessible. You can have a pint drawn for you at nearly any pub.

AVEBURY
The stone circle at Avebury is bigger (16 times the size), less touristy, and, I think, more interesting than Stonehenge. You're free to wander among 100 stones, ditches, mounds, and curious patterns from the past, as well as the village of Avebury, which grew up in the middle of this fascinating, 1,400-foot-wide neolithic circle.

In the 14th century, in a kind of frenzy of religious paranoia, Avebury villagers buried many of these mysterious pagan stones. Their 18th-century descendants broke up the remaining stones and used them for building material. Today the buried stones have been resurrected and concrete markers show where the broken-down stones once stood.

Take the mile walk around the circle. Visit the archaeology museum (£1.60, daily 10:00–18:00). Notice the pyramid-shaped Silbury Hill, a 130-foot-high, yet-to-be-explained mound of chalk just outside of Avebury. Nearly 5,000 years old, this mound is the largest man-made object in prehistoric Europe (with the surface area of London's Trafalgar Square and the height of the Nelson Memorial). It's a reminder that you've just scratched the surface of Britain's mysterious ancient and religious landscape.

The pleasant **Stones Café** serves healthy vegetarian meals and unhealthy cream teas (daily in summer, weekends only in winter, check out their mouthwatering £18 cookbook, next to the National Trust store, tel. 01672/539-514). The **Red Lion Pub** has good, inexpensive pub grub and a creaky, well-worn, dart-throwing ambience (cooking daily, also a B&B with three blah rooms, Db-£40, T-£60, CC:VM, tel. 01672/539-266).

For transportation connections, see Getting Around near Bath, above.

STONEHENGE

England's most famous stone circle, with parts older than the oldest pyramid, was built between 3100 and 1100 B.C. Many of these huge stones were brought all the way from Wales to form a remarkably accurate celestial calendar. Even today, every summer solstice (around June 21) the sun sets in just the right slot and Druids boogie. The monument is roped off, so even if you pay the £3.50 entry fee (which includes a worthwhile tape-recorded description) you're kept at a distance. Cheapskates see it free from the road (daily 10:00–18:00).

For transportation connections, see Getting Around near Bath, above.

SOUTH WALES

▲**Cardiff**—The Welsh capital (pop. 300,000) has a pleasant modern center across from its castle. A castle visit is interesting only if you catch one of the entertaining tours (every 30 minutes). The interior is a Victorian fantasy.

▲▲**St. Fagans' Welsh Folk Museum**—This best look at traditional Welsh folk life displays more than 30 carefully reconstructed old houses from all corners of this little country in a 100-acre park under a castle. Each is fully furnished and comes equipped with a local expert warming herself by a toasty fire and happy to tell you anything you want to know about life in this old cottage. Ask questions!

A highlight is the Rhyd-y-Car 1805 rowhouse, which displays ironworker cottages as they might have looked in 1805, 1855, 1895, 1925, 1955, and 1985, offering a fascinating zip through Welsh domestic life. You'll see traditional crafts in action and a great gallery displaying crude washing machines, the earliest matches, elaborately carved "love spoons," an impressive costume exhibit, and even a case of memorabilia from the local man who pioneered cremation. Everything is well explained, although the £2 museum guidebook is a good investment.

The museum has three sections: houses, museum, and castle/garden. If the sky's dry, see the scattering of houses first. Spend an hour in the large building's fascinating museum. The castle interior is royal enough and surrounded by a fine garden, but if you're tired it's not worth the hike. While the cafeteria near the entrance (Vale Restaurant) is handy, you'll eat light lunches better, cheaper, and with more atmosphere in the park at the Gwalia Tea Room. The Plymouth Arms pub just outside the museum serves the best food (£5.50, daily 10:00–18:00, until 17:00 off-season, tel. 01222/573-500). City bus #56 runs hourly between Cardiff Castle and the Welsh Folk Museum (which is in the village of St. Fagans). Drivers leave the M4 at junction 33 and follow the signs. Leaving the museum, jog left on the freeway, take the first exit, and circle back, following signs to the M4.

▲**Caerphilly Castle**—This impressive but gutted old castle is the second-largest in Europe (after Windsor). With two concentric walls, it was considered to be a brilliant arrangement of defensive walls and moats. Notice how Cromwell's demolition crew tried to destroy it, creating the leaning tower of Caerphilly (£2.40, daily 9:30–18:30, shorter hours in winter, nine miles north of Cardiff, 30 minutes from the Welsh Folk Museum, take train from Cardiff to Caerphilly—2/hrly, 20 minutes—and walk five minutes, tel. 01222/883-143).

▲▲**Tintern Abbey**—Inspiring monks to prayer, Wordsworth to poetry, Turner to a famous painting, and rushed tourists to a thoughtful moment, this poem-worthy ruined-castle-of-an-abbey is worth a five-mile detour off the motorway. Rent headphones (£1) for a tour that brings this richest abbey in Wales to life. Founded in 1131 on a site chosen by Norman monks for its tranquility, it functioned as an austere Cistercian abbey from 1131 until its dissolution in 1536. (£2.20, daily 9:30–18:30, until 16:00 in winter, tel. 01291/689-251, five buses/day from Chepstow, easy 15-minute walk up to St. Mary's church for a view of England just over the River Wye.) Visit late to miss crowds.

The abbey's shop sells the useful Wye-Cotswolds map, the

Welsh Tourist Board's *A Tourist Guide to North Wales*, fine Celtic jewelry, and other gifts. If seduced into spending the night, sleep in the 400-year-old **Wye Barn B&B** (three rooms, S-£20, Db-£44; no pets, smoking, or children, but still friendly; 200 yards from the abbey on the River Wye bank, tel. 01291/689-456). Judith Russill, the village historian, has made this former abbey tannery quiet and comfy. She serves a fine evening meal (£14, order in advance). Tintern TI: tel. 01291/689-566.

▲**Wye River Valley and Forest of Dean**—This land is lush, mellow, and historic. Local tourist brochures explain the Forest of Dean's special dialect, its strange political autonomy, and its oaken ties to Trafalgar and Admiral Nelson.

For a medieval night, check into the **St. Briavels' Castle Youth Hostel** (£9 beds in 8- to 12-bed dorms, members only, tel. 01594/530-272). An 800-year-old Norman castle used by King John in 1215 (the year he signed the Magna Carta), it's comfortable (as castles go), friendly, and in the center of the quiet village of St. Briavels just north of Tintern Abbey. For dinner, eat at the hostel or walk "just down the path and up the snyket" to the **Crown Pub** (decent food and local pub atmosphere).

Transportation Connections—Cardiff
By train to: Caerphilly (2/hrly, 20 min), **Bath** (hrly, 90 min, transfer in Bristol), **Birmingham** (8/day, 2 hrs), **London** (hrly, 2 hrs), **Chepstow** (hrly, 30 min, 6 miles to Tintern by bus). Train info: tel. 0345/484-950.

Route Tips for Drivers
Bath to South Wales: Leave Bath following signs for A4, then M4, then Stroud. It's 10 miles north (on A46 past a village called Pennsylvania) to the M4 superfreeway. Zip westward, crossing a huge suspension bridge into Wales (£4 toll westbound only). Stay on the M4 (not M48) past Cardiff, take exit 33, and follow the brown signs south to the Welsh Folk Museum. To get to Tintern Abbey, take the M4 to Exit 21 and get on M48. The abbey is six miles (up A466) off M48 at Exit 2, right where the northern bridge across the Severn hits Wales.

Cardiff to Cotswolds via Forest of Dean: On the Welsh side of the big suspension bridge, take the Chepstow exit and follow signs up A466 to Tintern Abbey and the Wye River Valley. Carry on to Monmouth and, if you're running late, follow the A40 and the M50 to the Tewksebury exit, where small roads will take you into the Cotswolds.

THE COTSWOLDS

The Cotswold Hills, a 25-by-50-mile chunk of Gloucestershire, are dotted with villages and graced with England's greatest countryside palace, Blenheim.

As with many fairy-tale regions of Europe, the present-day beauty of the Cotswolds was the result of an economic disaster. Wool was a huge industry in medieval England, and Cotswold sheep grew the best wool. The region prospered. Wool money built fine towns and houses. Local "wool" churches are called "cathedrals" for their scale and wealth. Stained-glass slogans say things like "I thank my God and ever shall, it is the sheep hath paid for all."

With the rise of cotton and the Industrial Revolution, the woolen industry collapsed. Ba-a-a-ad news. The wealthy Cotswold towns fell into a depressed time warp, so poor that nobody even bothered to knock them down. Today visitors enjoy a harmonious blend of man and nature—the most pristine of English countrysides decorated with time-passed villages, rich wool churches, tell-me-a-story stone fences, kissing gates you wouldn't want to experience alone, and the gracefully dilapidated homes of an impoverished nobility. Appreciated lately by hordes of 20th-century romantics, the Cotswolds are enjoying new prosperity.

Planning Your Time
The Cotswolds are an absolute delight by car (and a royal headache without one). With a car, on a three-week British trip, I'd spend two nights and a day in the Cotswolds (sleeping in Stow or Chipping Campden). The Cotswolds' charm has a softening effect on many tight itineraries. You could spend days of enjoyable walking from a home base here.

One-day driver's 100-mile Cotswold blitz (includes Blenheim; use a good map; reshuffle to fit your home base): 9:00—Browse through Stow, 10:00—Joyride through Bourton, the Slaughters, Guiting Power, Stanton, Stanway, and Snowshill, 13:00—Lunch and explore Chipping Campden, 15:00—Drive 30 miles to Blenheim Palace, take the hour-long tour (last tour departs at 16:45), 18:00—Drive home for pub dinner in home village.

Orientation

The north Cotswolds are best. Work-a-day Moreton-in-Marsh is the public transportation gateway to the region. Two of the region's coziest towns, Stow-on-the-Wold and Chipping Campden, are four and eight miles, respectively, from Moreton. Any of these three towns makes a fine home base for your exploration of the thatch-happiest of Cotswold villages and walks.

Cotswold Appreciation 101

Much history can be read into the names of the area. "Cotswold" could come from the Saxon phrase meaning "hills of sheeps' coats." Or it could mean shelter ("cot" like "cottage") on the open upland ("wold").

In the Cotswolds, a town's main street (called High Street) needed to be wide to accommodate the sheep and cattle being marched to market (and today, to park tour buses). Some of the most picturesque cottages were once humble rowhouses of weavers' cottages, usually along a stream for their water wheels (Bibury, Castle Combe). The towns run on slow clocks and yellowed calendars. An entire village might not have a phone booth that accepts a telephone card.

Fields of yellow (rapeseed) and pale blue (linseed) separate pastures dotted with black and white sheep. In just about any B&B, when you open your window in the morning you'll hear sheep baa-ing. The decorative "toadstool" stones that litter front yards throughout the region are medieval staddle stones. Buildings were set upon these to keep the rodents out.

Cotswold walls and roofs are made of limestone. The limestone roof tiles hang by pegs. To make the weight more bearable, smaller, lighter tiles are higher up. An extremely strict building code keeps towns looking what many locals call "overly quaint."

The area is provincial and gossipy. People are ever so polite but commonly catch themselves saying, "It's all very . . . ummm . . . yyya." Rich people open their gardens to support their favorite charities, while—until recently—the less couth enjoyed "badger baiting" (a gambling cousin of cockfighting in which a badger, with his teeth and claws taken out, is mangled by right-wing dogs).

This is walking country. The English love their walks and vigorously defend their age-old right to free passage. Once a year

Cotswold Villages and Surroundings

the Rambling Society organizes a "Mass Trespass," when each of the country's 50,000 miles of public footpaths is walked. By assuring each path is used at least once a year, they stop landlords from putting up fences. Any paths found blocked are unceremoniously unblocked.

Questions to ask locals: Does badger-baiting survive? Who are the Morris men? What's a kissing gate? What's the latest on the 11th Duke's attemps to disinherit the 12th Duke of Marlborough?

Getting Around the Cotswolds

By Bus: Moreton-in-Marsh is the train traveler's gateway and a bus hub. Except for two main lines, buses within the Cotswolds are miserable (e.g., two per week). There's a good Moreton–Chipping

Campden bus (5/day, 30 min) and a Moreton–Stow–Slaughter–Bourton–Cheltenham bus (8/day, 70 min). Moreton buses are generally timed to coincide with train arrivals.

By Bike: In Moreton-in-Marsh, Country Lanes Cycle Centre rents 21-speed bikes for £12 a day and offers bike tours (Easter–September Tuesday–Sunday 9:00–17:00, reserve ahead, at the train station, tel. 01608/650-065).

By Foot: Walking guidebooks abound, giving you a world of choices for each of my recommended stops. Villages are generally no more than three miles apart and most have pubs that would love to feed and water you.

By Car: Several nearby car rental companies offer one-day rentals from £25 (including insurance and everything but gas, figure £5 for a taxi or delivery, tel. 01608/661-681 or 01386/700-814).

Car hiking is great. Distances are minuscule. I've covered the postcard-perfect (but discovered) villages. With a car and the local Ordnance Survey map you can easily ramble about and find your own gems. The problem with having a car is that you are less likely to hike. Try to taxi or bus somewhere so you can hike back to your car and enjoy the scenery.

By Taxi: Two or three taxi trips can make more sense than renting a car. While taking a cab cross-country seems extravagant at £1.20 per mile, the distances are short (Stow–Moreton is four miles, Stow–Chipping Campden is 10) and one-way walks are lovely.

By Tour: From Bath, take a Mad Max tour to Castle Combe, the charming southernmost Cotswold town. From Stratford, catch the Guide Friday tour (£16.50, 13:45–17:00, drive through 15 villages and stop in Chipping Campden and Stow, six-person minimum, departs from Civic Hall, buy tickets at Civic Hall near Market Square or on bus, tel. 01789/294-466).

Sights—Central Cotswolds

▲▲**Stow-on-the-Wold**—Eight roads converge on Stow-on-the-Wold, but none interrupts the peacefulness of its main square. Stow-on-the-Wold (which means "meeting place on the uplands") has become a crowded tourist town. Most of these tourists, however, are day-trippers, so even summer nights are peaceful. Stow has no real sights other than itself, some good pubs, cutesy shops, and art galleries draped seductively around a big town square. At the TI on the main square (Monday–Saturday 9:30–17:30, less Sunday and off-season, tel. 01451/831-082), get the handy little 25p walking tour brochure called *Town Trail* (sold after-hours at the neighboring hostel). A visit to Stow is not complete until you've locked your partner in the stocks on the green. For accommodations, see Sleeping, below. You can generally find a parking spot on the main square (free for two hours).

▲**Moreton-in-Marsh**—This town makes a fine home base for

Stow-on-the-Wold

those without a car. It's Chipping Campden without the touristic sugar. Rather than gift and antique shops you'll find streets lined with real shops: ironmongers selling cottage nameplates and carpet shops strewn with the remarkable patterns that decorate B&B floors. A traditional market with 260 stalls filling High Street gets the town shin-kicking each Tuesday. There is an economy outside of tourism in the Cotswolds, and you'll feel it here. Moreton has a tiny, sleepy station two blocks from High Street, an unusually proficient—for the Cotswolds—tourist information office (Monday–Friday 9:00–17:00, offers £1 luggage check, tel. 01608/650-881), and two fine B&Bs. For accommodations, see Sleeping, below.

Bourton-on-the-Water—I can't figure out if they call this the "Venice of the Cotswolds" because of its quaint canals or its miserable crowds. If you can avoid the midday and weekend crowds it's worth a drive-through, a few cynical comments, and maybe a short stop. It's easiest to enjoy after dark. The Motor Museum shows off a lifetime's accumulation of vintage cars, old lacquered signs, a village life exhibit, threadbare toys, and pre-war memorabilia (£1.75, daily 10:00–18:00, in the Old Mill facing the town center, tel. 01451/821-255). Bourton is four miles south of Stow and a mile from the Slaughters.

Upper and Lower Slaughter—Lower Slaughter is a classic village with ducks, a working water mill, and usually an artist busy at her easel somewhere. Just behind the skippable Old Mill Museum, two kissing gates lead to the path that goes to nearby Upper Slaughter. In Upper Slaughter walk between the yew trees (sacred in pagan days) down a lane between the raised graveyard (a buildup of centuries of graves) to the peaceful church. In the back of the fine graveyard, a wistful woman looks over the tomb of an 18th-century rector (sculpted by his son). By the way, "Slaughter" has nothing to do with lamb chops. It comes from "sloe" tree (the one used to make "sloe gin"). From Bourton, Guide Friday buses do a handy loop through Upper and Lower Slaughter (£3.50, hrly in summer, handy for hikers who'd like to hop off here and on there). These towns are an easy one-hour round-trip walk from Bourton. You could also walk from Bourton through the Slaughters to Stow. The small roads from Upper Slaughter to Ford and Kineton are some of England's most scenic.

Sights—North Cotswolds
▲▲**Chipping Campden**—Ten miles north of Stow and less touristy, Chipping Campden is a working market town, home of some incredibly beautiful thatched roofs and the richest Cotswold wool merchants. Both the great British historian Trevelyan and I call Chipping Campden's High Street the finest in England.

Walk the full length of High Street (its width is characteristic of market towns) and around the block on both ends. On one end you'll find impressively thatched homes (out ugly Sheep Street, past the gas station—public WC, and right on Westington Street). Walking north on High Street you'll pass the Market Hall (built in 1627), the wavy roof of the first great wool mansion (the house of William Grevel, from 1380, on left), a fine and free memorial garden (on right), and, finally, the town's famous 15th-century Perpendicular "wool" church, down Church Street.

Chipping Campden's TI is opposite the town hall on High Street (tel. 01386/841-206, 10p town maps). Stop by the Guild of Handicrafts Museum on Sheep Street for an endearing look at Cotswold crafts from the late 1800s (downstairs) to today (upstairs). For accommodations, see Sleeping, below.
Stanton, Snowshill, and Guiting Power—Located between Stow and Broadway, these are my nominations for the cutest Cotswold villages. Like marshmallows in hot chocolate, they nestle side by side, awaiting your arrival.
▲▲**Stanway House**—Stanway is notable for its manor house. Lord Neidpath, whose family tree charts relatives back to 1270, occasionally opens his melancholy home to visitors (Tuesday and Thursday

North Cotswolds

TO STRATFORD

— MAJOR ROAD
— MINOR ROAD

N

HIDCOTE MANOR

A-46

MICKLETON

ILMING-TON

TO EVESHAM & M-5

CHIPPING CAMPDEN

SHIPSTON

B-4035

BROADWAY→

A-44

BROAD CAMPDEN

B-4081

STANTON

B-4479

COTSWOLD WAY FOOTPATH

BLOCK-LEY

A-429

MORETON -IN-MARSH

A-44

SNOWS-HILL

A-424

STANWAY

UPPER SWELL

WINCHE-COMBE

FORD

B-4077

A-44

A-34

TO OXFORD & BLENHEIM

LOWER SWELL

A-436

TO CHELTEN-HAM

GUITING POWER

B-4068

STOW-ON-THE-WOLD

A-436

TO OXFORD

UPPER + LOWER SLAUGHTER

A-429

BOURTON-ON-THE-WATER

A-424

TO BURFORD & OXFORD

5 MILES

TO CIRENCESTER

DCH

14:00–17:00 August–September, £3.50, tel. 01386/584-469). The 14th-century Tithe Barn predates the manor and was originally where monks—in the days before money—would accept one-tenth of whatever the peasants produced. Peek inside—this is a great hall for village hoedowns.

While the Tithe Barn is no longer used to greet motley peasants with their feudal "rents," the lord still collects rents from his vast landholdings. But the place feels musty and poor, even though the lord has recently remarried.

Ask the ticket-taker (inside) to demonstrate the spinning rent collection table. In the great hall marvel at the one-piece oak shuffleboard table and the 1780 Chippendale exercise chair (half an hour of bouncing on this was considered good for the liver).

Guests wander through Lord Neidpath's office strewn with bills (you're welcome to play the piano) and rummage through centuries of oil-on-canvas, black-and-white, and Kodak moments. The manor dogs have their own cutely painted "family tree," but

Lord Neidpath admits that his current dog, CJ, is "all character and no breeding."

The place has a story to tell. And so do the docents stationed in each room—modern-day peasants who, even without family trees, probably have relatives going back just as far in this village. Really. Talk to these people. Probe. Learn what you can about this side of England. Like you do at a new friend's house, psychoanalyze his lordship by his books. You'll find titles such as as: *The Last Tsar*, *The Medici of Florence*, *The Courtships of Catherine the Great*, and *The Enigmatic Edwardian*.

To get to Stanway, leave the B4077 at a statue of (Christian) George slaying the dragon (of pagan superstition); you'll round the corner and see the manor's fine 17th-century Jacobean gatehouse.

Stanway and Stanton are separated by a great oak forest and grazing land with parallel waves echoing the furrows plowed by medieval farmers. Centuries ago, farmers were allotted long strips of land (called a "furlong"—an attempt to dole out good and bad land equitably). Over centuries of plowing these furrows were formed. Let someone else drive so you can sit on the roof under a canopy of oaks as you pass stone walls and sheep. The first building outside Stanway (on the left) is a thatched cricket pavilion overlooking the village cricket green. Dating only from 1930, it's raised up on rodent-resistant staddle stones, like in the Middle Ages. Stanton's just ahead.

▲▲Stanton—Pristine Cotswold charm cheers visitors down this village's main street. Stanton's Church of St. Michael betrays a pagan past. It's safe to assume any church dedicated to St. Michael (the archangel who fought the devil) sits upon a sacred pagan site. Stanton is actually at the intersection of two ley lines (lines of prehistoric sights). You'll see St. Michael's well-worn figure (with a sundial) above the door as you enter. Inside, above the capitals in the nave, find the pagan symbols for the sun and the moon. While the church probably goes back to the ninth century, today's building is mostly 15th century with 13th-century transepts. On the north transept, medieval frescoes weakly show through the 17th-century whitewash. (Once upon a time, medieval frescos were considered too "papist.") Imagine the church interior colorfully decorated throughout. There's original medieval glass behind the altar. The list of rectors (left side wall) goes back to 1269. Finger the grooves in the back pews, worn away by sheepdog leashes. A man's sheepdog accompanied him everywhere.

▲Snowshill Manor—Another nearly edible little bundle of cuteness, Snowshill has a photogenic triangular square with a fine pub at its base. The Snowshill Manor is a dark and mysterious old palace filled with the lifetime collection of Charles Paget Wade. It's one big, musty celebration of craftsmanship, from finely carved spinning wheels to frightening samurai armor to tiny elaborate figurines carved by prisoners from the bones of meat served at dinner. Taking seriously his family motto, "Let Nothing Perish," Wade dedicated his life and fortune to preserving things finely crafted. The house (whose management made me promise not to promote it as an eccentric collector's pile of curiosities) really shows off Mr. Wade's ability to recognize and acquire fine examples of craftsmanship. It's all very . . . ummm . . . yyya. The manor overlooks the town square but, ridiculously—to stoke business for the overpriced manor shop 300 yards away—there's no direct access from the town square (£5.50, April–October Wednesday–Monday 13:00–17:00, closed Tuesday and off-season, car park and shop are a pleasant 500-yard walk from the house, tel. 01386/852-410).

Broadway—This very crowded town is worth a drive-through but not a stop. There won't be a parking place anyway (nine miles northwest of Stow).

▲**Hidcote Manor**—If you like gardens, the grounds around this manor house are worth a look. Garden designers here pioneered the notion of creating a series of outdoor "rooms," each with a unique theme and separated by a yew tree hedge. Follow your nose through a clever series of small gardens that lead delightfully from one to the next. Among the best in England, Hidcote gardens are at their fragrant peak in May, June, and July (£5.50, Saturday–Thursday 11:00–19:00, last entrance 18:00, closed Friday and off-season Tuesday, four miles northeast of Chipping Campden, tel. 01386/438-333).

Sights—South Cotswolds

▲**Cirencester**—Nearly 2,000 years ago, this was the ancient Roman city of Corinium. It's 20 miles from Stow down A429, which was called Foss Way in Roman times. In Cirencester (towns ending in "cester" were Roman camps), stop by the Corinium Museum to find out why they say, "If you scratch Gloucestershire, you'll find Rome" (£2.50, Monday–Saturday 10:00–17:00, Sunday 14:00–17:00, shorter hours and closed Monday off-season). The cutesy crafts center and workshops entertain visitors with traditional weaving, baking, potting in action, an interesting gallery, and a good coffee shop. Monday and Friday are general market days and Tuesday is cattle market day (TI tel. 01285/654-180).

▲**Bibury**—Six miles northeast of Cirencester, this is an entertaining but money-grubbing and not-very-friendly village with a trout farm, a Cotswolds museum, a stream teeming with fat trout and proud ducks, a row of very old weavers' cottages, and a church surrounded by rosebushes, each tended by a volunteer of the parish. Don't miss the scenic Coln Valley drive from A429 to Bibury through the enigmatic villages of Coln St. Dennis, Coln Rogers, Coln Powell, and Winson.

▲▲▲**Blenheim Palace**—Too many palaces can send you into a

furniture-wax coma. Visiting one is enough . . . as long as it's Blenheim. The Duke of Marlborough's home, the largest in England, is still lived in. And that's wonderfully obvious as you prowl through it. (Note: Americans who pronounce the place "blen-HEIM" are the butt of jokes. It's "BLEN-em.")

John Churchill, first duke of Marlborough, beat the French at the Battle of Blenheim in 1704. So the king built him this nice home, perhaps the finest Baroque building in England. Ten dukes of Marlborough later, it's as impressive as ever. The 2,000-acre yard, well-designed by "Capability" Brown, is as impressive to some as the palace itself. The view just past the outer gate as you enter is a classic. (The current 11th Duke considers the 12th more of an error than an heir and what to do about him is quite an issue.)

The well-organized palace tour begins with a fine Churchill exhibit centered around the bed in which Sir Winston was born in 1874 (prematurely . . . while his mother was at a Blenheim Palace party). Take your time in the Churchill exhibit. Then catch the guided tours (6/hrly, 1 hr, included with ticket, £8, mid-March–October 10:30–17:30, last tour at 16:45, tel. 01993/811-325).

For a more extensive visit, follow up the general tour with a 30-minute guided walk through the actual private apartments of the duke. Tours leave on the top and bottom of each hour (£4, noon–16:30, tickets are limited, buy from table in library—last room of main tour, enter in corner of courtyard to left of grand palace entry).

Kids enjoy the pleasure garden (a tiny train takes you from the palace parking lot to the garden, but if you're driving it's more efficient to simply drive there). A lush and humid greenhouse flutters with butterflies. A kid zone (£1) includes a few second-rate games and the "world's largest symbolic hedge maze." The maze is worth a look if you haven't seen one and could use some exercise.

Churchill fans can visit his tomb, a short walk away, in the Bladon town churchyard. The train station nearest Blenheim Palace (Hanborough) has no taxi or bus service. Your easiest train connection is to Oxford, where a bus goes from the station to the palace gate.

Blenheim Palace sits at the edge of the cute cobbled town of Woodstock. The grandmotherly Wishaw House B&B rents two big and comfortable rooms in a humble old house a five-minute walk from the palace (Db-£38, Browns Lane, tel. 01993/811-343).

Sleeping and Eating in the Cotswolds
(£1 = about $1.70)
Sleep Code: **S** = Single, **D** = Double/Twin, **T** = Triple, **Q** = Quad, **b** = bathroom, **t** = toilet only, **s** = shower only, **CC** = Credit Card (Visa, MasterCard, Amex).

Sleeping in Stow-on-the-Wold (tel. code: 01451)

The **Old Stocks Hotel**, the best hotel value in town, has 18 big comfy rooms in a classy historic building facing the town square. It's family-run but professional as can be (Db-£70 promised through 1999 with this book, CC:VM, The Square, Stow GL54 1AF, tel. 01451/830-666, fax 01451/870-014, Alan and Julie Rose).

Stow Lodge Hotel, on the town square in its own sprawling and peaceful garden, offers large, thoughtfully appointed rooms and stately public spaces (Sb-£63, Db-£85, CC:VM, GL54 1AB, tel. 01451/830-485, fax 01451/831-671). As in most Cotswold hotels, the prices are soft in case there's an opportunity for gouging.

The Pound is the quaint, restored, 500-year-old, low-ceilinged, heavy-beamed home of Patricia Whitehead. She offers two bright comfy twin-bedded rooms and a classic old fireplace lounge (D-£35, nonsmoking, downtown on Sheep Street, GL54 1AU, tel. 01451/830-229).

West Deyne B&B, with a garden and tiny conservatory overlooking the countryside, has fine rooms and a grandmotherly charm (D-£34, evening tea and biscuits, Lower Swell Road, GL54 1LD, tel. 01451/831-011, Joan Cave).

Rosemary Quinn's B&B, on a peaceful cul-de-sac two blocks off the main square in a tidy modern building, rents two no-nonsense, comfy rooms (S-£17, D-£34, nonsmoking, 22 Globe Close, tel. 01451/830042).

Top of the Wold B&B rents three spacious and well-appointed rooms. While warmly run, it lacks homeyness, being on the third floor of a furniture shop overlooking Stow's market square (Db-£48, nonsmoking, CC:VM, across from Queen's Head pub, tel. 01451/870-364, fax 01451/870717, e-mail: topofthewold @btinternet.com, Bob Whittock).

Tall Trees B&B, on the Oddington Road at the edge of Stow, rents three rooms in a modern annex on a farm (Db-£45, tel. 01451/831-296, Jennifer). The **Limes B&B** is a modern home two blocks out of town on the Tewkesbury Road (D-£36, Db-£40, tel. 01451/830-034, Helen and Graham).

The **Stow-on-the-Wold Youth Hostel**, on Stow's main square, has been completely renovated for 1999. It has a friendly atmosphere, good hot meals, and a do-it-yourself members' kitchen (£10 per bed with sheets, nonmembers £2 extra, 50 beds in 8 rooms, closed 10:00–17:00, no lockers, CC:VM, reserve long in advance in summer, tel. 01451/830-497, fax 01451/870-102).

B&Bs near Stow-on-the-Wold

Holmleigh B&B, in a farmhouse in the nearby hamlet of Donnington, rents two rooms, the cheapest around (D-£26, tel. 01451/830-792, Mrs. Garbett).

Fairview Farmhouse B&B feels more like a countryside mansion than a farmhouse. It's regally situated a mile outside Stow and comes with all the thoughtful touches (Db-45, deluxe Db-£50, nonsmoking, just down the Bledington Road from Stow, tel. & fax 01451/830-279, Susan and Andrew Davis).

Guiting Guest House, six miles west of Stow in the tiny village of Guiting Power, is my favorite sleepy-village alternative. Mrs. Yvonne Sylvester rents five modern, delightful doily rooms in her 400-year-old house (Sb-£28, Db-£52, CC:VM, Post Office Lane, Guiting Power, Cheltenham, GL54 5TZ, tel. 01451/850-470, fax 01451/850-034, Web site: freespace.virgin .net/guiting.guest_house/). If you're tired of pub grub, Yvonne serves a fine home-cooked dinner with the works for £15. Her husband, Bernie, is the local tourist board's B&B quality control man, so this place is either spot on . . . or gets away with murder. Guiting Power is a great base for walking excursions.

The **Vine B&B**, eight miles west of Stow in the postcard-pretty village of Stanton, is another idyllic hideaway. This classic Cotswolds home, run by Jill Gabb, is a block from the Stanton church. Jill's passion is horse riding. She rents horses by the hour (four rooms, Db-£40, CC:VM, most rooms with four-posters, WR12 7NE, tel. 01386/584-250, fax 01386/584-385).

Eating in Stow-on-the-Wold
The formal but friendly bar in the **Stow Lodge** serves fine £6 lunches and £8 dinners (daily noon–14:00 and 19:00–21:00). Next door, the more pub-esque **Queen's Head** serves an inexpensive decent meal and the local Cotswold brew, Donnington Ale (closed Monday). For non-pub grub in Stow, consider **The Prince of India** (Park Street, good Indian food) and the nearby **Fox** (English cuisine).

Those with a car are likely to eat well at any of these pubs (all near Stow): **The Plow Pub** in Ford, **The King's Head** (in Bledington, moderate, closed Sunday), **The Plough** (in Cold Aston, a 10-minute drive from Stow), or **The Fox** (two miles away in Oddington).

Sleeping in Chipping Campden
Sandalwood House B&B is a big, comfy, modern home with a royal lounge and a sprawling back garden. Its convenient location, just a five-minute walk from the center of town, is in a quiet, woodsy, pastoral setting. Its two cheery pastel rooms are bright and spacious (D-£42–45, family deals, evening tea and biscuits included, nonsmoking, GL55 6AU, tel. & fax 01386/840-091, well-run by Diana Bendall). Head south on High Street; at the church and Volunteer Inn turn right and right again; look for the sign in the hedge on your left, then head up the long driveway.

The **Kettle House B&B** offers four comfortable rooms above a furniture store (Db-£50, nonsmoking, near old church, High Street, Leysbourne, GL55 6HN, tel. 01386/840-328, fax 01386/841-740, Web site: www.kettlehouse.co.uk, Susie and Charles Holdsworth Hunt).

Dragon House B&B has two tight and tidy rooms right on the center of High Street with parking and a fine garden (Db-£45, near market hall, tel. & fax 01386/840-734, Valerie).

Taplins' B&B is a fine old house a five-minute walk from the town center renting a double and twin, each with antique furniture and fireplace (D-£42 with this book, CC:VM, nonsmoking, 5 Aston Road, GL55 6HR, tel. 01386/840-927, Rachel Hall).

Sparlings B&B, grandfather-clock tidy (perhaps similarly musty) and run by the very proper Mr. Black and Mr. Douglass, is a not-quite-cramped 17th-century townhouse (D-£48, Db-£51, nonsmoking, High Street, GL55 6HL, tel. 01386/840-505, fax 01386/841-676).

Badgers Hall Tea Room B&B has two cozy medieval attic rooms ideal for very short people but overpriced (Db-£45–50 with breakfast and afternoon tea and cakes, nonsmoking, center of High Street, tel. 01386/840-839).

The cheap **Lygon Arms Hotel** is musty and dumpy but likely to have space when all else fails (D-£45, Db-£50, CC:VMA, High Street, tel. 01386/840-318).

Eating in Chipping Campden
Badgers Bistro serves good food for around £10 (nonsmoking, in town center on High Street). **Lygon Pub** serves old English . . . "cuisine" (not quite the right word). **Volunteer Pub** serves cheap and smoky pub grub. In the Cotswolds House Hotel, the **Forbes Brasserie** (skip the formal restaurant) has good food, quick service, and vintage Cotswolds photos on its walls (12:00–20:00). Vegetarians and carnivores alike love the **Baker's Arms** for dinner (can be smoky and crowded, slow service, daily 18:00–21:30, Sunday only 19:00–21:00, live folk music every third Tuesday, indoor/outdoor seating, in Broad Campden, a mile out of Chipping Campden, tel. 01386/840-515). Since things change constantly, its important to take your B&B host's pub-grub advice seriously.

Sleeping in Broad Campden (tel. code: 01386)
A tiny village locally famous for its Baker's Arms Pub, Broad Campden has several very well-run B&Bs (one mile from Chipping Campden—addresses unnecessary, you'll see the signs, zip code: GL55 6UR).

Janet Rawling's **Marnic House B&B** is delightful with a cozy living room and prize-winning garden (Db-£42 two nights rate, nonsmoking, tel. 01386/840-014, fax 01386/840-441). **June Wadey's Wyldlands** is a comfortable modern house with a breezy, relaxing mini-Hidcote of a garden (Db-£42, Db-£40 for three nights, nonsmoking, tel. 01386/840-478).

Sleeping in Moreton-in-Marsh (tel. code: 01608)

There's a handy self-serve laundrette a block in front of the train station on New Road (Monday–Friday 7:30–20:00).

The Cottage is a 1620 cottage with low ceilings, an inglenooky lounge, and lots of character with no loss of comfort (S-£30, D-£36; charming, pastel, open-beamed "annex cottage" in the garden: Db-£45; nonsmoking, two blocks from the station on Oxford Street, GL56 0LA, tel. & fax 01608/651-740, e-mail: lcarter123@aol.com, Lorraine Carter). The twin is quieter and more spacious than the front double. I'd pay extra to sleep with Peter Rabbit in the garden.

Acacia B&B, with four tight but clean and cheery rooms on the third floor, is friendly and very handy (S-£20, D-£36, Db-£40, less for longer stays and off-season, bunky family deals, nonsmoking, on a quiet lane between the train station and High Street, at New Road, GL56 0AS, tel. 01608/650-130, Dot and Mick Ellwood).

Townend Cottage and Coach House is a fun and funky place enthusiastically run by Chris and Jenny Gant (four small, cozy rooms, D/Db-£42, less off-season, nonsmoking, fine garden, easy parking, end of High Street next to police station, GL56 0AD, tel. 01608/650-846).

Moreton House Guest House offers 11 basic rooms above an Old World lounge on the Stow end of High Street (S-£22, D-£42, Db-£48-52, CC:VM, High Street, GL56 0LQ, tel. 01608/650-747, fax 01608/652-747, run by the Dempster family).

The smoky **Redesdale Arms**, with dark and heavy carpets, is part of the Premier Lodge chain that has managed to give a classy old coaching inn the quality of a rundown American motel (Db-£43 without breakfast, CC:VMA, High Street, GL56 0AW, tel. 01608/650-308, fax 01608/651-843).

Eating in Moreton-in-Marsh

A stroll up and down High Street lets you survey your small-town options. Consider the **Marshmallow** (fun and basic) or the **Marsh Goose** (fine cuisine but dressy and designed for big shots on expense accounts). The friendly Indian restaurant (actually Bangladeshi), with tasty food, is a fine value and good for sit-down or takeout (tel. 01608/650-798).

Transportation Connections—Cotswolds

Moreton by train to: London's Paddington Station (£19, £20 round-trip after 8:00, 10/day, 90 min), **Heathrow** (10/day, 2.5 hrs, train to Reading, shuttle bus to airport), **Bath** (10/day, 2.5 hrs, transfers at Oxford and Didcot Parkway), **Oxford** (10/day, 40 min). Train info: tel. 0345/484-950.

Moreton by bus to: Chipping Campden (Castleways bus company conveniently connects with arriving trains and comes with chatty drivers, 5/day, 20 min, June–September, tel. 01242/603-715), **Stow** and **Bourton** (Pulhams, 5/day, 2 on Sunday, departs from a pub near city hall and from the station, tel. 01451/820-369).

Stagecoach Bus company does a regular run connecting **Bourton**, **Stow**, **Moreton**, **Broadway**, and **Stratford** (4/day, tel. 01788/535-555).

Chipping Campden by bus to: Stratford (6/day, 1 hr).

Cheltenham by train to: Bath (hrly, 1 hr, easy change in Bristol), **Birmingham** (hrly, 45 min). Birmingham, a major transportation hub, is your jumping-off point for Ironbridge Gorge, North Wales, northern England, and Scotland. Bus info: tel. 01452/425-543.

Drivers' Tips: Distances are wonderfully short (but only if you invest in the Ordnance Survey map of the Cotswolds—sold locally everywhere): Moreton to Broadway (10 miles), Chipping Campden (8 miles), Stratford (17 miles), Warwick (23 miles), Stow (4 miles).

NEAR THE COTSWOLDS: STRATFORD, WARWICK, AND COVENTRY

Shakespeare's hometown, Stratford . . . to see or not to see? A walking tour with a play's the thing to bring the bard to life in this touristy town. Explore Warwick, England's finest medieval castle, and stop by Coventry, a workaday town with a spirit that Nazi bombs couldn't destroy.

Planning Your Time

Stratford, Warwick, and Coventry are a made-to-order day for drivers connecting the Cotswolds with Ironbridge Gorge (IBG) or North Wales. While connections from the Cotswolds to IBG are tough, Stratford, Warwick, and Coventry are well served by public transportation.

Stratford is a classic tourist trap. But since you're passing through, it's worth a morning. (Don't spend the night.) Warwick is England's single most spectacular castle. It's very touristy but historic and fun for three hours. Lunch in Warwick town. Coventry, the least important stop on a quick trip, is most interesting as a chance to see a real, struggling, north-English industrial city (with some decent sightseeing).

The area is worth only a one-day drive-through. If you're speedy, hit all three sights. If you're more relaxed, do Stratford and Warwick and get to your Ironbridge Gorge B&B in time to enjoy the evening ambience of that more interesting stop.

STRATFORD-UPON-AVON

Stratford is the most overrated tourist magnet in England, but nobody back home would understand if you skipped Shakespeare's house. The old town is compact with the TI and theater along the riverbank and Shakespeare's birthplace a few blocks off the river; you can walk easily to everything except Anne Hathaway's and Mary Arden's places. The river has an idyllic yet playful feel, with a park along the opposite bank, paddleboats, and an old, one-man, crank-powered ferry just beyond the theater.

Tourist Information: The TI has an American Express office and a town map that welcomes you in seven languages (Monday–Saturday 9:00–18:00, Sunday 11:00–17:00; off-season 9:00–17:00 and closed Sunday, tel. 01789/293-127).

Sights—Stratford-upon-Avon

▲**Shakespeare's Birthplace**—This half-timbered Elizabethan building—entirely rebuilt in the 1900s—is furnished as it was when young William grew up, and is filled with bits about his life and work. This is most worthwhile if you get the attendants in each room talking. Ask questions. The attached Shakespeare exhibition gives a fine historical background.

While William Shakespeare (1564–1616) was born in this house, he spent most of his career in London, where he taught his playgoing public about human nature with plots that entertained the highest and the lowest minds at the same time. His tool was an unrivaled mastery of the English language. He retired—rich and famous—back in Stratford, spending his last five years at "New Place."

Little is known about Shakespeare the man. The scope of his brilliant work, his humble beginnings, and the fact that no original Shakespeare manuscripts survive raise a few scholarly eyebrows. But while some wonder who penned all these plays, most scholars accept his authorship (£4.50, daily 9:00–18:00, last admission an hour before closing, closes at 17:00 in winter, in the town center, tel. 01789/204-016).

▲**Four Other Shakespeare Properties**—Shakespeare's hometown is blanketed with opportunities for "Bardolatry." There are four other "Shakespearian properties," all run by the Shakespeare Birthplace Trust, in and near Stratford. Each comes with a garden and helpful docents who love to tell a story. **Anne Hathaway's Cottage,** a mile out of town in Shottery, is a picturesque thatched 12-room farmhouse where the bard's wife grew up. It has little to do with Shakespeare but offers an intimate peek at lifestyles in Shakespeare's day. Guides in each room do their best to lecture to the stampeding hordes. **Mary Arden's House**, the girlhood home of William's mom, is in Wilmcote, about three miles from town. This 16th-century farmhouse sees far fewer tourists, so the guides in each room have a chance to do a little better guiding. A 19th-century farming exhibit and a falconry demonstration are on the grounds. **Hall's Croft**, the home of Shakespeare's daughter, who married a doctor, is in the town. This fine old Tudor house, the richest house of the group, is interesting only if you're into 16th-century medicine. **Nash's House**, where the bard lived in retirement, is the least impressive of the properties. (Nash was the first husband of Shakespeare's granddaughter.) While Shakespeare's retirement home (New Place) is long gone, Nash's house has survived. It has the town's only general history exhibit—fascinating if you like chips of Roman pottery. All properties charge £3 to £4 each (pilgrims save money with a £10-for-all combo-ticket) and keep about the same hours (daily 9:00 or 9:30 to 17:00 or 17:30, off-season 10:00–16:00). **Shakespeare's grave** is in the riverside Holy Trinity Church (a 10-minute walk past the theater).

Avon Riverfront—The River Avon is a playground with swans and canal boats. These canal boats, which saw their workhorse days during a short window of time between the start of the Industrial Revolution and the establishment of the railways, are now mostly pleasure boats. They are long and narrow so two can pass in the narrow canals. There are 2,000 miles of canals here in the Midlands. These were built to connect centers of industry with seaports and provided vital transport during the early days of the Industrial Revolution.

▲▲**Guide Friday Bus Tours**—These open-top buses constantly make the rounds, allowing visitors to hop on and hop off at every sight in town. The full circuit takes about an hour and comes with a steady and informative live commentary (£8, buses leave from the TI every 15 minutes from 9:30, less frequent off-season, tel. 01789/294-466). Guide Friday offers longer tours of the Cotswolds (£16.50, 13:45–17:00, drive through 15 villages and stop in Chipping Campden and Stow, six-person minimum, departs from Civic Hall, buy tickets at Civic Hall near Market Square or on bus, tel. 01789/294-466).

▲▲**Walking Tour**—A guided walk makes this historic but oversold town endearing. Mrs. Pat Bouverat gives a great walk for £20 per group (tel. 01789/269-890).

▲▲**Royal Shakespeare Company**—The RSC, undoubtedly the best Shakespeare company on earth, splits its season between London (winter) and Stratford (summer). If you're a Shakespeare fan, see if the RSC schedule fits into your itinerary either here or in London. Tickets range from £7 to £47 (Monday–Saturday at 19:30, Thursday and Saturday matinees at 13:30). You'll probably need to buy your tickets in advance, although 50 restricted-view and standing-room places are saved to be sold each morning (from 9:30, £5), and returned tickets can often be picked up the evening of an otherwise sold-out show (box office tel. 01789/295-623, 24-hour ticket availability information tel. 01789/269-191). If you have a car, Stow and Chipping Campden are only 30 minutes from Stratford and an evening of classy entertainment.

Theater tours are given most days (£4, 13:30 and 17:30, not on matinee days, tours also given after performances but booked in advance). A huge collection of historical theatrical paintings is on display (Monday–Saturday 9:15–20:00, Sunday 12:00–17:00, tel. 01789/412602). The theater sponsors Shakespeare's Life in Stratford walks on Thursdays and Saturdays at 10:30 (£5, 2 hrs).

Transportation Connections— Stratford-upon-Avon

To: London (£15, £18 round-trip, 4 trains/day, 2.5 hrs, direct from Paddington Station, maybe 9:18–11:30 or 11:18–13:25), **Chipping Campden** (5 buses/day, 1 hr, tel. 01788/535-555), **Warwick** (hrly, 15 min, by bus or train), **Coventry** (hrly buses, 1 hr, tel. 01788/535-555). There is a Stratford–Warwick–Cambridge bus service (£12, 3/day, 2.5 hrs, tel. 01223/423-900). Train info: tel. 0345/484-950.

Driving is easy: Stow to Stratford (20 miles), Warwick (8 miles), Coventry (10 miles).

WARWICK AND COVENTRY

▲▲**Warwick Castle**—England's finest medieval castle is almost too groomed and organized, giving its hordes of visitors a decent value for the steep £10 entry fee. This cash-poor but enterprising lord hired the folks at Madame Tussaud's to wring maximum tourist dollars out of the castle. The latest marketing strategy is to build up the "kingmaker" reputation of the Earl of Warwick (WAR-ick).

With a lush, green, grassy moat and fairy-tale fornications, Warwick will entertain you from dungeon to lookout. Standing inside the castle gate, you can see the mound where the original Norman castle of 1068 stood. Under this "motte," the wooden stockade, or "bailey," defined the courtyard as the castle walls do today. The castle is a 14th- and 15th-century fortified shell holding an 18th- and 19th-century royal residence surrounded by another dandy "Capability" Brown landscape job.

There's something for every taste—a fine and educational armory, a terrible torture chamber, a knight in shining armor on a horse that rotates with a merry band of musical jesters, a Madame Tussaud re-creation of a royal weekend party with an 1898 game of statue-maker, a grand garden, and a peacock-patrolled, picnic-perfect park. The Great Hall and Staterooms are the sumptuous highlights. The new "King Maker" exhibit (it's 1471 and the town's folk are getting ready for battle . . .) is highly promoted but not quite as good as a Disney ride. Be warned: The tower is a one-way, no-return, 250-step climb offering a view not worth a heart attack. The £2 CD-ROM audiotour provides 60 easy-listening minutes of number-coded descriptions of the individual rooms (rent from kiosk on lane after turnstile). The £3 guidebook gives you nearly the same script in souvenir booklet form. Either are worthwhile if you want to understand the various rooms. If you tour without its help, pick the brains of the earnest and talkative docents (£10, daily 10:00–18:00, until 17:00 in winter, tel. 01926/406-600, 24-hour recorded message).

The Stables self-serve restaurant upstairs is much nicer than the cafeteria near the turnstiles. From the castle a lane leads into the old town center, a block away, where you'll find the TI (tel. 01926/492-212), doll museum, county museum, and several pubs serving fine lunches.

▲**Coventry's Cathedral**—The Germans bombed Coventry to smithereens in 1940. From that point on, the German word for "to really blast the heck out of a place" was "to coventrate" it. But Coventry rose from its ashes, and its message to our world is one of forgiveness and reconciliation. The symbol of Coventry is the bombed-out hulk of its old cathedral with the huge new one adjoining it. The inspirational complex welcomes visitors. Climb the tower (180 steps). If you're touring the church, first see the 18-minute movie, *The Spirit of Coventry*, downstairs (£1.25 for the movie, plus a requested donation at the church door, Monday–Saturday 10:00–16:00, closed Sunday, tel. 01203/227-597).

Coventry's most famous hometown girl, Lady Godiva, rode bareback through the town in the 11th century to help lower taxes. You'll see her bronze statue a block from the cathedral (near Broadgate). Just beyond that is the Museum of British Road Transport—the first, fastest, and most famous cars and motorcycles came from this British "Detroit" (free, daily 10:00–17:00). Browse through Coventry, the closest thing to normal workaday urban England you'll see. (TI tel. 01203/832-303.)

Route Tips for Drivers

Stratford to Ironbridge Gorge via Warwick and Coventry:
Entering Stratford from the Cotswolds, you cross a bridge. Veer right (following "through traffic," "P," and "Wark" signs), go around the block turning right and right and right over the speed humps, then enter the multistory garage (50p/hr, you'll find no place easier or cheaper). The TI and Guide Friday bus stop are a block away. Leaving the garage, circle to the right around the same block but stay on the "Wark" (Warwick, A439) road. Warwick is

eight miles away. The castle is just south of town on the right. If the free castle lot is full, you'll be directed to a city lot. You might lurk across the street until someone leaves. After touring the castle, carry on through the center of Warwick, following signs to Coventry (still A439, then A46). If stopping in Coventry, follow signs painted on the road into the "city centre" and then to cathedral parking. Grab a place in the high-rise car park. Leaving Coventry, follow signs to Nuneaton and M6 North through lots of sprawl and you're on your way. If skirting Coventry, M69 (Leicester) leads to M6. M6 threads through giant Birmingham. Try to avoid the 14:00-to-20:00 rush hour (see Ironbridge Gorge chapter for tips). From M6 (northwest), take M54 to the Telford/Ironbridge exit. Following the Ironbridge signs, you do-si-do through a long series of roundabouts until you're there.

IRONBRIDGE GORGE

The Industrial Revolution was born in the Severn River Valley. In its glory days, this valley (blessed with abundant deposits of iron ore and coal and a river for transport) gave the world its first iron wheels, steam-powered locomotive, and cast-iron bridge. The museums in Ironbridge Gorge (IBG) take you back into those days when Britain was racing into the modern age and pulling the rest of the West with her.

Planning Your Time

Without a car, IBG isn't worth the headache. Drivers can slip it in between Cotswolds/Stratford/Warwick and North Wales. For a short, reasonable visit, arrive in the early evening to browse the town and spend the morning and early afternoon touring the sights before driving on to North Wales (10:00—Visitors Centre, 11:00—Blists Hill Museum for lunch and sightseeing, 15:30—Drive to Wales).

Speed demons zip in for a midday tour of Blists Hill, look at the bridge, and speed out. With a month in Britain I'd spend two nights and a leisurely day: 9:30—Iron Bridge and the town, 10:30—Visitors Centre, 11:30—Coalbrookdale Museum of Iron, 14:30—Blists Hill Museum, dinner at Coalbrookdale Inn.

Orientation (tel. code: 01952)

The town is just a few blocks gathered around the Iron Bridge, which spans the Severn River. While the smoke-belching bustle is long gone, knowing that this sleepy river valley was the Silicon Valley of the 19th century makes wandering its brick streets almost a pilgrimage. The actual museum sites are scattered over three miles. While the modern cooling towers that loom ominously over these red-brick remnants (for coal, not nuclear energy) seem strangely appropriate, they're slated for destruction in 1999. Question to ask a local: What's a tontine?

Tourist Information: The TI is a block downhill from the Iron Bridge (Monday–Friday 9:00–17:00, weekends from 10:00, off-season closing at 17:00, tel. 01952/432-166).

Sights—Ironbridge Gorge

▲▲**Iron Bridge**—This first iron bridge was built in 1779, while England was at war with her American colonies, to show off a wonderful new building material. Lacking experience with iron, the builders erred on the side of sturdiness and constructed it as if it was made out of wood. The valley's centerpiece is free, open all the time, and thought-provoking. Walk across the bridge to the toll booth. Read the fee schedule and notice the subtle slam against royalty (England was not immune to the revolutionary sentiment brewing in the colonies at this time). Pedestrians paid half a penny to cross (poor people crossed cheaper by coracle—crude tub-like wood and canvas shuttle ferries). Walk upstream along the tow-path. Just above the bridge, peek through the dirty windows of a riverside shack to see a couple of these coracles.

▲▲▲**Ironbridge Gorge Industrial Revolution Museums**—Blists Hill admission is £6.80. Other sights are £3 or £4. The £9.50 combo ticket gets you into the seven sights, all of which have the same hours: daily 10:00 to 17:00, maybe until 18:00 in summer (tel. 01952/433-522 on weekdays, 01952/432-166 on weekends). Even though several of the sights may not be worth your time, seeing Blists Hill, the Visitors Centre, and the Museum of Iron costs £12 without the combo ticket.

Iron Bridge Visitors Centre: Orient yourself to the valley here in the Severn Warehouse (500 yards upstream, £1, 10:00–17:00, 18:00 in summer). See the 10-minute introductory movie, check out the exhibit and the model of the gorge in its heyday, and buy your guidebook and combination ticket. From the Visitors Centre parking lot a tiny tour boat does a 45-minute round-trip Severn River tour (£3.50, departs at the top of each hour, slow-moving taped commentary, peaceful photo opportunity for bridge, and lazy fisherman along riverbanks, tel. 01952/418-844). Farther upstream is the fine riverside Dale End park with picnic areas and a playground.

Coalbrookdale: This is the birthplace of the Industrial Revolution. Abraham Darby's blast furnace sits like a shrine inside a big glass pyramid (free), surrounded by the evocative Industrial Age ruins. This is where, in 1709, Darby first smelted iron using coke as fuel. If you're like me, "coke" is a drink and "smelt" is the past tense of smell. . . . Nevertheless, this event kicked off the modern Industrial Age.

Ironbridge Gorge

The Recipe: All the ingredients of big industry were here in abundance—iron ore, top-grade coal, and water for power and shipping. Wander around Abraham Darby's furnace. Before this furnace was built, iron ore was laboriously melted by charcoal. With a huge waterwheel-powered billows, Darby burned top-grade coal super hot (burning off the impurities to make "coke"). Local iron ore was dumped into the furnace and melted. Impurities floated to the top while the pure iron sank to the bottom of a clay tub in the bottom of the furnace. Twice a day the plugs were knocked off allowing the "slag" to drain away on the top and the molten iron to drain out on the bottom. The low-grade slag was used locally on walls and paths. The high-grade iron trickled into molds formed in the sand below the furnace. It cooled into pig iron (named because the molds look like piglets suckling their mother). The pig iron "planks" were broken off by sledgehammers and shipped away. The Severn River became one of Europe's busiest, shipping pig iron to distant foundries where it was remelted and made into cast iron (for projects such as the Iron Bridge) or to forges where it was worked like toffee into wrought iron.

The Coalbrookdale Museum of Iron: This does a fine job of explaining the original iron-smelting process (£4.20, opposite Darby's furnace). Rosehill House, just up the hill, is the 18th-century Darby mansion furnished as a Quaker ironmaster's home would be in 1850 (daily 10:00–17:00). The adjacent Dale House from the 1780s is less interesting.

Blists Hill Open-Air Museum: Save most of your time and energy for this wonderful museum. You'll wander through 50 acres of Victorian industry, factories, and a re-created community from the 1890s, complete with Victorian chemists, candy shop, an ancient dentist's chair, candlemakers, a working pub, a fascinating squatter's cottage, and a snorty, slippery pigsty. Don't miss the explanation of the winding machine at the Blists Hill Mine (first demonstration at 11:15). Walk along the canal to the "inclined plane." Grab lunch in the Victorian Pub or the cafeteria near the squatter's cottage and old-time children's rides. The board by the entry lists which exhibits are staffed and lively. The £2 *Blists Hill* guidebook gives a good step-by-step rundown (admission is £7).

Coalport China Museum and Jackfield Tile Museum: Housed in their original factories, these showcase the region's porcelain and decorated tile industries. These industries were developed to pick up the slack when the iron industry shifted away from Severn Valley. The museums feature finely decorated pieces and low-energy workshops.

Skiing, Swimming, and Fishing—There's a small, brush-covered ski slope with two poma lifts in Madeley, two miles from Ironbridge Gorge; you'll see signs as you drive into IBG (£7.30/hr including gear, less for kids, daily until 20:00 or 22:00, Telford Ski Centre, tel. 01952/586-862). There's a public swimming pool next door. The Woodlands Farm, on Beech Road, runs a private fishing business where only barbless hooks are used and locals toss their catch back to hook again (kind of a fish Hell).

Sleeping in Ironbridge Gorge
(£1 = about $1.70, tel. code: 01952)
Sleep Code: **S** = Single, **D** = Double/Twin, **T** = Triple, **Q** = Quad, **b** = bathroom, **t** = toilet only, **s** = shower only, **CC** = Credit Card (**V**isa, **M**asterCard, **A**mex).

Hill View Farm is a peaceful, thrifty, brave, clean and reverent farmhouse B&B run by Rosemarie Hawkins while her husband John raises a "beef suckler herd." If you're looking for calm and country—Auntie Em–style—this is it, in a great rural setting overlooking the ruins of a 12th-century abbey (S-£17.50, D-£32, nonsmoking, Buildwas, Ironbridge, Shropshire, TF8 7BP, tel. 01952/432-228). It's just outside of Ironbridge on the Much Wenlock road (A4169); pass the huge modern power plants, take a left over the bridge, and go about a quarter mile (sign on right).

If you like the country and Hill View Farm is full, try **Grove**

Farm House B&B (S-£21, D-£35, Db-£40 less for two nights, nonsmoking, three miles from IBG on road to Shrewsbury in Buildwas, tel. 01952/433-572, fax 01952/433-650, Pat and Clive Pygott).

The **Library House** is "better-homes-and-gardens" elegant. In the town center, right across from the bridge, it's classy but friendly and a fine value. Chris and George Maddocks run a smoke-free place and their breakfast won a "healthy heartbeat" award (Sb-£40, Db-£50, Tb-£65, family price-£65, 11 Severn Bank, 1B, Shropshire TF8 7AN, tel. 01952/432-299, fax 01952/ 433-967, e-mail: libhouse@enta.net).

Severn Lodge offers three rooms in an 1832 captain-of-industry mansion with a garden and views of the lush hills (but not of the river where the sweatshops used to groan). This spacious place has all the hotel extras and easy parking. Nita and Alan Reed won the coveted "Deluxe" (top 1 percent) category—so rare, people don't even know it's a category (three rooms, Db-£54; from the Wharfage Cottage go one block up the steep New Road, Ironbridge, Shropshire TF8 FAX, tel. & fax 01952/432-148).

Three places right in the town center overlook the bridge: **Eley's Bridge View B&B** rents five bright and comfy rooms (Db-£40 with this book through 1999, CC:VM, tel. & fax 01952/432-541, Jo or Rich). The **Post Office House B&B** is literally above the post office. The postmaster's wife, Ann Jones, rents three fine rooms (Db-£36, 6 The Square, Iron Bridge, Shropshire TF8 7AQ, tel. 01952/433-201). The **Tontine Hotel** is the town's big, musty, Industrial Age hotel (S-£20, Sb-£34, D-£38, Db-£52, 10 percent discount promised with this book, CC:VMA, tel. 01952/432-127, fax 01952/432-094). Check out the historic photos in the bar.

Hostels

Coalport Youth Hostel is a plush new hostel filling an old factory at the China Museum in Coalport (most beds are in quads but they have plenty of bunkbed Ds for £22 including sheets). The **Ironbridge Gorge Youth Hostel**, built in 1859 as the grand Coalbrookdale Institute, is another fine hostel (a 20-minute walk from the Iron Bridge down A4169 toward Wellington, four- to six-bed rooms). Each hostel charges £10 per bed with sheets, serves meals, has a self-serve laundry service, is closed from 10:00 to 17:00, welcomes travelers without memberships, and uses the same telephone number: tel. 01952/588-755.

Wilderhope Manor Youth Hostel, a beautifully remote and haunted 500-year-old manor house, is one of Europe's best hostels. One day a week, tourists actually pay to see what we hostelers sleep in for £9 (closed Sunday night, dinner served at 19:00, tel. 01694/771-363). It's six miles from Much Wenlock down B4371 toward Church Stretton.

Eating in Ironbridge Gorge

The best values and most local crowds are found outside of the IBG town. For a local crowd, fine spit-and-sawdust ambience, excellent ales, and surprisingly good food, try the **Coalbrookdale Inn** (dinner served 18:00–20:00 except Sunday, occasional folk music, across the street from the Museum of Iron a mile from IBG, tel. 01952/433-953; run by Corrine and Mike, who's on the quest for the perfect pint). This former "best pub in Britain" (1995) has a tradition of offering free samples from a lineup of featured beers. Each are listed on a blackboard with their price and alcohol content. Ask a local to explain . . . or ask if he's ever tried a brew called The Prior's Piddle. For a classier and more subdued atmosphere, eat well at the **Meadow Inn**, a local favorite with prize-winning pub grub (a pleasant 15-minute walk along the riverside park from the town center, dinners nightly 18:00–21:45, tel. 01952/433-193).

For a break from pub grub, you have these options in the town center: **Coracle Restaurant** (Tuesday–Saturday 19:00–21:30, reservations smart, tel. 01952/433-913), **Oliver's** (a smoke-free vegetarian place, reservations always necessary, tel. 01952/433-086), and **Old Vaults Wine Bar** (a hipper, younger place, plenty of indoor/outdoor seating, healthy food, real ale, tel. 01952/432-716).

For a pleasant evening, drive down Wenlock Edge on B4371. At the Wenlock Edge Inn, park and walk to the cliff for a marvelous view of Shropshire at sunset (made nearly famous by the poet A.E. Housman). Then drive farther to Much Wenlock and eat with a fun local crowd at **George and Dragon Pub**.

Transportation Connections— Ironbridge Gorge

Public transportation is miserable. Buses (every two hours) and cabs run the seven miles between Ironbridge and the nearest train station at Telford. Adding insult to injury, the Telford bus and train stations are a 15-minute walk apart.

Telford by train to: Birmingham (hrly, 45 min), **Blackpool** (hrly, 4.5 hrs, with four transfers: Birmingham–Shrewsbury, hrly, 1 hr; Shrewsbury–Crewe, hrly, 40 min; Crewe–Preston, 2/hrly, 45 min; Preston–Blackpool, 2/hrly, 20 min), **Lake District** (allow up to 6.5 hrs total; follow directions toward Blackpool, above; transfer at Preston for Penrith, 2/hrly, 75 min, and bus into Keswick, 6/day, 40 min), **Edinburgh** (8 hrs, with several transfers). Train info: tel. 0345/484-950.

By Car: Driving in from the Cotswolds and Stratford, take M6 through Birmingham, then M54 to the Telford/Ironbridge exit. Follow the brown Ironbridge signs through lots of roundabouts to Ironbridge Gorge. The traffic north through Birmingham is miserable from 14:00 to 20:00, especially on Fridays. From Warwick, consider the M40, M42, Kidderminster alternative, coming into IBG on the A442 via Bridgnorth to avoid the B'ham traffic. Driving from IBG to Ruthin in North Wales is an easy two hours. IBG to Conwy is 2.5 hours.

NORTH WALES

Wales' top historical, cultural, and natural wonders are found in the north. From towering Mount Snowdon to lush forests to desolate moor country, North Wales is a poem written in landscape. For sightseeing thrills and diversity, North Wales is far and away the most interesting slice of Britain's Celtic crescent. But be careful not to be waylaid by the many gimmicky sights and bogus "best of" lists. The region's economy is poor, and they're wringing every possible pound out of the tourist trade. Sort carefully through your options.

Welsh

Language: The Welsh language, Cymru, has been a written language since about A.D. 600 and was spoken 300 years before French or German. It remains alive and well. Although English imperialism tried to kill it, today Welsh and those who speak it are protected by law. In Northwest Wales well over half the population is fluent in Welsh. It's either the first or the required second language in the public schools. Tourists hardly notice that the locals chatter away in Welsh and, as they turn to you, switch seamlessly to English. Listen in.

Welsh is a Celtic language (like Irish) and most closely related to the Breton language in western France. The common "ll" is pronounced as if you were ready to make an "l" sound and then blew it out. The language is phonetic but comes with a few tricks: the Welsh "dd" sounds like the English "th," f = v, ff = f, w = oo, and y = i. In a pub, impress your friends (or make some) by toasting the guy who just bought your drink. Say "*Yeach-hid dah*" ("Good health to you") and "*Dee olch*" ("Thank you") or "*Dee olch un vowr*" ("Thanks very much"). If the beer's bad, just make something up.

Choirs: Every town has a choir (men's or mixed) that prac-
tices weekly. Visitors are usually welcome to observe and very
often follow the choir down to the pub afterward for a good, old-
fashioned, beer-lubricated singsong. Ask your B&B hostess for
specifics. Choirs welcome visitors and practice weekly in the
towns of **Ruthin** (mixed choir at the Tabernacle Church, Thursday 19:30–21:30), **Llangollen** (men's choir Monday and Friday at
19:30 at the Hand Hotel, 21:00 pub singsong afterward, tel.
01978/860-303), **Denbigh** (Cormeibion men's choir Monday at
19:00), and **Wrexham** (Rhos Orpheus men's choir Wednesday
and Friday at 19:30 in the Grango Rhos school).

Planning Your Time

Give North Wales two nights and a day (on a three-week British
trip) and it'll give you a medieval banquet, a mighty castle, giant
slate mines, and some of Britain's most beautiful scenery. Many
visitors are charmed and find an extra day. Drivers interested in
the medieval banquet should set up in Ruthin and do this loop:

9:00—Drive over Llanberis mountain pass to Caernarfon
(with possible short stops in Trefriw Mill, Betws-y-Coed, Pen-y-
Gwryd Hotel, and Llanberis), 12:00—Caernarfon Castle. Catch
noon tour and 13:00 movie in Eagle Tower. See Prince Charles
(of Wales) exhibit. Climb to top for view. Walk through Caernarfon town, lunch, shop. 14:30—Drive the scenic road (A4085) to
Blaenau Ffestiniog, 15:30—Tour Llechwedd Slate Mine, 17:30—
Drive home to Ruthin, 19:00—Arrive at home, 19:45—Medieval
banquet at castle (if not last night).

With a car and no interest in the banquet, skip Ruthin and
shorten your drive time by spending two nights in Conwy. Without a car, skip Ruthin. From Conwy you can tour Snowdonia and
Caernarfon by bus and train.

With a second day, add the train up Snowdon (or take a hike)
and visit Conwy. With more time and a desire to hike, consider
using the mountain village of Beddgelert as a base.

Getting Around North Wales

North Wales (except Ruthin) is well-covered by a combination of
buses and trains. A main train line zips along the north coast from
Chester to Holyhead via Llandudno Junction, Conwy, and Bangor
(hrly). From Llandudno Junction the Conwy Valley line goes
scenically south to Betws-y-Coed and Blaenau Ffestiniog (5/day,
1 hr). With these two train lines, public buses (get the Gwynedd
Public Transport Guide), and Arriva buses (which circle Snowdonia National Park with the needs of hikers in mind, tel. 01492/
596-969), those without a car should manage fine. Day passes such
as Rover (all day on Sherpa buses, £2, buy ticket from driver) or
Ranger (bus and train) save money if you're traveling a lot.

North Wales

RUTHIN

Ruthin (rith-in) is a low-key workaday market town whose charm is in its ordinary Welshness. The people are the sights. Admission is free if you start the conversation. The market square, castle, TI, bus station, and in-town accommodations are all within five blocks of each other. Ruthin is Welsh as can be, makes a handy base for drivers doing North Wales, and serves up a great medieval banquet. The TI (daily 10:00–17:30 in summer, until 17:00 off-season, tel. 01824/703-992) is in a busy crafts center.

Sights—Ruthin

▲▲**Ruthin Castle Welsh Medieval Banquet**—English, Scottish, Irish, and Welsh medieval banquets are all variations on the same touristy theme. This one is fun, more culturally justifiable (if that's necessary), and less expensive than most. You'll be greeted with a chunk of bread dipped in salt, which the maiden explains will "guarantee your safety." Your medieval master of ceremonies then seats you and the candlelit evening of food, drink, and music rolls gaily on. You'll enjoy harp music, angelic singing, and lots of entertainment, including insults slung at the Irish, Scots, English, and even us brash colonists. With fanfare (and historic explanation), wenches serve mead, spiced wine, and four hearty traditional courses. Drink from a pewter goblet, wear a bib, and eat with your fingers and a dagger. Food and mead are unlimited—just ask for more (£27.75, CC:VMA, starts at 19:45, two to five nights a week depending upon demand, vegetarian options, smoke-free, easy doorstep parking, down Castle Street from the town square, call for reservations, tel. 01824/703-435 or, after hours, the hotel at 01824/702-664).

Walks—For a scenic and interesting one-hour walk, try the Offa's Dyke Path to Moel Famau (the "Jubilee Tower," a 200-year-old war memorial on a peak overlooking stark moorlands). The trailhead is a 10-minute drive from Ruthin. Dave Murray is a local guide who takes visitors on walks (tel. 01824/705-032).

▲▲**Welsh Choir**—The mixed choir performs at the Tabernacle Church on Thursday from 19:30 to 21:30.

Sleeping in Ruthin
(£1 = about $1.70, tel. code: 01824)

Sleep Code: **S** = Single, **D** = Double/Twin, **T** = Triple, **Q** = Quad, **b** = bathroom, **t** = toilet only, **s** = shower only, **CC** = Credit Card (**V**isa, **M**asterCard, **A**mex).

Bryn Awel, a warm, traditional, charming farmhouse B&B with a paradise garden, is run by Beryl and John Jones in the hamlet of Bontuchel just outside of Ruthin (Db-£34, £37 for one-nighters, nonsmoking, LL15 2DE Bontuchel, tel. 01824/702-481). Beryl, a prize-winning quilter, is helpful with touring tips, nearby walks, booking the medieval banquet, and key Welsh words. (From Ruthin, take Bala road, #494, then B5105 Cerrigydrudion road. Turn right after church, at Bontuchel/Cyffylliog sign. It's on the right, 1.8 fragrant miles down a narrow road. If you get to the Bridge Hotel, backtrack 200 yards.)

Gorphwysfa Guest House, in a cozy 15th-century Tudor home between the castle and the town square, serves a royal breakfast and has a library, grand piano, and three huge, comfortable rooms (Db-£38, Tb-£50, Qb-£60, family deals, 8a Castle Street, tel. & fax 01824/702-748, Margaret O'Riain).

Margaret Ranson's B&B is friendly, comfortable, and moderately priced (three rooms, Db-£36, entirely smoke-free, Rhianfa, Ffordd Llanrhydd, Ruthin, Clwyd, LL15 1PP, a 10-minute walk from the castle; from Anchor Pub drive 100 yards toward the hospital; it's the first big red-brick house on right; Rhianfa sign on stone wall, tel. 01824/702-971). Margaret's husband, John, a natural tour guide, will lend you an excellent North Wales road map. Or you can just play croquet in their sprawling backyard.

The **Castle Hotel**, not to be confused with the Ruthin Castle Hotel, is a well-worn, 24-room hotel on the town square (Db-£38 with this book promised through 1999, family suites, front rooms are larger and overlook the town square, some nonsmoking rooms, reasonable evening meals, CC:VMA, St. Peter's Square, LL15 1AA, tel. 01824/702-479, fax 01824/703-488).

Ruthin

Moelfa B&B on the busy Denbigh Road is modern and non-descript but comfortable and friendly (D-£30 with this book, leave town on Denbigh Road, first B&B sign on left, tel. 01824/702-468, Meg Jones).

Ruthin Castle is the ultimate in creaky Old World elegance for North Wales (Sb-£72, Db-£92, show this book for 10 percent off room rates or 10 percent off their two-night-with-a-banquet deal, CC:VMA, tel. 01824/702-664, fax 01824/705-978). Enjoy lavish public places, armor, antlers, ghosts, and your private snooker table (giant billiards, £1/hour). Explore the fascinating grounds complete with a drowning pool and 40 peacocks. You'll wake up to their cry thinking it's a loony-tune damsel in distress.

For cheap beds go to the **Llangollen Youth Hostel** (15 miles from Ruthin, see below).

Eating in Ruthin

There's no reason to rush home for dinner in Ruthin if you're not going to the medieval banquet. No one place is a clear winner, but you'll eat reasonably well at the **Anchor Pub**, the **Wynnstay Arms**, the **Middleton Arms Pub** on the main square, and at the classier **Castle Hotel** or **Manor House Hotel Restaurant**. For fish 'n' chips, locals paddle over to **Finns** on Clwyd Street (take-away only).

LLANGOLLEN

Worth a stop if you have a car, Llangollen is famous for its musical **International Eisteddfod** (July 6–11 in 1999), a very popular and very crowded festival of folk songs and dance. Monday and Friday nights throughout the year is men's choir practice (19:30 at the Hand Hotel, 21:00 pub singsong afterward, tel. 01978/860-303).

You can walk or ride a horse-drawn boat down the old canal (£3, 45-minute, three-mile round-trip, summer only, tel. 01978/860-702) toward the lovely 13th-century **Cistercian Vale Crucis Abbey** (£1.70) near the even older cross called **Eliseg's Pillar** (TI: tel. 01978/860-828).

Llangollen has a handful of other amusements and attractions including scenic steam train trips, the world's largest permanent exhibition of model railways, and the biggest "Doctor Who" exhibition anywhere.

Gale's Hotel is a decent value (15 rooms, Db-£50, £42.50 for two nights, good food, CC:VMA, Bridge Street, tel. 01978/860-089, fax 01978/861-313) and the **Llangollen Youth Hostel** is cheap (£9 per bed in 4- to 20-bed rooms, tel. 01978/860-330).

Llangollen is 15 miles and a 30-minute drive from Ruthin (no bus connection). Hourly buses connect Llangollen with train stations at Chirk, Ruabon, and Wrexham.

KING EDWARD'S CASTLES

In the 13th century the Welsh, under two great princes named Llywelyn, created a united and independent Wales. The English King Edward I fought hard to end this Welsh sovereignty. In 1282 Llywelyn was killed (and went to where everyone speaks Welsh). King Edward spent the next 20 years building or rebuilding 17 great castles to consolidate his English foothold in troublesome North Wales. The greatest of these (such as Conwy Castle) were masterpieces of medieval engineering with round towers (tough to undermine by tunneling), a castle-within-a-castle defense (giving defenders a place to retreat and wreak havoc on the advancing enemy . . . or just wait for reinforcements), and sea access (safe to stock from England). These were English islands in the middle of angry Wales. Most were built with a fortified grid-plan town attached and were filled with English settlers. (With this blatant abuse of Wales, you have to wonder, where was Greenpeace 700 years ago?)

Castle lovers will want to tour each of Edward's five greatest castles. With a car and two days this makes one of Europe's best castle tours. I'd rate them in this order: **Caernarfon** is most entertaining and best presented (described below). **Conwy** is attached to the cutest medieval town and the best public transport (described below). **Harlech** is the most dramatic (£3, daily 9:30–18:30, tel. 01766/780-552). **Beaumaris**, surrounded by a swan-filled moat, was the last, largest, and most romantic (daily 9:30–18:30, tel. 01248/810-361). **Criccieth**, built in 1230 by Llywelyn, is also dramatic and remote (daily 10:00–18:00, tel. 01766/522-227).

CONWY

This garrison town was built at the same time as the castle in the 1280s to give Edward I an English toehold on Wales (see above). What's left today are the best medieval walls in Britain, surrounding a humble workaday town and crowned by the bleak and barren hulk of a castle awesome in its day. Conwy's charming High Street leads from Lancester Square (with the tiny bus and train station and a column honoring the town's founder, Welsh prince Llywelyn the Great) down to a fishy harborfront that permitted Edward to safely restock his castle.

Since the highway was tunneled under the town, a strolling ambience has returned to Conwy. Much of the wall is walkable (free). Stroll the harbor past Britain's smallest house (see below), the tour boat (£2.50, 30 min), an aquarium, the town lifeboat house, and a fresh-fish trailer selling 15p crab sticks. Beyond the castle, the mighty Telford suspension bridge is a 19th-century slice of English imperialism, built in 1826 to better connect (and control) the route to Ireland. The newly restored bridge is open to pedestrians only (£1).

Tourist Information: The TI is between the castle and the town center (daily 9:30–18:30, less off-season, tel. 01492/592-248). Don't confuse it with the tacky "Visitors Centre" near the station with its goofy little 80p video show.

Sights—Conwy

▲**Conwy Castle**—Built dramatically on a rock overlooking the sea with eight linebacker towers, it has an interesting story to tell (£3.50, daily 9:30–18:30, less in winter, tel. 01492/592-358). Guides wait inside ready to take you on a 40-minute, £1 tour. If the booth is empty, look for the group and join it. (These guides do city tours as well.)

St. Mary's Parish Church—Built in 1186, it's still the core of the town and worth a look for its fine interior and wispy graveyard. Originally a Cistercian church, it is actually older than the town.

Conwy and Snowdonia National Park

Old Houses—By the harbor, the tiniest house in Britain is 72 inches wide, 122 inches high, and 50p to see. Two old houses on High Street may tempt you. **Plas Mawr**, billed as the oldest house in Wales, offers a frail look at domestic life in 16th-century Wales (£4, Tuesday–Sunday 10:00–18:00, closed Monday). The **Aberconwy House** at the bottom of the street is even less exciting (£2).

▲**Bodnant Garden**—This sumptuous display of floral color—set in the lush green of Snowdonia—is one of Britain's best. It's famous for its magnolias, rhodies, camellias, and floral arch (£4.60, daily 10:00–17:00 in season, best spring–June, six miles south of Conwy, tel. 01492/650-460).

Sleeping in Conwy
(£1 = about $1.70, tel code: 01492)
Conwy has several decent budget B&Bs each located within a

three-minute walk from the bus and train station. There's no Laundromat in town.

Gwynedd Guest House, spacious, thoughtfully decorated, and charmingly run by Margaret Young, is Conwy's best value (S-£17, D-£30, T/Q-£45, family deals, two blocks from bus and train station, 10 Upper Gate Street, LL32 8RF, tel. & fax 01492/596-537).

Llys Llywelyn Hotel is well-worn but stately with nine rooms, easy parking, a big lounge, and some views (Db-£35, just outside the town wall at Mount Pleasant, tel. 01492/593-257, Karen Morton).

Rose Hill House B&B rents three small, tidy rooms directly across from the train station (S-£15, D-£26, 20 Rose Hill Street, tel. 01492/593-435, Mrs. Curran). **Swan Cottage B&B** is a homey place near the harborfront renting three fine rooms (D-£28 with this book, 18 Berry Street, tel. 01492/596840, Mr. and Mrs. Roberts).

The big, musty old **Castle Hotel** rents 29 overpriced rooms (Db-£90 minimum two-night stays, 10 percent discount with this book, CC:VMA, High Street, tel. 01492/592-324, fax 01492/583-351).

Conwy's new **hostel** is a 15-minute walk from the castle (£9 per bed in two-, four-, and six-bed rooms, all with showers and lockers, family rooms, Larkhill, Sychnant Pass Road, tel. 01492/593-571, fax 01492/593-580).

Eating in Conwy

When hungry in Conwy, stroll up High Street comparing the cute teahouses and smoky pubs. At the top, on Lancaster Square, is **Alfredo's Restaurant**, a family-friendly place that serves good and reasonable Italian food nightly (tel. 01492/592-381). The tiny **Wall Place** on Chapel Street is good for vegetarian meals. The gritty **Malt Loaf** pub hosts the Conwy Folk Music Club each Monday from 20:30 on (across from the station). At the bottom of High Street two fish-'n'-chips joints brag they're the best. The best cheap meal in town is either a picnic from the grocery store (top of High Street, open until 22:00) or fish and chips on the harborfront with the locals.

CAERNARFON

The small and lively little town of Caernarfon (ka-NAR-von) is famous for its striking castle—the place where the Prince of Wales is "invested." The old garrison town still marches out from the castle following the original medieval grid plan laid within its well-preserved ramparts.

But Caernarfon is mostly a 19th-century town and the most important thing in town is not the castle but the parking lot that sprawls below the castle. This was once a booming slate port shipping tidy bundles of slate from North Wales mining towns to roofs all over Europe.

The statue of local boy David Lloyd George looks over the town square. A member of parliament from 1890 to 1945, he was the most important politician Wales ever sent to London and ultimately became Britain's prime minister. Boy George began his career as a noisy nonconformist liberal advocating Welsh rights. He ended up an eloquent spokesperson for the notion of Great Britain, convincing his slate-mining constituents that only as part of the Union would their slate industry boom.

A small but lively town, Caernarfon bustles with shops, cafés, and people. Market day activities fill its main square each Monday and Saturday. The charming grid-plan medieval town is worth a wander.

Tourist Information: The TI, across from the castle entrance, has a wonderful town map/guide (tel. 01286/672-232). Donna "Caernarfon is more than a castle" Goodman leads historic walks several times a week (£3, call 01286/677-059 for her schedule).

Sights—Caernarfon

▲▲**Caernarfon Castle**—Edward I built this impressive castle 700 years ago to establish English rule over North Wales. Modeled after the striped and angular walls of ancient Constantinople, the castle—while impressive—was never finished and never really used. From the inner courtyard you can see the notched walls ready for more walls that were never built. Its fame is due to its physical grandeur and from its association with the "Prince of Wales." The English king got the angry Welsh to agree that if he presented them with "a prince, born in Wales who spoke not a word of English," that they would submit to the crown. In time, Edward had a son . . . born in Wales . . . who spoke not a word of English, Welsh, or any other language. In modern times, as another political maneuver, the Prince of Wales has been "invested" (given his title) here. This "tradition" actually dates only from this century and only 2 of 21 Princes of Wales have taken part.

In spite of its disappointing history, it's a great castle to tour. An essential part of any visit is the guided tour (50-minute tours for £1 leave on the hour from the center of the courtyard in front of entry; if you're late, ask to join one in progress). In the huge Eagle Tower (on the seaward side) see the history exhibit (ground floor), watch the 20-minute movie (broad mix of Welsh legend and history, on the half-hour, upstairs, comfortable theater seats), and climb the tower for a great view. The opposite tower has an exhibit about the investiture of Prince Charles in 1969 (£4, daily 9:30–18:30, winter 9:30–16:00, Sunday 11:00–16:00, tel.

01286/677-617). Martin de Lewandowicz gives mind-bending tours of the castle (01286/674-369).

Men's Choir—If spending the night, consider dropping by the local men's choir practice (Tuesday 19:30–21:30, Conservative Club on High Street).

Sleeping in Caernarfon
(£1 = about $1.70, tel code: 01286)

Isfryn B&B is just down the street from the castle, overlooking the water (S-£19, D-£36, Db-£41, family deals, 11 Church Street, L5 51SW, tel. & fax 01286/675-628, Graham). **Totters Hostel** is a creative little hostel well-run by Bob and Henriette (30 beds in five dorm rooms, £9.50 per bed with bedding, continental breakfast, and lockers; couples can have their own room when available; open all day, welcoming game room/lounge, use of kitchen, a block from the castle at 2 High Street, tel. 01286/672-963). There's a fine traditional old fish-and-chips joint on High Street.

SNOWDONIA NATIONAL PARK

Snowdonia National Park is Britain's second-largest national park, with Mount Snowdon—the tallest mountain in England and Wales—as its centerpiece. Each year half a million people choose one of seven different paths to the top of 3,560-foot Snowdon. Hikes take from five to seven hours. If you're reasonably fit and the weather cooperates, it's an exciting day. Trail info abounds. As you explore the area, notice the slate roofs—they're the local specialty.

Sights—Snowdonia

Betws-y-Coed—The resort center of Snowdonia National Park, Betwys-y-Coed (bet-us ee coyd) bursts with tour buses and souvenir shops. It has a good National Park and Tourist Information office (daily 10:00–18:00, tel. 01690/710-426), but I don't understand why everyone seems to stop here. As you drive west out of town on A5, you'll see the car park for scenic Swallow Falls, a pleasant five-minute walk from the road. A mile or so past the falls, on the right, you'll see "The Ugly House," built overnight to take advantage of a 15th-century law that let any quickie building avoid fees and taxes. A regular bus service connects Conwy and Betws-y-Coed. Trains run from the north coast through Betws-y-Coed to Blaenau (6/day).

Trefriw Woolen Mills—The mill in Trefriw, five miles north of Betws-y-Coed, is free and surprisingly interesting if the machines are running (Monday–Friday 9:30–13:00 and 14:00–17:30, tel. 01492/640-462). Follow the 11 stages of wool transformation: warping, weaving, carding, hanking, spanking, spinning, and so on. The handspinning house (next to the WC) has a charming spinster and a petting cupboard of all the fibers that can be spun into cloth. Then enjoy the fine woolen shop, pleasant town (more so than Betws-y-Coed), and coffee shop. The woolen mill at Penmachno (also near Betws-y-Coed) is smaller and less interesting.

Beddgelert—This is the quintessential Snowdon village, packing a scenic mountain punch without the tourist crowds (17 miles from Betws-y-Coed). Set on a river in the shadow of Snowdon and her sisters, with a fine variety of hikes from its doorstep and pretty good bus service, Beddgelert makes a good stop for those wanting to experience the peace of Snowdonia.

Locals can recommend walks. You can follow the lane along the river (three miles round-trip), walk down the river and around the hill (three hours, six miles, 900-foot gain, via Cwm Bycham), hike along (or around) Llyn Gwynant Lake and four miles back to Beddgelert (ride the bus to the lake), or try the more dramatic higher ridge walks on Moel Hebog (Hawk Hill).

Sleeping in Beddgelert: Plas Tan Y Graig Guest House, at the village bridge, is a good value (D-£32 with breakfast, family room, LL55 4LT, tel. 01766/890-329). They have a fine lounge and loaner hiking maps. Also just over the bridge, Brian Wheatley rents rooms at **Plas-Gwyn** (D-£34, Db-£36, nonsmoking, tel. 01766/890215). The **Royal Goat Hotel** offers well-worn, chandeliered, woody elegance in a grand hotel built for the rugged 19th-century aristocrat (Db-£78, some nonsmoking rooms, CC:VMA, tel. 01766/890-224, fax 01766/890-422).

Mountaineers note that this area was used by Sir Edmund Hillary and his men as they practiced for the first ascent of Mount Everest. The **Pen-y-Gwryd Hotel Pub** (at the top of the pass north of Beddgelert) is strewn with fascinating Hillary and Mount Everest memorabilia (D-£42, Db-£52, saggy beds, smoky, old-time-elegant public rooms, those in D rooms get to use museum-piece Victorian tubs, grand five-course dinners-£16, tel. 01286/870-211). Situated in the peaceful middle of nowhere, with a crampon ambience, this is ideal for well-bred hikers.

Llanberis—A town of 2,000 people with as many tourists on a sunny day, Llanberis is a popular base for Snowdon activities. Along with the station for the Snowdon train, there is a good information center, a few touristy museums, pony trekking, and good bus connections.

▲▲Mount Snowdon and the Mountain Railway—The easiest and most popular ascent of Mount Snowdon is by the Snowdon Mountain Railway, a rack-and-pinion railway from 1896 that climbs 3,000 feet over 4.5 miles from Llanberis to the summit of Snowdon (£15 round-trip, family discounts on early departures, 2.5 hours including a 30-minute stop at the summit, CC:VM, tel. 01286/870-223). First departure is usually at 9:00. While the schedule flexes with weather and demand, they try to run several trips a day mid-March through October (two departures per hour in peak season). Off-season trains often stop short of the summit. On sunny summer days trains fill up (waits are longer in the afternoon, arrive early and get a departure appointment time—usually a wait of an hour or two). While they "don't really do this," you might telephone and see if you can get your name on the list.

BLAENAU FFESTINIOG
This quintessential Welsh slate-mining town is notable for its slate-mine tour and its old steam train. The town—a dark, poor place—seems to struggle on, oblivious to the tourists who nip in and out. Take a walk. The shops are right out of the 1950s. Long rows of humble "two up and two down" houses (four rooms) feel pretty grim. There are some buses from the town to the slate mines; the road isn't pedestrian-friendly. (TI open daily 10:00–18:00, tel. 01766/830-360.)

Sights—Blaenau Ffestiniog
▲▲**Llechwedd Slate-Mine Tour**—Slate mining played a block-buster role in Welsh heritage, and this mine on the northern edge of the bleak town of Blaenau Ffestiniog does a fine job of explaining the mining culture of Victorian Wales. The Welsh mined and split most of the slate roofs of Europe. And for every ton of usable slate found, 10 tons were mined. The exhibit comes in three parts: a tiny Victorian mining town (free and worthwhile) and two 30-minute tours. The "deep mine" tour features a tape-recorded dramatization of social life, a serious descent, and a half-mile of walking. The "tramway" tour is a level train ride with two stops, no walking, and a live guide; it focuses on working life and traditional mining techniques. Both are different and, considering the cheap combo-ticket, worthwhile. Don't miss the slate-splitting demonstration, open to all, at the end of the tramway tour (£6.50 for one tour or £10 for both, daily 10:00–18:00, last tour starts at 17:15, closes at 17:00 in winter, tel. 01766/830-306). Dress warmly—I mean it. You'll freeze underground without a sweater.
▲**Gloddfa Ganol Slate Mine**—The world's largest slate mine, across the street from the Llechwedd Mine, offers a less commercial visit for a serious look at today's mining operations. After an A-V presentation, hard-hatted visitors are basically free to roam the 150-year-old main tunnel and gaze into the open pit (£5.50, Monday–Friday 10:00–17:30, closed winter, tel. 01766/830-664).
▲**Ffestiniog Railway**—This 13-mile narrow-gauge train line was built in 1836 for small horse-drawn wagons to transport the slate from the Ffestiniog mines to the port of Porthmadog. In the 1860s horses gave way to steam trains. Today hikers and tourists enjoy these tiny titans (£13 round-trip, hrly, 2.5 hrs round-trip; diesel trains are £2 cheaper, first-class observation cars are £5 extra, tel.

01766/512-340). This is a novel steam train experience, but the full-size Llandudno–Blaenau Ffestiniog train is more scenic and works better for hikers.

Portmeirion—Ten miles southwest of Blaenau Ffestiniog, this "Italian Village" was the lifework of a rich local architect who began building it in 1925. Set idyllically on the coast just beyond the poverty of the slate-mine towns, the extravagance of this flower-filled fantasy is particularly striking. Surrounded by lush Welsh greenery and a windswept mudflat at low tide, the village is an artistic glob of palazzo arches, fountains, gardens, and promenades filled with cafés, tacky shops, a hotel, and local tourists who always wanted to go to Italy (or who are fans of the cultish British 1960s TV series *The Prisoner*). The architect explains his purpose in a videotaped slide presentation. Not worth the £3.50 (daily 9:30–17:30, two miles from Porthmadog, tel. 01766/770-228).

Transportation Connections—North Wales

Conwy to: Llandudno Junction (to catch the Conwy Valley train; 2 buses/hrly, 5 min, or walk 20 min), **Trefriw–Betws-y-Coed–Penygwryd–Llanberis** (bus 19, 2/hrly in summer).

 Llandudno Junction by train to: Chester (2/hrly, 1 hr), **Birmingham** (2/hrly, 2.5 hrs), **London**'s Euston Station (hrly, 3.5 hrs). Train info: tel. 0345/484-950.

 Caernarfon to: Conwy (direct hrly bus, 75 min, buy ticket on bus; or train then bus, 2/hrly, 75 min), **Llanberis** (2 buses/hrly, 30 min), **Beddgelert** (hrly buses, 30 min, summer only), **Blaenau–Ffestiniog** (hrly buses, 80 min), **Beddgelert–Penygwryd–Llanberis** (bus 95, every 2 hrs, 90 min).

 Llanberis to: Beddgelert (buses hrly, 45 min, £11.50).

 Ruthin to: Llangollen (15 miles; connections are doable, but discouraging), **Betsw-y-Coed** (30 miles; doable but time-consuming with transfers), **Chester** (6 buses/day, 30 min, or a £15 taxi).

 Chester by train to: London (hrly, 3 hrs), **Liverpool** (2/hrly, 50 min), **Birmingham** (2/hrly, 2 hrs), points in **North Wales** (2/hrly).

Ferry Connections—North Wales and Ireland

Holyhead and Dun Laoghaire: Stena Line sails between Holyhead (North Wales) and Dun Laoghaire near Dublin (4/day, 100 min, £25–36 one-way walk-on fare, £24 round-trip in a day if you have no baggage, plus £5 tax if buying ticket in Ireland, reserve by phone as soon as you can—they book up long in advance on summer weekends, Dublin tel. 01/204-7722, Holyhead tel. 01407/606-606).

 Holyhead and Dublin: Irish Ferries sails between Holyhead (North Wales) and Dublin (2/day, 3 hrs, £20 one-way walk-on fare, £30 round-trip, Dublin tel. 01/661-0511, Holyhead tel. 0990-329-129, Web site: www.iol.ie/irishferries, e-mail: info@irish-ferries.ie).

Car fares vary from £250 to £350 (with up to five passengers, depending on season, cheapest on Wednesdays).

Sleeping near Holyhead dock: The fine **Monravon B&B** has seven smoke-free rooms (Db-£35, family deals, Porth-Y-Felin Road, 10-minute walk from dock, CC:VM, tel. & fax 01407/762-944).

Route Tips for Drivers

Ironbridge Gorge to Ruthin: Drive for an hour to Wales via A5 through Shrewsbury, crossing into Wales at the pretty castle town of Chirk. There, take A5 to Llangollen. Cross the bridge in Llangollen, turn left, and follow A542 and A525 past the romantic Valle Crucis abbey, over the scenic Horseshoe Pass, and into Ruthin. Driving to Conwy is faster via Wrexham and then the A55.

Ruthin to Caernarfon (56 miles) to Blaenau (34 miles) to Ruthin (35 miles): This route connects the top sights with the most scenic routes. From Ruthin take B5105 (steepest road off main square) and follow signs to Cerrigydrudion. Then follow A5 into Betws-y-Coed with a possible quick detour to the Trefriw Woolen Mill (five miles north on B5106, well signposted). Climb west on A5 through Capel Curig, then take A4086 over the rugged Pass of Llanberis, under the summit of Mount Snowdon (to the south, behind those clouds), and on to Caernarfon. Park under the castle in the harborside car park (£2).

Leaving Caernarfon, take the lovely A4085 southeast through Beddgelert to Penrhyndeudraeth. (Make things even more beautiful by taking the little B4410 road from Garreg through Rhyd.) Then take A487 toward What Maentwrog, and A496 to Blaenau Ffestiniog. Go through the dark, depressing mining town of Blaenau Ffestiniog on A470 into hills of slate and turn right into the Llechwedd Slate Mine.

After the mine, continue uphill on A470, snapping photos north through Dolwyddelan (passing a fine old Welsh castle ruin) and back to A5. For a high and desolate detour, return to Ruthin via the windy, curvy A543 road over the stark moors to the Sportsman's Arms Pub (the highest pub in Wales, good food), through Denbigh, and home.

BLACKPOOL

This is Britain's fun puddle. It's England's most-visited attraction, the private domain of its working class, a faded and sticky mix of Coney Island, Las Vegas, and Woolworth's. Juveniles of any age love it. My kids declared it better than Disneyland.

Blackpool grew up with the Industrial Revolution. In the mid-1800s entire mill towns would close down and take a two-week break in Blackpool. They came for the fresh air—much needed after a hard year in the mills—and to drink the seawater. Back then they figured it was healthy to drink the seawater. Blackpool's heydays are past now as more and more working people can afford the cheap charter flights to sunny Spain. Still, this is an accessible and afford-able fun zone for the Anne and Andy Capps of northern England. People come year after year. They stay for a week and they love it.

Most Americans don't even consider a stop in Blackpool. Many won't like it. It's an ears-pierced-while-you-wait, tipsy-toupee kind of place. Tacky, yes. Lowbrow, OK. But it's as English as can be, and that's what you're here for. An itinerary should feature as many facets of a culture as possible. Blackpool is as English as the Queen—and considerably more fun.

Spend the day "muckin' about" the beach promenade of fortune-tellers, fish-and-chips joints, amusement piers, warped mirrors, and Englanders wearing hats with built-in ponytails. A million greedy doors try every trick to get you inside. Huge arcade halls advertise free toilets and broadcast bingo numbers into the streets; the wind machine under a wax Marilyn Monroe blows at a steady gale; and the smell of fries, tobacco, and sugar is everywhere. Milk comes in raspberry or banana in this land where people under incredibly bad wigs look normal. If you're bored in Blackpool, you're just too classy.

Planning Your Time

Ideally, get to Blackpool around lunchtime for a free afternoon and evening to make bubbles in this cultural mudpuddle. Blackpool is easy by car or train. Speed demons with a car can treat it as a midday break (it's just off the M6) and continue north. If you have kids, they'll want more time here (hey, it's cheaper than Disneyland). If you're into nightlife, this town is a slam dunk. If you're before or beyond kids and not into kitsch and greasy spoons, skip it. If the weather's great and you love nature, the lakes are just a few hours north. A visit to Blackpool does sharpen the wonders of Windermere.

Orientation (tel. code: 01253)

Everything clusters along the six-mile beachfront promenade, a tacky, glittering strip mall of fun. Each of the three amusement piers has its own personality: north—sedate, central—young fun, south—family. The piers were built for Victorian landlubbers who wanted to go to sea but were afraid of getting seasick. The Pleasure Beach rides are near the south pier. Jutting up near the north pier is Blackpool's stubby Eiffel-type tower. The most interesting shops, eateries, and theaters are inland from the north pier.

Tourist Information: There are two TIs near the tower, one on Clifton Street, one on the Promenade (Monday–Saturday 9:00–17:00, Sunday 10:00–16:00, shorter hours off-season, tel. 01253/478-222, the same number gives recorded entertainment info after hours). Get the city map (50p), pick up brochures on the amusement centers, and ask about special shows.

Arrival in Blackpool: The train station is just three blocks from the town center. The motorway funnels you down Yeadon Way into a giant parking zone (formerly the central station).

Getting Around Blackpool

Vintage trolley cars run 13 miles up and down the waterfront, connecting all the sights. This first electric tramway in Europe dates from 1885 (80p–£1.50, depending on the length, £4.25 for an all-day pass; they come every five minutes or so, just jump on and pay the conductor). Taxis are easy to snare in Blackpool.

Sights—Blackpool

▲**Blackpool Tower**—This mini–Eiffel Tower is a 104-year-old vertical fun center. You pay £6 to get in; after that, the fun is free. Work your way up from the bottom through layer after layer of noisy entertainment: circus (two acts a day, usually at 14:30, the big show is at 19:30, not on Friday, you can return on a ticket), space world, dinosaur land, aquarium, and a wonderful old ballroom with barely live music and golden oldies dancing to golden oldies all day. Enjoy a break at the dance floor–level pub or on a

Blackpool

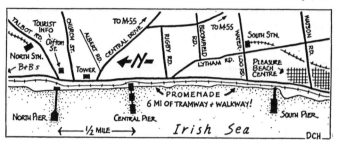

balcony perch. Kids love this place. With a little marijuana, adults would, too. Ride the elevator to the tip of the 500-foot-tall symbol of Blackpool for a smashing view, especially at sunset (daily 10:00–23:00, tower closed when windy, tel. 01253/622-242).

▲**Pleasure Beach**—These 42 acres, littered with more than 80 rides (including "the best selection of white-knuckle rides in Europe"), ice-skating shows, cabarets, and amusements attract 7 million people a year. The most talked-about attraction is the Pepsi Max Big One, "the world's fastest and highest" roller coaster (235 feet, 85 mph). The newest sensation is "Play Station," which rockets you straight up before letting you bungee down. Also memorable is a frightening race called "Steeple Chase" (imagine carousel horses stampeding down a roller coaster track) and the new "Pasaje de Terror." Admission is free and rides cost a couple of pounds each (hours vary with weather and season, tel. 01253/ 341-033). There are several other major amusement centers, including a popular water park called Sand Castle (across the street from Pleasure Beach).

▲▲▲**People-Watching**—Blackpool's top sight is its people. You'll see England here as nowhere else. Grab someone's hand and a big stick of "rock" (candy), and stroll. Grown men walk around with huge teddies looking for "bowlingo" places. Ponder the thought of actually retiring here to spend your last years, day after day, surrounded by Blackpool and wearing a hat with a built-in ponytail. Blackpool puts people in a talkative mood. Ask someone to explain the difference between tea and supper.

▲▲**Variety Show**—Blackpool always has a few razzle-dazzle music, dancing-girl, racy-humor, magic, and tumbling shows. Box offices around town can give you a rundown on what's available (tickets £5–12). I enjoy the old-time music hall shows. They're corny—neither hip nor polished—but it's fascinating to be surrounded by hundreds of partying British seniors, swooning and waving their hankies to the predictable beat. Busloads of happy widows come from all corners of North England to giggle at jokes

I'd never tell my grandma. Your B&B has the latest. If that's too lowbrow, Blackpool is second to London in theater. You can always watch a good play.

▲▲**Funny Girls**—Blackpool's current hot bar is just a block from the North Pier. Every night from 20:30 to 23:30 Funny Girls puts on a "glam bam thank you ma'am" burlesque-in-drag show that delights footballers and grannies alike. Cover is only £3. Get your drinks at the bar unless the transvestites are dancing on it. The show, while racy, is not raunchy. The music is very loud. The crowd is young, old, straight, gay, very down-to-earth, and fun-loving. Go on a weeknight. Friday and Saturday are jammed. You can pay £5–£10 for VIP seats to avoid any weekend lines and look down on the show and crowded floor from a mezzanine level (tel. 01253/291-144).

Blackpool's clubs and discos are cheap, with live bands and an interesting crowd (22:00–1:00). The pubs of Blackpool have a unique tradition of "and your own, luv." Say that here and your barmaid will add 20p to your bill and drop it into her tip jar. (Say it anywhere else and they won't know what you mean.)

▲**Illuminations**—Blackpool was the first town in England to "go electric." Now, every September and October, Blackpool stretches its tourist season by illuminating its six miles of waterfront with countless lights, all blinking and twinkling. The American in me kept saying, "I've seen bigger and I've seen better," but I filled his mouth with cotton candy and just had some simple fun like everyone else on my specially decorated tram.

Sleeping in Blackpool
(£1 = about $1.70, tel. code: 01253)
Sleep Code: **S** = Single, **D** = Double/Twin, **T** = Triple, **Q** = Quad, **b** = bathroom, **t** = toilet only, **s** = shower only, **CC** = Credit Card (Visa, MasterCard, Amex).

Blackpool's 140,000 people provide 120,000 beds in 3,500 mostly dumpy, cheap, nondescript hotels and B&Bs. Remember, the town's in the business of accommodating the people who can't afford to go to Spain. Most have the same design—minimal character, maximum number of springy beds—and charge £12 to £18 per person. Empty beds abound except during September through November and summer weekends. It's only really tight on Illumination weekends. The first three listings below are on the waterfront in the quiet area they call "the posh end," a mile or two north of the Tower, with easy parking and easy access to the center by trolley. The last two are near the train station. Prices go up during the Illuminations and are soft off-season.

Robin Hood Hotel is a super place, cheery and family-run, with a big, welcoming living room and 10 newly and tastefully refurbished rooms with the only sturdy beds I found (Sb-£20,

Db-£36, less for two nights, family deals, CC:VM, entirely non-smoking, trolley stop: St. Stevens Avenue, 1.5 miles north of Tower across from a peaceful stretch of beach, 100 Queens Promenade, North Shore FY2 9NS, tel. 01253/351-599, Pam and Colin Webster).

Beechcliffe Private Hotel is clean, smoke-free, and family-run with more charm than average (S-£15, D-£30, Dt-£33, Tt-£50, less for two nights, trolley stop: Uncle Tom's, walk a block away from the beach, 16 Shaftesbury Avenue, North Shore FY2 9QQ, tel. 01253/353-075, David and Brenda).

Prefect Hotel is all smiles and pink-flamingo pretty. Shabby, but spacious-for-Blackpool with all the fun touches, this place is the appropriate springboard for the town (Sb-£17, Db-£34, ask for a view room, trolley to Bispham, two miles north of Tower at 204 Queens Promenade, FY2 9JS, tel. 01253/352-699, Bill and Pauline Acton).

Valentine Private Hotel is a bit smoky but has a smoke-free breakfast room (S-£12, D-£24, Db-£28, family deals, plenty of showers, CC:VMA, three blocks from the station at 35 Dickson Road, FY1 2AT, tel. 01253/622-775, Denise and Garry Hinchliffe). **Sandylands Guest House** is a plain "homely" little place two blocks from the station (S-£12, D-£24, smoky, 47 Banks Street, tel. 01253/294-670, Kevin Poole).

Eating in Blackpool

Your hotels may serve a cheap, early-evening meal. The following places are all between the Tower and the North Pier: For mushy peas and good fish and chips, go to the "world famous" **Harry Ramsden's** near the tower (60 The Promenade, tel. 01253/294-386). Their advertising brings out the smart aleck in you. The **Oyster Bar** at the corner of West Street and the Promenade is a fixture that actually pre-dates the resort (as do some of its employees). Around the corner on West Street is the **Mitre Bar**—drop in to survey the great photos of old Blackpool. Across the street from the bar, **The Scullery** is a humble, hardworking pantry serving healthy/hearty food for great prices (10 West Street). Food in the tower is terrible, but it's not much better elsewhere.

Transportation Connections—Blackpool

If you're heading to (or from) Blackpool by train, you'll usually need to transfer at Preston (2/hrly, 30 min). Train info: tel. 0345/484-950.

Preston to: Keswick, the Lake District (hrly trains, 30 min to Penrith, transfer to bus, 6 buses/day, 40 min to Keswick), **York** (hrly trains, 4.5 hrs, change at Manchester), **Edinburgh** (8/day, 3 hrs).

Points south: For **Ironbridge Gorge, Cotswolds, Bath,** and

North Wales, you'll have several transfers but find fast and frequent trains. To **London**, change in Manchester (2/hrly, 5 hrs).

   Drivers entering and leaving Blackpool: Approaching Blackpool, the motorway dumps you right onto Yeadon Way, which funnels you into a huge city parking lot. Day-trippers need to park here. The quickest way out of town is to drive the Promenade to the Central Pier and turn inland. Under the bridge take an immediate left (take exit for M55). This gets you into the huge parking lot that leads directly to the motorway.

NEAR BLACKPOOL: LIVERPOOL

Liverpool, a gritty but surprisingly enjoyable city, is a fascinating stop for Beatles fans and those who would like to look urban England straight in its problem-plagued eyes.

   The TI is with everything else—on Albert Dock (tel. 0151/708-8854). The bus and train stations are central.

Sights—Liverpool

▲**Albert Dock**—Opened in 1852 by Prince Albert and enclosing seven acres of water, the dock is surrounded by five-story-high brick warehouses. In its day, Liverpool was England's greatest seaport. It prospered as one corner of the triangular commerce of the 18th-century slave trade. As England's economy boomed, so did the port of Liverpool. From 1830 to 1930, 9 million emigrants sailed from Liverpool to find their dreams in the New World. But the port was not deep enough for the big new ships; trade declined after 1890, and by 1972 it was closed entirely. Like Liverpool itself, the docks have enjoyed a renaissance, and today they are the featured attraction of the city. The city's main attractions are lined up here out of the rain and padded by lots of shopping mall–type distractions. There's plenty of parking.

▲**Merseyside Maritime Museum**—This museum, which tells the story of this once-prosperous shipping center, gets an A for effort but feels designed for visiting school groups. The ships section is pretty dull, but the smuggling and customs, slavery, and emigration sections are interesting. The associated **Museum of Liverpool Life** offers a good look at the workaday story of the town (one £3 ticket for both, daily 10:00–17:00).

Tate Gallery Liverpool—This prestigious 20th-century gallery is next to the Maritime Museum. It won't entertain you as well as its London sister, but if you're into modern art, any Tate's great (free, Tuesday–Sunday 10:00–18:00, closed Monday, tel. 0151/709-0507).

▲**The Beatles Story**—It's kind of sad to think the Beatles are stuck in a museum (and Ringo's in reruns of *Shining Time Station*). While overpriced and not very creative, the story's a great one and even an avid fan will pick up some new information (£6.50 but discount

coupons abound, try not to pay full fare, daily 10:00–18:00, tel. 0151/709-1963). The shop is an impressive pile of Beatles buyables. Die-hard Beatles fans may want to invest a couple of hours in one of several Beatles "Magical Mystery" bus tours (the lads' homes, Penny Lane, and so on, £9, two hours). The TI has specifics on the big bus that goes daily. You may want a more fun and intimate mini-bus Beatles tour from Phil Hughes (£8 per person, minimum £40 per group, three-hour Beatles tours; also offers Liverpool and regional tours; tel. & fax 0151/228-4565, mobile phone 0961-511-223).
▲**Matthew Street**—Beatles fans will want to explore Matthew Street (a 15-minute walk into the center from Albert Dock), including the site of the famous Cavern Club, the new "Cavern Club" nearby, and the Beatles Shop at #31.

Transportation Connections—Liverpool
By train to: Blackpool (hrly, 2 hrs, transfer at Preston), **York** (hrly, 2.5 hrs), **London** (hrly, 2.5 hrs), **Crewe** (18/day, 45 min). Train info: tel. 0345/484-950.

Route Tips for Drivers
Ruthin to Blackpool via Liverpool: From Ruthin, get to the M53, which tunnels under the Mersey River (£1). Once in Liverpool, follow signs to City Center, Pier Head, and Albert Dock, where you'll find a huge car park next to all the sights. Leaving Liverpool, drive north along the waterfront following signs to M58 (Preston), then M6, and finally M55 into Blackpool.
　　Ruthin to Blackpool (100 miles): From Ruthin, take A494 through the town of Mold and follow the blue signs to the motorway. M56 zips you to M6, where you'll turn north toward Preston and Lancaster. Don't miss your turnoff: A few minutes after Preston take the not-very-clearly-signed next exit (#32, M55) into Blackpool and drive as close as you can to the stubby Eiffel-type tower in the town center. Downtown parking is terrible. If you're not spending the day, head for one of the huge £6/day garages. If you're spending the night, drive to the waterfront and head north. My top B&Bs are north on the Promenade (easy parking).

LAKE DISTRICT

In the pristine Lake District, Wordsworth's poems still shiver in trees and ripple on ponds. This is a land where nature rules and man keeps a wide-eyed but low profile. Relax, recharge, take a cruise or a hike, maybe even write a poem. Renew your poetic license at Wordsworth's famous Dove Cottage.

The Lake District, about 30 miles long and 30 miles wide, is nature's lush, green playground. Explore it by foot, bike, bus, or car. While not impressive in sheer height (Scafell Pike, the tallest peak in England, is only 3,206 feet), there's a walking-stick charm about the way nature and the local culture mix. Walking along a windblown ridge or climbing over a rock fence to look into the eyes of a raga-muffin sheep, even tenderfeet get a chance to feel very outdoorsy.

You'll probably have rain mixed with brilliant bright spells. Drizzly days can be followed by delightful evenings. Pubs offer atmospheric shelter at every turn. As the locals are fond of saying, "There's no such thing as bad weather, only unsuitable clothing."

While the south lakes (Windermere, Bowness, Beatrix Potter's cottage) get the promotion and tour crowds and are closer to London, the north lakes (Ullswater, Derwentwater, Buttermere) are less touristy and at least as scenic.

This chapter should actually be called the "North Lakes District." The town of Keswick, the lake called Derwentwater, and the vast time-passed Newlands Valley will be our focus. The area works great by car or train/bus. And Wordsworth and Potter fans can easily side-trip south to see their homes.

Planning Your Time
If great scenery is commonplace in your life, the Lake District can be more soothing (and rainy) than exciting. To save time you

could easily make this area a one-night stand—or even a quick drive-through. With a car and a three-week trip in Britain, I'd spend two days and two nights in the area. The quickest way in is to leave the motorway at Penrith.

Here's the most exciting way for drivers to pack their day of arrival: Get an early start from Blackpool or North Wales, leave the motorway at Kendal by 10:30, drive along Windermere and through Ambleside, 11:30—Tour Dove Cottage, 12:30— Backtrack to Ambleside, where a small road leads up and over the dramatic Kirkstone Pass (far more scenic northbound than southbound, get out and bite the wind) and down to Glenridding on Ullswater. You could catch the 14:40 boat. Hike six miles (15:15–18:45) from Howtown back to Glenridding. Drive to your farmhouse B&B near Keswick with a stop as the sun sets at Castlerigg Stone Circle.

On your second day, explore Buttermere Lake, drive over Honister Pass, explore Derwentwater, and do the Cat Bells High Ridge walk. Spend the evening at the same B&B.

Those without a car will use Keswick as a springboard. Cruise the lake and hike in the Cat Bells area. If you need a vacation from your vacation, this is a fine day to simply vegetate.

Getting Around the Lake District

Those based in Keswick without a car can manage fine. Be sure to pick up the excellent *Lakeland Explorer* magazine (free from TIs and hotels), which explains all the local bus and boat schedules and outlines some great walks for the first-time visitor.

By Foot: Piles of hiking information are available everywhere you turn. Consider buying a detailed map (such as Ordnance Survey). For easy hikes, the fliers at TIs and B&Bs detailing particular routes are very helpful. The best ridge walk is immediately outside of town (see Cat Bells High Ridge Hike, below).

By Boat: A circular boat service glides you easily around Derwentwater (for a sail/hike option, see Derwentwater, below).

By Bus: Buses take you quickly and easily (if not very frequently) to all nearby points of interest. Pick up the free 30-page Lakeland Explorer bus brochure for schedules, prices, and suggested bus/hike outings.

By Bus Tour: Mountain Goat Tours run an interesting variety of half-day (£12) and all-day (£23) minibus tours daily in summer from Keswick. They are rugged, informative (led by established mountain guides), and great for people with bucks who'd like to see the area without hiking or messing with public transport. Unfortunately, you may not know if your tour will reach its minimum number of six passengers until shortly before departure (office at Keswick central car park, tel. 017687/73962, Web site: www.lakes-pages.co.uk).

Lake District

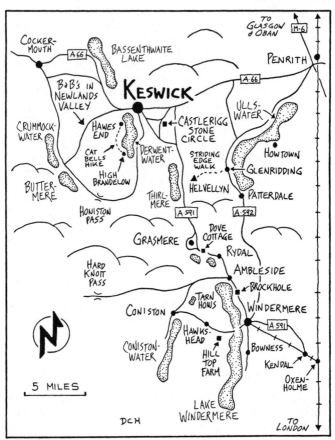

By Car: Nothing is very far from Keswick and Derwentwater. Get a good map, get off the big roads, and leave the car, at least occasionally, for some walking. In summer, the Keswick–Ambleside–Windermere–Bowness corridor (A591) suffers from congestion.

KESWICK

As far as touristy lake-district centers go, Keswick (kezz-ick, pop. 5,000) is far more enjoyable than Windermere, Bowness, or Ambleside. An important mining center (slate, copper, lead) through the Middle Ages, Keswick became a resort in the 19th century. Its fine Victorian buildings recall those romantic days when city slickers first learned about "communing with nature." Today the compact town is lined with tea shops, pubs, gift shops, and hiking-gear shops. For up-to-date Lake District weather, call 017687/75757.

Keswick is the ideal home base: plenty of good B&Bs (see Sleeping, below), an easy bus connection to the nearest train station at Penrith, and a prime location on the best lake in the area, Derwentwater. In Keswick everything is within a five-minute walk of each other: the market square, tourist and hiking information office (daily 9:30–17:30, winter 10:00–16:00, tel. 017687/72645, great 25p brochures outlining nearby hikes), recommended B&Bs, bike rental shop, municipal pitch-and-putt golf course, bus station, Mountain Goat minibus tour starting point, lakeside boat dock, post office (with Internet access), and a central car park. Saturday is market day and the town square is packed and lively.

Sights—Keswick

▲**Pencil Museum**—Graphite was first discovered centuries ago in Keswick. A hunk of the stuff proved great for marking sheep in the 15-century, and the rest is history (which you can learn all about here). While you can't tour the 150-year-old factory where the famous Derwent pencils are made, the charming museum on the edge of Keswick is a good way to pass a rainy hour (£2, daily 9:30–16:00, rentable headsets are not necessary but the fine and free 20-minute film is; cheap brass-rubbing in the shop, tel. 017687/73626).

Walks—The TI organizes daily walks of varying levels of difficulty with local guides (£4, daily 10:00–17:00, tel. 017687/72645).

▲**Plays**—Locals are proud of their Century Theater, which is moving into a new playhouse and offers plays nearly nightly during summer. This is a fine opportunity to do something completely local (£10, three different plays by professional actors, tel. 017687/74411).

▲**Golf**—A lush nine-hole pitch 'n' putt golf course separates the town from the lake and offers a classy, cheap, and convenient chance to golf near the birthplace of the sport (daily 9:30–20:00, £2.25 for nine holes).

Swimming—The Leisure Center has a pool kids love, with a huge water slide (a short walk from the town center, tel. 017687/72760 for hours).

Sights—Derwentwater Area

▲▲**Derwentwater**—This is one of the region's most photographed and popular lakes. With four islands, good circular boat service, plenty of trails, and the pleasant town of Keswick at its north end, Derwentwater entertains.

The roadside views aren't much, so walk or cruise. You can

Keswick

To Newlands Valley B+B's
To A-66
Crosthwaite
Pencil Museum
Fitz Park
Art Museum
High Hill
River Greta
Main
B+B's
Laundry
Stanger
Bank
To Penrith
Station Rd
Victoria
Bus Station + Supermarket
Camping
Headlands
Heads
Market Pl.
Post
Penrith Road
B+B Area
The Heads
Borrowdale Rd
Southey
St. Johns
Ambleside
To Castlerigg Stone Circle
Hope Park Pitch + Putt Golf
Crow Park
Lake Road
Nat'l Park Info
To Windermere via A-591
To Buttermere via B-5289
Derwent Water
Dock
DCH
¼ mile

walk around the lake (fine trail, but floods in heavy rains, nine miles, three hours), cruise it (50 minutes), or do a hike/sail mix. I suggest a hike/sail trip around the lake. Boats run from Keswick about every 30 minutes (alternating clockwise and "anti-clock-wise") from 10:00 to 19:30, making seven stops on each 50-minute round-trip. The best hour-long lakeside walk is the 1.5-mile path between the docks at High Brandlehow and Hawse End. You could continue on foot along the lake back into Keswick. The boat trip costs £5 per circle with free stopovers, or 70p per segment. Stand on the pier or the boat may not stop (tel. 017687/72263).

▲▲**Cat Bells High Ridge Hike**—For a great (and easy) "king of the mountain" feeling, sweeping views, and a close-up look at the weather blowing over the ridge, hike about two hours from Hawes End up along the ridge to Cat Bells (1,480 feet) and down to High

Brandlehow. From there you can catch the boat or take the easy path along the shore of Derwentwater to your Hawes End starting point. This is probably the most dramatic family walk in the area. From Keswick, the lake, or your farmhouse B&B, you can see silhouetted stick figures hiking along this ridge. Drivers can park free at Hawes End (not particularly safe) or at the Littletown Farm on the Newlands Valley side of Cat Bells (£1).

Cat Bells is just the first of a series of peaks all connected by a fine ridge trail. Heartier hikers continue up to nine miles along this same ridge, enjoying valley and lake views as they arc around the Newlands Valley toward (and even down to) Buttermere. After High Spy you can descend an easy path into Newlands Valley. An ultimate day plan would be to bus to Buttermere, climb Robinson, and follow the ridge around to Cat Bells and back to Keswick.

▲▲**Car Hiking from Keswick**—Distances are short, roads are narrow with turnouts, and views are rewarding. Ask your B&B host for advice. Particularly scenic drives include Latrigg (from a car park just north of Keswick, walk a few minutes to the top of the hill for a commanding view of the town and lake). Two miles south of Keswick on the lakeside B5289 Borrowdale Valley Road, take the small road left (signposted Watendlath) for a half mile to a packhorse bridge (a quintessential Lake District scene) and, a half-mile farther, to a car park and the "surprise view" of Derwentwater. Following the road to its end, you hit the idyllic farm hamlet of Watendlath, where you can ponder the tiny lake and lazy farm animals. (Free shuttle buses—offered in hopes of minimizing traffic congestion—go from Keswick to Watendlath on Sundays hourly in summer. Ride to the end and hike home.) Return down to B5289 and back to Keswick or farther south to the scenic Borrowdale and over the dramatic pass to Buttermere.

▲▲**Buttermere**—This ideal little lake with a lovely, encircling four-mile stroll offers nonstop, no-sweat, Lakeland beauty. If you're not a hiker but kind of wish you were, take this walk. If you're very short on time, at least stop here and get your shoes dirty. (Parking and pubs are in Buttermere village.) Buttermere is connected with Borrowdale and Derwentwater by a great road over the rugged Honister Pass, strewn with glacial debris and curious shaggy Swaledale sheep (looking more like goats with their curly horns). In the other direction you can explore the cruel Newlands Valley or carry on through gentler scenery along Crummock Water and through the forested Whinlatter Pass (fine new Visitors Centre with a café the flying squirrels love) and back to Keswick.

▲▲**Castlerigg Stone Circle**—These 38 stones, 90 feet across and 3,000 years old, are mysteriously laid out on a line between the two tallest peaks on the horizon. For maximum goose-pimples (as they say here), show up at sunset (free, open all the time, just east of Keswick, follow brown signs, three minutes off A66, easy parking).

▲▲**More Hikes**—The area is riddled with wonderful hikes. B&Bs all have fine advice. From downtown Keswick you can walk the seven-mile Latrigg hike, which includes the Castlerigg Stone Circle (pick up 25p map/guide from TI). From the car park at Newlands Pass, at the top of Newlands Valley, an easy one-mile walk to Knottrigg probably offers more thrills per calorie burned than any walk in the region.

▲**Lakeland Sheep and Wool Centre**—If you're from farm country this is nothing special. But for a city slicker, the Sheep and Wool Centre offers an interesting and entertaining introduction to the region's most famous residents: its sheep. In the 50-minute show you'll meet 19 different breeds of sheep, watch one sheared, and see sheep dogs do their impressive thing. Afterward you'll meet the stars of the show. It's a hands-on experience kids enjoy (£3, four shows daily: 10:30, 12:00, 14:00, and 15:30, Wednesday–Sunday only in winter, unimpressive exhibition but good sheep-stuff shop, drive west from Keswick 15 minutes on A-66, at A-5086 roundabout you'll see the 300-seat auditorium on left).

Sights—Windermere Area

▲**Brockhole National Park Visitors Centre**—Check the events board as you enter. The center offers a 20-minute introduction-to-the-lakes slide show (played upon request), an information desk, organized walks, exhibits, a bookshop, a good cafeteria, gardens, nature walks, and a large car park. It's in a stately old lakeside mansion between Ambleside and the town of Windermere on A591 (daily April–October 10:00–17:00, free entry but £3 to park, tel. 015394/46601). The bookshop has an excellent selection of maps and guidebooks. I enjoyed Hunter Davies' refreshingly opinionated (but now a bit dated) *Good Guide to the Lakes* (£6).

▲▲**Dove Cottage**—William Wordsworth, the poet whose appreciation of nature and back-to-basics lifestyle put this area on the map, spent his most productive years (1799–1808) in this well-preserved old cottage on the edge of Grasmere. Today it's the obligatory sight for any Lake District visit. Even if you're not a fan, Wordsworth's "plain living and high thinking," his appreciation of nature, his romanticism, and the ways his friends unleashed their creative talents are very appealing. The 20-minute cottage tour (departures every few minutes—rarely a wait) and adjoining museum are excellent. In dry weather the garden where the poet was much inspired is worth a wander. Even a speedy, jaded museum goer will want at least an hour here (£4.40, daily 9:30–17:30, tel. 015394/35544).

Rydal Mount—Wordsworth's final, higher-class home with a lovely garden and view lacks the charm of Dove Cottage. Just down the road from Dove Cottage, it's worthwhile only for Wordsworth fans (£3.50, daily 9:30–17:00, tel. 015394/33002).

▲**Beatrix Potter's Hill Top Farm and Other Sights**—Many come to the lakes on a Beatrix Potter pilgrimage. Sensing that, entrepreneurial locals have dreamed up a number of BP sights. This can be confusing. Most important (and least advertised) is **Hill Top Farm**, the 17th-century cottage where Potter wrote many of her Peter Rabbit books (£3.80, Saturday–Wednesday 11:00–17:00 April–October, closed Thursday and Friday, next to Sawrey, near Hawkshead, tel. 015394/36269). Small, dark, and crowded, it gives a good look at her life and work.

The **Beatrix Potter Gallery** (in the neighboring, likeable town of Hawkshead) shows off BP's original drawings and water-color illustrations used in her children's books, and tells more about her life and work (£2.80, Sunday–Thursday 10:30–16:30, closed Friday and Saturday, Main Street, tel. 015394/36355). The gimmicky **World of Beatrix Potter** tour—which features a five-minute video trip into the world of Mrs. Tiggywinkle and com-pany, a series of tableaus starring the same imaginary gang, and a 15-minute video biography of BP—is a hit with children (not worth £3, daily 10:00–18:00, in Bowness near Windermere town, tel. 015394/88444).

Hard Knott Pass—Only 1,300 feet above sea level, this pass is a thriller, with a narrow, winding, steeply graded road. Just over the pass are the scant but evocative remains of the Hard Knott Roman fortress. There are great views and miserable rainstorms, but it can be very slow and frustrating when the one-lane road with turnouts is clogged by traffic (avoid in summer).

Sights—Ullswater Area

▲▲**Ullswater Hike and Boat Ride**—Long, narrow Ullswater offers eight miles of diverse and grand Lake District scenery. While you can drive it or cruise it, I'd ride the boat from the south tip halfway up and hike back. Boats leave Glenridding regularly (£2.80, 10:00–16:30, until 17:45 in July and August; get there a little early in summer; 35-minute ride, cheap and safe parking lot, pick up their 25p map/guide for the walk, tel. 017684/82229). Ride to the first stop, Howtown, halfway up the lake. Then spend four hours hiking and dawdling along the well-marked path by the lake south to Patterdale and then along the road back to Glenridding. This is a serious seven-mile walk with good views, varied terrain, and a few bridges and farms along the way. Wear good shoes and be prepared for rain. For a shorter hike, consider a circular walk from Howtown Pier. (Round-trip boat rides cost only 60p more than one-way.) There are several steamer trips daily up and down Ullswater. A good rainy-day plan is to ride the covered boat up and down the lake (two hours) or to Howtown and back (£3.10, one hour).

Helvellyn—Often considered the best high-mountain hike in the Lake District, this breathtaking, round-trip route from Glenridding includes the spectacular Striding Edge ridge walk. Be careful; do this six-hour hike only in good weather, and get advice from the Glenridding tourist office. While there are shorter routes, the Glenridding ascent is best.

Sleeping in the Lake District
(£1 = about $1.70, tel. code: 017687)

Sleeping in Keswick
Sleep Code: **S** = Single, **D** = Double/Twin, **T** = Triple, **Q** = Quad, **b** = bathroom, **t** = toilet only, **s** = shower only, **CC** = Credit Card (Visa, MasterCard, Amex).

The Lake District abounds with attractive B&Bs, guest houses, and hostels. It needs them all when summer hordes threaten the serenity of this romantic mecca. With the mobility of a car, you should have no trouble finding a room. But to get a particular place (especially on a Saturday), call ahead. Those using public transportation should stay in Keswick. With a car, drive into a remote farmhouse experience. Lakeland hostels are fine money-savers and filled with an interesting crowd. The Keswick TI can give you phone numbers of places with vacancies if you call.

In Keswick I've featured two streets, each within three blocks of the bus station and town square. "The Heads" is a classier street lined with proud Victorian houses, close to the lake, overlooking a golf course. Stanger Street, a bit humbler but also quiet and handy, has smaller homes. All of my Keswick listings are strictly smoke-free. The launderette is around the corner from the bus station on Main Street (daily 7:30–19:30, £3 wash and dry, change machine and coin-op flake dispenser, £2 extra for full-service by 10:00 or earlier; just leave clothes by door in rear with note and she'll do them for you).

Sleeping on The Heads
Berkeley Guest House, a big slate mansion enthusiastically run by Barbara Crompton, has a pleasant lounge, cramped hallways, and carefully appointed, comfortable rooms. The chirpy, skylight-bright £32 double in the attic is a fine value if you don't mind the stairs (small D-£30, Db-£40–44, The Heads, Keswick, Cumbria, CA12 5ER, tel. 017687/74222).

The Parkfield is thoughtfully run and decorated by Fay and Bob Watson. This big house is bright and pastel with a fine and restful view lounge (eight rooms, one on the ground floor, Db-£44-48 with this book through 1999, CC:VM, car park, strictly non-smoking, The Heads, CA12 5ES, tel. 017687/72328, e-mail: parkfield@kencomp.net).

Howe Keld Lakeland Hotel offers more of a small hotel feel with 15 rooms, a wide variety of breakfast selections, evening meals, and a bar (S-£21, Sb-£26, small Db-£40, big Db-£46 minimum two nights, prices with this book through 1999, two ground-floor rooms, 5-7 The Heads, CA12 5ES, tel. & fax 017687/72417, e-mail: howekeld@globalnet.co.uk, David and Valerie Fisher).

West View Guest House, next door, is smaller—only seven rooms—simpler, and also a decent value (D-£36, Db-£48, tel. 017687/73638, Carole and John).

Sleeping on Stanger Street

Abacourt House is an old Victorian slate townhouse completely redone by Sheila and Bill Newman. Bill, who just finished climbing all the "Wainwright" peaks, is a wealth of Lakeland sightseeing information and happy to point you in the most scenic direction. All five doubles have firm beds, TVs, and shiny, modern bathrooms (Db-£42, no children, 26 Stanger Street, Keswick, CA12 5JU, tel. 017687/72967, e-mail: abacourt@aol.com).

Dunsford Guest House, a few doors down, is another small, cheery place run by a young couple who get their exercise fellrunning (Db-£39, veggie breakfast options, 16 Stanger Street, tel. 017687/75059, e-mail: dunsford@clara.net, Pat and Peter Richards).

Fell House B&B is a charming place. Proprietor Barbara Hossack serves tea and homemade cakes each evening (six rooms, S-£17, D-£34, Db-£40, 28 Stanger Street, CA12 5JU, tel. 017687/72669).

Badgers Wood B&B is at the top of the street (S-£17, D-£34, Db-£38 with this book, 30 Stanger Street, tel. 017687/72621, e-mail: badgers.wood@kencomp.net, Irene and David).

Two former hotels now operate as hostels with £8 dorm beds: **Keswick** (4- to 12-bed rooms, center of town just off Station Road, tel. 017687/72484) and **Derwentwater** (two miles south of Keswick, tel. 017687/77246).

Sleeping in Newlands Valley

With a car, I'd drive 10 minutes past Keswick down the majestic Newlands Valley. Hiking opportunities are wonderful. If the place had a lake it would be packed with tourists. But it doesn't—and it isn't. The valley is studded with 500-year-old farms that have been in the same family for centuries. Shearing day is reason to rush home from school. Sons get school out of the way ASAP and follow their dads. Neighbor girls marry sons and move in. Grandparents retire to the cottage next door. With the price of wool depressed, most of the wives supplement the family income by running B&Bs. Traditionally, farmhouses lacked central heating, and while they are now heated, you can still request a hot-water bottle to warm up your bed.

Newlands Valley is just over the Cat Bells ridge from Derwentwater between Keswick and Buttermere. Leave Keswick heading west on the Cockermouth Road (A66). Take the second Newlands Valley exit through Braithwaite and follow signs through Newlands Valley (drive toward Buttermere). You'll pass Stoneycroft B&B and Ellas Crag first, then the curious purple house (and the turnoff to Low Skelgill), then Birkrigg Farm B&B, and finally Keskadale Farm (about four miles before Buttermere). The road is one-lane with passing turnouts.

Birkrigg Farm is the ideal farmhouse B&B. Mrs. Margaret Beaty offers visitors a comfy lounge, evening tea (good for socializing with her other guests), a classy breakfast, a territorial view, and perfect peace on this 220-acre working farm. Take your toast and last cup of tea out to the front yard bench (£17 per person in S, D, T, or Q, family deals, one shower and one tub for six rooms, March–November, Birkrigg Farm, Newlands Pass Road, Keswick, Cumbria, CA12 5TS, tel. 017687/78278).

Keskadale Farm B&B is another great farmhouse experience with valley views and ponderosa hospitality. This is a working farm with lots of curly-horned sheep and three rooms to rent (£18 per person in D or T, March–November, nonsmoking, one minute farther down Newlands Pass Road to Buttermere Road on a hairpin turn, Keskadale Farm, Newlands, Keswick CA12 5TS, tel. 017687/78544, Margaret Harryman). One of the oldest farms in the valley, it's actually made from 500-year-old ship beams.

Low Skelgill Farm, with three rooms sharing one bathroom, is immediately under Cat Bells. This is ideal for hikers since you can leave your car there for the Cat Bells ridge walk (S-£16, D-£32, take the Buttermere Road to Stair and then follow the "narrow-gated" road to Skelgill, tel. 017687/78453, Ann Grave). She also runs a rustic "camping barn" with mattresses for £3.50 a night (no bedding provided).

Stoneycroft B&B, an elegant old farm with a "new" 100-year-old extension, rents six spacious rooms—the most comfortable in the valley (D-£38, Db-£46, nonsmoking, CA12 5TS, tel. 017687/78240, e-mail: stoneycroft.newlands@btinternet.com, Sue and Mike Felton). While the other farms feel more rural, this place is posher, with more garden and fewer children.

Ellas Crag B&B, while in the same glorious setting, is a more comfortable stone house and not a farm. This homey place, with a good mix of modern and traditional, is enthusiastically run by Tony, Jean, and Catherine Hartley (S-£20, Ds-£40, no twin beds, only doubles, nonsmoking, dinner available, Stair, Newlands Valley, CA12 5TT, tel. 017687/78217).

Sleeping in Buttermere

The Bridge Hotel, just beyond Newlands Valley at Buttermere, offers a classy, musty, Old World countryside hotel experience (22 rooms, £65 per person with a five-course dinner, cheaper for longer stays, £45 per person B&B only upon request, CC:VM, Buttermere, Cumbria, CA13 9UZ, tel. 017687/70252, fax 017687/70215). There are no shops within 10 miles—only peace and quiet a stone's throw from one of the region's most beautiful lakes. Buttermere also has a hostel (see below).

Lake District Hostels
The Lake District's inexpensive hostels, usually located in great old buildings, are handy sources of information and social fun (£6–9 a bed). Local TIs have lists. The Lake District's free booking service (daily 9:00–18:00, tel. 015394/31117) can tell you which of the area's 30 hostels have beds available and can even book a place on your credit card (no more than seven days in advance). Since most hostels don't answer their phones during the day and many are full, this is a helpful service.

The **Buttermere King George VI Memorial Hostel**, a quarter-mile south of Buttermere village on Honister Pass Road, has good food, family rooms, and a royal setting (tel. 017687/70245). The well-run Borrowdale Hostel is secluded in Borrowdale Valley just south of Rosthwaite (drying rooms, tel. 017687/77257).

Eating in the Lake District

Eating in Keswick
The bus station faces a fine **supermarket** (Monday–Saturday 10:00–19:00, Sunday 10:00–16:00) which has a smoke-free Coffee Shop Café popular with locals. It features regional specialties and a menu that's healthy for your body and your pocketbook (last hot service at 17:30). **Maysons Whole Food Restaurant** is favored for its home cooking: curry, Cajun, vegetarian options, and not a chip in sight. It feels Californian (£6 meals, family-friendly, on Lake Road, tel. 017687/74104). **Keswick Lodge Pub** is popular for its fine pub meals and atmosphere (nightly, just off the main square on Main Street, tel. 017687/74584). For fish and chips, Keswickians go to **The Old Keswickian** (nightly, facing the TI, take-out or a restaurant upstairs).

Locals will tell you that Keswick restaurants have it too easy and you need to drive for a really good meal. The **Old Posting House**, a 20-minute drive west of Keswick, serves excellent meals in a non-smoky pub setting (just beyond Cockermouth at Dean-scales, tel. 01900/823-278).

Eating in Newlands Valley
Since most farmhouses don't serve dinner to their guests, take the lovely 10-minute drive to Buttermere for your evening meal at the **Fish Hotel** pub (£5, nightly 18:00–21:00, family-friendly, limited menu, good fish, *beaucoup* chips, no vegetables) or the

more expensive but much cozier and tastier **Bridge Hotel** pub (£6 or £7, nightly 18:00–21:30, more interesting menu, crunchy veggies). On the Keswick side of Newlands Valley, the **Farmer's Arms** pub in Portinscale also serves good pub grub. **Swinside Inn**, the only pub actually in Newlands Valley, is a little tatty but serves decent meals.

Transportation Connections—Lake District

Keswick by bus to: Buttermere (4/day via Whinlatter Forestry Centre and Crummock Water, 40 min), **Borrowdale** (8/day to the powerfully scenic valley south of Derwentwater, Grange, and Seatoller, 30 min), **Grasmere/Ambleside/Windermere** (hrly, 1 hr), **Penrith** (£3, 6/day 8:00–18:20, fewer on Sunday, 40 min, offered by X5 Lakes Link buses). Buses run from the Penrith train station to Ullswater and Glenridding (5/day, 1 hr). Bus info: tel. 01946/63222.

Penrith by train to: Oban (hrly to Glasgow, 2 hrs; then to Oban, 3/day, 3 hrs), **Edinburgh** (8/day, 2 hrs), **Blackpool** (hrly, 2 hrs, transfer in Preston), **Liverpool** (hrly, 2.5 hrs), **Birmingham** (hrly, 3 hrs), **London**'s Euston Station (hrly, 4.5 hrs). Train info: tel. 0345/484-950.

Route Tips for Drivers

North Wales or Blackpool to the Lake District: The direct, easy way to Keswick is to leave the M6 at Penrith and take the A66 highway 16 miles to Keswick. For the scenic sightseeing drive through the south lakes to Keswick, exit the super M6 on A590/A591 through the towns of Kendal and Windermere to reach Brockhole National Park Visitors Centre. From Brockhole, the A road to Keswick is fastest but the high road—the tiny road over Kirkstone Pass to Glenridding and lovely Ullswater—is much more dramatic.

For the drive north to **Oban**, see the Highlands chapter.

YORK

Historical York is loaded with world-class sights. Marvel at the York Minster, England's finest Gothic church. Ramble through the Shambles, York's wonderfully preserved medieval quarter. Enjoy a walking tour led by an old Yorker. Hop a train at Europe's greatest Railway Museum, travel to the 1800s in the York Castle Museum, and head back a thousand years to Viking York at the Jorvik exhibit.

York has a rich history. In A.D. 71 it was Eboracum, a Roman provincial capital. Constantine was proclaimed emperor here in A.D. 306. In the fifth century, as Rome was toppling, a Roman emperor sent a letter telling England it was on its own, and York became Eoforwic, the capital of the Anglo-Saxon kingdom of Northumbria. A church was built here in 627, and the town was an early Christian center of learning. The Vikings later took the town and from about 860 to 950 it was a Danish trading center called Jorvik. The invading and conquering Normans destroyed then rebuilt the city, giving it a castle and the walls you see today. Medieval York, with 9,000 inhabitants, grew rich on the wool trade and became England's second city. Henry VIII spared the city's fine minster and used York as his Anglican church's north-ern capital. The Archbishop of York is second only to the Arch-bishop of Canterbury in the Anglican Church. In the Industrial Age, York was the railway hub of North England. When it was built, York's train station was the world's largest. Today, except for its huge chocolate factory (Kit-Kats are made here), York's leading industry is tourism.

Planning Your Time
York rivals Edinburgh as the best sightseeing city in Britain after London. On even a 10-day trip through Britain, it deserves two

nights and a day. For the best 36 hours, follow this plan: Catch the 19:00 city walking tour on the evening of your arrival. The next morning be at Jorvik at 9:00 when it opens (to avoid the midday crowds). The nearby Castle Museum is worth the rest of the morning (10:00–noon, I could spend even more time here). Three options for your early afternoon: shoppers browse the Shambles, train buffs tour the National Railway Museum, and scholars do the Yorkshire Museum. Tour the Minster at 16:00 before catching the 17:00 evensong service. Finish your day with an early evening stroll along the wall and perhaps through the abbey gardens. This schedule assumes you're there in the summer (evening orientation walk) and that there's an evensong on. Confirm your plans with the TI.

Orientation (tel. code: 01904)

The sightseer's York is small. Virtually everything is within a few minutes' walk: the sights, train station, TI, and B&Bs. The longest walk a visitor might take (from a B&B across the old town to the Castle Museum) is 15 minutes.

Bootham Bar, a gate in the medieval town wall, is the hub of your York visit. At Bootham Bar (and on Exhibition Square facing it) you'll find the TI, the starting points for most walking tours and bus tours, handy access to the medieval town wall, Gillygate (lined with good eateries), and Bootham Street, which leads to the recommended B&Bs. (In York, a "bar" is a gate and a "gate" is a street. Go ahead, blame the Vikings.)

Tourist Information: The TI at Bootham Bar sells a 75p "York Map and Guide." Ask for the free monthly *What's On* guide and the monthly "gig guide" for live music (July–August Monday–Saturday 9:00–19:00, Sunday 9:00–18:00; September–June Monday–Saturday 9:00–17:00, Sunday 10:00–17:00, tel. 01904/621-756). The train station TI is smaller but provides all the same information and services (9:00–20:00, less on Sunday).

Arrival in York: Upon arrival, grab a bench at the station and enjoy the enchanting voice of the woman announcer singing the train arrivals. The station is a five-minute walk from town; turn left down Station Road and follow the crowd toward the Gothic towers of the Minster. After the bridge, a block before the Minster, signs to the TI send you left. Recommended B&Bs are a five-minute walk from there. Buses #1, 2, and 3 go from the station to near the TI (St. Leonards Place). With luggage, consider a quick taxi ride (£3).

Tours of York

▲▲▲**Walking Tours**—Charming local volunteer guides give energetic, entertaining, and free two-hour walks through York (daily, 10:15 all year and 14:15 April–October, plus 19:00

York

BEST B&B AREA

KING'S MANOR, MUSEUMS & ST. MARY'S ABBEY IN NICE PARK

BOOTHAM BAR

BOOTHAM ROAD

Medieval Walls

MINSTER

MONK BAR

NATIONAL RAILWAY MUSEUM

RIVER OUSE

THE SHAMBLES

JORVIK

TRAIN STATION

LENDAL BRIDGE

RIVER FOSS

OUSE BRIDGE

YORK STORY

Medieval Walls

BLOSSOM ST.

CLIFFORD'S TOWER

CASTLE MUSEUM

MICKLEGATE BAR

to Cambridge via A-64 & A-1

WALMGATE BAR

FISHERGATE BAR

0   ¼
MILES

DCH

June–August, from Exhibition Square across from the TI). There are many other commercial York walking tours. YorkWalk Tours, for example, has reliable guides and many themes to choose from (£3, TI has schedule). The various ghost tours, all offered after nightfall, are more fun than informative. York's voluntary guide association can be reached only from 9:30 to 11:30 at 01904/640-780).

▲**Guide Friday Hop-on and Hop-off Bus Tours**—York's Guide Friday offers tour guides on speed who can talk enthusiastically to three sleeping tourists in a gale on a topless double-decker bus for an hour without stopping. Buses make the hour-long circuit, covering secondary York sights that the city walking tours skip—the workaday perimeter of town. Tickets cost £7.50 on the bus, £6.50 from the TI (hop on and off all day, departures every 10 or 15 minutes from 9:20 until around 18:00, tel. 01904/640-896). While you can hop on and off where you like, the York route is of no value from a transportation-to-the-sights point of view. I'd catch it at the Bootham Bar TI and ride it for an orientation all the way around (one hour) or get off at the Railway Museum, skipping the last five minutes. Guide Friday's competitors give you a little less for a little less.

Sights—York

▲**City Walls**—The historic walls of York provide a fine two-mile walk. Walk from Bootham Bar (gate) to Monk Bar for outstanding cathedral views. Open until dusk (barring attacks) and free.

▲▲▲**York Minster**—The pride of York, this largest Gothic church north of the Alps (540 feet long, 200 feet tall) is a brilliant example of how the High Middle Ages were far from dark. The word "minster" means a place from where people go out to minister or spread the word of God.

Your first impression might be the spaciousness and brightness of the nave (built 1280–1350). The nave—from the middle period of Gothic, called "Decorated Gothic"—is one of the widest Gothic naves in Europe. Notice the Great West Window (1338) above the entry. The heart in the tracery is called "the heart of Yorkshire." The mysterious dragon's head (sticking out over the nave) was probably used as a crane to lift a font cover.

The north and south transepts are the oldest part of today's church (1220–1270). The oldest complete window in the minster, with the modern-looking grisaille pattern, is the Five Sisters' Window in the north transept (1260).

The fanciful choir and the east end (high altar) is from the last stage of Gothic, Perpendicular (1360–1470). The Great East Window (1405), the largest medieval glass window in existence, shows the beginning and the end of the world with scenes from Genesis and the Book of Revelation. A chart (on the right, with a tiny, more helpful chart within) highlights the core Old Testament scenes in this hard-to-read masterpiece. Enjoy the art close up on the chart, then step back and find the real thing.

The "foundations" (£2) give you a chance to climb down—archaeologically and physically—through the centuries to see the roots of the much smaller but still huge Norman church (Romanesque, 1100) that stood on this spot, and below that, the Roman excavations. Constantine was proclaimed Roman emperor here in A.D. 306. Peek also at the modern concrete save-the-church foundations and the church treasury.

There are three more extra visits to consider. The chapter house, an elaborately decorated 13th-century Gothic dome, features playful details carved in the stonework (pointed out in the flier that comes with the 70p admission). You can step into the crypt—an actual bit of the Romanesque church excavated in modern times—which features 12th-century Romanesque art (70p), or scale the tower (£2, long climb, great view).

The cathedral is open daily from 7:30 to 20:30 (tel. 01904/624-426). The chapter house, tower, and "foundations" have shorter hours, usually 9:30 to 18:30, less off season. Follow the *Welcome to the York Minster* flyer and ask about a free guided tour (they go frequently; you can join one in progress). The helpful blue-armbanded

Minster guides are happy to answer your questions. While a donation of £2 to visit the church is reasonably requested, by visiting all the small extra spots inside I give that (and more) in the form of those admissions. Just pay for and enjoy all the little extras.

Evensong is a chance to experience the cathedral in musical and spiritual action. Evensong services are held weekdays at 17:00, and 16:00 on Saturday–Sunday (but usually spoken on Monday and when the choir is off).

▲**The Shambles**—This is the most colorful old York street in the half-timbered, traffic-free core of town. Ye olde downtown York, while very touristy, is a window-shopping, busker-filled, people-watcher's delight. Don't miss the more frumpy Newgate Market or the old-time candy store just opposite the bottom end of the Shambles.

▲▲▲**York Castle Museum**—Truly one of Europe's top museums, this is a Victorian homeshow, the closest thing to a time-tunnel experience England has to offer. It includes the 18th-century Kirkgate: a fine collection of old shops well-stocked exactly as they were 150 years ago, along with costumes, armor, an eye-opening Anglo-Saxon helmet (from A.D. 750), and the entertaining "every home should have one" exhibit showing the evolution of vacuum cleaners, toilets, TVs, bicycles, stoves, and so on, from their crude beginnings to now. Follow the arrows to cover everything: a working watermill, prison cells, man traps, WWII fashions, and old toys (£5, Monday–Saturday 9:30–18:00, Sunday 10:00–18:00, less off-season, 1960s cafeteria, shop, car park; the £2.50 guidebook, while not necessary, makes a nice souvenir, tel. 01904/653-611). Clifford's Tower (across from the Castle Museum, not worth the £1.70) is all that's left of York's castle (13th century, site of a 1190 massacre of local Jews—read about this at base of hill). While a stupid stunt, the current record for racing up and down the stairs is 22 seconds.

▲**Jorvik**—Sail the "Pirates of the Caribbean" north and back 800 years and you get Jorvik—more a ride than a museum. Innovative 10 years ago, the commercial success of Jorvik inspired copycat ride/museums all over England. You'll ride a little Disney-type train car for 13 minutes through the re-created Viking street of Copper-gate. It's the year 948 and you're in the village of Jorvik. Next your little train takes you through the actual excavation sight that inspired this. Finally you'll browse through a small gallery of Viking shoes, combs, locks, and other intimate glimpses of that redheaded culture (£5, daily from 9:00, last entry at 17:30, November–March last entry at 15:30, tel. 01904/643-211). Avoid hour-long midday waits by going very early or very late. Even past the turnstile there's a 25-minute wait. Some love this "ride"; others call it a gimmicky rip-off. If you're looking for a serious museum, see the Viking exhibit at the Yorkshire Museum. It's better. If you're thinking

Disneyland with a splash of history, Jorvik's great. I like Jorvik, but it's not worth a long line.

▲▲**National Railway Museum**—This thunderous museum shows 150 fascinating years of British railroad history. Fanning out from a grand roundhouse are an array of historic cars and engines, including Queen Victoria's lavish royal car and the very first "stagecoaches on rails." There's much more, including exhibits on dining cars, post cars, sleeping cars, train posters, and videos. This biggest and best railroad museum anywhere is interesting even to people who think "Pullman" is Japanese for "tug-o-war" (£5, daily 10:00–18:00, tel. 01904/621-261).

▲**Yorkshire Museum**—Located in a lush and lazy park next to the stately ruins of St. Mary's Abbey, Yorkshire Museum is the city's forgotten serious "archaeology of York" museum. While the hordes line up at Jorvik, the best Viking artifacts are here—with no crowds and in a better historical context. You have to walk through this museum, but the stroll takes you through Roman, Saxon, Viking, Norman, and Gothic York. Its prize piece is the delicately etched 15th-century pendant called the "Middleham Jewel." The video about the creation of the abbey is worth a look (£3.60, daily 10:00–17:00, tel. 01904/629-745).

The Theatre Royal—Fine plays, usually British comedies, entertain the locals (20:00 almost nightly, tickets easy to get from £6–13, St. Leonard's Place next to the TI and a five-minute walk from recommended B&Bs, info tel. 01904/610-041, tickets tel. 01904/623-568).

Honorable Mention—York has a number of other sights and activities (described in TI material) which, while interesting, pale in comparison to the biggies. **Fairfax House** is perfectly Georgian inside (£3.75, Monday–Saturday 11:00–17:30, Sunday 13:30–17:30, closed non-summer Fridays). The **York Story** offers a 45-minute video on the history of York—it's good, straight history (£2, associated with, across the street from, and pushed by the Castle Museum, 10:00–17:00, Sunday 13:00–17:00). The **Hall of the Merchant Adventurers** claims to be the finest medieval guild hall in Europe (from 1361). It's basically a vast half-timbered building with marvelous exposed beams and 15 minutes worth of interesting displays about life and commerce back in the days when York was England's second city (£2, daily 9:00–17:00, less in winter, below the Shambles off Piccadilly). The **Richard III "Museum"** at Monk Bar is interesting only for Richard III enthusiasts (£1). **The ARC** (Archaeological Resource Center) is a big former church full of genuine archaeological artifacts that visitors—mostly school groups—can study as pretend archaeologists (£3.60, Monday–Friday 10:00–17:00, last admission 15:30; great for kids; welcomes adults; plenty of microscopes, hands-on fun, and helpful volunteers; just off the Shambles on St. Saviourgate, tel. 01904/643-211). The **York Dungeon** is gimmicky but, if you insist on papier-mâché gore, is better than the

London Dungeon. The **Antiques Centre** is a fun browse (41 Stonegate near the Minster). Visitors are welcome to buy a pint of beer and watch the action at the **bowling green** near recommended B&Bs (Sycamore Place).

Sleeping in York
(£1 = about $1.70, tel. code: 01904)
Sleep Code: **S** = Single, **D** = Double/Twin, **T** = Triple, **Q** = Quad, **b** = bathroom, **t** = toilet only, **s** = shower only, **CC** = Credit Card (**V**isa, **M**asterCard, **A**mex).

I've listed peak-season book-direct prices. Don't use the TI. Outside of July and August some prices go soft.

Sleeping in B&Bs near Bootham Gate
These recommendations are in the handiest B&B neighborhood, a quiet residential neighborhood just outside the old-town wall's Bootham gate, along the road called Bootham. All are within a five-minute walk of the Minster and TI and a 10-minute walk or £3 taxi ride from the station. If driving, head for the cathedral and follow the medieval wall to the gate called Bootham Bar. Bootham "street" leads away from Bootham Bar. These B&Bs are all small, smoke-free, family-run, and come with plenty of steep stairs but no traffic noise. For a good selection, call well in advance. They will generally hold a room with a phone call, and work hard to help their guests sightsee and eat smartly. Most have permits for street parking. And most take no credit cards. Regency Dry Cleaning does small loads for £7 (8:30–18:00, Saturday 9:00–17:00, closed Sunday, 75 Bootham, tel. 01904/613-311). The laundrette beyond Gillygate (10-minute walk from B&Bs) is cheaper.

Airden House, the most central of my Bootham-area listings, has eight spacious rooms, a grandfather clock–cozy TV lounge, and brightness and warmth throughout. Susan and Keith Burrows keep their place simple, comfortable, and friendly. They are a great source of local travel tips (D-£40, Db-£48, 1 St. Mary's, York Y03 7DD, tel. 01904/638-915).

The Sycamore, run by Margaret and David Tyce, is a fine value with homey rooms strewn with silk flowers and personal touches. It's at the end of a dead-end opposite a fun-to-watch bowling green (D-£32, Db-£40, family deals, 19 Sycamore Place off Bootham Terrace, YO3 7DW, tel. & fax 01904/624-712).

The Hazelwood is my most hotelesque listing. Ian and Carolyn McNabb run this aggressively spacious old 14-room place in an entrepreneurial way, paying careful attention to details and serving a classy breakfast (Db-£50–53, Db with four-poster-£5 extra, two ground-floor rooms; a fridge, ice, and great travel library in the plush basement lounge; CC:VM, 24 Portland Street,

York, Our Neighborhood

Gillygate, YO3 7EH, tel. 01904/626-548, fax 01904/628-032, e-mail: hzwdyok@aol.com).

Abbeyfields Guest House, with cozy, bright rooms and a quiet lounge, is run and decorated with a masculine sensibility (S-£20, Sb-£28, Db-£48, 19 Boothham Terrace, YO3 7DD, tel. & fax 01904/636-471, Richard and Gwen).

Claremont Guest House is a friendly house offering two delightful rooms and many thoughtful touches. Gill and Martyn Cornell offer laundry service (D-£32, Db-£42, 18 Claremont Terrace off Gillygate, YO3 7EJ, tel. 01904/625-158, e-mail: claremont.york@dial.pipex.com).

White Doves is a cheery little Victorian place with a comfy lounge and four fine rooms (Db-£42–45, family deals, 20 Claremont Terrace off Gillygate, YO3 7EJ, tel. 01904/625-957, Pauline and David Pearce).

23 St. Mary's is a rococo riot. Mrs. Hudson has done everything super-correctly, and offers nine comfortable rooms, a classy lounge, and all the doily touches (Sb-£30–34, Db-£58–64 depending on season and size, 23 St. Mary's, YO3 7DD, tel. 01904/622-738).

Queen Anne's Guest House has six compact, clean, and cheery rooms (D-£30, Db-£34 through 1999 with this book, family deals, 24 Queen Anne's Road, tel. 01904/629-389, Judy and David West).

Crook Lodge B&B is a bit more elegant than the rest with tight and charming rooms (Db-£46–50, 26 St. Mary's, tel. 01904/655-614, Susan and John Arnott).

Alcuin Lodge is also good (Db-46, one small top floor D-£35, no kids, CC:VM, 15 Sycamore Place, tel. 01904/632-222, e-mail: Alcuinlodg@aol.com, Susan Taylor).

York's Youth Hotel is well run, with lots of extras like a kitchen, laundrette, games, and bar (S-£14, D-£26, £11 in four- to six-bed dorms, sheets and breakfast extra, £1 less for multinight stays, CC:VM, 10-minute walk from station at 11 Bishophill Senior Road, York YO1 1EF, tel. 01904/625-904 or 01904/612-494, e-mail: youth-hotel@ymn.co.uk).

Sleeping in Hotels in the Center of York
Dean Court Hotel, facing the Minster, is a big stately place run by Best Western with classy lounges and spacious rooms (small Db-£99, Db-£115, fancy Db-£125, super-fancy Db-£145, CC:VMA, some nonsmoking rooms, elevator, Doncombe Place, YO1 2EF, tel. 01904/625-082, fax 01904/620-305).

Galtres Lodge Hotel, a block from the Minster, offers cramped hallways but comfy rooms above a restaurant in the old town center (Dt-£50, Db-£65, CC:VM, no kids under 14, nonsmoking, 54 Low Petergate, tel. 01904/622-478, fax 01904/627-804).

Eating in York

Lunch in the Shambles
For cuteness, consider the tiny **St. Crux Parish Hall**, a medieval church now used by a medley of charities selling tea and snacks (at bottom end of the Shambles). For a smoky place with the floor still sticky from last night's spilled beer, the **Golden Fleece** pub is busy at lunch, serving famous Yorkshire pudding and hearty meals. Twee eateries line the street called Pavement. **Ye Olde Starre Inn**, the oldest pub in town, has yet to learn the art of cooking.

Traditional Tea
York is famous for its elegant teahouses. Drop into one around 16:00 for tea and cakes. Ladies love **Betty's Teahouse** (£4, daily 9:00–21:00, mostly nonsmoking, St. Helen's Square, fine people-watching from a window seat, usually a line, wait for a main-floor table), but several others can satisfy your king- or queen-for-a-day desires.

Eating near the Minster
Café **Concerto** has a loyal following for good reason. Their £15 three-course meal is the best I've had in York (nightly until 22:00, traditional English or Continental cuisine, on Petergate, under Bootham Bar, smart to reserve at 01904/610-478). The **Viceroy of India**—just outside Monkgate and therefore outside the tourist

zone—serves great Indian food at good prices to mostly locals (nightly, £8 plates, friendly staff, just past the big old "Bile Beans keep you healthy, bright-eyed, and slim" sign at 26 Monkgate, tel. 01904/622-370). If you've yet to eat Indian on your trip, do it here. **St. Williams Restaurant,** just behind the great east window of the Minster in a wonderful half-timbered 15th-century building, serves quick and tasty lunches and elegant candlelit dinners (two courses-£10, three courses-£15, traditional and Mediterranean, tel. 01904/634-830).

Eating near Bootham Bar and Your B&B
Walk along Gillygate and choose from an enjoyable array of eateries: For authentic Italian, consider **Mama Mia's** (£6–9, daily 11:30–14:00, 17:30–23:00, fun, *domani* service, indoor/outdoor patio, 20 Gillygate, tel. 01904/622-020). **Gillygate Fisheries** is a wonderfully traditional little fish-and-chips joint where tattooed people eat-in and housebound mothers take-out (Mel serves £3 meals, eat your mushy peas; closed Sunday, smoke-free seating, 59 Gillygate). For the closest you'll get to Mexico in Britain, consider **Fiesta Mehicana** (17:30–19:00, sit-down or take-out, 14 Clifford Street, tel. 01904/610-243). There's a pub serving grub on every block. The **Horse and Wagon** on Gillygate has local color and £5 meals. Eat where you see lots of food or go to the **Coach House** (nightly 18:30–21:30, 20 Marygate, tel. 01904/652-780). The people who run your B&B know the latest on what's good.

Transportation Connections—York
By train to: Durham (2/hrly, 40 min), **Edinburgh** (2/hrly, 2 hrs, £43), **London** (2/hrly, 2 hrs, £50), **Bath** (via Bristol, hrly, 5 hrs), **Cambridge** (nearly hrly, 2 hrs with a change in Petersborough), **Birmingham** (8/day, 3 hrs). Train info: tel. 0345/484-950.
      By bus to: Keswick (1/day, 4 hrs, tel. 0990-808-080).

Route Tips for Drivers
As you near York (and your B&B) you'll hit the A1237 ring road. Follow this to the A19/Thirsk roundabout (next to river on northeast side of town). From roundabout, follow signs for York City traveling through Clifton into Bootham. All recommended B&Bs are four or five blocks before you hit the medieval city gate (see neighborhood map).
      If you're nearing the end of your trip, consider dropping your car upon arrival in York. The money saved by turning it in early nearly pays for the train ticket that whisks you effortlessly to Edinburgh or London. Avis (tel. 01904/610-460), Hertz (tel. 01904/612-586), Kenning, and Budget all have car rental offices in York. Beware, car rental agencies close Saturday afternoon and all day Sunday (when dropping off is OK but picking up is impossible).

NEAR YORK: NORTH YORK MOORS

The North York Moors are a vacant lot compared with the Cumbrian Lake District. But that's unfair competition. In the lonesome North York Moors you can wander through the stark beauty of its time-passed villages, bored sheep, and powerful landscapes.

Sights—North York Moors

▲**The Moors**—Car hike across the moors on any small road. You'll come upon tidy villages, old Roman roads, and maybe even a fox hunt. Danby Lodge, the North York Moors Visitors Centre, provides the best orientation for exploring the moors. It's a grand old lodge offering exhibits, shows, nature walks, an information desk with plenty of books and maps, brass-rubbing, a cheery cafeteria, and brochures on several good walks that start right there (free, daily April–October 10:00–17:00, off-season weekends 11:00–16:00, a half-mile from the train station, tel. 01287/660-654).

▲**North Yorkshire Moors Railway**—This 18-mile, one-hour steam engine ride from Grosmont and Goathland to Pickering goes through some of the best parts of the moors almost hourly. Even with the windows small and dirty (wipe off the outside of yours before you roll) and the track mostly in a scenic gully, it's a good ride (£9 round-trip, tel. 01751/472-508).

Pickering, with its rural-life museum, castle, and Monday market, is worth a stop. You could catch the York–Pickering bus (hrly, 75 min), see Pickering, ride the train with a stop along the way to take a moors walk, and carry on to Grosmont, which is on a regular train line with good connections to Whitby and points north.

▲**Hutton-le-Hole**—This postcard-pretty town is home of the fine Ryedale Museum, which illustrates "farm life in the moors" through reconstructed and furnished 18th-century local buildings (£3, daily 10:00–17:30 April–October, tel. 01751/417-367).

Castle Howard—Especially popular since the filming of *Brideshead Revisited*, this fine palatial home is about half as interesting as the Cotswolds' Blenheim Palace (open late March–October, two buses a day from York, 30 minutes).

Rievaulx Abbey—It's a highlight of the North York Moors and beautifully situated, but if you've seen other fine old abbeys, this is a rerun.

▲**James Herriot Country**—Herriot fans will be more interested in the Yorkshire Dales than the neighboring moors. Local booklets at the TI lay out the route for drivers. The easy way to make your *All Creatures Great and Small* pilgrimage is to take one of several all-day bus tours from York (done once a week by various companies) that cover all the sights, with commentary, for around £14.

Staithes/Whitby—See Durham and Northeast England chapter.

DURHAM AND NORTHEAST ENGLAND

Some of England's best history is harbored in the northeast. Hadrian's Wall reminds us that Britain was an important Roman colony 2,000 years ago. After a Roman ramble, you can make a pilgrimage to Holy Island, where Christianity gained its first toehold in Britain. The logical next stop is Durham, to marvel at England's greatest Norman church and enjoy an evensong service. And, for a trip into the less distant past, spend a morning in the year 1913 at the Beamish Open-Air Folk Museum.

Planning Your Time

Of the sights described in this chapter, only Durham is convenient and worth a stop on a three-week British train trip. By car you'll be driving right by Hadrian's Wall, Holy Island, Bamburgh, and the Beamish Folk Museum. Whitby and Staithes are seaside escapes worth a stop only for the seagulls and surf. Whitby is accessible by train, but Staithes makes sense only with a car.

By car, connect Edinburgh and York by this string of sights, spending a night near Hadrian's Wall and a night in Durham on a one-month trip, just a night in Durham on a three-week trip. For drivers with 36 hours between Edinburgh and York, leave Edinburgh early, tour Hadrian's Wall and Housesteads Fort, take a walk and have lunch, and get to Durham in time to tour the cathedral and enjoy the 17:15 evensong service. Sleep in Durham. Tour Beamish (15 minutes north of Durham) or drive through the North York Moors the next day, arriving in York by late afternoon.

DURHAM

Without its cathedral it would hardly be noticed. But this magnificently situated cathedral is hard not to notice (even if you're zooming by on the train). Durham sits, seemingly happy to go nowhere, along its river and under its castle and famous cathedral. It has a workaday, medieval, cobbled atmosphere and a scraggly peasant's market just off the main square. While Durham is the home of England's third-oldest university, the town feels rough and working-class, surrounded by newly closed coal mines and filled with tattooed and stapled people in search of job security.

Orientation (tel. code: 0191)

Tidy little Durham clusters everything safely under its castle within the tight, protective bend of its river. The longest walk you'd make would be a 15-minute walk from the train station to the cathedral.

Tourist Information: The TI, located on the town square, organizes £3 90-minute city walks Wednesday and Saturday in season (Monday–Saturday 10:00–17:30, summer Sundays 14:00–17:00, less off-season, tel. 0191/384-3720).

Sights—Durham

▲▲▲**Cathedral**—Built to house the much-venerated bones of St. Cuthbert from Lindisfarne, the cathedral is the best look at Norman architecture in England (free, daily 7:15–20:00, less off-season, limited access during services; the tower, treasury, and monks' dorm are open 10:00–16:00, shorter hours Sunday).

St. Cuthbert, an inspirational leader of the early Christian church in North England, lived in the Lindisfarne monastery on Holy Island (100 miles north of Durham). He died in 687. Eleven years later his body was exhumed and found to be miraculously preserved. This stoked the popularity of his shrine, and pilgrims came in growing numbers. When Vikings raided Lindisfarne in 875, the monks fled with his body (and the famous illuminated Lindisfarne Gospels). After 120 years of roaming, they settled in 995 in Durham on an easy-to-defend hairpin bend in the Wear River. The cathedral was built over Cuthbert's tomb.

The architecture of the nave is particularly harmonious because it was built in a mere 40 years (1093–1133). Few additions were made and the bulk of what you see today is Norman (that's British for Romanesque). The round arches and zigzag carved decorations are textbook Norman. The church was also proto-Gothic, built by well-traveled French masons and architects who knew the latest innovations from Europe. Its stone and ribbed roof, first pointed arches, and first flying buttresses were revolutionary in England. It's not as cluttered as other churches for several reasons. Out of respect for St. Cuthbert, for centuries no one else was buried here. During Reformation times, sumptuous Catholic decor was high risk. And subsequent fires and wars destroyed what Protestants didn't.

Durham

B+B's:
- **❶** CASTLEVIEW
- **❷** GEORGIAN TOWN HOUSE
- **❸** CASTLEDENE
- **❹** PARK VIEW

A Tour Plan: From the cathedral green, notice how this fortress of God stands boldly across from the Norman keep of Durham's fortress of man. (The castle, now part of the university, is not worth touring.) At the cathedral door the big bronze lion-faced knocker, a replica of the 12th-century original (in treasury), was used by criminals seeking sanctuary (read the explanation).

Immediately inside you'll see the information desk. Church attendants happily answer questions. Ideally, follow a church tour (Monday–Friday at 10:30 or other times by appointment; there's usually one in session somewhere that you're welcome to join, £2.50 donation). The 50p "walkabout" guide pamphlet is informative but dull.

The black marble strip on the floor was as close to the altar as women were allowed in the days when this was a Benedictine church (until 1540). Sit down (ignoring the black line) and let the fine proportions of England's best Norman (and arguably Europe's best Romanesque) nave stir you. Any frilly woodwork and stonework were added in later centuries.

Notice the modern window with the novel depiction of the Last Supper (above and to the left of the entry door, given to the church by a local department store in 1984) and remember that the cathedral remains a living part of the community.

Enter the Galilee Chapel in the back of the nave (late Norman, from 1175). Notice the paintings of St. Cuthbert and St. Oswald (7th-century king of Northumbria) on the side walls of the altar niche, rare examples of Romanesque or Norman paintings. In the center is the tomb of the Venerable Bede, "the father of English learning," who died in 735 and was buried here in the 11th century.

Back in the main church, stroll down the nave to the center under the highest bell tower in Europe (218 feet). Gaze up. The ropes pull hammers that ring the bells. Continuing east (all medieval churches faced east), you enter the choir. Monks worshiped many times a day, and the choir in the center of the church provided a cozier place to gather in this vast, dark, and cold building. This is the heart of the cathedral where Mass has been said daily for 900 years. The fancy wooden chairs are from the 17th century. The Norman choir leads to the Gothic east end of the church. Passing the lacy Neville Screen (1380) and climbing a few stairs, you'll find the tomb of St. Cuthbert.

Finally, step into the relatively extravagant, 13th-century Gothic Chapel of the Nine Altars—taller, lighter, and more vertical than the Norman nave.

The treasury (well worth £1) is filled with medieval bits and holy pieces. It fleshes out this otherwise stark building. The actual relics from St. Cuthbert's tomb are at the far end. The view from the tower will cost you 325 steps and £2. The "Monks' Dormitory" is now a library with an original 14th-century timber roof filled with Anglo-Saxon stones (worth 80p). The unexceptional A-V show in the unexceptional undercroft tells about St. Cuthbert (80p). The fine cafeteria (smoke-free, serving lunch 12:00–14:30), bookshop, and WCs are next to the treasury.

Evensong: For a thousand years this cradle of English Christianity has been praising God. To really experience the cathedral, go for an evensong service. Arrive early and ask to be seated in the choir. It's a spiritual Oz as 40 boys sing psalms—a red-and-white-robed pillow of praise, raised up by the powerful pipe organ. If you're lucky and the service went well, the organist runs a spiritual musical victory lap as the congregation breaks up (begins at 17:15 almost nightly, Sunday at 15:30, one hour, normally not sung on Monday or during the mid-July-through-August school break, tel. 0191/386-2367).

Riverside Walk—For a 20-minute woodsy escape, walk Durham's riverside path from busy Framwelgate Bridge to sleepy Prebends Bridge. Just beyond the Prebends Bridge on the old-town side of the river, you'll find The Upper Room, a cluster of trees carved to show the Last Supper when seen from the tree-trunk throne provided. Where are the apostles? Count the tree trunks.

Sleeping in Durham
(£1 = about $1.70, tel code: 0191)

Sleep Code: **S** = Single, **D** = Double/Twin, **T** = Triple, **Q** = Quad, **b** = bathroom, **t** = toilet only, **s** = shower only, **CC** = Credit Card (Visa, MasterCard, Amex).

My recommended B&Bs are along or near Crossgate (between the train station and cathedral; from the city center, cross Framwelgate Bridge, take the first left, up the hill). They are within a 5- or 10-minute walk of both the town square and train station.

Castleview Guest House, 400 yards off Framwelgate Bridge, is a good bet. It's renovated but still creaky, with eight comfortable smoke-free rooms and a classy lounge (Sb-£38, Db-£50, 4 Crossgate, DH1 4PS, tel. & fax 0191/386-8852, Mike and Anne Williams).

The **Georgian Town House**, next door, has a cheery bossanova ambience with a breezy garden, plush lounge, and comfortable rooms (Db-£55 with this book, nonsmoking, 10 Crossgate, tel. & fax 0191/386-8070, Jane Weil).

Castledene B&B is tidy, simple, and friendly (twin-£38, past Crossgate to Palatine View, cross street, up 10 steps to pedestrian lane, walk 100 yards parallel to and above Crossgate Path to last house, 37 Nevilledale Terrace; drivers find Nevilledale Terrace via Summerville Street, tel. & fax 0191/384-8386, Lorna and Brian Byrne).

Park View B&B is an unremarkable place with three rooms and a handy location (Db-£40 with book, family deals, 1 Allergate Terrace, tel. 0191/386-7034, June Buxton).

Consider the simpler **Bromme Farm Guest House**, which is good but out of town (four rooms, D-£35, across from Love's Pub in Broom Park, tel. 0191/386-4755).

Durham Castle, a student residence actually on the castle grounds facing the cathedral, rents 100 singles and 30 doubles

(July–September only, £20 per person, £30 with private facilities, elegant breakfast hall; parking, with luck, on the cathedral green; tel. 0191/374-3863). Request a room in the classy old main building or you may get bomb shelter–style modern dorm rooms.

Eating in Durham

Trust your host's advice, or stroll from Framwelgate Bridge through Market Place up Saddler and take what looks good. Consider these places: **La Trattoria** for Italian, near the Market Place; **Shaheens**, healthy Indian in the old post office up Saddler Street; **Hogshead** on Saddler Street for pub grub; **The Almshouse** on the cathedral green for tasty light meals; **Bistro 21** out of town for those with a car looking for an nontouristy splurge; and the **Duke of Wellington** for hearty eating with great pub atmosphere (1.5 miles down the A1050/Darlington Road).

Transportation Connections—Durham

By train to: Edinburgh (5/day, 2 hrs), **York** (hrly, 1 hr), **London** (hrly, 3 hrs), **Newcastle** (hrly, 15 min, then trains or buses to Hadrian's Wall). Train info: tel. 0345/484-950.

   Parking in Durham: Parking in old Durham is nearly impossible. You're best off simply following the signs into the big public parking lots at the bottom end of town (£1.60 per day).

HADRIAN'S WALL

This is one of England's most thought-provoking sights. Around A.D. 130, during the reign of Emperor Hadrian, the Romans built this great stone wall. Its actual purpose is still debated. While Rome ruled Britain for 400 years, it never quite ruled its people. The wall may have been used to define the northern edge of the empire, protect Roman Britain from invading Scottish tribes (or at least cut down on pesky border raids), monitor the movement of people, or simply give an otherwise bored army something to do. (Nothing's more dangerous than a bored army.) Stretching 74 miles coast to coast across the narrowest stretch of northern England, it was built and defended by nearly 20,000 troops. The wall was flanked by ditches, and a military road lies on the south side. At every mile of the wall a castle guards a gate, and two turrets stand between each castle. The mile castles are numbered. (Eighty of them cover the 74 miles because a Roman mile was slightly shorter than our mile.) Today, several chunks of the wall, ruined forts, and museums thrill history buffs.

Sights—Hadrian's Wall

▲▲**Housesteads Fort**—With its tiny museum, national park information center, powerful scenery, and the best-preserved segment of the wall, this is your best single stop. All such Roman forts were the

Durham and Northeast England

same shape and design—very logical with public toilets on lower corner (£2.70 for site and museum, daily 10:00–18:00, less off-season, car park, snack bar, tel. 01434/344-363).

▲▲**Hiking the Wall**—From Housesteads, hike west along the wall speaking Latin. For a good, craggy, three-mile walk along the wall, hike between Housesteads and Steel Rigg. You'll pass a castle sitting in a nick in a crag (castle #39, called Castle Nick). There's a car park near Steel Rigg (take the little road up from Twice Brewed Pub).

▲**Vindolanda**—This larger Roman fort (which actually predates the wall by 40 years) and museum is just south of the wall and worth a visit only if you've devoured the Housesteads museum and are still hungry. From the car park you'll walk through 600 meters of grassy parkland decorated by the foundation stones of the Roman fort and a full-size replica chunk of the wall. At the far side of the site is the best Roman museum in the area. Eight forts were built on this spot. By carefully sealing the foundations from each successive fort, Roman demolition teams left 20th-century archaeologists seven meters of remarkably well-preserved artifacts to excavate. The earliest examples of Roman writing were recently discovered here, shining a new light on life on the northern fringe of the Empire. While the actual fragments are in London's British Museum, see the interesting, detailed video here (£3.50, £5.25 combo ticket includes Roman Army Museum, daily 10:00–18:00, closes earlier off-season, tel. 01434/344-277). The **Roman Army Museum**, a few miles farther west at Greenhead, is redundant if you've seen Vindolanda (£2.80, or buy combo ticket, above, same hours).

Sleeping near Hadrian's Wall
(£1 = about $1.70, tel code: 01434)
Crindledykes Farm is a classy old farmhouse in an idyllic and peaceful setting a mile south of the wall (small D-£34, spacious twin room with view-£36, room for a child's bed, WC down the hall, nonsmoking, accessible by car only, signposted from the B6318 at Housesteads, Bardon Mill, Hexham, NE47 7AF, tel. 01434/344-316, Judy Davidson).

   East Wharmley Farm rents two spacious rooms in a wonderfully rural setting six miles from Housesteads on the A69 midway between Haydon Bridge and Hexham (D-£34, nonsmoking, tel. 01434/674-259, Dorothy Foster).

   Crow's Nest B&B offers three rooms in a remodeled farmhouse a quarter-mile from the wall (D-£34, on B6318 road 500 meters from the Once Brewed TI and hostel at East Twice Brewed, Bardon Mill, Hexham, tel. 01434/344-348).

   The nearby **Mile Castle Pub** cooks up all sorts of exotic game and offers the best dinner around, according to hungry national park rangers. Two miles west of Housesteads, the **Twice Brewed Pub and Hotel** serves decent pub grub nightly to a local darts-and-pool crowd (S-£18, D-£36, Db-£45, dreary rooms, rarely full, tel. 01434/344-534). Next door to the Twice Brewed Pub is the comfortable **Once Brewed Youth Hostel** (£13 per bed, with sheets and breakfast, four to seven beds per room, tel. 01434/344-360).

Transportation Connections—Hadrian's Wall
To reach Hadrian's Wall, catch a train from Durham to Newcastle (hrly, 15 min), then head east on the Newcastle–Carlisle line (6/day) to Bardon Mill (45 min from Newcastle), the stop nearest Housesteads Fort; from Bardon Mill, catch a taxi to the fort or your B&B

(your host can arrange this). In summer, special Hadrian's Wall buses go between the Hexham and Haltwhistle train stations connecting the various wall sights (4/day, tel. 01434/344-396). Train info: tel. 0345/484-950.

If you're driving, take B6318; it parallels the wall and passes several viewpoints, minor sights, and "severe dips." (If there's a certified nerd or bozo in the car, these road signs add a lot to a photo portrait.)

Other Sights near Durham

▲▲**Beamish Open-Air Museum**—This huge museum, which re-creates the year 1913 in northeast England, takes at least three hours to explore. A vintage tram shuttles visitors around the park, stopping at each of the four stations: Coal Mine Village, Home Farm, The Town, and an 1820s Manor House. This isn't wax. If you touch the exhibits, they may smack you. Attendants at each stop explain everything.

Start with the colliery village (company village around a coal mine), with school, church, miners' homes, and a fascinating—if claustrophobic—20-minute tour into a real "drift" mine. "The Town" (along with the mine tour) is the highlight. This bustling street features a 1913 candy shop, dentist's office, garage, working pub (fun for a smoky beer), and a 1990s smoke-free cafeteria. The old train station isn't much. The Pockerley Manor (first part of a new section re-creating the 1820s) is barely worth the climb. The Home Farm is the least interesting section. (£8, daily 10:00–17:00, until 18:00 July–August, shorter hours as the season wanes, closed in winter Monday and Friday, check events schedule as you enter, last tickets two hours before closing, tel. 01207/231-811.)

Durham–Beamish buses go hourly, stopping 700 yards from the museum. The X79 summer-only museum shuttle bus (Durham station to museum door) leaves three times each morning and returns three times each afternoon. Drivers find the museum well signposted, located between the villages of Stanley and Chester-le-Street. From Durham, drive north on the M1 to the first exit (Chester-le-Street) and follow the signs.

▲**Whitby**—On the coast of the North York Moors, Whitby is a fun resort town with a busy harbor and steep and salty old streets, a carousel of Coney Island–type amusements overseen by the stately ruins of its seventh-century abbey. Whitby has been an important port since the 12th century. The **Captain Cook Memorial Museum** offers an interesting look at the famous hometown sailor and his exotic voyages (£2.30, daily 9:45–17:00, closed in winter, in the old town just over the bridge). Two of Captain Cook's boats (*Resolution* and *Endeavour*) were built in the Whitby shipyards. The TI (daily 9:30–18:00, tel. 01947/602-674) is on the harbor next to the train and bus stations.

Whitby has plenty of rooms. August is the only tight month. **Crescent House** has six rooms with modern bathrooms. Most rooms come with sea views (Db-£40, family deals, nonsmoking, on the bluff just south of the harbor at 6 East Crescent, YO21 3HD, tel. & fax 01947/600-091, Janet and Mike Paget). The **Dolphin Hotel**, in the old-town center at the bridge overlooking the harbor, is a pub with a few rooms upstairs (Db-£50, three blocks from train station, pub closes at 23:00, tel. 01947/602-197). The **hostel** is next to the abbey above the town (£10 per bed, 70 beds in 10 rooms, closed 10:00–17:00, tel. 01947/602-878).

Buses connect Whitby and York (5/day, 2 hrs, tel. 01653/692-556). Trains connect Durham with Middlesbrough (8/day, 50 min); the Middlesbrough–Whitby train (4/day, 90 min) stops at Grosmont (where you can catch the Moors steam train) and Danby (half-mile from the Moors info center).

▲**Staithes**—Staithes is a short drive north of Whitby and worthwhile by car. Whitby–Staithes buses run hourly (30 min). A poor and not particularly pretty village where the boy who became Captain James Cook got his first taste of the sea, Staithes is a salty tumble of cottages bunny-hopping down a ravine into a tiny harbor. Ten years ago the town supported 20 fishing boats—today, only three. But fishermen (who pronounce their town "steerths") still outnumber tourists in undiscovered Staithes. There's nothing to do but drop by the lifeboat house (these are a big deal in England; page through the history book, read the not-quite-stirring accounts of every time the boats were called to duty; drop a coin in the box), walk the beach, and relax to the tune of seagulls singing its praise.

I sleep in Staithes. The town is struggling. Tourists just aren't coming. It's changed little since Captain Cook's days. There are no fancy rooms. Each of these three- or four-bedroom places is cramped with old carpets, bad wallpaper, lumpy beds, and tangled floorplans that make you feel like a stowaway. The first is on the harborfront (worth the extra money for the view but not the rooms).

Harborside Guest House provides basic beds, four sea-view rooms, breakfast in a fish-and-chips shop, and the sound of waves to lull you to sleep (D-£40, tel. 01947/841-296). Also consider the **Endeavour Restaurant B&B** (D-£42, Db-£50, tel. 01947/840-825, Lisa Chapman) and **Salmon Cottage** (a £36 twin and a family room, tel. 01947/841-193, Geoff and Isabel Elliott). Staithes' zip code is TS13 5BH.

The oddly-classy-for-this-town **Endeavour Restaurant** offers excellent £15 dinners (fresh seafood, vegetarian, reservations at 01947/840-825). The **Cod and Lobster Pub** serves dinner overlooking the harbor with outdoor benches and a cozy living room warmed by a coal fire. There's bar food at the **Royal George** on High Street (dinners daily 19:00–21:00, throw darts while you wait).

▲**Holy Island and Bamburgh**—Twelve hundred years ago this "Holy Island" was Christianity's toehold on England. It was the home of St. Cuthbert. We know it today for the Lindisfarne Gospels, decorated by monks in the seventh century with some of the finest art from Europe's "Dark Ages" (now in the British Museum). It's a pleasant visit, a quiet town with an evocative priory and striking castle (not worth touring), reached by a two-mile causeway that's cut off daily by high tides. Tidal charts are posted, warning you when this holy place becomes Holy Island and you become stranded (for TI and tide information, tel. 01289/330-733). For a peaceful overnight, a few good B&Bs cluster in the town center (Britannia Guest House, D-£32, Db-£36, four rooms, tel. 01289/389-218).

A few miles farther south down the coast from Holy Island is the grand **Bamburgh Castle**, overlooking the loveliest stretch of beach in Britain. Its impressive interior is worth touring (£3.50, daily 11:00–17:00 April–October, tel. 01668/214-515). Berwick TI tel. 01289/330-733. This area is only worthwhile for those with a car.

EDINBURGH

Edinburgh, the colorful city of Robert Louis Stevenson, Walter Scott, and Robert Burns, is Scotland's showpiece and one of Europe's most entertaining cities. Historical, monumental, fun, and well-organized, it's a tourist's delight.

Promenade down the Royal Mile through the Old Town. Historic buildings pack the Royal Mile between the castle (on the top) and Holyrood Palace (on the bottom). Medieval skyscrapers stand shoulder-to-shoulder, hiding peaceful courtyards connected to High Street by narrow lanes or even tunnels. This colorful jumble—in its day the most crowded city in the world—is the tourist's Edinburgh.

Edinburgh (ED'n-burah) was once two towns divided by a lake. To alleviate crowding, the lake was drained and a magnificent Georgian city, today's New Town, was laid out to the north. Georgian Edinburgh, like the city of Bath, shines with broad boulevards, straight streets, square squares, circular circuses, and elegant mansions decked out in colonnades, pediments, and sphinxes in the proud, neoclassical style of 200 years ago.

While the Georgian city celebrated the union of Scotland and England (with streets and squares named after English kings and emblems), "devolution" is the latest craze. In a 1998 election the Scots voted for more autonomy and to bring their parliament home. Though Edinburgh has been the historic capital of Scotland for centuries, parliament has not met in Scotland since 1707. In 2000—while London will still call the strategic shots—Edinburgh will resume its position as home to the Scottish Parliament. And a strikingly modern new parliament building, opening in 2002, will be one more jewel in Edinburgh's crown.

Planning Your Time

While the major sights can be seen in a day, on a three-week tour of Britain I'd give Edinburgh two days.

Day 1: Orient yourself with a Guide Friday bus tour. Do the whole loop, getting off only to tour the Georgian House. After lunch, catch a 14:00 walking tour of the Royal Mile. Finish the afternoon at the National Gallery or browsing through the New Town. Evening: Scottish show, folk pub, or literary pub crawl or haunted walk.

Day 2: Spend the morning touring the castle. The rest of the day is easily spent exploring (downhill) the Royal Mile—museum-going or shopping. If you tour the Holyrood Palace, do it at the end of the day and the bottom of the mile. Family or fun options: Hike up Arthur's Seat or go swimming at the Commonwealth Pool.

Orientation (tel. code: 0131)

The center of Edinburgh holds the Princes Street Gardens park and Waverley Bridge, where you'll find the TI; Waverley Shopping and Eating Center; train station; bus info office, the starting point for most city bus tours; festival office; the National Gallery; and a covered dance-and-music pavilion. Weather blows in and out—bring your sweater.

Tourist Information: The crowded TI has become a profit-seeking business with advice colored by kickbacks. It's central as can be atop the Waverley Market on Princes Street (Monday–Saturday 9:00–19:00, Sunday 10:00–19:00, shorter hours and closed Sunday in off-season, tel. 0131/557-1700, airport TI tel. 0131/333-2167). Ideally, skip it and telephone if you have questions. They have the monthly entertainment *Gig Guide* (free) and brochures on the various Scottish folk shows and walking tours. Their misnamed *Essential Guide to Edinburgh* (which costs £1 and shuffles a little information between lots of ads) has a cruddy little map. *The List*, the best monthly entertainment listing, is sold for £1.50 at newsstands. Book your room direct without the TI's help.

For real information without the sales push, visit the **Old Town Information Centre** at Tron Church (Easter–September, South Bridge at the Royal Mile, great free Royal Mile maps). The **Backpackers' Centre** is a good source of budget travel information (just off High Street at 5 Blackfriars Street).

Sunday Activities: Many sights close on Sunday, but there's still a lot to do: Royal Mile walking tour, city bus tour, Edinburgh Castle, St. Giles Cathedral, Holyrood Palace, Royal Botanic Gardens, and Arthur's Seat hike. The Georgian House and National Gallery open Sunday afternoon.

Arrival in Edinburgh: Arriving by train at Waverley Station puts you in the city center, a few steps from the TI and the city

Edinburgh

GEORGIAN HOUSE · QUEEN STREET · GEORGE STREET · ROSE STREET · PRINCES ST. · PRINCES ST. GARDENS · QUEENSFERRY STREET · to A.90 & Highlands · LOTHIAN ROAD · GRASSMARKET · MELVILLE DRIVE · UNIVERSITY · SCOTT MONUMENT · BUS STN. · C+A · POST · ROYAL MILE · ST. GILES · SOUTH BRIDGE · CALTON HILL · REGENT ROAD · QUEEN'S DRIVE · Salisbury Crags · to Dalkeith Rd. B&B area · HOLYROOD PARK · Arthur's Seat

N

0 — 1/4 MILES

❶ CASTLE ❷ NATIONAL GALLERY ❸ WAVERLEY MARKET +TOURIST INFO ❹ TRAIN STN. ❺ HOLYROOD PALACE

bus to my recommended B&Bs. Both National Express and Scottish Citylink buses use the bus station a block from the train station in the Georgian town on St. Andrew Square.

Edinburgh's slingshot-of-an-airport is 10 miles northwest of the center and well-connected by shuttle buses (LRT "Airline" bus, 4/hrly, 30 min, from Waverley Bridge, £3.20 or £4 with all-day city bus pass, flight info tel. 0131/333-1000, British Midlands tel. 0345/554-554, British Air tel. 0345/222-111). Taxi to airport: £14.

Getting Around Edinburgh
Nearly all Edinburgh sights are within walking distance. City buses are handy and inexpensive (average fare-65p, LRT info office, Old Town end of Waverley Bridge, tel. 0131/555-6363). Tell the driver where you're going, drop exact change into the box or lose the excess, grab your ticket as you board, push the stop button as you near your stop (so your stop isn't skipped), and exit from the middle door. All-day "Freedom Ticket" passes are sold on buses (£2.20—four rides make it worthwhile). Taxis are reasonable (easy to flag down, £1.20 drop charge, 80p extra after 18:00, average ride between downtown and B&B district—£4).

Bus Tours of Edinburgh
▲Hop-on and Hop-off City Bus Tours—Two companies, Guide Friday and LRT's "Edinburgh Classic Tour," offer buses that circle the town center—Waverley Bridge, around the castle, Royal Mile, Calton Hill, Georgian New Town, and Princes Street—in about an hour, with pick-ups about every 15 minutes and an informative narration. You can hop on and off all day on

one ticket (not for 24 hours). Overlapping can be interesting, since each guide has her own story to tell. On sunny days they go top-less (the buses), but can suffer from traffic noise and congestion. First and last buses leave Waverley Bridge at 9:00 and 19:00 in summer. (Guide Friday, £7, tel. 0131/556-2244; Classic Tour, £5.50, tel. 0131/555-6363.)

▲**City Bus Tours**—"City, Sea, and Hills" is the best 90-minute tour of greater Edinburgh (£3.50, Friday and Sunday at 10:30, information at LRT office, on Waverley Bridge, tel. 0131/555-6363). Several all-day bus tours go as far as Loch Ness.

Sights—Edinburgh

▲▲▲**Edinburgh Castle**—The fortified birthplace of the city 1,300 years ago, this imposing symbol of Edinburgh sits proudly on a rock high above the city. While the castle has been both a fort and a royal residence since the 11th century, most of the buildings today are from its more recent use as a military garrison (£6, daily 9:30–18:00, until 17:00 in winter, cafeteria, tel. 0131/225-9846; consider avoiding the long uphill walk from the nearest bus stop by taking a cab to the castle gate).

Entry Gate: Start with the wonderfully droll 30-minute guided introduction tour (free with admission, departs twice an hour from entry, see clock for the next departure). The CD-ROM audio guide is excellent, with four hours of quick digital dial descriptions (free with admission, pick up at entry gate before meeting the live guide). Don't miss the fine WC at the entry (three-time "British Loo of the Year" winner, award plaques near men's entry—ask janitor why they lost last year).

In the castle there are four essential stops: Crown Jewels, Great Hall, National War Memorial, and St. Margaret's Chapel with city view. All are at the highest and most secure point—on or near the castle square—and where your guided tour ends.

The Royal Palace (facing castle square under the flag pole) has two unimpressive rooms (through door reading 1566). Remember, Scottish royalty only lived here when safety or proto-col required. They preferred the Holyrood Palace at the bottom of the Royal Mile. The line of tourists leads from the square directly to the jewels. Skip this line and enter the building around to the left where you'll get to the jewels via a wonderful *Honors of Scotland* exhibition about the crown jewels.

Scotland's Crown Jewels are older than England's. While Cromwell destroyed England's, the Scots hid theirs successfully. Long-time symbols of Scottish nationalism, they were made in Edinburgh—of Scottish gold, diamonds, and gems—in 1540 for a 1543 coronation. They were last used to crown Charles II in 1651. Apparently there was some anxiety about the Act of Union, which dissolved Scotland's parliament into England's to create the

United Kingdom in 1707—the Scots locked up and hid their jewels. In 1818 Walter Scott and a royal commission rediscovered the jewels intact.

The **Stone of Scone** sits plain and strong next to the jewels. This is the coronation stone of Scotland's ancient kings (ninth century). Swiped by the English, it sat under the coronation chair at Westminster Abbey from 1296 until 1996. With major fanfare, Scotland's treasured Stone of Scone returned to Edinburgh on November 15, 1996. Talk to the guard for more details.

The Great Hall was the castle's ceremonial meeting place in the 16th and 17th centuries. In modern times it was a barracks and a hospital. While most of what you see is Victorian, two medieval elements survive: the fine hammerbeam roof and the iron-barred peephole (above fireplace on right). This allowed the king to spy on his partying subjects.

The imposing **Scottish National War Memorial** commemorates 148,000 Scottish soldiers lost in WWI, 57,000 lost in WWII, and 750 lost in British battles since. Each bay is dedicated to a particular Scottish regiment. The main shrine, featuring a green Italian marble memorial containing the original WWI rolls of honor, actually sits upon an exposed chunk of the castle rock. Above you, the archangel Michael is busy slaying the dragon. The bronze frieze accurately shows the attire of various wings of Scotland's military. The stained glass starts with Cain and Abel on the left and finishes with a celebration of peace on the right.

St. Margaret's Chapel, the oldest building in Edinburgh, is dedicated to Queen Margaret, who died here in 1093 and was sainted in 1250. Built in the Romanesque style of the Norman invaders in 1130, it is wonderfully simple, with classic Norman zigzags decorating the round arch that separates the tiny nave from the sacristy. Used as a powder magazine for 400 years, very little survives. You'll see an 11th-century Gospel book of St. Margaret's and small windows featuring St. Margaret, St. Columba (who brought Christianity to Scotland via Iona), and William Wallace (the brave defender of Scotland). The place is popular for weddings and, since it seats only 20, particularly popular with brides' fathers.

Belly up to the bannister (across the terrace outside the chapel) to enjoy the great view. Below you are the guns that fire the one o'clock salute and a sweet little line of doggie tombstones— the soldier's pet cemetery. Beyond stretches the Georgian New Town (read the informative plaque).

The castle could keep you entertained all day (for instance, below, in the vaults, you can see a fine military museum and Mons Meg—a huge 15th-century siege cannon that fired 500-pound stones nearly two miles). But you've seen the essentials.

When leaving the castle, turn around and look back at the

gate. There stand King Robert the Bruce (on the left, 1274–1329) and Sir William Wallace (Braveheart—on the right, 1270–1305). Wallace (newly famous, thanks to Mel Gibson) fought long and hard against English domination before being executed in London—his body cut to pieces and paraded through the far corners of jolly olde England. Bruce beat the English at Bannockburn in 1314. Bruce and Wallace still defend the spirit of Scotland.

Sights—Along the Royal Mile
(In walking order from top to bottom.)

▲▲▲**Royal Mile**—This is one of Europe's most interesting historic walks. Start at the top and amble down to the palace. I've listed the top sights of the Royal Mile—working downhill.

The Royal Mile, which consists of a series of four different streets—Castlehill, Lawnmarket, High Street, and Canongate—is actually 100 yards longer than a mile. And every inch is packed with shops, cafés, and lanes leading to tiny squares. By poking down the many side-alleys, you'll find a few rough edges of a town well on its way to becoming a touristic mall. See it now. In a few years tourists will be slaloming through the postcard racks on bagpipe skateboards.

Royal Mile Terminology: A "close" is a tiny alley between two buildings (originally with a door that closed it at night). A close usually leads to a "court" or courtyard. A "land" is a tenement block of apartments. A "pend" is an arched gateway. A "wynd" is a narrow winding lane. And "gate" is from an old Scandinavian word for street.

Royal Mile Walking Tours: Mercat Tours offers two-hour guided walks of the mile—more entertaining than historic (£5, daily at 11:00 and 14:00, from Mercat Cross on the Royal Mile, tel. 0131/661-4541). The guides, who enjoy making a short story long, ignore the big sights, taking you behind the scenes with piles of barely historic gossip, bully-pulpit Scottish pride, and fun but forgettable trivia. For a private guide, consider Robin Sinton (tel. 0131/661-7722) or the Voluntary Guides Association (0131/664-7180).

Castle Esplanade—At the top of the Royal Mile, the big parking lot leading up to the castle was once a military parade ground. It's often cluttered with bleachers under construction for the military tattoo—a spectacular massing of the bands that fills the square nightly for most of August (see Edinburgh Festival, below). At the bottom, on the left, the tiny witch's fountain memorializes 300 women who were accused of witchcraft and burned here. Scotland burned more witches per capita than any other country—17,000 between 1479 and 1722. But in a humanitarian gesture, rather than burning them alive as was the custom in the rest of Europe, Scottish "witches" were strangled to death before they were

Royal Mile

burned. The plaque shows two witches: one good and one bad. (For 90 minutes of this kind of Royal Mile trivia, take the guided tour described above.)

Scotch Whiskey Heritage Centre—This touristy ambush is designed only to distill £5 out of your pocket. You get a video history, a little whiskey-keg train-car ride, and a free sample before finding yourself in the shop. People do seem to enjoy it, but that might have something to do with the sample (tel. 0131/ 220-0441). The **Camera Obscura**, across the street, is just as rewarding.

▲▲Gladstone's Land—Take a good look at this typical 16th- to 17th-century merchant's house, complete with a lived-in furnished interior and guides in each room who love to talk (£3, Monday–Saturday 10:00–17:00, Sunday 14:00–17:00). For a good Royal Mile photo, lean out the upper-floor window or climb the entry stairway with the golden eagle.

▲Writers' Museum at Lady Stair's House—This interesting house, built in 1622, is filled with manuscripts and knickknacks of Scotland's three greatest literary figures: Robert Burns, Sir Walter Scott, and Robert Louis Stevenson. It's worth a few minutes for anyone and is fascinating for fans (free, Monday–Saturday 10:00–17:00, closed Sunday). Wander around the courtyard here. Edinburgh was a wonder in the 17th and 18th centuries. Tourists came here to see its skyscrapers, which towered 10 stories and higher. No city in Europe was so densely populated as "Auld Reekie."

Deacon Brodie's Tavern—This is a decent place for a light meal (see Eating, below). Read the story of its notorious namesake on the wall facing Bank Street.

▲St. Giles Cathedral—Wander through Scotland's most important church. Stepping inside, find John Knox's statue. Look into his eyes from 10 inches away. Knox, the great reformer and founder of austere Scottish Presbyterianism, first preached here in

1559. His insistence that every person should be able to read the word of God gave Scotland an education system 300 years ahead of the rest of Europe. For this reason it was Scottish minds who led the way in math, science, medicine, engineering, and so on. Voltaire called Scotland "the intellectual capital of Europe."

The neo-Gothic Chapel of the Knights of the Thistle (from 1911, in far corner) was built in two years entirely with Scottish material and labor. Find the angel tooting the bagpipes (above the door on right). The Scottish crown steeple from 1495 is a proud part of Edinburgh's skyline (daily 9:00–19:00, until 17:00 off-season, fine café downstairs).

John Knox is buried out back—austerely, under the parking lot, at spot 44. The statue among the cars shows King Charles II riding to a toga party back in 1685.

Parliament House—Stop in to see the grand hall with its fine 1639 hammer-beam ceiling and stained glass. This housed the Scottish Parliament until the Act of Union in 1707 (explained in history exhibition adjacent). Today it's busy with wigged and robed lawyers hard at work in the old library (peek through the door) or pacing the hall deep in discussion. Greater eminence . . . longer wig. The friendly doorman is helpful (free, public welcome Monday–Friday 9:00–16:30, best action mid-mornings Tuesday–Friday, open-to-the-public trials 10:00–16:00—doorman has day's docket, entry behind St. Giles Cathedral near parking spot 21).

Mercat Cross—This stands on the downhill side of the church. Royal proclamations were read from here in the 14th century. Today it's the meeting point of various walking tours. Pop into the police information center, a few doors downhill, for a little local law-and-order history (free, daily 10:00–22:00).

▲**Tron Kirk**—This fine old building houses an interesting (free) Old Town history display and the genuinely helpful Old Town tourist information center (open Easter–September). No crowds. No conflict of interests. Just caring help by an outfit working to better organize and show off Edinburgh's historic Old Town.

▲**Museum of Childhood**—This five-story playground of historical toys and games—called the noisiest museum in the world because of its delighted tiny visitors—is rich in nostalgia and history (free, Monday–Friday 10:00–17:00, closed Sunday). Just downhill is a fragrant fudge shop offering free samples.

▲**John Knox House**—Fascinating for Reformation buffs, this fine 16th-century house offers a well-explained look at the life of the great reformer (£2, Monday–Saturday 10:00–16:30, closed on Sunday). While Knox never actually lived here, it was called "his house" to save it from the wrecking ball in 1850.

▲**People's Story**—This interesting exhibition traces the lot of the working class through the 18th, 19th, and 20th centuries (free, Monday–Saturday 10:00–17:00, closed Sunday). Curiously, while this museum is dedicated to the proletariat, immediately around the back is the tomb of Adam Smith—the author of *Wealth of Nations* and the father of modern capitalism (1723–1790).

▲**Huntly House**—Another old house full of old stuff, Huntly is worth a look for its early Edinburgh history and handy ground-floor WC. Don't miss the original copy of the National Covenant (written in 1638 on an animal skin) or the sketches of pre-Georgian Edinburgh with its lake still wet (free, Monday–Saturday 10:00–17:00, closed Sunday). Just a toot farther downhill is Bagpipes Galore.

White Horse Close—Step into this 17th-century courtyard (bottom of Canongate, on the left, a block before Holyrood Palace). It was from here that the Edinburgh stagecoach left for London. Eight days later, the horse-drawn carriage pulled into its destination: Scotland Yard.

▲**Holyrood Palace**—The palace marks the end of the Royal Mile. The queen spends a week in Scotland each summer and this is her official residence and office. The abbey—part of a 12th-century Augustinian monastery—stood here first. It was named for a piece of the cross brought here as a relic by queen-then-saint Margaret. Scotland's royalty preferred living here to the blustery castle on the rock and, gradually, the palace grew. The building is rich in history and decor. But without information or a guided tour ("there's none of either," snickered the guy who sells the boring £3.70 museum guidebooks), you're just another peasant in the dark. Docents in each room are happy to give you the answer if you know the question. After wandering through the elegantly furnished rooms and a few dark older rooms filled with glass cases of historic bits and Scottish pieces that must be fascinating, you're free to wander through the ruined abbey and the queen's gardens (£5.30, daily 9:30–18:00, shorter hours off-season, closed when the queen's home—usually 10 days in early July, tel. 0131/556-7371).

More Bonnie Wee Sights

▲**Georgian New Town**—Cross Waverley Bridge and walk through Georgian Edinburgh. The grand George Street, connecting St. Andrew and Charlotte Squares, was the centerpiece of the elegantly planned New Town. The entire city plan—laid out in the late 18th century when George was king—celebrates the notion of the United Kingdom. Look at the map. You'll see George Street. Queen Street, Hanover Street (the royal family surname), and even Thistle and Rose Streets are emblems of the two happily paired nations.

▲▲**Georgian House**—This refurbished Georgian house, set on Edinburgh's finest Georgian square, is a trip back to 1796. A volunteer guide in each room is trained in the force-feeding of stories and trivia. Start your visit with two interesting videos

Scottish Words

aye	yes	**inch, innis**	island
ben	mountain	**inver**	river, mouth
bonnie	beautiful	**kyle**	strait
carn	heap of stones	**loch**	lake
creag	rock, cliff	**neeps**	turnips
tattie	potato		
haggis	rich assortment of oats and sheep organs stuffed into a chunk of sheep intestine, liberally seasoned, boiled, and eaten mostly by tourists. Usually served with "neeps and tatties." Tastier than it sounds.		

(architecture/Georgian lifestyles) totaling 30 minutes (£4.30, Monday–Saturday 10:00–17:00, Sunday 14:00–17:00, 7 Charlotte Square, tel. 0131/225-2160).

Princes Street Gardens—This grassy park, a former lake-bed, separates Edinburgh's New and Old Towns and offers a wonderful escape from the city. There are plenty of free concerts and country dances in the summer, and the oldest floral clock in the world. Join the local office workers for a picnic-lunch break.

▲**National Gallery**—This elegant neoclassical building has a small but impressive collection of European masterpieces from Raphael to van Gogh and offers the best look you'll get at Scottish paintings (free, Monday–Saturday 10:00–17:00, Sunday 14:00–17:00, tel. 0131/624-6200).

▲**Walter Scott Monument**—Built in 1840, this elaborate, neo-Gothic monument honors the great author, one of Edinburgh's many illustrious sons. The 200-foot monument shelters a marble statue of Scott. He is surrounded by busts of 16 great Scottish poets and 64 characters from his books. Climb 287 steps for a fine view of the city (£1, Monday–Saturday 9:00–18:00, until 17:00 off-season, closed Sunday).

Royal Botanic Garden—Britain's second-oldest botanical garden, established in 1670 for medicinal herbs, is now one of Europe's best (free, daily 9:30–20:00 in season, £2 "rainforest to desert" tours daily at 11:00 and 14:00, one mile north of the center at Inverleith Row, tel. 0131/552-7171).

▲▲**Arthur's Seat Hike**—A 45-minute hike up the 822-foot volcanic mountain (surrounded by a fine park overlooking Edinburgh), starting from the Holyrood Palace, Commonwealth Pool, or your B&B, gives you a rewarding view. It's the easiest "king of the mountain" feeling I've ever had. You can drive up most of the way from behind (follow the one-way street from the palace, park by the little lake) or run up like they did in *Chariots of Fire*. Ask a local for the best way up.

Brush Skiing—If you'd rather be skiing, the Hillend Ski Centre is an open-all-year hill on the edge of town with a chairlift, T-bar, and rentable skis, boots, and poles (£6/hr with gear, daily 9:30–21:00, less on weekends, probably canceled if it snows, tel. 0131/445-4433).

▲**Royal Commonwealth Games Swimming Pool**—The biggest pool I've ever seen is open to the public, with Café Aqua (overlooking the pool), weight room, sauna (£6 extra), and plenty of water rides, including Europe's biggest waterslide flume (£2.50, Monday–Friday 9:00–21:00, Saturday and Sunday 10:00–16:00, tel. 0131/667-7211).

Edinburgh Crystal—Blowing, molding, cutting, polishing, and engraving, the Edinburgh Crystal Company glassworks tour smashes anything you'll see in Venice (£3, 35-minute tours offered Monday–Friday 9:15–15:30, Saturday and Sunday 11:00–14:30, children under age eight and large dogs are not allowed in for safety reasons). There is a shop full of "bargain" second-quality pieces, a video show, and a cafeteria. A free red minibus shuttle service from Waverley Bridge departs hourly (10:00–15:00) in summer; or you can drive 10 miles south of town on A701 to Penicuik. You can schedule a more expensive super tour where you actually blow and cut glass (tel. 01968/675-128).

Shopping—The best shopping is along Princes Street (don't miss elegant old Jenner's Department Store), Victoria Street (antiques galore), and the Royal Mile (touristy but competitively priced, shops usually open 9:00–17:30, later on Thursday).

Edinburgh Festival

One of Europe's great cultural events, Edinburgh's annual festival turns the city into a carnival of culture. There are enough music, dance, art, drama, and multicultural events to make even the most jaded traveler drool with excitement. Every day is jammed with formal and spontaneous fun. The official and fringe festivals rage simultaneously for about three weeks each summer, with the Military Tattoo starting a week earlier. Many city sights run on extended hours and those that normally close on Sunday stay open. It's a glorious time to be in Edinburgh.

The official festival (August 15–September 4 in 1999) is more formal and serious, with entertainment by festival invitation only. Major events sell out well in advance (show office at 21 Market Street, £4–45, CC:VMA, booking from April on, tel. 0131/473-2000).

The less-formal **Fringe Festival** features "on the edge" comedy/theater (August 8–30, 1999, ticket/info office just below

St. Giles Cathedral on the Royal Mile, tel. 0131/226-5257, bookings tel. 0131/226-5138). Its many events have, it seems, more performers than viewers. Tickets are usually available at the door (or strewn on the streets).

The **Military Tattoo** is a massing of the bands, drums, and bagpipes with groups from all over what was the British Empire. Displaying military finesse with a stirring lone-piper finale, this grand spectacle fills the castle esplanade nightly except Sunday, normally from a week before the festival starts until a week before it finishes: August 6–28 in 1999 (£8–16, CC:VMA, booking starts in January, tel. 0131/225-1188, Friday and Saturday shows sell out, Monday–Thursday shows rarely do). If nothing else, it is a really big show. The BBC airs the Tattoo in a grand TV spectacle throughout Britain once each season (worth watching from anywhere in Britain).

If you do manage to hit Edinburgh during the festival, extend your stay by a day or two and book a room far in advance. While Fringe tickets and most Tattoo tickets are available the day of the show, you may want to book an official event or two in advance. Do it directly by telephone, leaving your credit-card number. Pick up your ticket at the office the day of the show or at the door just before curtain time. Several publications—including the festival's official schedule, the *Festival Times*, *The List*, *Fringe Program*, and the *Daily Diary*—list and evaluate festival events.

Entertainment in Edinburgh

▲▲**Evening Walking Tours**—These walks, more than a pile of ghost stories, are an entertaining and cheap night out (offered nightly, usually 19:00 and 21:00, easy socializing for solo travelers). The theatrical and creatively staged Witchery Tours are the most established of the ghost tours (£7, 90 min, leave from the Royal Mile, reservations required, book your spot by calling 0131/225-6745). The fascinating-for-those-who-care Literary Pub Tour leaves from the Beehive Pub on Grassmarket (£6, two hours with two actors and three pub stops, nightly in July and August at 18:00 and 20:30, Thursday–Sunday at 19:30 otherwise, Friday only in winter, tel. 0131/226-6665).

▲**Scottish Folk Evenings**—These £35 to £40 dinner shows, generally for tour groups, are held in huge halls of expensive hotels. (Prices are bloated to include 20 percent commissions.) Your "traditional" meal is followed by a full slate of swirling kilts, blaring bagpipes, and Scottish folk-dancing with an "old-time music hall"–type emcee. You can often see the show without dinner for about half-price. The TI has fliers on all the latest venues. Carlton Highland Hotel offers a Scottish folk evening without dinner (£12, at High Street and North Bridge, tel. 0131/556-7277).

▲▲**Folk Music in Pubs**—Edinburgh is a good place for folk

music. There's always a pub or two with a folk evening on. The free monthly *Gig Guide* lists most of the live music action. Just off the Royal Mile on South Bridge, the **Tron Tavern and Ceilidh House** is home of the Tron Folk Club. They have nightly ad-lib traditional music from about 22:00 (but doesn't really get going until later, smoky) and a £3–6 candlelit folk concert on Saturday nights (smoke-free, tel. 0131/226-0931). **Whistle Binkies** offers live folk music several nights a week (also near High Street South Bridge at Niddry Street, tel. 0131/557-5114).

Grassmarket Street (below the castle) is sloppy with live music—mostly folk. This noisy nightlife center is fun to just wander through late at night. By the noise and crowds you'll know where to go and where not to. The **Fiddlers Arms** (fiddling on Monday and Thursday, tel. 0131/229-2665), **Biddy Mulligan**, and **White Hart Inn**, among others, all feature regular live folk music. **Finnigan's Wake** specializes in Irish folk music (a block off Grassmarket at 9 Victoria Street, tel. 0131/226-3816).

Theater—Even outside of festival time, Edinburgh is a fine place for lively and affordable theater. Pick up *The List* for a complete rundown of what's on.

Sleeping in Edinburgh
(£1 = about $1.70, tel. code: 0131)
Sleep Code: **S** = Single, **D** = Double/Twin, **T** = Triple, **Q** = Quad, **b** = bathroom, **t** = toilet only, **s** = shower only, **CC** = Credit Card (Visa, MasterCard, Amex).

The annual festival fills Edinburgh each August. Conventions, school holidays, and other surprises can make room-finding tough at almost any time. Call in advance or pay 30 percent extra for a relative dump. For the best prices, book direct (rather than through the greedy TI) and, again, call in advance! "Standard" rooms, with toilets and showers a tissue-toss away, save you £10 a night.

My recommendations are south of town near the Royal Commonwealth Pool, just off Dalkeith Road. This comfortably safe neighborhood is a 20-minute walk or short bus ride from the Royal Mile. All listings are on quiet streets, a two-minute walk from a bus stop, and well-served by city buses. Near the B&Bs you'll find plenty of eateries (see Eating, below), easy free parking, and a handy Laundromat (Monday–Saturday 9:00–17:00, £4 for a self-serve load, £5 if they do it, June–September they'll deliver your clean clothes at the B&B for £1 extra, 208 Dalkeith Road, tel. 0131/667-0825).

To reach the hotel neighborhood from the train station, TI, or Scott Monument, cross Princes Street and wait under the C&A sign (65p, buses #14, #21, #33, #82, #86, or C3; red bus: exact change or pay more; green bus: makes change; ride 10 minutes to first stop 100 yards after the pool, push the button, exit

Edinburgh, Our Neighborhood

middle door). These buses also stop at the corner of North Bridge and High Street on the Royal Mile. Taxi fare from the station or Royal Mile to the B&Bs is about £4. Room prices are for peak-season 1999 (but not festival time, when they can go higher) and assume you are booking directly and not through a tourist office. Off-season prices go soft. All recommended B&Bs have no traffic noise and are strictly nonsmoking in the bedrooms and breakfast room.

Millfield Guest House, run by Liz and Ed Broomfield, is thoughtfully furnished with antique class, a rare sit-and-chat ambience, and a comfy TV lounge. Since the showers are down the hall, you'll get spacious rooms and great prices (S-£21, D-£35–36, T-£48–52, CC:VM, CC reservation allows for late arrival, 12 Marchhall Road, EH16 5HR, tel. 0131/667-4428). Decipher the breakfast prayer by Robert Burns. Then try the "Taste of Scotland" breakfast option. See how many stone (14 pounds) you weigh in the elegant throne room. This place is worth calling well in advance.

Turret Guest House is teddy-on-the-beddy cozy with a great bay-windowed family room and a vast breakfast menu that includes haggis and vegetarian options (S-£18–24, D-£36–40, Db-£42–54,

£2-per-person discount with this book, cheaper off-season, 8 Kilmaurs Terrace, tel. 0131/667-6704, Mrs. Jackie Cameron).

Kenvie Guest House, well and warmly run by Dorothy Vidler, comes with lots of personal touches (one small twin-£36, D-£39, Db-£47, family deals, 3 percent more with CC, 16 Kilmaurs Road, EH16 5DA, tel. & fax 0131/668-1964).

The comfortable and very Victorian **Ravensneuk Guest House** is also good (D-£42, Db-£52, 5 percent discount with cash and this book, family deals, CC:VMA, great lounge, 11 Blacket Avenue, EH9 1RR, tel. & fax 0131/667-5347, Chris and Toni Henry).

Highland Park House is simple, bright, and friendly (S-£20, D-£38 with this book, family deals, 16 Kilmaurs Terrace, tel. 0131/667-9204, Margaret and Brian Love).

Ard-Na-Said B&B is an elegant 1875 Victorian house with a comfy lounge and fine rooms (Db-£44–48, family deals, 5 Priestfield Road, EH16 5HH, tel. 0131/667-8754, fax 0131/271-0960, enthusiastically run by Jim and Olive Lyons).

● **Salisbury Hotel** fills a classy old Georgian building with 12 rooms, a large cushy lounge, and even a dumbwaiter in the breakfast room. It's more like a hotel than its neighbors but run with B&B warmth by Brenda Wright (D-£46, Db-£50; D-£48 and Db-£54 in July and August; 5 percent off with cash and this book, CC:VM, 45 Salisbury Road, EH16 5AA, tel. & fax 0131/667-1264, e-mail: brenda.wright@btinternet.com).

Dunedin Guest House is bright, Scottish, and a good value (seven rooms, S-£22–27, Db-£44–54, family deals, strong showers, NASA lighting, TVs with satellite channels in rooms, e-mail access, Scotland and Edinburgh videos in lounge, 8 Priestfield Road, EH16 5HH, tel. 0131/668-1949, fax 0131/668-2181, Annette and Max Preston).

Dorstan Private Hotel is small and personable, but professional and hotelesque with all the comforts. Several of its 14 prim rooms are on the ground floor (Ds-£58, Db-£66, family rooms, CC:VMA, 7 Priestfield Road, EH16 5HJ, tel. 0131/667-6721, fax 0131/668-4644, e-mail: reservations@dorstan-hotel.demon.co.uk, Mairae Campbell).

Priestville B&B is a big old place with charming rough edges (D-£38, Db-£44, family deals, 10 Priestfield Road, tel. 0131/667-2435).

Belford House is a tidy and simple place offering good rooms and a warm welcome (D-£40, Db-£50, family deals, CC:VM, 13 Blacket Avenue, tel. 0131/667-2422, Isa and Tom Borthwick).

Big, Modern, Cheap Hotels in the Center

Ibis Hotel, mid–Royal Mile behind Tron Church, is perfectly located with 97 soulless but clean and comfy rooms and American charm (Db-£55 all year, breakfast is extra, CC:VMA, some non-smoking rooms, elevator, 6 Hunter Square, EH1 1QW, tel. 0131/240-7000, fax 0131/240-7007). Considering its location and the costs of other hotels in town, this is a great deal.

Travel Inn, the biggest hotel in Edinburgh, has even less character but a great price and a mediocre location about a mile from the Mile. Each of its 280 rooms are modern and comfortable, with a sofa that folds out for two kids if necessary (Db-£40 for two adults and up to two kids under 15, breakfast is extra, CC:VMA, elevators, non-smoking rooms, weekends booked long in advance, near Haymarket station just west of the castle at 1 Morrison Link, EH3 8DN, tel. 0131/228-9819, fax 0131/228-9836, Web site: www.travelinn.co.uk).

Hostels

Although Edinburgh's hostels are well run, open to all, and provide £10 bunk beds (an £8-12 savings over B&Bs), they don't include breakfast and are scruffy.

Castle Rock Hostel is hip and easygoing, offering cheap beds, plenty of friends, and a great central location just below the castle and above the pubs with all the folk music (15 Johnston Terrace, tel. 0131/225-9666). They run another backpackers' place at 105 High Street.

For more regulations and less color, try the IYH hostels: **Bruntsfield Hostel** (on a park, 6 to 10 beds per room, 7 Bruntsfield Crescent, buses #11, #15, and #16 to and from Princes Street, tel. 0131/447-2994) and **Edinburgh Hostel** (4 to 22 beds per room, 18 Eglinton Crescent, tel. 0131/337-1120).

Eating in Edinburgh

Eating Along the Royal Mile

Historic pubs and doily cafés with reasonable, unremarkable meals abound. But, since chefs seem to come and go with the seasons, I have no splurge meals to recommend. These are simply handy, affordable places for a good bite to eat (listed in downhill order). **Deacon Brodie's Pub** serves soup, sandwiches, and snacks on the ground floor and good £7 meals upstairs (daily 12:00–22:00, tel. 0131/225-6531). Or munch prayerfully in the **Lower Aisle** restaurant under St. Giles Cathedral (Monday–Friday 10:00–16:30). **Bann's Vegetarian Café** serves carnivore-pleasing veggie cuisine that goes way beyond tofu and granola (daily 10:00–23:00, just off South Bridge behind the Tron Church at 5 Hunter Square, tel. 0131/226-1112). For a break from the touristic grind, consider the **Elephant House** where locals browse newspapers, listen to classic rock, and sip coffee or munch a light meal (daily, three blocks south of Royal Mile at 21 George IV Bridge, tel. 0131/220-5355). **Food Plantation** has good, inexpensive fresh sandwiches to eat-in or take-out (274 Canongate). **Brambles Tea Room** serves light lunches and Starbucks coffee (next to Huntley House at 158 Canongate). **Clarinda's Tea Room**, near the bottom of the Royal Mile, is a charming and tasty place for a break after touring the Mile or palace (daily 9:00–16:45).

Grassmarket Street, below the castle, is lined with sloppy eateries and noisy pubs. This is the place for live folk music. If you want dinner to melt into your beer, eat here.

Lunch in the New Town
Waverley Center Food Court, below the TI and above the station, is a food circus of sticky fast-food joints (including **The Scot's Pantry** for quick traditional edibles) littered with paper plates and shoppers. Local office workers pile into **Lanterna** for good Italian food (family-run, fresh and friendly for lunch or dinner, 83 Hanover Street, two blocks off Princes Street, tel. 0131/226-3090). For a generation, New Town vegetarians have munched salads at **Henderson's Salad Table and Wine Bar** (Monday–Saturday 8:00–22:45, closed Sunday, nonsmoking section, strictly vegetarian, between Queen and George Streets at 94 Hanover Street, tel. 0131/225-2131). Rose Street has tubs of pubs.

Eating in Dalkeith Road Area, near Your B&B
The following places are within a five-minute walk of the recommended B&Bs. Most are among a cluster of simple eateries within a block of the corner of Newington and Preston Streets. For a fun local atmosphere that makes up for the food and smoke, the **Wine Glass Pub** serves filling "basket meals" (£4, Sunday–Thursday 18:00–20:30). **Chinatown**, next to the Wine Glass, is a delightful little Chinese restaurant (moderate prices, 17:30–23:30, closed Monday, reservations are wise, tel. 0131/662-0555). **Brattisanis** is your basic *chippie* (lousy milkshakes, great haggis, 87 Newington Road). **Chatterbox** is fine for a light meal with tea (8:30–20:00, down East Preston from the pool). **Jade Palace** has tasty Chinese food (take-out only, closed Tuesday, 212 Dalkeith Road). The huge Commonwealth Pool's **Café Aqua** is a noisy cafeteria for hungry swimmers and budget travelers (pass the entry without paying, sit with a poolside view). **Minto Hotel's bar/restaurant** serves a good high tea—hot bar dinner with tea and scones—for £8 (daily 17:00–21:00, corner of Mayfield Terrace and Minto Street, tel. 0131/668-1234).

Transportation Connections—Edinburgh
By train to: Inverness (7/day, 4 hrs), **Oban** (3/day, change in Glasgow, 4.5 hrs), **York** (hrly, 2.5 hrs), **London** (hrly, 5 hrs), **Durham** (hrly, 2 hrs), **Lake District** (south past Carlisle to Penrith, catch bus to Keswick; 6/day, 40 min), **Birmingham** (6/day, 4.5 hrs), **Crewe** (6/day, 3.5 hrs). Train info: tel. 0345/484-950.

By bus to: Oban (3/day, 4 hrs, £12), **Fort William** (3/day, 4 hrs, £12), **Inverness** (4/day, 4 hrs, £12). For bus info, call National Express (tel. 0990-808-080) or Scottish Citylink (tel. 0990-505-050).

Route Tips for Drivers

Arriving in Edinburgh from the north: Rather than drive through downtown Edinburgh to the recommended B&Bs, circle the city on the new A720 City Bypass road. Approaching Edinburgh on the M-9, take the M-8 (direction Glasgow) and quickly get onto the A720 City Bypass (direction Edinburgh South). After four miles you'll hit a roundabout. Ignore signs directing you into Edinburgh North and stay on A720 for 10 more miles to the next roundabout named "Sheriffhall." Exit the roundabout on the first left (A7, Edinburgh). From here it's four miles to the B&B neighborhood (see Arriving from the south, below, and B&B neighborhood map).

Arriving from the south: Coming into town on A68 from the south, take the "A7 Edinburgh" exit off the roundabout. A7 becomes Dalkeith Road. If you see the huge swimming pool, you've gone a couple of blocks too far (avoid this by referring to B&B neighborhood map above).

Leaving Edinburgh, heading south: Edinburgh to Hadrian's Wall is 100 miles; to Durham it's another 50 miles. From Edinburgh, Dalkeith Road leads south and eventually becomes A68 (handy Cameron Toll supermarket with cheap gas is on left as you leave Dalkeith Town, 10 minutes south of Edinburgh; gas and parking behind store). A68 takes you to Hadrian's Wall in two hours. You'll pass Jedburgh and its abbey after one hour. (For one last shot of shop-Scotland, there's a coach tour's delight just before Jedburgh, with kilt-makers, woolens, and a sheepskin shop.) Across from Jedburgh's lovely abbey is a free parking lot, a good visitors center, and public toilets (20p to pee). The England/Scotland border is a fun, quick stop (great view, ice cream, and tea caravan). Before Hexham, roller-coaster two miles down A6079 to B6318, following the Roman wall westward. (See Hadrian's Wall in Durham chapter for more driving instructions.)

OBAN, ISLANDS, AND HIGHLANDS

Filled with more natural and historical mystique than people, the Highlands are the essence of extreme Scotland. Legends of Bonnie Prince Charlie swirl around crumbling castles as pipers and kilts swirl around tourists. The harbor of Oban is a fruit crate of Scottish traditions, and the wind-bitten Hebrides are just an island hop, skip, and jump away.

The Highlands are cut in two by the impressive Caledonian Canal, with Oban at one end and Inverness at the other. The major sights cluster along the scenic 120-mile stretch between these two towns. Oban is a fine home base for western Scotland, and Inverness makes a good overnight stop on your way through eastern Scotland.

Planning Your Time

While Ireland has more charm and Wales has better sights, this area provides your best look at rural Scottish culture. There are a lot of miles, but they're scenic, the roads are good, and the traffic's light. In two days you can get a feel for the area with the car hike described below. To do the islands, you'll need more time. Iona is worthwhile, but adds a day to your trip. Generally, the region is hungry for the tourist dollar and everything overtly Scottish is designed to woo the tourist. You'll need more than a quick visit to get away from that.

With a car and two days to connect the Lake District and Edinburgh, consider this plan:

Day 1: 9:00—Leave Lake District (see Castlerigg Stone Circle if you haven't yet), 12:00—Rest stop on Loch Lomond, then joyride on, 13:00—Lunch in Inveraray, 16:00—Arrive in Oban, tour whiskey distillery, and drop by the TI, 20:30—Have dinner

with music at McTavish's Kitchen or dinner with class at
The Studio.

Day 2: 9:00—Leave Oban, 10:00—Explore the valley of Glencoe,
11:00—Drive to Fort Augustus, 12:00—Follow Caledonian Canal,
stopping at Loch Ness to take care of any monster business,
15:00—Visit the evocative Culloden Battlefield near Inverness,
16:00—Drive south, 19:00—Set up in Edinburgh.

With more time, spend a second night in Oban and tour
Iona; get to know Arthur Smith at Glencoe; or sleep in Inverness
or Pitlochry, both fun and entertaining towns.

OBAN

Oban, called the "gateway to the isles," is a busy little ferry-and-
train terminal with no important "sights" but a charming shiver-
and-bustle vitality that gives you a feel for small-town Scotland.
Wind, boats, gulls, several layers of islands, and the promise of a
wide-open Atlantic beyond give it a rugged and salty charm.

Orientation (tel. code: 01631)

Oban's business action, just a couple of streets deep, stretches
along the harbor and its promenade. Everything's close together
and the town seems eager to please its many visitors. There's live,
touristy music nightly in several bars and restaurants, shops sell
woolen and tweed with cash registers cocked (open until 20:00
and on Sunday), and posters announce a variety of enticing day
tours to Scotland's wild and rabbit-strewn western islands.

Tourist Information: The TI has brochures on everything
from saunas to launderettes to horseback riding to rainy-day activities, and a fine bookshop (Argyll Square, Monday–Saturday
9:00–21:00, Sunday 9:00–19:00, less off-season, just off harbor in
city center a block from train station, tel. 01631/563-122). Wander through their exhibit on the area (pick up a few phones to
hear old-timers talk about their life on the west edge of Scotland).
Check the TI "What's On" board for the latest on Oban's small-
town evening scene (free live entertainment nightly at the Great
Western Hotel with a Scottish Night every Wednesday, tug-o-
war on the pier, American line dancing, etc.).

Helpful Hints

Oban Rentals rents bikes downtown on Craigard Road (£2/hour,
£10/day, daily 8:00–18:30, tel. 01631/566-996). There's a Laundromat downtown on Stevenson Street (Monday–Saturday
9:00–17:00, closed Sunday, self-serve or £5 for full-serve). The
Oban Lawn Bowling Club has welcomed visitors since 1869. This
elegant green is the scene of a wonderfully British spectacle of old
men tiptoeing wishfully after their balls. It's fun to watch and—if
there's no match—for £2 each you can rent shoes and balls and

Oban

actually play (two blocks above the recommended B&Bs on Dalriach Road, tel. 01631/570-808).

Sights—Oban

▲**West Highland Malt Scotch Whiskey Distillery Tours**—
The 200-year-old Oban Whiskey Distillery produces 14,000
liters a week. They offer serious and fragrant 40-minute, £3
tours explaining the process from start to finish, with a free,
smooth sample in the middle and a discount coupon for the shop
at the end. The free exhibition preceding the tour gives a quick,
whiskey-centric history of Scotland. This is the handiest whiskey
tour you'll see, just a block off the harbor and better than anything in Edinburgh (Monday–Friday and, in-season, Saturday
9:30–17:00; last tour at 16:15; to avoid a wait, call to reserve a
place, tel. 01631/564-262).
McCaig's Tower—The unfinished "colosseum" on the hill overlooking the town was an "employ-the-workers-and-build-me-a-
fine-memorial" project undertaken by an early Oban tycoon in
1906. While the structure itself is nothing to see close up, a 10-
minute hike through a Victorian residential neighborhood gets
you to a peaceful garden and a mediocre view.
▲▲**Day Trip to the Islands of Iona and Mull**—See below.
Kerrera—This stark but very green island, nearly opposite Oban,
offers a quick, easy opportunity to get that romantic island experience (£2.50 round-trip, 50p for bikes, sails upon request, at Gallanach's dock, two miles south of Oban, tel. 01631/563-665).
Isle of Seil—Enjoy a drive, walk, solitude, and the sea. Drive 15
miles south of Oban on A816 to B844 to the Isle of Seil, connected to the mainland by a bridge. Just over the bridge on the

Isle of Seil is a pub called Tigh-an-Truish ("house of trousers"). After a 1745 English law forbade the wearing of kilts on the mainland, Highlanders used this pub to change from kilts to trousers before crossing the bridge. The pub serves great meals to those in kilts or pants (daily 12:00–14:15 and 18:00–20:30, darts anytime, good seafood dish, crispy vegetables, tel. 01852/300-242). Five miles across the island, on a tiny second island, is Easdale, a historic, touristy, windy, little slate-mining town facing the open Atlantic (shuttle ferry goes the 300 yards; slate-town museum, incredibly tacky egomaniac's "Highland Arts" shop).

Sleeping in Oban
(£1 = about $1.70, tel. code: 01631)
Sleep Code: **S** = Single, **D** = Double/Twin, **T** = Triple, **Q** = Quad, **b** = bathroom, **t** = toilet only, **s** = shower only, **CC** = Credit Card (Visa, MasterCard, Amex).

The first four places are well-located on a quiet street two blocks off the harbor, three blocks from the center, and a six-minute walk from the train station. By car, as you enter town, turn left after King's Knoll Hotel and take first right onto Breadalbane. Each has parking from an alley behind the buildings.

Strathlachlan Guest House is a winner. Mrs. Rena Anderson's place is stocking-feet cozy, crackerjack friendly, and chocolate-box tidy. It's a spacious, uncluttered place with six rooms, solid beds, and a rest-awhile TV lounge (S-£15, D-£30, family deals, entirely smoke-free, 2 Breadalbane Street, Oban, Argyll, tel. 01631/563-861).

Tanglin B&B, next door, is another fine value. Liz and Jim Montgomery offer a bright, nonsmoking, and homey place, TVs in the rooms, and an easygoing atmosphere (S-£15, D-£29, Db-£36, off-season rates and family deals, 3 Strathaven Terrace, Breadalbane Street, tel. 01631/563-247, e-mail: jimtanglin@aol.com).

Gramarvin Guest House is small, comfy, friendly, and quiet (small D-£25, D-£30, Db-£37, Breadalbane Street, tel. 01631/564-622, Mrs. Hill).

Sleepable: Try **Raniven Guest House** (Db-£35–40 with this book, some nonsmoking rooms, Strathlachlan Terrace, tel. 01631/562-713, Jessie Turnbull), **Glengorm B&B** (S-£17, D-£30, £34 in August, firm beds, noisy street, around the corner on Dunollie Road, tel. 01631/565-361, MacColl), and **West Mount B&B**, just up the hill (D-£36, smoke-free rooms, across from lawn bowling on Dalriach Road, tel. 01631/562-884, Christina Adams).

Kimberley Hotel, a few blocks above town, is a stately Victorian mansion—originally a hospital—that is half-elegant, half-spooky. The 17 rooms have fairy-tale furnishings, dark hardwood floors, and modern baths (Db-£50, except Db-£70 in July and August, CC:VMA, just above The Studio restaurant at 13 Dalriach Road, tel. 01631/571-115, fax 01631/571-008, e-mail: reception@kimberley-hotel.demon.co.uk).

Barriemore Hotel is the last place (and best value) on Oban's grand waterfront esplanade. It has a classy, dark, woody, equestrian feel with 13 spacious and comfortable nonsmoking rooms furnished like living rooms (Db-£44–56, grand views, CC:VM, The Esplanade, PA34 5AQ, tel. 01631/566-356, Evelyn and Jim McLean).

Hostels and Dorm Beds in Oban

Oban offers plenty of £10 dorm beds. Your choice: orderly, fun, or spacey. The orderly **IYHF hostel**, on the waterfront esplanade, is in a grand building with a smashing harbor/island view (4- to 16-bed rooms, great facilities and public rooms, closed winter, tel. 01631/562-025). **Oban Backpackers** is laid-back and fun with 6 to 10 bunks per room (fine, central location, five-minute walk from the station on Breadalbane Street, tel. 01631/562-107). The **Jeremy Inglis B&B**, a block from the TI and train station, is least expensive and feels more like a commune than a youth hostel (21 Airds Crescent, tel. 01631/565-065 or 01631/563-064).

Eating in Oban

Oban has plenty of fun eating options. Downtown is full of cheap eateries and pubs serving decent grub: consider the harborfront **Oban Inn** (the oldest building in town) and the **Argyle Hotel Pub** next door.

To mix a folk show inexpensively with dinner, eat at **McTavish's Kitchen**. This huge eating hall is an Oban institution featuring live but tired folk music and dancing nightly (May–September). Like anything so Scottishly clichéd, this is your basic tourist trap filled with English vacationers. The food is inexpensive and edible (£6 basic plate; £7 for good haggis, neeps, and tatties; £13 for a super Scottish multicourse menu). The piping, dancing, and singing happen nightly from 20:30 to 22:30 (mostly a fiddle and two accordians with precious little dancing and bagpiping, the last hour is most interesting, tel. 01631/563-064). The show costs £3 without a meal, £1.50 with dinner, or free with dinner with a coupon from your B&B. No reservations required. Nonsmokers get the best harbor views. Smokers are closest to the stage.

Everyone's favorite nice dinner out is at **The Studio**, a small, candlelit restaurant featuring serious, first-class Scottish cooking (£12 for a full Scottish meal, nightly 17:00–22:00, meals £1 off until 18:30, reservations smart, tel. 01631/562-030). It has great trout, salmon, and a prawn-and-clam chowder that hits the spot on a stormy day.

For a genteel dining experience—pricey but worthwhile for a waterfront splurge—eat at the **Manor House Hotel** (a short drive or taxi ride south of town on the waterfront, Gallanach Road, tel. 01631/562-087).

For creative continental and vegetarian cuisine, consider the **Boxtree Restaurant** (£10 meals, nightly until 22:00, 108 George Street). You'll eat good seafood at **The Waterfront Restaurant** (#1 The Pier, tel. 01631/563-110). For a seafood appetizer drop by the **Local Shellfish** shack at the ferry dock (often free salmon samples, inexpensive coffee, open until the 18:00 boat unloads from Mull—pleasant way to cap off your day trip to the islands).

THE ISLANDS OF IONA AND MULL

For the best one-day look at the dramatic and historic Hebrides island scenery around Oban, take the Iona/Mull tour from Oban (£16, daily 10:00–17:40). Several companies offer the same tour, schedule, and prices from Oban: Bowman & MacDougall's Tours, tel. 01631/563-221; Gordon Grant Tours, tel. 01631/562-842; and Highlands and Islands Tours, tel. 01631/566-999.

Each morning travelers gather on the Oban pier and pile onto the huge Oban–Mull ferry (40 min). On board, if it's a clear day, ask a local to point out Ben Nevis, the tallest mountain in Great Britain. The ferry has a fine cafeteria and a bookshop (though guidebooks are cheaper in Oban). Five minutes before landing on Mull, you'll see the striking Duart castle on the left.

Upon arrival in Mull, you'll find your company's bus for the entertaining and informative 35-mile bus ride across the Isle of Mull (90 min, single-lane road). All drivers spend the entire ride chattering away about life on Mull. They are hardworking local boys who know how to spin a yarn; they make historical trivia fascinating, or at least fun. The Isle of Mull, the third-largest in Scotland, has 300 scenic miles of coastline and castles, and a 3,169-foot-high mountain. Called Ben More ("big hill" in Gaelic), it was once much bigger. The last active volcano in northern Europe, it was 14,000 feet tall—the entire island of Mull—before it blew. Mull has a notably laid-back population. My bus driver reported there are no deaths from stress and only a few from boredom.

On the far side of Mull the caravan of tour buses unloads at a tiny ferry town. The ferry takes about 200 walk-ons. (If there's a big crowd, line up quickly to avoid the 30-minute delay if you don't make the first trip over.) After the 10-minute ride, you wash ashore on sleepy Iona. This tiny island, just three miles by 1.5 miles with a population of about a hundred, is famous as the birth-place of Christianity in Scotland. You'll have about two hours here on your own before you retrace your steps, docking back in Oban by about 17:40. While the day is spectacular in good weather, it's worthwhile in any weather.

Iona's history: St. Columba, an Irish scholar, soldier, priest, and founder of monasteries, got into a small war over the possession of an illegally copied Psalm book. Victorious but sickened by the bloodshed, Columba left Ireland vowing never to return. According to legend, the first bit of land out of sight of his homeland was Iona. He stopped here in 563 and established the abbey.

Columba's monastic community flourished and Iona became the center of Celtic Christianity. Iona missionaries spread the gospel through Scotland and North England while scholarly monks established Iona as a center of art and learning. The Book of Kells—perhaps the finest piece of art from "Dark Age" Europe—was probably made on Iona in the eighth century. The island was so important that it was the legendary burial place for ancient Scottish and Scandinavian kings (including Shakespeare's Macbeth).

Slowly the importance of Iona ebbed. Vikings massacred 68 monks in 803. Fearing more raids, the monks evacuated most of Iona's treasures (including the Book of Kells, which is now in Dublin) to Ireland. Much later, with the Reformation, the abbey was abandoned and most of its finely carved crosses were destroyed. In the 17th century locals used the abbey only as a handy quarry for other building projects.

Iona's population peaked at about 500 in the 1830s. In the 1840s a potato famine hit. In the 1850s a third of the islanders emigrated to Canada or Australia. By 1900 the population was down to 210, and today it's only around 100.

But in our generation a new religious community has given the abbey new life. The Iona community is an ecumenical community of men and women seeking new ways of living the Gospel in today's world, with a focus on worship and peace and justice issues. A center on the island welcomes guests (tel. 01681/700-404, Web site: www.iona.org.uk, e-mail: ionacomm@iona.org.uk).

A pristine light and a thoughtful peace pervade the stark car-free island and its tiny community. While the present abbey, nunnery, and graveyard go back to the 13th century, much of what you'll see was rebuilt in the last century. But with bouyant clouds bouncing playfully off of distant bluffs, sparkling white sand crescents, and lone tourists camped thoughtfully atop huge rocks just looking out to sea, it's a place perfect for meditation. Climb a peak—nothing's higher than 300 feet above the sea.

The village, Baile Mor, has a shop, tiny eateries, enough beds, and a meager heritage center. The Finlay Ross Shop rents bikes (near ferry dock, £3.50/hr, £8/day).

Sleeping in Iona: Enjoy the serenity of Iona by spending the night. When the day-trippers leave, you'll find that special peace. **Argyll Hotel**, built in 1868, sits proud and classy overlooking the waterfront with basic rooms above a fine grassy yard and public spaces (17 rooms, Db-£82–90, CC:VM, tel. 01681/700-334, fax

01681/700-510). **Finlay B&B** rents 11 basic rooms immediately in front of the ferry dock (D-£42, Db-£46, reception at the Finaly Ross Shop, tel. 01681/700-357, fax 01681/700-562).

Other Island Tours—The Oban tour companies offer an array of tours. You can spend an entire day on Mull. Those more interested in nature than church history will enjoy trips to the wildly scenic Isle of Staffa with Fingal's Cave. Trips to Treshnish Island (brimming with puffins, seals, and other critters) cause nature lovers to say "awesome" a lot.

Transportation Connections—Oban

Oban to: Inverness (6 buses/day, 4 hrs), **Glasgow** (3 trains/day, 3 hrs). Ferries fan out from Oban to the southern Hebrides. Train info: tel. 0345/484-950. Bus info: tel. 01631/562-856. Caledonian MacBrayne Ferry info: tel. 01631/566-688.

Transportation Connections—Glasgow

Glasgow is one of the region's major transportation hubs.

Glasgow to: Edinburgh (2 trains/hrly, 1 hr), **Inverness** (hrly buses, 4.5 hrs), **Penrith** (9 trains/day, 2 hrs; 6 buses/day from Penrith to Keswick, Lake District), **London** (8 trains/day, 6 hrs). Train info: tel. 0345/484-950.

THE HIGHLANDS: FROM OBAN TO INVERNESS

Discover Glencoe's dark secrets in the Weeping Glen where Britain's highest peak, Ben Nevis, keeps its head in the clouds. Explore the locks and lochs of the Caledonian Canal while the Loch Ness monster plays hide-and-seek. Hear the music of the Highlands in Inverness and the echo of muskets in Culloden, where the English put down Bonnie Prince Charlie and any hopes for Scottish independence.

Getting Around the Highlands

The trains are scenic, but if schedules frustrate, take the bus. Six buses a day connect the towns from Oban to Inverness (four hours). Ask at the station to see how schedules work for sight-hopping. One great option is to ride with the postman. The post bus or car allows people on its route for a nominal fee. While locals do this to get somewhere, tourists do it to chat with the postman—great gossip on the entire neighborhood! This works well in Glencoe.

Sights—Scottish Highlands

▲▲**Glencoe**—This valley is the essence of the wild, powerful, and stark beauty of the Highlands (and, I think, excuses the hurried tourist from needing to go north of Inverness). Along with its scenery, Glencoe offers a good dose of bloody clan history.

Oban, Islands, and Highlands

Glencoe town is just a line of houses. One is a tiny thatched building jammed with local history. The huggable **Glencoe and North Lorn Fold Museum**, purely a homegrown effort, is filled with humble exhibits gleaned from the town's old closets and attics. For instance, when one house was being rethatched, its owner found a cache of old rifles hidden there from the British Redcoats after the disastrous battle of Culloden (£1, Monday–Saturday 10:00–17:30, closed Sunday).

A couple miles into the dramatic valley you'll find the **Visitors Centre**. While little more than a café, WC, and bookshop, it does show a 14-minute video about the 1692 massacre when the Redcoats killed the sleeping MacDonalds and the valley got its nickname, "The Weeping Glen" (50p, daily 9:30–17:30, shorter hours or closed off-season, just east of town on A82, tel. 01855/811-307).

Walks: For a steep one-mile hike, climb the **Devil's Staircase** (trail leaves from A82, eight miles east of Glencoe). For a three-hour hike, ask at the Visitors Centre about walking to the **Lost Valley of the MacDonalds** (trail leaves from A82, three miles east of Glencoe).

Sleeping in Glencoe: Many find Glencoe more interesting than Oban for an overnight stop. In Glencoe village, Arthur Smith runs the **Cala Sona B&B**, aptly named "haven of happiness" in Gaelic. He entertains his guests with a peat fire, ghost stories, and tales of the Glencoe massacre (S-£15, D-£30, less if necessary, on the main street, tel. 01855/811-314). If Arthur's place is full, try the **Mack-Leven House B&B** (D-£30, Db-£32 with this book, family deals, smoke-free rooms, Lorn Drive, Glencoe, tel. 01855/811-215, Mackintosh family) or **Greenhill B&B** (D-£28, flexible on price when slow, nonsmoking, just before Cala Sona B&B, tel. 01855/811-391, Ann Blake). The nearest TI is in Ballachulish (tel. 01855/811-296).

Ben Nevis—From Fort William, take a peek at Britain's highest peak, Ben Nevis (over 4,400 feet). Thousands of visitors walk to its summit each year. On a clear day you can admire it from a distance. Scotland's only mountain cable cars can take you to the not-very-lofty, 2,150-foot level of a nearby peak (£6.50, daily 10:00–17:00, later in summer, 15-minute ride, signposted on A82, tel. 01397/705-825).

▲**Caledonian Canal**—Three lochs and a series of canals cut Scotland in two. Oich, Lochy, and Ness were connected in the early 1800s by the great British engineer Thomas Telford. For a good look at the locks, see "Neptune's Staircase," where you'll find a park built along a series of 10 locks (two miles north of Fort William, detour one mile on A830). Fort Augustus is another good lock stop. Traveling between Fort William and Inverness (60 miles), you'll follow Telford's work—20 miles of canals and locks between 40 miles of lakes, raising ships from sea level to 51 feet (Ness) to 93 feet (Lochy) to 106 feet (Oich).

Loch Ness—I'll admit it. I had my zoom lens out and my eyes on the water. The local tourist industry thrives on the legend of the Loch Ness monster. It's a thrilling thought, and there have been several seemingly reliable "sightings" (monks, policemen, and sonar images). The loch, 24 miles long, less than a mile wide, and the third-deepest in Europe, is deepest near the Urquhart Castle. Most monster sightings are in this area.

The Nessie commercialization is so tacky that there are two "official" Loch Ness Exhibition Centres within 100 yards of each other. Each has a tour-bus parking lot and more square footage devoted to their shop than to the exhibit. The exhibits are fascinating but way overpriced. The exhibition in the big stone mansion (closest to Inverness) is the better one, with a 40-minute series of video bits on the geological and historical environment that bred the monster story and the various searches (£4.50, daily 9:00–20:30). The other (closest to Oban) is a high school–quality photo report followed by the 30-minute "We believe in the Loch Ness monster" movie, featuring credible-sounding locals explaining what they saw and a review of modern Nessie searches (£4, daily 9:00–19:30). The nearby Urquhart Castle ruins are gloriously situated with a view of virtually the entire lake (£3.50, daily 9:30–18:30, tel 01456/450-551). It's an empty shell of a castle with crowds and parking problems.

▲**Culloden Battlefield**—Scottish troops under Bonnie Prince Charlie were defeated here by the English in 1746. This last land battle fought on British soil spelled the end of Jacobite resistance and the fall of the clans. Wandering the battlefield, you feel that something terrible happened here. Locals still bring flowers and speak of "46" as if it were this century.

The excellent Visitors Centre shows a stirring 16-minute audiovisual every 20 minutes. Wander through a furnished old cottage and around the memorial battlegrounds (£3, daily 9:00–18:00, off-season 10:00–16:00, closed January, good tearoom, tel. 01463/790-607).

INVERNESS

The only sizable town in the north of Scotland, with 42,000 people, Inverness is pleasantly located on a river at the base of a castle (not worth a look) with a free little museum (worth a look, cheap café). Its **Highland Music Museum** traces local music from heroic warrior songs to Gaelic rock (£2 to scan six hours of music, daily 10:00–17:00, until 20:00 in July and August, closed Mondays, live bagpiping at 17:00 during summer, Balnain House, tel. 01463/715-757). Check out the bustling pedestrian downtown and central TI (tel. 01463/234-353). Ask about the very informative "Gordon's" minibus tours to Loch Ness (£11, most days 10:30–16:30). Guide Friday buses connect Inverness and Culloden. Trains link Inverness, Pitlochry, and Edinburgh (9/day, 3.5 hrs, tel. 01463/238-924), and buses run betwen Oban and Inverness (6/day, 4 hrs, tel. 01463/233-371). Consider the Scottish evening at the Cummings Hotel.

Sleeping in Inverness
(£1 = about $1.70, tel. code: 01463)

These rooms are all a short walk from the train station and town center. The first two are on a quiet street just up the steps from the pedestrian High Street. **Ardconnel House** is tasteful, bright, spacious, and classy (Sb-£22, D-£38, Db-£42, CC:VM, family deals, nonsmoking, TVs in rooms, 21 Ardconnel Street, IV2 3EU, tel. & fax 01463/240-455, Mrs. MacKenzie). **The Hollies** is much simpler, but still a fine value, with only three rooms and sturdy beds (S-£16, D-£32, T-£48, family deals, 24 Ardconnel Street, tel. 01463/231-291, run by friendly and helpful Mrs. Proudfoot). **The Melness Guest House** is also a good value with a cozy lounge and three fine rooms (D-£38, Db-£46, less off-season, near the hostel at 8 Old Edinburgh Road, tel. 01463/220-963). For £10 beds in six-bed rooms downtown within a 10-minute walk from the train station, consider the **IYHF hostel** (up the street from the castle on Victoria Drive, tel. 01463/231-771) and the much more friendly and laid-back **Inverness Student Hotel** (8 Culduthel Road, tel. 01463/236-556).

PITLOCHRY

This likable tourist town, famous for its whiskey, makes an enjoyable overnight stop. Its cute **Edradour Scotch Distillery**—the smallest in Scotland—offers a free one-hour guided tour, 10-minute audiovisual show, and, of course, tasting (3/hrly, Monday–Saturday 9:30–17:00, summer Sundays 12:00–16:15, a lovely 20-minute walk through the forest from downtown, tel. 01796/472-095). The big **Blair Athol Distillery** gives £2 hour-long tours with a sample at the end (2/hrly, Monday–Saturday 9:30–16:15, Sunday 12:00–16:15, half-mile from town, tel. 01796/472-234). Pitlochry also has plenty of forest walks and a salmon ladder (jumping May and June, free viewing area, three-minute walk from town). The town theater offers a different play every night (£10). For a unique look at pressed heather stems jewelry, tour Heather-gems (behind the TI). The helpful TI is open daily from 9:00 to 20:00 (tel. 01796/472-215).

Sleeping in Pitlochry
(£1 = about $1.70, tel. code: 01796)

Try **Craigroyston House**, a big Victorian country house with eight smoke-free Laura Ashley–style rooms run by charming Gretta Maxwell (Db–£40–54, flexing with demand, next to the church and TI at 2 Lower Oakfield, PH16 5HQ, tel. & fax 01796/472-053). Mrs. Maxwell can find you another B&B if her place is full. For a cheaper, simpler, more rural alternative, drive two miles south of town on the old A9 to the **Donavourd Farmhouse B&B** (D–£30, evening meals, near the Edradour distillery, tel. 01796/472-254, Mrs. Somersal). Pitlochry's fine **hostel** is on Knockard Road above the main street (£8 bunks, tel. 01796/472-308).

Route Tips for Drivers

Lake District to Oban (220 miles): From Keswick, take A66 for 18 miles to M6 and speed nonstop north (via Penrith and Carlisle), crossing Hadrian's Wall into Scotland. The road stays great, becoming the M74 south of Glasgow. To slip quickly through Glasgow, leave M74 at Junction 4 onto M73, following signs to M8/Glasgow. Leave M73 at Junction 2, exiting onto M8. Stay on M8 west through Glasgow, exit on Junction 30, cross the Erskine Bridge (60p), and turn left on A82, following signs to Crianlarich. (For a scenic drive through Glasgow, take exit 17 off M8 and stay on A82 toward Dumbarton.) You'll soon be driving along scenic Loch Lomond. The first picnic turnout has the best lake views, lots of benches, a grassy park, and a kids' playground. Halfway up the loch, at Tarbet, take the "tourist route" left onto A83, drive along saltwater Loch Long toward Inveraray via Rest-and-Be-Thankful Pass. (This colorful name comes from the 1880s, when second- and third-class coach passengers got out and pushed the coach and first-class passengers up the hill.) Stop in **Inveraray,** a lovely castle-town on Loch Fyne. Park near the pier. (TI tel. 01499/302-063.) The town jail, now a museum, is a "19th-century living prison" (£4.50, daily 9:30–18:00, last admission 17:00, tel. 01499/302-381). Leaving Inveraray, drive through a gate (at the Woolen Mill) to A819, through Glen Aray, and along scenic Loch Awe. A85 takes you into Oban.

Oban to Glencoe (45 miles) to Loch Ness (75 miles) to Inverness (20 miles) to Edinburgh (150 miles): Barring traffic, you'll make great time on good, mostly two-lane roads. Americans are generally timid about passing. Study the British. Be careful, but if you don't pass, diesel fumes and large trucks might be your memory of this drive. From Oban follow the coastal A828 toward Fort William. At Loch Leven and Ballachulish Village, leave A828, taking A82 into Glencoe. Drive through the village up the valley (Glencoe) for 10 minutes for a grand view and a chance to hear a bagpiper in the wind—Highland buskers. At the top of the valley you hit the vast Rannoch Moor—500 square and desolate miles with barely enough decent land to graze a sheep. Then make a U-turn and return through Glencoe. Continue north on A82, over the bridge, past Fort William toward Loch Ness. Follow the Caledonian Canal on A82 for 60 miles, stopping at Loch Ness, then continuing on A82 to Inverness.

Leaving Inverness, follow signs to A9 (south toward Perth). Just as you leave Inverness, detour four miles east off A9 on B9006 to visit the Culloden Battlefield Visitors Centre. Back on A9 it's a wonderfully speedy and very scenic highway (A9, M90, A90) all the way to Edinburgh. If traffic is light and your foot is heavy, you can drive from Inverness to Edinburgh in three hours.

For a scenic shortcut, head north only as far as Glencoe (Loch Ness is not much to see), then cut over to Edinburgh via Rannoch Moor and Tyndrum. To get to the Edinburgh B&Bs, see driving instructions in Edinburgh chapter.

DUBLIN

With reminders of its stirring history and rich culture on every corner, Ireland's capital and largest city is a sightseer's delight. Dublin's fair city will have you humming "Alive, alive-O."

Founded as a Viking trading settlement in the ninth century, Dublin grew to be a center of wealth and commerce second only to London in the United Kingdom. Dublin, the seat of English rule in Ireland for 700 years, was the heart of a "civilized" Anglo-Irish area (eastern Ireland) known as "the Pale." Anything "beyond the Pale" was considered uncultured and almost barbaric . . . purely Irish.

The Golden Age of English Dublin was the 18th century. Britain was on a roll and Dublin was Britain's second city. Largely rebuilt during this Georgian era, Dublin became an elegant and cultured capital. Everything was OK until nationalism and human rights got in the way. The ideas of the French Revolution inspired Irish intellectuals to buck British rule and, after the revolt of 1798, life in Dublin was never quite the same. But the 18th century left a lasting imprint on the city. Georgian (that's British for neoclassical) squares and boulevards gave the city a grand elegance. The National Museum, National Gallery, and many government buildings are in the Georgian section of town. Few buildings (notably St. Patrick's Cathedral and Christchurch Cathedral) predate this Georgian period.

In the 19th century, with the closing of the Irish Parliament, the famine, and the beginnings of the struggle for independence, Dublin was treated and felt more like a colony than a partner. The tension culminated in the Rising of 1916 and the battle that followed. While many of Dublin's grand streets were left in ruins, the city emerged as the capital of the only former colony in Europe.

While bullet-pocked buildings and dramatic statues keep

Ireland

memories of Ireland's recent struggle for independence alive, the city is looking to a bright future. Visitors enjoy a big-town cultural scene wrapped in a small-town smile.

Planning Your Time

On a two-week trip through Ireland, Dublin deserves three nights and two days. Consider this sightseeing plan:

Day 1: 9:30—Dublin Experience, 10:30—Trinity College walk, 11:00—Book of Kells and Old Library, 12:00—Browse Grafton Street, lunch there or picnic on St. Stephen's Green, 13:30—National Museum, 15:00—Historical town walk, 17:00—Return to hotel, rest, dinner, 19:30—Evening walk (literary or musical), 22:00—Irish music in Temple Bar area.

Day 2: 10:00—Kilmainham Jail, 12:00—Guinness Brewery tour, 13:30—Lunch (with a faint buzz), 15:00—Tour Dublin Castle, Evening—Catch a play or concert.

Orientation (tel. code: 01)

Greater Dublin sprawls with about 1 million people—nearly a third of the country's population. But the center of touristic interest is a tight triangle between O'Connell Bridge, St. Stephen's Green, and Christchurch Cathedral. Within this triangle you'll find Trinity College (Book of Kells), Grafton Street (top pedestrian shopping zone), Temple Bar (trendy nightlife center), Dublin Castle, and the hub of most city tours and buses.

The River Liffey cuts the town in two. Focus on the southern half (where nearly all your sightseeing will take place). Dublin's main drag, O'Connell Street (near the Abbey Theater and outdoor produce market), stretches from the very central O'Connell Bridge north of the river. Over the river this main city axis continues—mostly as Grafton Street—to St. Stephen's Green. Only the Kilmainham Jail and the Guinness Brewery (both west of the center) are outside your home triangle.

Tourist Information

The TI fills an old church on Suffolk Street (a block off Grafton Street). While packed with tourists, promotional brochures, an American Express office, a café, and traditional knickknacks, it's short on hard info. Less crowded but equally helpful TI branches are on Baggot Street and at the airport (daily 8:00–22:00). To talk to the TI on the phone, you'll pay 60p per minute (1-850-230-230)—welcome to Dublin. The TI gives a free newspaper with a lousy map, lots of advertisements, and the fliers that fill racks all over town. The best extensive publication they offer is *Dublin's Top Visitor Attractions* (which you can buy for £2.50 at the TI bookshop without any wait). This has a map and the latest on all the town's sights (many more than I list here). For a schedule of happenings in town, buy the excellent *In Dublin* at any newsstand (fortnightly, £1.95).

Helpful Hints

Cyber Cafés: On the north side of town, try Global Internet Café (£5/hr, 8 Lower O'Connell St., tel. 01/878-0295). On the south side, try Planet Cybercafé (£4.50/hr, 23 South Great George's Street, tel. 01/679-0583).

Bikes: Bikes can be rented at Dublin Bike Hire (27 North Great Georges Street, tel. 01/878-8473).

Arrival in Dublin

By Train: Trains arrive at Heuston Station (serving the west and southwest) on the west end of town. Dublin's second train station, Connolly Station (serving the north, northwest, and Rosslare), is closer to the center—a 10-minute walk from O'Connell Bridge. Each station has a luggage-check facility.

Bus 90 connects both train stations and the bus station and the city center (60p flat fee, 6/hrly, runs along river).

By Bus: Bus Eireann, Ireland's national bus company, uses the Busaras Central Bus Station next to Connolly Station (catch bus 90 to the city center).

By Ferry: Irish Ferries dock at the mouth of the River Liffey (near the town center) while the Stena Line docks at Dun Laoghaire (easy DART train connections into Dublin, at least 3/hrly, 15 min).

By Plane: From the airport, milk-run buses 41 and 41C go to O'Connell Bridge (£1.10, 3/hrly). The faster Airlink direct bus connects the airport with the Heuston train station and Busaras bus station near Connolly Station (£2.50, 4/hrly, 30 min). Taxis from the airport into Dublin cost about £10.

Getting Around Dublin

You'll do most of Dublin on foot. Big green buses are cheap and cover the city thoroughly. Most lines start at the four Quays nearest O'Connell Bridge. Tell the driver where you're going and he'll ask for 60p (one to five stops) or 80p (5 to 10 stops). The bus office at 59 Upper O'Connell Street has free "route network" maps and sells bus passes (one-day pass-£3.30 adults, £5.50 per family, four-day adult Explorer pass-£10.00, bus information tel. 01/873-4222). DART trains connect Dublin with Dun Laoghaire (ferry terminal and recommended B&Bs, at least 3/hrly, 15 min, £1.10). Taxis seem honest, and they are plentiful, friendly, and good sources of information (£4 for most downtown rides).

Tours of Dublin

While the physical treasures of Dublin are mediocre by European standards, the city has a fine story to tell and people with a natural knack for telling it. It's a good town for walking tours—and the competition is fierce for your business. You'll find pamphlets touting creative walks all over town. There are medieval walks, literary walks, Georgian Dublin walks, and more. The two evening walks are great ways to meet other travelers.

Historical Walking Tour—This is your best introductory walk. A group of hardworking history graduates—many who claim to have done more than just kiss the Blarney Stone—fill Dublin's basic historic strip (Trinity College, Old Parliament House, Dublin Castle, and Christchurch Cathedral) with the story of their city from its Viking origin to the present. You stand in front of buildings that aren't much to see but are lots to talk about and listen to your guide's story. Guides talk at length about "the Troubles" and the roots of Ireland's struggle with Britain (£5, two hours, depart from gate of Trinity College, daily 11:00, 12:00, 15:00; Saturday and Sunday only 12:00 in winter; tel. 01/878-0227).

Jameson Literary Pub Crawl—Two actors take 30 or so tourists on a walk stopping at four pubs. Half the time is spent enjoying their entertaining banter which introduces the novice to the high *craic* (conversation) of Joyce, O'Casey, and Yeats. The 2.5-hour tour is punctuated with 20-minute pub breaks (free time). It can be great fun socially, but the content suffers. Meet any night at 19:30 (plus Sunday at noon) in the Duke Pub off Grafton on Duke Street (£6, runs three nights a week in winter, tel. 01/670-5602).

Traditional Irish-Music Pub Crawl—This is like the Literary pub crawl but features music. You meet at 19:30 at Gogarty's Pub (in the Temple Bar area) and spend 20 minutes in the upstairs rooms of four pubs listening to two musicians talk about, play, and sing traditional Irish music. While having only two musicians makes the music a bit thin and Irish music aficionados will tell you you're better off just finding a good session, the evening—while touristy—is not gimmicky. The musicians demonstrate four instruments and really enjoy introducing rookies to their art (£6 plus beer, nightly May–October, weekends only in winter, allow 2.5 hours, tel. 01/478-0191).

Hop On/Hop Off Bus Tours—Several companies offer the basic center-of-Dublin orientation. Dublin City Tour (£7, tel. 01/873-4222) and Guide Friday (£7, tel. 01/676-5377) do identical 90-minute circuits of the town allowing you to hop on and hop off at your choice of 10 stops (two buses/hour—mostly topless—with running commentaries; they go to Guinness Brewery but not to Kilmainham Jail). Just hop on and pay the driver. Your ticket's good for the entire day. Buses, which leave about every 10 minutes from about 9:30 to 18:00, are especially enjoyable for photographers on sunny days. One ticket gets you on either company's buses.

Sights—Dublin's Trinity College
▲**Trinity College**—Started in 1592 by Queen Elizabeth I to establish a Protestant way of thinking about God, Trinity has long been Ireland's most prestigious college. Originally the student body was limited to rich, Protestant males. Women were admitted in 1903 and Catholics, while allowed entrance by the school much earlier, were given permission to study at Trinity in the 1970s. Today half of Trinity's 11,000 students are women and 70 percent are culturally Catholic (although only about 20 percent of Irish youth are churchgoing).

▲**Trinity College Tour**—Inside the gate of Trinity, students organize and lead 30-minute tours of their campus. You'll get a rundown on the mostly Georgian architecture, a peek at student life, both in the early days and today, and mostly enjoy a chance to hang out with a witty Irish college kid as he talks about his school (daily 10:00–15:30, the £4.50 tour fee includes the £3.50 fee to see the Book of Kells where the tour leaves you).

▲▲▲**Book of Kells/Trinity Old Library**—The 65-meter-long main chamber of the Old Library (from 1732) is home to an original copy of the 1916 Proclamation of the Irish Republic,

Dublin

WRITER'S MUSEUM ■

GREAT DENMARK ST.

STREET

PARNELL

←HEUSTON STN.
(TO GALWAY)

MARKET→

HENRY ST.

CONNOLLY STN.

TALBOT ST.

CHRISTCHURCH CATHEDRAL

POST ABBEY ST.

ABBEY THEATRE

O'CONNELL BRIDGE

DUBLINIA→

RIVER

BUSARAS BUS STN.

LIFFEY

TO GUINNESS BREWERY & KILLMAINHAM JAIL

JURY'S INN

■ TEMPLE BAR

COLLEGE

TOWNSEND ST.

TARA ST. STN.

VIKING ADVENTURE

TOURIST INFO

TRINITY COLLEGE

DUBLIN CASTLE

NASSAU ST.

PEARSE STN.

NAT'L GALLERY

GRAFTON ST.

✳ NOT TO SCALE—
O'CONNELL BRIDGE
TO WRITER'S MUSEUM
OR ST STEPHEN'S GREEN
IS A 15 MIN. WALK

ST. STEPHEN'S GREEN

NAT'L MUSEUM

MERRION SQUARE

TO DUN LAOGHAIRE

BAGGOT ST.

TO TOURIST INFO & BALLSBRIDGE B&B'S

the oldest Irish harp (from the 15th century), and, stacked to its towering ceiling, 200,000 of the library's oldest books. The artistic prize of the library—and all Ireland—is the magnificent Book of Kells, stored in the treasury. A first-class exhibit puts the 680-page illuminated manuscript in its historical and cultural context and prepares you for the original book and other precious manuscripts in the collection.

Written on vellum (baby sheepskin) in the ninth century— probably by Irish monks in Iona (Scotland)—and taken to the Irish monastery at Kells in 806 after a series of Viking raids, this enthusiastically decorated copy of the four gospels is arguably the finest piece of art from what is generally called the Dark Ages. It shows how monastic life in this far fringe of Europe was far from dark. The book has been bound into four separate volumes. At any given time, two of the gospels are on display. You'll see four richly decorated 1,200-year-old pages—two text and two decorated cover pages—under glass (£3.50, at Trinity College Library, Monday– Saturday 9:30–17:00, Sunday 9:30–16:30, shorter hours off-season,

tel. 01/608-1171). The library also displays the Book of Armagh
(A.D. 807) and the Book of Durrow (A.D. 680), neither of which
can be checked out.

▲▲**The Dublin Experience**—Shown in a modern building next
to the Trinity Old Library, this 40-minute video giving a historic
introduction to Dublin is one more tourist movie with the sound
turned up. It's good—offering a fine sweeping introduction to the
story of Ireland—but pricey and riding on the coattails of the
Book of Kells (£3, save a little with a combo Kells/video ticket,
daily 10:00–17:00 on the hour, in the modern arts building next to
Trinity College Library).

More Sights—Dublin

▲▲**Dublin Castle**—Built on the spot of the first Viking fortress,
this castle was the seat of British rule in Ireland for 700 years
(until 1922). Located where the Poddle and Liffey Rivers came
together making a black pool ("*dubh linn*" in Irish), Dublin Castle
was the official residence of the Viceroy, who implemented the
will of the British royalty. Today it's used for fancy state and char-
ity functions. The 45-minute tours offer a room-by-room walk
through the lavish state apartments of this most English of Irish
palaces (£2.50, about 4/hrly, Monday–Friday 10:00–17:00, weekends 14:00–17:00, tel. 01/677-7129). The tour finishes with a look
at the foundations of the Norman tower and the best remaining
chunk of the 13th-century town wall.

▲**Dublin's Viking Adventure**—This really is an adventure. You
start in a box of seats that transforms into a Viking ship. Your chieftain joins you and suddenly you're in a storm, waves splash, smoke
rolls, and you land in a kind of Viking summer camp where you
spend 30 minutes being shuttled from one friendly original Dubliner
to the next (a trader, a sassy maiden, a monk building a church, and
so on). A short film about the Vikings follows with a look at artifacts
recently uncovered in the adjacent excavation sight. It feels hokey,
but the cast is certainly hardworking and you leave feeling if not
having visited a Viking town, at least having visited the set for a
B-grade Viking movie. It's on Essex Street a block off the riverside
Essex Quay in Temple Bar—exactly where the Vikings established
their first Dublin settlement in 841 (£4.75, Tuesday–Saturday
10:00–16:30, closed Sunday and Monday, tel. 01/679-6040).

Dublinia—This tries and fails to be a "bridge to Dublin's medieval
past." The amateurish look at the medieval town starts with a goofy
12-minute Walkman tour followed by a few rooms of medieval
exhibits, and finishes with a hard-to-follow movie dramatizing
medieval political wrangling. Possibly entertaining for a school field
trip, it just isn't worth the £4 or time (daily 10:00–17:00, less in winter, tel. 01/679-4611). The ticket does get you a tower-top city view
and into Christchurch Cathedral (£1 otherwise).

Christchurch Cathedral—The oldest building in Dublin, the cathedral marks the spot where the Vikings established their town on the river. The first church here was built of wood in 1038 by King Sitric. The present structure dates from a mix of periods: Norman, Gothic, and mostly Victorian neo-Gothic (1870s restoration work). Because of its British past, neither of Dublin's two top churches are Catholic. Christchurch Cathedral and the nearby St. Patrick's Cathedral are both from the Church of Ireland. In Catholic Ireland they feel hollow and are more famous than visit-worthy.

▲▲▲**National Museum**—Showing off the treasures of Ireland from the Stone Age to the 20th century, this museum is wonderfully digestible under one dome. Ireland's Bronze Age gold fills the center. The prehistoric Ireland exhibit rings the gold, and in a corner you'll find the treasury with the most famous pieces (brooches, chalices, and other examples of Celtic metalwork) and an 18-minute video giving an overview of Irish art through the 13th century. Jumping way ahead, a special corridor features *The Road to Independence* with guns, letters, and death masks recalling the fitful birth of the "Terrible Beauty" (1900–1921 with a focus on the Easter Rising of 1916). The best Viking artifacts in town are upstairs (museum is free, Tuesday–Saturday 10:00–17:00, Sunday 14:00–17:00, closed Monday, between Trinity College and St. Stephen's Green on Kildare Street, tel. 01/677-7444). Greatest-hits tours are given several times a day (£1, 45 minutes, call for schedule).

National Gallery—Along with a hall featuring the work of top Irish painters, this has Ireland's best collection of paintings by the European masters. It's impressive—unless you've been to London or Paris (free, Monday–Saturday 10:00–17:30, Thursday until 20:30, Sunday 14:00–17:00, tel. 01/661-5133).

Streets, Squares, and Parks—Dublin
▲**Grafton Street**—Once filled with noisy traffic, today Grafton Street is Dublin's liveliest pedestrian shopping mall. You'll find colorful pubs, fancy shops, singing buskers, and lots of browsers. The Powerscourt Townhouse Shopping Centre (nearby on William Street South) is a hit with shoppers. Grafton Street connects Trinity College with St. Stephen's Green.

▲**St. Stephen's Green**—This city park, originally a medieval commons, was enclosed in 1664 and gradually surrounded with fine Georgian buildings. Today it provides 22 acres of grassy refuge for Dubliners.

Merrion Square—This square offers an insider's look at Georgian Dublin. Tour the carefully restored house at **Number 29 Lower Fitzwilliam Street** for a walk through a Dublin home in 1790 (£2.50, Tuesday–Saturday 10:00–17:00, Sunday 14:00–17:00,

closed Monday). Notice the fine doors around the square—a Dublin trademark—and the elegant Georgian knobs and knockers.
▲**O'Connell Street and surroundings**—Dublin's grandest street leads from O'Connell Bridge through the heart of north Dublin. Since the 1740s it's been a 45-meter-wide promenade. Ever since the first O'Connell Bridge connected it to the Trinity side of town in 1794, it's been Dublin's main drag. The street, while lined with fast-food and souvenir shops, echoes with history. Much of the fighting during the 1916 Easter Rising and the Civil War a few years later took place here. The imposing **General Post Office** is where Patrick Pearse read the Proclamation of Irish Independence. The GPO building itself—a kind of Irish Alamo—was the rebel headquarters and scene of a five-day bloody siege during the Rising. While there's little to see, its facade remains pockmarked with bullet holes.

The statues lining the street celebrate great figures in Ireland's fight for independence. One monument that didn't—a tall column crowned by a statue of the British hero of Trafalgar, Admiral Nelson—was blown up in 1966 as locals celebrated the 50th anniversary of the Rising.

Make a point to get away from tourists' Dublin. A good way to do that is to stroll the smaller streets north of the Liffey. Just a block west of O'Connell Street, the **Moore Street Market** is a colorful commotion of produce and hawkers. For workaday Dublin, the long pedestrian mall of Mary Street, Henry Street, and Talbot Street is a people-watchers' delight.

Explore. The prestigious **Abbey Theatre**, now a modern, ugly building, is still the much-loved home of the Irish National Theater (a block off the river on Abbey Street). **St. Mary's Pro-Cathedral** is the leading Catholic church in town, but curiously not a cathedral since Christchurch was made one in the 12th century (the pope chose to ignore the fact that it hasn't been Catholic for centuries). The Georgian **Parnell Square** has a Garden of Remembrance honoring the victims of the 1916 Rising.

The **Dublin Writers' Museum** is a must for anyone interested in Irish literature; it features the lives and works of Dublin's greats (£3, daily 10:00–18:00, 18 Parnell Square North, tel. 01/872-2077). With hometown wits such as Swift, Yeats, Joyce, and Shaw, literary fans will have a checklist of residences and memorials to see.

▲▲**Temple Bar**—For many visitors the heart of Dublin is its hot and much-promoted nightlife center, the Temple Bar district. While promoted as Dublin's "Left Bank," it's actually on the right bank (as central as can be and just south of the river). It's a pedestrians-only hive of creative energy day and night. The central Meeting House Square (just off Essex Street) hosts free street theater and is surrounded by interesting cultural centers. For a listing of events, visit the Temple Bar Information Centre (Eustace Street, tel. 01/671-5717). Trendy shops, cafés, theaters, galleries, pubs with live music, and restaurants (Italian, American, and even Irish) vie for your attention. Rather than follow particular recommendations, simply wander the main drag and venture down a few side lanes to see what looks good. Touristy **Gallagher's Boxty House** is a good bet for traditional Irish food (call to get your name on the waiting list at peak times, 01/677-2762). You'd eat their boxty (a stuffed dinner pancake) or Irish stew in anticipation of a famine. The **Bad Ass Café** remains as popular as can be (students-in-a-warehouse ambience, vegetarian and Italian). Pub grub abounds. (To get some folk music away from the tourist crowds, walk five minutes up the river to **Merchants Quay** where, on Lower Bridge Street, you'll find the Merchants Pub and the Brazen Head.) The pedestrian-only Ha' Penny Bridge, named for the half-pence toll originally levied from those who walked it, leads over the Liffey to Temple Bar. ("*Bar*" means a walkway along the river.)

Sights—Outer Dublin

The Jail and the Guinness Brewery are the only sights outside of the old center. Combine these in one visit.

▲▲▲**Kilmainham Gaol (Jail)**—Opened in 1796 as the Dublin County Jail and a debtors' prison and considered a model in its day, it was used frequently as a political prison by the British. Many of those who fought for Irish independence were held or executed here, including leaders of the rebellions of 1798, 1803, 1848, 1867, and 1916 (most notably Robert Emmett and Charles Stewart Parnell). The last prisoner to be held here was Eamon de Valera (later president of Ireland). He was released on July 16, 1924, the day Kilmainham was finally shut down. The buildings, virtually in ruins, were restored in the 1960s. Today it's a shrine to the Nathan Hales of Ireland.

Your visit starts with an excellent exhibit on Ireland's fight for independence, followed by a 30-minute video. Then a guide shows you around for another 30 minutes. Touring the cells and places of execution while hearing tales of terrible colonialism and heroic patriotism—alongside Irish schoolkids who know these names well—is moving. Finally the museum explains Victorian prison life and the battle for independence. Don't miss the dimly lit hall off the second floor displaying the stirring last letters patriots sent to loved ones hours before facing the firing squad (£3, daily 9:30–18:00, tours on the hour except last tour at 16:45; off-season Sunday–Friday 10:00–17:00, closed Saturday; £4 taxi, bus #51 or #79 from Aston Quay, tel. 01/453-5984).

▲**Guinness Brewery**—A visit to the Guinness Hop Store is almost a pilgrimage for many. The home of Ireland's national beer welcomes visitors (for £4) with a museum, video, and drink. Arthur Guinness began brewing the famous stout here in 1759. By 1868 it was the biggest brewery in the world. Today the sprawling brewery fills several city blocks. Around the world Guinness brews more than 10 million glasses a day. You can learn as much or as little about the brewing process as you like. Highlights are the cooperage (with old film clips showing the master wood-kegmakers plying their now extinct trade) and a display of the brewery's clever ads. The video is a well-done ad for the brew that makes you feel almost patriotic as you run down to the sample bar to turn in your coupons for a pint of the real thing (£4, Monday–Saturday 9:30–17:00, Sunday 10:30–16:30, enter on Crane Street off Thomas Street, bus #78A from Aston Quay near O'Connell Bridge, or bus 123 from Dame Street and O'Connell Street, tel. 01/453-6700 ext. 5155). Hop on, hop off bus tours stop here. (Why is there no museum of Irish alcoholism, which is a serious but rarely discussed problem in this land where the social world seems to float in a sea of beer?)

Entertainment and Theater in Dublin

Ireland produced some of the finest writers in both English and Gaelic, and Dublin houses some of Europe's finest theaters. While Handel's *Messiah* was first performed in Dublin (1742), these days Dublin is famous for its rock bands (U2, Thin Lizzie, and Sinead O'Conner all got started here).

You have much to choose from: Abbey Theatre is Ireland's national theater. Gate Theatre does foreign plays as well as Irish classics. Point Theatre, once a railway terminus, is now the country's top live music venue. At the National Concert Hall, the National Symphony Orchestra performs most Friday evenings. Street theater takes the stage in Temple Bar on summer evenings. Folk music rings in the pubs, and street entertainers are everywhere. For the latest, pick up the free *Dublin Event Guide* or a copy of the twice-monthly *In Dublin* (£2, any newsstand).

Irish Music in nearby Dun Laoghaire

For an evening of pure Irish music, song, and dance, check out the **Comhaltas Ceoltoiri Eireann**, an association working to preserve this traditional slice of Irish culture. It got started when Elvis and company threatened to steal the musical heart of the new generation. Judging by the pop status of traditional Irish music these days, Comhaltas accomplished its mission. Their "Fonntrai" evening is a costumed stage show mixing traditional music, song, and dance (£5, Monday–Thursday at 21:00 mid-June–August). These are followed by an informal music session at 22:30. Fridays all year long they have a Cailidh where everyone dances (£5, 21:30–00:30). Saturday nights feature an informal session by the fireside. Performances are held in the Cuturlann na Eireann, near the Seapoint DART stop or a 20-minute walk from Dun Laoghaire, at 32 Belgrave Square, Monkstown (tel. 01/280-0295). Their bar is free, and often filled with music.

Sleeping in Dublin
(£1 = about $1.50, tel. code: 01)
Sleep Code: **S** = Single, **D** = Double/Twin, **T** = Triple, **Q** = Quad, **b** = bathroom, **t** = toilet only, **s** = shower only, **CC** = Credit Card (**V**isa, **M**asterCard, **A**mex).

Dublin is popular and rooms can be tight. Big and practical places (both cheap and moderate) are most central at Christchurch on the edge of Temple Bar. For classy, older Dublin accommodations you'll pay more and stay a bit farther out in the direction of Ballsbridge (embassy row). For a small-town escape with the best budget values, side-trip by the convenient DART train (at least 3/hrly, 15 min) from nearby Dun Laoghaire (see below).

Sleeping in Christchurch
These places each face Christchurch Cathedral, a great locale a five-minute walk from the best evening scene at Temple Bar and eight minutes from the sightseeing center (Trinity College). Buses 50, 54, 65, and 77 stop here. For an easy meal near your hotel, try the popular Leo Burdocks Fish & Chips (2 Werburgh Street, off Christchurch).

Jurys Christchurch Inn, like its sister in Galway, is well-located offering business-class comfort in all its identical rooms. This no-nonsense, modern, American-style hotel has a winning keep-it-simple-and-affordable formula. If old is getting old (and you don't mind big bus-tour groups), you won't find a better value in town. All 180 rooms cost the same: £60 for one, two, or three adults, or two adults and two kids, breakfast not included. Each room has a modern bathroom, direct-dial telephone, and TV. One floor is strictly nonsmoking. Request a room far from the noisy elevator (CC:VMA, Christchurch Place, Dublin 8, tel. 01/454-0000, fax 01/454-0012, United States tel. 800/843-3311). A 234-room **Jurys Custom House Inn** (£60, tel. 01/607-5000) is on Custom House Quay in Dublin.

Kinlay House, across the square from Jurys Christchurch Inn, is its backpackers' equivalent—definitely the place to go for cheap beds with a good location, privacy, and an all-ages-welcome atmosphere. This huge, red-brick, 19th-century Victorian building has 120 metal, prison-style beds in spartan, smoke-free rooms: singles, doubles, and four- to six-bed dorms (generally coed). It fills up most days. Call well in advance, especially for summer weekends (S-£20, D-£30, Db-£34, dorm beds-£13, includes continental breakfast, self-catering kitchen, launderette, left luggage, and so on, Christchurch,

2-12 Lord Edward Street, Dublin 2, tel. 01/679-6644, fax 01/679-7437, e-mail: kindub@usit.ie). If Kinlay is full, a similar place is the well-located **Avalon House** (D-£30, Db-£32, dorm beds-£7.50–10.50, south of Temple Bar at 55 Aungier Street, tel. 01/475-0001, fax 01/475-0303, Web site: www.avalon-house.ie, e-mail: info@avalon-house.ie).

Harding Hotel is a hardwood, 20th-century, Viking-style place with 53 hotelesque rooms. The hotel is as comfortable as Jurys but on a more intimate scale and without the tour-group scene (Sb-£45, Db/Tb-£60, breakfast extra, CC:VM, Copper Alley across the street from Christchurch, tel. 01/679-6500, fax 01/679-6504, Web site: www.iol.ie/usitaccm/, e-mail: harding@usit.ie).

Sleeping East of St. Stephen's Green

The Fitzwilliam rents 13 hotelish rooms in a classy guesthouse (Sb-£45, Db-£80, CC:VMA, 41 Upper Fitzwilliam Street, Dublin 2, tel. 01/662-5155, fax 01/676-7488).

Mespil Hotel is a huge, modern, business-class hotel renting 153 identical three-star rooms, each with all the comforts and at a very good price. Half the rooms overlook a canal greenbelt (Sb, Db, or Tb-£78, continental breakfast-£6, Irish breakfast-£9, elevator, one nonsmoking floor, CC:VMA, Mespil Road, Dublin 4, tel. 01/667-1222, fax 01/667-1244, e-mail: mespil@leehotels.ie).

Albany House is Georgian throughout and completely smoke-free. Each of the 33 rooms are tastefully designed with old elegance and modern comfort. Request the huge "superior" rooms which are the same price (Sb-£70, Db-£100, £80 in slow times, back rooms are generally bigger and quieter, the included breakfast is a healthy first-class continental buffet, CC:VMA, one block south of St. Stephen's Green at 84 Harcourt Street, Dublin 2, tel. 01/475-1092, fax 01/475-1093, e-mail: albany@indigo.ie).

Kilronan House, a classy Georgian-style B&B on a whispy tree-lined street, comes with lots of marble, gilding, chandeliers, and a professional staff (Sb-£50, Db-£80, CC:VM, two blocks south of St. Stephen's Green at 70 Adelaide Road, Dublin 2, tel. 01/755-266, fax 01/782-841).

The next three listings are on Northumberland Road. While Trinity College is only a 15-minute walk away, buses 7, 7A, and 8 (to O'Connell Street) lumber down Northumberland Road to the city center every 10 minutes.

Northumberland Lodge is a quiet, elegant mansion. Bridget and Tony Brady run a tight, comfortable, and friendly ship (Sb-from £55, Db-from £90, CC:VM, 68 Northumberland Road, Ballsbridge, Dublin 4, tel. 01/660-5270, fax 01/668-8679). **Glenveagh Town House** has 13 classy rooms—Victorian upstairs, modern downstairs (Sb-£42, Db-£72, less in slow times, CC:VMA, 31 Northumberland Road, tel. 01/668-4612, fax 01/668-4559). **Bush**

Dun Laoghaire

Map labels (not to scale):

MRS. KANE'S B&B · INNISFREE B&B · LYNDON B&B · ROSMEEN GARDENS RD. · GLENGEARY RD. · CLARINDA PARK · UMBER · NORTH · MULGRAVE · PATRICK ST. · CONVENT RD. · DE SELBY'S RESTAURANT · TO COMHALTAS IRISH MUSIC HOUSE → · TO BRAY · SANDYCOVE DART STN. · TEN. CTS. · GEORGES ST. (UPPER) (LOWER) · FERRY HOUSE B&B · DUNCREE B&B · EBLAND · SANDYCOVE HOUSE · PARK ROAD · MARINE RD. · THE OLD SCHOOL HOUSE HOSTEL · CROFTON RD. · TO DUBLIN · MELLIFONT · PROMENADE · WINDSOR · QUEENS PARK · ROAD · DART TRAIN STATION · T.I. · EAST PIER · STENA SEALINK DOCK · WEST PIER · *NOT TO SCALE - A WALK DOWN TO DOCK FROM GEORGES ST. IS ABOUT 5 MIN. · TO HOLYHEAD (N. WALES) ←

House, next door, is small and homey with a pleasant lounge and garden and four rooms mostly on the ground floor (Sb-£46, Db-£66–70, maybe less off-season, CC:VMA, 33 Northumberland Road, tel. & fax 01/668-3927, Diane Armstrong).

Sleeping near the Station

The Townhouse of Dublin is a fine basic and comfortable hotel with new furnishings but small rooms located midway between the train station and O'Connell Bridge (Sb-£35–47, D-£50–60, Db-£60–80 depending on season and day of the week, weekends are most expensive, CC:VMA, 47 Lower Gardiner Street, Dublin 1, tel. 01/878-8808, fax 01/878-8787, e-mail: grotter@indigo.ie).

Sleeping in nearby Dun Laoghaire
(tel. code: 01, mail: County Dublin)

The first three listings are a three-minute walk to the Sandycove DART station and a seven-minute walk to the Dun Laoghaire DART station/ferry landing. The rest are closest to the Dun Laoghaire DART station. Except for the first place, all are a bit tattered around the edges. While buses go into Dublin, the DART is much faster (6/hrly in peak times, at least 3/hrly otherwise, 15 min, Eurail valid, £1.10; for a longer stay consider the four-day Explorer ticket covering DART and Dublin buses). The **Dun**

Laoghaire TI is in the ferry terminal (daily 10:00–21:00, 9:00–17:00 off-season). The Society of the Preservation of Irish Folk Music has a lively branch in Dun Laoghaire (see above).

Mrs. Kane's B&B is a modern house with three big, cheery rooms and a welcoming guests' lounge. While a few blocks farther out than the others, it's worth the walk for its great, bright, friendly feeling (Db-£45, completely smoke-free, past Rosmeen Gardens to 2 Granite Hall, tel. & fax 01/280-9105).

Sandycove House, a comfortable old place overlooking a park and the harbor, is run in a no-nonsense kind of way. Its 12 rooms are generally large and fluffy (Sb-£30, Db-£45–47, Db overlooking the sea-£50, CC:VM, a £3 taxi or seven-minute walk from the ferry landing and two blocks from the Sandycove DART station, Marine Road, Sandycove, tel. & fax 01/284-1600).

Lynden B&B, with a classy 150-year-old interior hiding behind a somber front, offers four big rooms run by the charming and energetic Maria Gavin (one S-£17, D-£34, Db-£38, past Mulgrave Street to 2 Mulgrave Terrace, tel. & fax 280-6404). Next door, the similar **Belmont B&B** rents three rooms (D-£34, Db-£39, tel. 01/280-1422).

Innisfree B&B has a fine lounge and six big, bright, and comfy rooms (D-£32, Db-£37, CC:VM, from George Street follow the "Yellow Fever Vaccination Centre" sign to 31 Northumberland Avenue, tel. 01/280-5598, Brendan and Mary Smith).

Duncree B&B is similar with four mostly large rooms on a quiet street (S-£19.50, D-£35, Db-£39, 16 Northumberland Avenue, tel. 01/280-6118, Mrs. O'Sullivan).

Ferry House B&B is a stately old place facing a quiet square with a tennis court with seven huge rooms and a cozy lounge (D-£42, Db-£46, CC:VM, 15 Clarinda Park North, tel. 01/280-8301, fax 01/284-6530).

The Old School House Hostel is a shoestring traveler's dream-come-true. It's just two blocks from the DART station and ferry landing with incredibly cheap beds in two- to eight-bed rooms and a hardworking and creative staff. The only problem is that it's a hostel: old carpets, bare walls, and a general scruffiness. Having said that, it's clean with good beds and plenty of privacy and feels secure and safe (£9 bunks in six-bed dorms, £10 in a quad, £24 doubles, less off-season, showers down the hall or in your room for 50p extra, breakfast not included, nonsmoking rooms, self-catering kitchen, restaurant, £3 laundry service, 24-hour staff; CC:VMA; from ferry, go up Marine Road, take first right onto Eblana Avenue; tel. 01/280-8777, fax 01/284-2266, e-mail: info@hostel.ie).

Eating in Dun Laoghaire

George Street, the town's main drag and three blocks inland, has plenty of eateries and pubs, many with live music. Probably the best bet for a good mid-range meal is **De Selby's Restaurant,** serving traditional Irish food, stew, and seafood (£12 meals, nightly 17:00–23:00, a block off George Street at 17 Patrick Street, tel. 01/284-1761). **Scott's** is an Art Nouveau Irish pub with good Irish and Cajun food (nightly until midnight, Georges St. Upr. 17B). The **Purty Kitchen Pub/Restaurant** has good seafood.

Transportation Connections—Dublin
By bus to: Belfast (7/day, 3 hrs), Ennis (7/day, 4.5 hrs), **Galway** (10/day, 3.5 hrs), **Limerick** (10/day, 3 hrs), **Tralee** (5/day, 6 hrs). Bus info: tel. 01/836-6111.

By train to: Rosslare (3/day, 3 hrs), **Tralee** (6/day, 4 hrs), **Galway** (4/day, 3 hrs, talking timetable tel. 01/805-4222), **Ennis** (4/day, 4 hrs), **Portrush** (5/day, 5 hrs, £20 one-way, £28 round-trip; stops in Belfast on the way south), **Belfast** (8/day, 2.25 hrs, talking timetable tel. 01/855-4477). The new Dublin–Belfast train connects the two Irish capitals in just over two hours at 90 mph on one continuous welded rail (£17 one-way, £26 round-trip; round-trip the same day only £17, except Friday and Sunday; from the border to Belfast one-way £9, £12 round-trip). Train info: tel. 01/836-6222.

The **Dublin Airport** is well connected to the city center, 12 miles away (see Arrival in Dublin). British Air flies to London's Gatwick Airport (4/day, from £69 return, toll-free tel. 800/626-747 in Ireland, 800/247-9297 in the United States), as do Aer Lingus (tel. 01/705-6705) and British Midland (tel. 01/283-8833 in Ireland, 800/788-0555 in the United States). Dublin Airport info: tel. 01/814-4222. Ryanair is a new Irish cut-rate airline with unbelievable fares to European destinations (tel. 01/609-7800).

Transportation Connections— Ireland and Britain
Dublin and London: The boat/rail journey takes eight hours (4/day, £40–75). Dublin train info: tel. 01/836-6222.

Dublin and Holyhead: Irish Ferries sails between Dublin and Holyhead in North Wales (2/day, 3 hrs, £25 one-way walk-on fare, Dublin tel. 01/661-0511, Holyhead tel. 0990-329-129).

Dun Laoghaire and Holyhead: Stena Line sails between Dun Laoghaire (near Dublin) and Holyhead in North Wales (5/day, under 2 hrs with new *HSS Catamaran*, £36 one-way walk-on fare, £18 round-trip in a day if you have no baggage, reserve by phone early—they book up long in advance on summer weekends, Dublin tel. 01/204-7777, recorded information tel. 01/204-7799).

Ferry Connections—Ireland and France
Irish Ferries connect Ireland (Rosslare) with France (Cherbourg, and Roscoff) every other day (except January–March). While Cherbourg

has the quickest connection to Paris, your overall time between Ireland and Paris is about the same regardless of which port is used on the day you sail. One-way fares vary from £35 to £70 (round-trips are much cheaper). Except for a £4 port tax, Eurailers go half-price and also get beds or cabins for half-price (depending on availability). In both directions departures are generally between 16:00 and 23:00 and arrivals are around midday of the following day. While passengers can nearly always get on, reservations are wise in summer. If you anticipate a crowded departure you can reserve a seat for £5. Beds in a quad start at £10. Doubles (or singles) start at £23. The easiest way to get a bed (except during summer) is from the information desk upon boarding. The cafeteria serves bad food at reasonable prices. Upon arrival in France, buses and taxis connect you to your Paris-bound train (Irish Ferries: Dublin tel. 01/661-0511, recorded info tel. 01/661-0715, Paris tel. 01 44 94 20 40, Web site: www .irishferries.ie, e-mail: info@irishferries.ie, European Ferry Guide Web site: www.youra.com/ferry/intlferries.html).

NEAR DUBLIN: WICKLOW MOUNTAINS AND GLENDALOUGH

While only 10 miles south of Dublin, the Wicklow Mountains feel remote—remote enough to have provided a handy refuge for opponents to English rule. Rebels who took part in the 1798 Irish uprising hid out here for years. When the frustrated British built a military road in 1800 to help flush out the rebels, the area became more accessible. Now known as the R115, this same road takes you through the Wicklow area to Glendalough at its south end. While the darling of the Dublin day trip tour organizers, the valley itself doesn't live up to its hype. But two blockbuster sights make a visit worth considering.

Getting Around the Wicklow Mountains

By car or tour, it's easy. If you lack wheels, it's not worth the trouble.

By Tour: Several tour companies run day trips through the Wicklow Mountains from Dublin (Dublin Bus is cheapest). Mary Gibbon's Tours visit both the monastery and the gardens in a four-hour trip (£17, be careful—they spend an hour picking up tourists at Dublin hotels before leaving, tel. 01/283-9973). Wild Wicklow Tours—funny, irreverent, packed with information—takes small groups in minibuses daily to the most scenic corners of the mountains with time to get out and visit top attractions (£22, 8:40 pick up at the Dublin TI, 9:30 pick up at the Dun Laoghaire TI, home by 18:00, tel. 01/280-1899, Web site: www.arantours.ie-wildwicklow).

By Car: It's a joy. You might consider detouring through the Wicklow area as you drive between Dublin and the west coast. Take the freeway south to Enniskerry, your gateway to the Wicklow

Mountains. Signs direct you to the gardens. From Glendalough you can leave the valley (and pick up the highway to the west) over the famous but dull mountain pass called the Wicklow Gap.

Sights—Wicklow Mountains

▲▲**Gardens of Powerscourt**—While the mansion around which they were built was gutted by a fire in 1974, these meticulously kept aristocratic gardens are the most beautiful in Ireland. Commissioned in the 1730s by Richard Wingfield, first viscount of Powerscourt, the gardens are called "the grand finale of Europe's formal gardening tradition . . . probably the last garden of its size and quality ever to be created." I'll buy that.

Upon entry you'll get a flyer laying out 40-minute and 60-minute walks. Do the "hour walk" (which takes 30 minutes at a slow amble). With the impressive summit of the Great Sugar Loaf Mountain as a backdrop and a fine Japanese garden, Italian garden, and a goofy pet cemetery along the way, this garden provides the scenic greenery I hoped to find in the rest of the Wicklow area. The lush movie *Barry Lyndon* was filmed in this well-watered aristocratic fantasy.

The gardens, a mile above the village of Enniskerry, cover several thousand acres within the 16,000-acre estate. The driveway alone is a mile long. It's an easy stop by car, but probably not worthwhile if relying on public transport (£3.50, daily 9:30–17:30 March–October, tel. 01/286-7676). Skip the associated waterfall (£2, three miles away).

▲▲**Glendalough**—The steep wooded slopes of Glendalough (glen-da-lock, which means "valley of the two lakes"), at the south end of Wicklow's military road, hides one of Ireland's most impressive monastic settlements. Founded by St. Kevin in the sixth century, the monastery flourished (despite repeated Viking raids) throughout the "Age of Saints and Scholars" until the English destroyed it in 1398. While it was finally abandoned during the Dissolution of the Monasteries in 1539, pilgrims kept coming, especially on St. Kevin's Day, June 3. (This might have something to do with the fact that a pope said seven visits to Glendalough had the same indulgence value as one visit to Rome.) While much restoration was done in the 1870s, most of the buildings date from the eighth through the 12th centuries.

The valley sights are split between the two lakes. The lower lake has the visitors center and the best buildings. The upper lake, with scant ruins, feels like a state park with a grassy lakeside picnic area, school groups, and fine walks.

General Glendalough plan: Park free at the visitors center (£2, daily 9:00–18:30 in summer, closes earlier off-season, tel. 0404/45325). For a complete visit, begin with the video and history exhibit in the center, wander the ruins around the Round

Tower, walk the traffic-free Green Road one mile to the upper lake, and then walk back to your car. (You can drive to the upper lake, but it's £1.50 to park). If you're rushed, skip the upper lake. While tour-bus crowds are terrible all day on weekends, during the week crowds are a problem only from 11:00 to 14:00.

Glendalough Visitors Centre: Start your visit here. The 20-minute video provides a good thumbnail background on the monastic society in medieval Ireland. While the video is more general than specific to Glendalough, the adjacent museum room features this particular monastic settlement. The model in the center of the room re-creates the fortified village in the year 1050 (although there were no black-and-white Frisian cows in Ireland back then—they would have been red cows). A browse here shows the contribution these monks made to intellectual life in Dark Age Europe (such as Irish minuscule, a more compact alphabet developed in the seventh century, and illuminated manuscripts such as the Book of Kells from the ninth century). From the center, a short and scenic walk along the Green Road takes you to the Round Tower.

The Monastic Village: Easily the best ruins of Glendalough gather around its famous 110-foot-tall Round Tower. Towers like this (60–110 feet tall, standard features in such settlements) functioned as beacons for pilgrims, bell towers, storage lofts, and places of final refuge during Viking raids. They had a high door with a pull-up ladder. Several ruined churches (8th–12th centuries) and a sea of grave markers complete this evocative scene. Markers give short descriptions of the ruined buildings.

In an Ireland without cities, these monastic communities were mainstays of civilization. They were remote outposts where ascetics (with a taste for scenic settings) gathered to commune with God. In the 12th century, with the arrival of grander monastic orders such as the Franciscans and the Dominicans, and with the growth of cities, these monastic communities were eclipsed. Today Ireland is dotted with the reminders of this age—illuminated manuscripts, simple churches, carved crosses, and about 100 round towers.

Upper Lake: The Green Road continues peacefully one mile farther up the valley to the upper lake (where the marriage scene from the movie *Braveheart* was filmed). The oldest ruins—scant and hard to find—lie near this lake. If you're looking for a scenic Wicklow walk, this is the place to start.

DINGLE PENINSULA

Dingle Peninsula, the westernmost tip of Ireland, offers just the right mix of far and away beauty, ancient archaeological wonders, and desolate walks or bike rides all within convenient reach of its main town. Dingle Town is just big enough to have all the necessary tourist services and a steady nocturnal beat of Irish folk music.

While the big tour buses clog the neighboring Ring of Kerry before heading east to slobber all over the Blarney Stone, Dingle—while crowded in the summer—still feels like the fish and the farm matter. Fifty fishing boats sail from Dingle, and a faint whiff of peat still fills its nighttime streets.

For 15 years my Irish dreams have been set here on this sparse but lush peninsula where locals are fond of saying "The next parish is Boston." There's a closeness to the land on Dingle. When I asked a local if he was born here, he thought for a second and said, "No, it was about six miles down the road." When I told him where I was from, a faraway smile filled his eyes, he looked out to sea and sighed, "Ah, the shores of Americay."

Dingle feels so traditionally Irish because it's a Gaeltacht, a region where the government subsidizes the survival of the Irish language and culture. While English is always there, the signs, menus, and songs come in Gaelic. Even the local preschool brags "ALL Gaelic."

Of the peninsula's 10,000 residents, 1,300 live in Dingle Town. Its few streets, lined with ramshackle but gaily painted shops and pubs, run up from a rain-stung harbor always busy with fishing boats and yachts. During the day kids—already working on ruddy beer-glow cheeks—roll kegs up the streets and into the pubs in preparation for another night of music and *craic* (fun conversation).

Dingle History

The wet sod of Dingle is soaked with medieval history. In the darkest depths of the Dark Ages, peace-loving, bookwormish monks fled the chaos of the Continent and its barbarian raids. They sailed to the drizzly fringe of the known world—places like Dingle. These monks kept literacy alive in Europe. Charlemagne, who ruled much of Europe in the year 800, imported Irish monks to be his scribes.

It was from this peninsula that the semi-mythical explorer monk, St. Brandon, is said to have set sail in the sixth century in search of a legendary western paradise. Some think he beat Columbus to North America by nearly a thousand years.

Dingle (An Daingean in Gaelic) was a busy seaport in the late Middle Ages. Along with Tralee, it was the only walled town in Kerry and a gateway to northern Spain—a three-day sail due south. Many 14th- and 15th-century pilgrimages left from Dingle for Santiago di Compostela in Spain.

When its position as a medieval trading center ended, Dingle faded in importance. In the last century it was a linen-weaving center. Until 1970 fishing dominated. The only visitors were scholars and students of old Irish ways. In 1970 the movie *Ryan's Daughter* introduced the world to Dingle. The trickle of Dingle fans has grown to a flood in the 1990s as word of its musical, historical, gastronomical, and scenic charms—not to mention its friendly dolphin—has spread.

Planning Your Time

For the shortest visit, give Dingle two nights and a day. It takes about six hours to get there from Dublin, Galway, or the boat dock in Rosslare. I like two nights because you feel more like a local on your second evening in the pubs. You'll need the better part of a day to explore the 30-mile loop around the peninsula by bike, car, or tour bus (see Circular Tour, below). To do any serious walking or relaxing you'll need two or three days. It's not uncommon to find Americans slowing way, way down in Dingle.

Orientation (tel. code: 066)

Dingle is extremely comfortable on foot. The town hangs on a medieval grid of streets between the harborfront (where the Tralee bus stops) and Main Street (three blocks inland). Nothing in town is more than a five-minute walk away. Dingle is so small that street numbers are used only when more than one place is run by a family of the same name. Most locals know most locals, and people on the street are fine sources of information. Remember, tourism is what puts soda bread on the table here and the locals offer a warm and sincere welcome.

Tourist Information: The Bord Failte (TI) is on Strand

Southwest Ireland

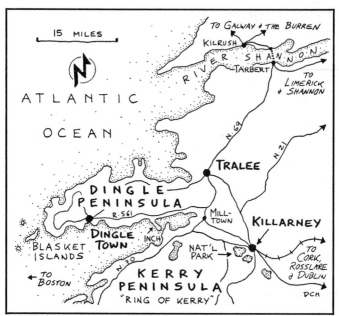

15 MILES

ATLANTIC

OCEAN

TO GALWAY & THE BURREN

KILRUSH

RIVER SHANNON

TARBERT

TO LIMERICK & SHANNON

N. 69

N. 21

TRALEE

DINGLE PENINSULA

R. 561

MILL-TOWN

KILLARNEY

Dingle Town

INCH

BLASKET ISLANDS

NAT'L PARK

TO CORK, ROSSLARE & DUBLIN

TO BOSTON

N. 70

KERRY PENINSULA

"RING OF KERRY"

DCH

Street, by the water (March–October Monday–Saturday 9:00–19:00, Sunday 10:00–13:00 and 14:15–18:00, off-season shorter hours and closed Sunday, tel. 066/51188, Web site: www.dingle-peninsula.ie). In the summer the TI organizes town walks. For more creative help, drop by the Mountain Man shop (on Strand Street, see below).

Helpful Hints

Crowds: Dingle gets so crowded during summer holiday weekends that the police actually close down the road access. July 15 to August 30 is bad (you might consider the less-discovered Beara Peninsula, south of the Ring of Kerry). The absolute craziest are the Dingle Races (second weekend in August) and Dingle Regatta (third weekend in August). Dingle's dead before May 1: no music, activities, tours, or tourists.

Banking: There are two banks in town, both uphill from the TI on Main Street (Monday–Friday 10:00–12:30 and 13:30–16:00). Both have cash machines.

Supermarket: The Super Valu supermarket/department store is at the base of town (Monday–Saturday 8:00–21:00, Sunday 8:00–18:00, less off-season).

Launderette: At this full-service shop you can drop off a load and pick it up three hours later (small-£3.50, large-£5.50, Monday–Saturday 9:00–17:30, on Green Street behind El Toro restaurant, tel. 066/51837).

Internet Café: Dingleweb, Monday–Saturday 10:00–22:00, less on Sunday, £5/hour, Main Street around the corner from Grapevine Hostel, tel. 066/52477, e-mail: postmaster @dingleweb.com).

Bike Rental: Bike rental shops abound in Dingle. You can get good mountain bikes at Paddy's Bike Hire (daily 9:00–19:00, £5/day, £6/24 hrs, on Dykegate next to Grapevine Hostel), Sciuird Tours, the Mountain Man, and the Ballintaggert Hostel. If you're biking the peninsula, get a bike with skinny street tires, not slow and fat mountain bike tires. Plan on leaving a credit card, driver's license, or passport as security.

Dingle Activities: The Mountain Man, a hiking shop run by two local guides, Con and Mike, is a clearinghouse for information, local tours, and excursions (located just off the harbor at Strand Street, tel. 066/52400, fax 066/52396). Pick up the free *Kerry Gems* booklet or, for longer outdoorsy stays, the more complete *Easy Guide to the Dingle Peninsula*. For bike rentals and ideas on biking, hiking, horse riding, climbing, peninsula tours (which they offer), and trips to the Blaskets, stop by here. They are the Dingle Town contact for the Dunquin–Blasket Islands boats (see Blasket Islands, below).

Sights—Dingle Town

▲**Oceanworld**—The only place charging admission in Dingle is worth considering. This new aquarium offers a little peninsula history, 160 different local fish and other sea creatures in thoughtfully described tanks (including a chance to walk under the fish in the "ocean tank"), and the easiest way to see Fungi the dolphin—on video (£4.50, £12 for families, daily 10:00–20:30 in summer, until 18:00 or earlier in off-season, just past the harbor on the west edge of town, tel. 066/52111).

Fungi—In 1983 a dolphin moved into Dingle Harbor and became a local celebrity. Fungi is now the darling of the town's tourist trade and one reason you'll find so many tour buses parked along the harbor. With a close look at Fungi as bait, tour boats are thriving—£6, book behind the TI. While she's too cute to kill, I'll happily give a free copy of the next edition of this book to anyone who can make Fungi leave.

▲**Short Harbor Walk from Dingle**—For an easy stroll along the harbor out of town (and a chance to see the dolphin) head east from the roundabout on R561. Just after Bambury's B&B, take a right following signs to Skelligs Hotel. At the beach, climb the steps over the wall and follow the seashore path to the mouth of Dingle harbor (marked by a tower—some 19th-century fat cat's

Dingle Town

1 SMEARA DUBHA	21 DICK MACK
2 OCEANWORLD	22 CAFE CEO
3 DINGLE SAILING CLUB	23 LAUNDRY
4 CRUISEBOAT OFFICES	24 EL TORO
5 MAIRE DE BARRA RESTAURANT	25 GRAPEVINE HOSTEL
6 MOUNTAIN MAN	26 BANK
7 BUS STATION	27 BIKE RENTAL
8 GREANY'S RESTAURANT	28 AN CAFE LITEARTA
9 SUPER VALUE	29 TOURIST INFORMATION
10 TIG LISE	30 CAPTAIN'S HOUSE B&B
11 O'FLAHERTY'S	31 CINEMA
13 BAMBURY'S B&B	32 ADAM'S BAR & RESTAURANT
14 TRAIL TO LIGHTHOUSE	33 SMALL BRIDGE BAR
15 BALLINTAGGERT HOSTEL	34 DOYLE'S & HALF DOOR RESTAURANTS
16 ALPINE HOUSE	35 SRAID EOIN B&B
17 SCIUIRD TOURS & KIRRARY B&B	36 KELLIHER'S BALLYEGAN HOUSE
18 CORNER HOUSE B&B	37 GREENMOUNT HOUSE
19 CONNORS B&B	38 HILLGROVE HOTEL
20 CITY PARK	39 ARD NA GREINE HOUSE B&B

folly). Ten minutes beyond that is a lighthouse. This is Fungi's neighborhood. If you see tourist boats out, you're likely to see her. If you continue walking, you'll get to a dramatic cliff.

The Harbor—The harbor is on land reclaimed (with imported Dutch expertise) five years ago. The new roundabout allows traffic to skirt the town center. The string of old stone shops facing the harbor was the loading station for the narrow-gauge railway that hauled the fish from Dingle to Tralee (1891–1953). The Esk Tower on the distant hill is a marker built in 1847 during the famine as a make-work project. In pre-radar days, it helped ships locate Dingle's hidden harbor. The fancy mansion across the harbor is Lord Ventry's 17th-century manor house.

Cruises—The Dingle Marina Center offers diving, sailing, and traditional currach rowing. One-man sailboats can be lent to those wanting to blow around the bay with a day membership in the Sailing Club (£15, tel. 066/52422). Currachs are Ireland's traditional lightweight fishing boats, easy to haul and easy to make: Cover a wooden frame with canvas and paint with tar. Stacked near the Sailing Club, the currachs are owned by the Dingle Rowing Club and go out most evenings. You can take a sailing trip to the Blaskets on the 41-foot cutter "Kimberly Laura" (£40, book in advance, tel. 066/59882). The beaches nearby are popular in the summer.

Entertainment

▲▲▲**Folk Music in Dingle Pubs**—Even if you're not into pubs, take a nap and then give these a whirl. Dingle is renowned among traditional musicians as a place to get work ("£30 a day, tax-free, plus drink"). The town has 50 pubs. There's music every night (and never a cover charge). The scene is a decent mix of locals, Americans, and Germans. Music normally starts around 21:30, and the last call for drinks is "half eleven" (23:30). For a seat near the music, arrive early. If the place is chockablock, power in and find breathing room in the back. By midnight the door is closed and the chairs are stacked. While two pubs, the Small Bridge Bar (An Droicheed) and O'Flahertys, are the most famous for their good beer and folk music, make a point to wander the town and follow your ear. Smaller pubs may feel a bit foreboding to a tourist, but people—locals as well as travelers—are out for the *craic*. Pubs are smoky and hot (leave your coat home). The more offbeat pubs are more likely to erupt into leprechaun karaoke.

The best pub crawl is along the Strand to O'Flaherty's (rough-and-tumble Murphy's is liveliest, offering rock as well as traditional music). Then head up Green Street. Dick Mack is a tiny leather shop by day and a pub by night with two snugs (private booths), reliably good beer, and a strangely fascinating ambience; notice the Hollywood-type stars on the sidewalk recalling famous visitors. Wander up and down Main Street (Small Bridge Bar at the bottom is best) and then up Spa Road a few doors to An Conair, a pub attracting a more alternative Celtic folk talent (often less crowded but with good music). During the day, music lovers will enjoy dropping by Danlann Gallery, a music shop on Dykegate Street (Monday–Saturday 10:00–22:00, Sunday 11:00–18:00, less off-season).

More Evening Fun—Somewhere almost every night, a pub

hosts "Set Dancing" with live music (An Conair Bar does it on Monday after 21:30). The music office on Dykegate has the lastest on musical happenings. Hillgrove Hotel (up Spa Road a few hundred meters) is a modern hotel with traditional dances every Thursday and pop dancing other nights in summer. Locals say the Hillgrove "is a good time if you're pissed." Dingle has a great little theater (The Phoenix on Dykegate). The film club (50 or 60 locals) meets for coffee, cookies, and a film every Tuesday at 20:30 (October–June).

Sleeping in Dingle Town
(£1 = about $1.50, tel. code: 066, mail: Dingle, County Kerry)
Sleep Code: **S** = Single, **D** = Double/Twin, **T** = Triple, **Q** = Quad, **b** = bathroom, **t** = toilet only, **s** = shower only, **CC** = Credit Card (**V**isa, **M**asterCard, **A**mex).

Sraid Eoin B&B, on the quiet end of town with four spacious and modern pastel rooms and giant bathrooms, is warmly run by Kathleen and Maurice O'Connor (Sb-£25, Db-£34, family deals, CC:VM, John Street, tel. 066/51409, fax 066/52156). Maurice runs Galvin's Travel Agency on the ground floor (same phone number).

Kellihers Ballyegan House is a big, plain building with six comfortable rooms on the edge of town, run by friendly Mrs. Hannah Kelliher (Sb-£18, Db-£36, no CC or smokers, Upper John Street, tel. 066/51702).

Greenmount House sits among palm trees at the top of town, in the countryside with a commanding view of the bay and mountains but just three minutes' walk from the town center. John and Mary Curran run one of Ireland's classiest B&Bs with six fine rooms (Db-£40) and six sprawling suites (Db-£60) in a modern building with lavish public areas and breakfast in a solarium (no singles during high season or children under eight ever, lower prices off-season, CC:VM, up John Street to Gortonora, reserve in advance, tel. 066/51414, fax 066/51974).

Corner House B&B is my longtime Dingle home. It's a simple, traditional place with five rooms run with a twinkle and a smile by Kathleen Farrell (S-£18, D-£32, T-£45, plenty of plumbing but it's down the hall, no CC, reserve with a phone call and reconfirm a day or two ahead or risk losing your bed, central as can be on Dykegate Street, tel. 066/51516).

Captain's House B&B is a salty-feeling place in the town center with seven classy rooms (Sb-£30, Db-£44, CC:VMA, the Mall, tel. 066/51531, fax 066/51079, e-mail: captigh@tinet.ie, Jim and Mary Milhench).

Connors B&B, well-located and likely to have a room available, has 15 big, basic rooms (£25 per person in July and August, £18 other months, CC:VMA, in the center on Dykegate Street, tel. 066/51598, fax 066/52376, Mrs. Connor).

Ard Na Greine House B&B is a charming, wind-blown, modern house on the edge of town. Mrs. Mary Houlihan rents four well-equipped, comfortable rooms to nonsmokers (Sb-£24, Db-£36, Tb-£50, CC:VM, on the edge of town a 10-minute walk up Spa Road, three doors beyond the Hillgrove Hotel, tel. 066/51113, fax 066/51898).

Ballintaggert Hostel, a backpacker's complex, is housed in a stylish old manor house used by Protestants during the famine as a soup kitchen (for those hungry enough to renounce their Catholicism). It comes complete with horse riding, bike rental, laundry service, kitchen, café, classy study, family room with a fireplace, a shuttle into town, and a resident ghost (166 beds, £7 in 8- to 12-bed dorms, £10 in quads, £13 in singles and doubles, breakfast extra, one mile east of town on Tralee Road, tel. 066/51454, fax 066/52207, e-mail: btaggert@iol.ie).

Grapevine Hostel is a clean and friendly establishment with a cozy fireplace lounge and a fine members' kitchen. Each four- to eight-bed dorm has its own bathroom. Dorms are coed but there's usually a girls' room established. No curfew or lockout (32 beds, £8–9 each, Dykegate Lane, tel. 066/51434).

Alpine House Guest House (tel. 066/51250) and **Bambury's B&B** (tel. 066/51244), both big, modern buildings on the main Tralee Road a block or so from the roundabout, might have a reasonable bed when the others are full.

Ocean View B&B rents three tidy rooms in a little waterfront rowhouse overlooking the the bay (S-£15, D-£26, five-minute walk from the center, 100 meters past Ocean World at 133 The Wood, tel. 066/51659, Mrs. Brosnan).

Eating in Dingle Town

For a rustic little village, Dingle is swimming in high and fun cuisine. Many of the best values close after 18:00. Most pubs also stop serving food early (to make room for maximum beer). The town's grocery stores stay open until about 21:00.

Adam's Bar and Restaurant serves traditional food at great prices. Try their corned beef and cabbage (last meal at 20:30, earlier in low season, Upper Main Street).

Tig Lise offers a good, simple menu with a tasty lasagna-and-salad meal and good vegetarian selections (meals are £5, closed at 21:00, earlier off-season, near the roundabout at Holyground).

An Cafe Litearta, a popular and friendly eatery hiding behind an inviting bookstore, has good sandwiches, salads, and hot food (10:00–17:30, Dykegate Street).

Greany's Restaurant, just off the roundabout, is a local hit serving good, basic food at decent prices in a cheery, modern atmosphere (12:30–22:00, Holyground).

El Toro offers a candlelit splash of Italy with good seafood, salads, and pizzas (17:30–20:00, Green Street, tel. 066/51820). **Maire De Barra** has simple traditional food and seafood (£5, the Pier).

Smeara Dubha is a small vegetarian restaurant down by the harbor (evenings only, 18:00–21:00, The Wood, Dingle).

Dingle's long-established top-notch restaurants are **Doyle's Seafood Bar** (more famous, John Street, tel. 066/51174) and the **Half Door** (heartier portions, pay in cash to avoid Visa card scam, John Street, tel. 066/51600). Both offer three-course early-dinner specials for £15 between 18:00 and 18:30 and more expensive dining after that. Reservations are necessary in both places.

Transportation Connections—Dingle Town

The nearest train station is in Tralee. Buses connect Dingle and Tralee nine times a day in summer, less off-season and on Sunday (75 min, £6). Dingle has no bus station and only one stop, on the waterfront behind the Super Valu supermarket (bus info tel. 066/23566). See Tralee Transportation Connections, below, for more information.

Drivers choose two roads into town, the easy southern route or the much more dramatic and treacherous Conor Pass (see Tralee Transportation Connections, below). It's 30 miles from Tralee either way.

Dingle Peninsula: Circular Tour by Bike or Car

A ▲▲▲ sight, the Dingle Peninsula loop trip is about 30 miles long (seven hours by bike, three hours by car, including stops; do only in clockwise direction). While you can take a guided tour of the peninsula (below), it's not necessary with the route described in this section. A fancy map is also unnecessary with my instructions. I've keyed in mileage to help locate points of interest. If you're driving, as you leave Dingle, reset your odometer at Oceanworld. Even if you get off track or are biking, derive distances between points from these numbers. To get the most out of your circle, read through this entire section before departing. Then go step by step (staying on R559 and following the "The Slea Head Drive" signs). Note: Roads are very congested in August.

The Dingle Peninsula is 10 miles wide and runs 40 miles from Tralee to Slea Head. The top of its mountainous spine is Mount Brandon—at 3,130 feet, the second-tallest mountain in Ireland. While only tiny villages lie west of Dingle Town, the peninsula is home to 500,000 sheep.

Leave Dingle Town west along the waterfront (0.0 miles at Oceanworld). There's an eight-foot tide here. The seaweed was used to nourish reclaimed land. Across the water the fancy Milltown House B&B was Robert Mitchum's home for a year during the filming of *Ryan's Daughter*.

Dingle Peninsula Tour

0.4 miles: Turn left over the bridge. The building on the right was a corn-grinding mill in the 18th century.

0.8 miles: The Milestone B&B is named for the pillar stone (*Gallaun* in Gaelic) in its front yard. This may have been a prehistoric grave marker or a boundary marker between two tribes. The stone goes down as far as it sticks up. Another pillar stone stands in the field across the street in the direction of the yellow manor house of Lord Ventry. The peninsula, literally an open-air museum, is dotted with more than 2,000 monuments dating from the Bronze Age through early Christian times.

2.1 miles: Pass through a rare grove of trees and turn left ("Leather Workshop" sign). After 100 yards enter the **Lord Ventry's Manor**, take the first left (unmarked, through white gate), and go up the long one-lane drive past small 18th-century estate houses and the palms, magnolias, fuschias, and exotic flora introduced to Dingle by Lord Ventry. Because of the mild climate (cradled by the gulf stream), fuschias line the roads all over the peninsula and fill the countryside with red from June to September. At the fork in the road, turn right. Fifty yards before the yellow mansion, stop at the six stones.

The **Ogham Stones** (dating from the third to seventh century, named for the Celtic goddess of writing) decorating the drive are rare examples of early Celtic writing. With variations on five straight lines, they could make 20 letters—the original bar code. Of the 380 known Ogham Stones, 80 are in Dingle. Lord Ventry, whose family came to Dingle as landlords in 1666, built this mansion in about 1750. Today it houses an all-Gaelic boarding school for 140 high school–age girls. Return to the main road and turn left (3.1 miles).

4.1 miles: Stay off the "soft margin" as you enjoy views of **Ventry Bay** and its four-mile-long beach. Mt. Eagle (1,660 feet), the end of Ireland, is beyond. In the little town of Ventry, Gaelic is the first language.

6.0 miles: The rushes on either side of the road are the kind used to make the local thatched roofs. Thatching, which nearly died out because of the fire danger, is more popular now that anti-flame treatments are available. Magpies fly.

6.6 miles: The Irish football star Paidi O Se (Paddy O'Shea) is a household name in Ireland. He now trains the Kerry team and runs the pub on the left.

6.9 miles: The blue house hiding in the trees on the left (view through the white gate) was kept cozy by Tom Cruise and Nicole Kidman during the filming of *Far and Away*.

7.9 miles: "*Taisteaal go Mall*" means "go slowly"; there's a peach-colored schoolhouse on the right. On the left is the Celtic and Prehistoric Museum, a strange private collection of dinosaur eggs, Celtic and Viking tools, coins, weapons, and a very odd mechanical sheep (£3.50, closed Monday).

8.2 miles: The circular mound on the right is a late–Stone Age ring fort. In 500 B.C. it was a petty Celtic chieftain's head-quarters, a stone-and-earth stockade filled with little stone houses. These survived untouched through the centuries because of super-stitious beliefs that they were "fairy forts." While this is unexca-vated, recent digging has shown that people have lived on this peninsula since 4000 B.C.

8.6 miles: The Hungarian red deer on the right are the work of the European Community (easier on the land, but higher fences are needed). Grass-fed deer (venison) are in the Euro cards, not more sheep.

9.0 miles: **Dunbeg Fort,** a series of defensive ramparts and ditches around a central *clochan*, while ready to fall into the sea, is open to tourists. While there are no carvings to be seen, the small (*beg*) fort (*dun*) is dramatic (£1, daily 9:00–20:00, descriptive hand-out). Forts like this are the most important relics left from Ire-land's Iron Age (500 B.C. to A.D. 500). Since erosion will someday take this fort, it has been excavated.

9.6 miles: The Fahan group of **beehive huts**, or *clochans*, is a short walk uphill. These mysterious stone igloos cluster together within a circular wall (£1, daily 9:00–19:00, WC). These are a better sight than the Fahan beehive huts a mile down the road. Farther on, you'll ford a stream. There has never been a bridge here; the road was designed as a ford.

10.6 miles: Pull off to the left at this second group of beehive huts. Look downhill at the scant remains of the scant home that was burned as the movie equivalent of Lord Ventry tried to evict the tenants in *Far and Away*. Even without Hollywood, this is bleak, godforsaken land. Look above at the patches of land slowly reclaimed by the inhabitants of this westernmost piece of Europe. Rocks were moved and piled into fences. Sand and seaweed were laid on the clay and in time it was good for grass. The created land was generally not tillable. Much has fallen out of use now.

11.4 miles: At **Slea Head**, marked by a crucifix, a pullout, and great views of the Blasket Islands (described below), you turn the corner on this tour.

11.9 miles: Pull out here to view the Blaskets and Dunmore Head (the westernmost point in Europe) and to review the roadside map (which traces your route) in the parking lot. The scattered village of Dunquin has many ruined rock homes—abandoned during the famine. They were built with small windows to minimize taxation. Some have been fixed up, as this is a popular place these days for summer homes. (The lead singer of the Irish rock band The Cranberries has a huge home a mile or so down the road.) You can see more good examples of land reclamation, patch by patch, climbing up the hillside.

13.4 miles: The Blasket Islanders had no church or cemetery on the island. This was their cemetery. The famous Blasket storyteller Peig Sayers (1873–1958) is buried in the center. Just past a washed-out bit of road, a lane leads left (100 yards) to a marker remembering the 1588 shipwreck of the *Santa Maria de la Rosa* of the Spanish Armada. Below that is the often tempestuous Dunquin Harbor, from where the Blasket ferry departs.

13.5 miles: Back on the main road, follow signs to the Great Blasket Centre.

15 miles: Leave the Slea Head Road left for the modern Blasket Centre (described below).

15.7 miles: Back at the turnoff, head left (sign to Louis Mulcahy Pottery).

16.4 miles: Passing land that was never reclaimed, think of the work it took to pick out the stones, pile them into fences, and bring up sand and seaweed to nourish the clay and make soil for growing potatoes. On the left is a shadow of the main street of the fake poor village built to film *Far and Away*. Beyond that is the "Sleeping Giant" island—with hand resting happily on his beer belly.

16.8 miles: The view is spectacular, especially when the waves are "racing in like white horses." Ahead on the right, study the top fields, untouched since the planting of 1845, when the potatoes rotted in the ground. The vertical ridges of the potato beds can still be seen—a reminder of the famine. Before the famine, 60,000 people lived on this peninsula.

20.2 miles: **Ballyferriter** (Baile an Fheirtearaigh), established by a Norman family in the 12th century, is the largest town on this end of the peninsula. The pubs serve grub and the old schoolhouse is a museum (£1.50, daily in summer 10:00–17:30, off-season Monday–Friday 10:00–12:00 and 14:00–16:00). The early Christian cross looks real. Tap it . . . it's a fiberglass prop from *Ryan's Daughter*.

21.0 miles: At the T-junction, signs direct you to Dingle (An Daingean 11 km) either way. Go left, via Gallarus. Take a right over the bridge, still following signs to Gallarus.

21.4 miles: Just beyond the bridge and a few yards before the sign to Mainistir Riaise (Riasc Monastic enclosure), detour right up the lane. After .2 miles (the unsigned turnout on your right) you find the scant remains of the walled **Riasc Monastery** (dating from the fifth to 12th centuries). Step over the rocks and go inside. The inner wall divided the community into work and religious sections. The layer of black felt marks where the original rocks stop and the excavators' reconstruction begins. The pillar stone is Celtic (from 1000 B.C.). When the Christians arrived in the fifth century, they didn't throw out the Celtic society. Instead, they carved a Maltese-type cross over the Celtic scrollwork. The square building was an oratory (church). The round buildings would have been dwellings. The monasteries had cottage industries. Just outside the wall (opposite the oratory), find a stone hole with a passage facing the southwest wind. This was a kiln. Locals would bring their grain to be dried and ground. The monks would keep a "tithe." With the arrival of the Normans in the 12th century, these small religious communities were replaced by relatively big-time state and church governments.

21.9 miles: Back on the main road, continue to the right.

23.0 miles: At the big pink restaurant, turn left.

23.7 miles: At another restaurant, go right up an unmarked one-lane road.

24.0 miles: The Gallarus Oratory (£1), built about 1,300 years ago, is one of Ireland's best-preserved early-Christian churches. Its shape is reminiscent of an upturned boat, and the dry-stone walls are so perfectly fitted together that they are still waterproof. Notice the holes for some covering at the door and the fine alternating stonework on the corners. Your ticket includes a 17-minute *Story of the Dingle Peninsula* video, which gives an interesting overview of the historic sights. (Drivers can avoid the £3 parking fee by grabbing one of four spots up the hill and taking the public access path to the oratory (free, but no video). Continue up the rugged one-lane road.

24.6 miles: Turn left on the two-lane road, then right (to An Daingean, 7 km) where you'll crest and enjoy a three-mile coast back into Dingle Town in the direction of the Esk Tower.

27.6 miles: At the intersection just look for the happy dolphin. Head that way, over the bridge and back into Dingle Town (28.4 miles). Well done.

Dingle Peninsula Tours

Sciuird Archaeology Tours are offered by the Sciuirds, a family that has Dingle history—and a knack for sharing it—in its blood. Tim Coileain (a retired Dingle policeman) and his son Michael give serious 2.5-hour, £7 minibus tours at 11:00 and 14:00, depending upon demand. Drop by the Kirrary B&B (at intersection of Dykegate and Grey's Lane in Dingle Town) or call 066/51937 or 066/51606 to put your name on the list. Call early. Tours fill quickly in summer. Off-season you may have to call back to see if the necessary four people signed up to make a bus go. While skipping the folk legends and the famous sights (such as Slea Head), your guide will drive down tiny farm roads (the Gaelic word for road is "cow path"), over hedges, and up ridges to hidden Celtic forts, mysterious stone tombs, and forgotten castles with sweeping seaside views. The running commentary gives an intimate peek into the history of Dingle. Sit as close to the driver as possible to get all the information. They do two completely different tours: west (Gallarus Oratory) and east (Minard Castle and a wedge tomb). I enjoyed both. Dress for the weather. In a literal gale with horizontal winds my guide kept saying, "You'll survive it."

Moran's Tour does three-hour guided minibus trips around the peninsula with a more touristic slant (£7, normally at 10:30 and 14:30 from the Dingle TI, tel. 066/51155). The **Mountain Man** also offers three-hour minibus tours of the peninsula (tel. 066/52400). **Guide Friday** makes the circuit about hourly in its familiar "hop on and off the topless bus" style.

Blasket Islands

This rugged group of six islands off the tip of Dingle Peninsula seems particularly close to the soul of Ireland. The population of Great Blasket Island, home to as many as 160 people, dwindled until the last handful of residents were moved by the government to the mainland in 1953. These people were the most traditional Irish community of the 20th century—the symbol of antique Gaelic culture. Their special closeness to their island—combined with their knack for vivid storytelling—is inspirational. From this poor, primitive but proud fishing/farming community came three writers of international repute whose Gaelic work—basically tales of life on Great Blasket—is translated into many languages. You'll find *Peig* (by Peig Sayers), *Twenty Years a-Growing* (Maurice O'Sullivan), and *The Islander* (Thomas O'Crohan) in shops all over the peninsula.

In the summer there may be a café, shop, and hostel on the island, but it's little more than a ghost town overrun with rabbits on a peaceful, grassy, three-mile-long poem. The ferry schedule is dictated by demand and weather. In 1999 there should be two or three buses a day from Dingle Town to Dunquin (usually around 9:00, 14:00, and 16:00, returning about 10:00, 14:30, and 18:00) coordinated with ferry departures; check at the Mountain Man shop in Dingle Town (£3 each way by bus, £10 round-trip with boat trip to Blasket, Dunquin ferry tel. 066/56455). There is a hostel in Dunquin.

▲▲**Great Blasket Centre**—This state-of-the-art Blasket and Gaelic heritage center gives visitors the best look possible at the language, literature, and way of life of the Blasket Islanders. See the fine video (shows on the half-hour), hear the sounds, read the poems, browse through old photos, and then gaze out the big windows at those rugged islands and imagine. Even if you never got past limericks, the poetry of these people—so pure and close to each other and nature—will have you dipping your pen into the cry of the birds (£2.50, daily 10:00–18:00 Easter–October, until 19:00 July and August, on the mainland facing the islands, well signposted, tel. 066/56444). Visit this center before visiting the islands.

Sights—East of Dingle Town

▲**Minard Castle**—Three miles southwest of Annascaul is Minard Castle, the largest fortress on the peninsula. Built by the Norman Knights of Kerry in 1551, it was destroyed by Cromwell in about 1650.

Wander around the castle. With its corners undermined by Cromwellian explosives, it looks ready to split. Look up the garbage/toilet chute. As you enter the ruins, find the faint scallop in the doorway—the symbol of St. James. The castle had a connection to Santiago de Compostela in Spain. Medieval pilgrims would leave from here on a seafaring pilgrimage to northern Spain. Inside, after admiring the wall flowers, re-create the floorplan: ground floor for animals and storage; main floor with fireplace; thin living quarters floor; and, on top, the defensive level.

The setting is dramatic with the Ring of Kerry across the way and Storm Beach below. Storm Beach is notable for its sandstone boulders that fell from the nearby cliffs. Grinding against each other because of the wave and tidal action, the boulders eroded into cigar-shaped rocks. Some of these rocks, inscribed by prehistoric people, became the Ogham Stones (see Circular Tour, above).

▲**Puicin Wedge Tomb**—While pretty obscure, this is worth the trouble for its evocative setting. Above the hamlet of Lispole in Doonties, park your car and hike 10 minutes up a ridge. At the summit is a pile of rocks made into a little room with one of the finest views on the peninsula. Beyond the Ring of Kerry you may just make out the jagged Skellig Rock, noted for its sixth-century monastery.

Inch Strand—This four-mile sandy beach, shaped like a half-moon, was made famous by *Ryan's Daughter*.

TRALEE

While Killarney is the tour-bus capital of county Kerry, Tralee is its true leading city. Except for the tourist complex around the TI and during a few festivals, Tralee feels like a bustling Irish town.

Tralee's famous **Rose of Tralee International Festival** (a week in late August), while a celebration of arts and music, climaxes with the election of the "Rose of Tralee"—the most beautiful woman at the festival. While the rose garden in the Castle Gardens surrounding the TI is in bloom from summer through October, Tralee's finest roses are going about their lives in the busy streets of this workaday town.

Orientation (tel. code: 066)

For the tourist, the heart of Tralee is Ashe Memorial Hall, housing the TI and Kerry the Kingdom, located near the rose garden and surrounded by the city park. Beyond the park is the Aqua Dome and steam railway which, if you were here 50 years ago, would chug-chug you to Dingle. Today it goes only to the touristy windmill.

Tourist Information: The TI is in Ashe Memorial Hall (daily 9:00–18:00, shorter hours off-season, tel. 066/21288).

Arrival in Tralee: From the train and bus station (located in the same building, with bike rental available) the TI is a 10-minute walk through the center of town. From the station head down Edward Street, then turn right on Castle Street and left on Denny. The TI is at the end of Denny. Drivers should knock around the town center until they find a sign to the TI. Parking on the street requires a disc (40p per hour, sold at TI and newsstands, have them date it for you).

Sights—Tralee

▲▲**Kerry the Kingdom**—This is the place to learn about life in Kerry. The museum has three parts: Kerry slide show, museum, and medieval town train ride. Get in the mood by relaxing for 20 minutes through the Enya-style slideshow of Kerry's spectacular scenery (continuous), then wander through 7,000 years of Kerry history. The Irish say that when a particularly stupid guy moved from Cork to Kerry, he raised the IQ in both counties—but this is pretty well done. The museum starts with good background on the archaeological sights of Dingle and goes right up to a video showing highlights of the Kerry football team (a fun look at Irish football). The attempted finale is a 15-minute four-person train ride down Tralee's Main Street in 1450 (£5, daily 10:00–18:00, until 19:00 in August, less in winter, tel. 066/27777, 40p disk at TI for one-hour parking). Before leaving, garden enthusiasts will want to ramble through the rose garden in the adjacent park.

Blennerville Windmill—On the edge of Tralee, just off the Dingle road, spins a restored mill originally built in 1800. Its 10-minute video tells of the famine (£3, daily 10:00–18:00 April–October, tel. 066/27444). A restored narrow-gauge steam railway runs hourly from Tralee's Ballyard Station to the windmill (tel. 066/21064 for services). In the 19th century Blennerville was a major port for America-bound immigrants.

Blennerville's Jeanie Johnston Shipyard—This features a life-size replica of the tall ship that made 16 successful voyages to North America during the famine (1847–58). (Visitors Centre daily 9:00–18:00).

Siamsa Tire Theatre—The National Folk Theater of Ireland stages two-hour dance and theater performances based on Gaelic folk traditions. They're in Irish, but work as mime (£9, 20:30 most evenings May–mid-October, next to TI in park, tel. 066/23055).

Swimming—The Aqua Dome is a modern swim center—the largest indoor water world in Ireland—at the Dingle end of town. Families enjoy the huge slide, wave pool, and other wet amusements (£6, £4 for kids, daily 10:00–22:00 June–August, less in winter, tel. 066/29150).

Music and Other Distractions—Tralee has a fine pub scene with several pubs within a few blocks of each other offering live traditional music most evenings. There's greyhound racing (Tuesday, Friday, and Saturday at 20:00, 10-minute walk from the station or town center, tel. 066/80008). It costs a few pounds plus what you lose gambling. At just about any time of day you can drop into a betting office to see the local gambling scene.

Sleeping in Tralee
(£1 = about $1.50, tel. code: 066, mail: Tralee, County Kerry)
O'Shea's B&B, a simple, tidy, modern house, rents four comfy rooms (Sb-£20, Db-£32, Tb-£45, leaving the station, walk five minutes up Oakpark Drive to #2 Oakpark, tel. & fax 066/80123, Mairead O'Shea).

Two good and central hostels with £8 dorm beds and £20 doubles without breakfast are **Finnegan's Hostel** (in a stately Georgian house from 1826, a block in front of the TI in the town center at 17 Denny Street, rustic celler restaurant serving fine meals, CC:VM, tel. 066/27610) and the homey **Lisnagree Hostel** (two quads and five doubles, from the center follow Boherboy to Ballinorig Road, tel. 066/27133). **Atlas House Budget Accommodation** also offers cheap dorms and tidy doubles (D-£30, Db-£33, £10 beds in four- to eight-bed rooms, with continental breakfast, CC:V, two blocks from the train station, just off Castle Street, tel. 066/20722, fax 066/20747, e-mail: atlashousetralee@tinet.ie).

Collis-Sandes House, a mile or so north of the station and town center, is a neo-Gothic mansion in a peaceful forest with 100 cheap beds (£7 beds in four- to eight-bed rooms, D-£18, Db-from £22, sheets included, breakfast not included, CC:VMA, from the station head up Oakpark Drive, after about eight blocks you'll see the sign on the left, tel. & fax 066/28658). They have a free shuttle service when the minibus is working.

Transportation Connections—Tralee

By train to: Dublin (4/day, 3/day on Sunday, 4 hrs), **Rosslare** (1/day, 5 hrs). Train info: tel. 066/23522.

By bus to: Dingle (7/day, less off-season and on Sunday, 75 min, £6), **Galway** (5/day), **Limerick** (5/day, 2 hrs), **Doolin/Cliffs of Moher** (daily at 9:30 and 15:30), **Ennis** (5/day, 3 hrs), **Rosslare** (3/day, 7 hrs, £16), **Shannon** (5/day). Tralee's bus station is at the train station. Bus info: tel. 066/23566.

Car Rental: Duggan's Garage Practical Car Hire rents Fiat Unos (£35/24 hours, £70/48 hours, CC:VM, three blocks from the station on Ashe Street, tel. 066/21124, fax 066/27527).

Kerry Airport, a 45-minute drive from Dingle Town, now offers direct flights to Dublin, London (daily, £86), and even points on the Continent (tel. 066/64644).

Route Tips for Drivers

Between Tralee and Dingle: Drivers choose between the narrow, but very exciting, Conor Pass road or the faster, easier, but still narrow N86 through Lougher and Anascaul. On a clear day Conor Pass comes with incredible views over Tralee Bay and Brandon Bay, the Blasket Islands, and the open Atlantic. Pull over at the summit viewpoint to look down on Dingle Town and the harbor. While in Kerry listen to Radio Kerry FM 97. To practice your Gaelic, tune into FM 94.4.

Between Tralee and Galway/Burren/Doolin: The Killimer–Tarbert ferry connection allows those heading for the Cliffs of Moher to avoid the 80-mile detour around the Shannon River. If you're going to Galway, the Limerick route is faster but the ferry route is more scenic (hrly trips, 20 min, £9/carload, leaves on the half-hour going north and top of the hour going south in peak times, tel. 065/53124).

GALWAY, ARAN ISLANDS, AND COUNTY CLARE

GALWAY

Galway feels like a boomtown—rare in western Ireland. With 52,000 people, it's the area's main city—a lively university town and the county's industrial/administrative center. Amid the traditional regions of Connemara, James Joyce country, and the Aran Islands, it's also a Gaelic cultural center.

For the tourist, Galway is well-connected to Dublin, a traditional music capital, and the convenient jumping-off point for a visit to the Aran Islands.

While Galway has a long and interesting history, its British overlords (who ruled here until 1922) had little use for anything important to the Irish heritage and, consequently, precious little from old Galway survives. What does survive has the interesting disadvantage of being built by the local limestone which, even if medieval, looks like modern stone construction. A spirit of preservation came with the city's quincentennial celebration in 1984.

What Galway lacks in turnstile sights, it makes up for in ambience. Just to wander its medieval streets with their delightfully ramshackle mix of colorful facades, labyrinthine pubs, weather-resistant buskers, and steamy eateries is an entertaining way to while away an afternoon.

Galway gets even better after dark with fine theaters and a pub scene Dubliners travel for. Visitors mix with old-timers and students as the traditional music goes round and round.

If you hear a strange language on the streets and wonder where those people are from . . . it's Irish and so are they.

Galway History

The medieval fishing village of Galway went big-time when the Normans captured the territory from the O'Flaherty family in 1234. Making the town a base, they invited in their Anglo friends, built a wall (1270), and kicked out the Irish. Galway's Celtic name (Gaillimh) comes from an old Irish word, *gall*, which means foreigner. Except for a small section in the Eyre Square Shopping Center and a chunk at the Spanish Arch, that Norman wall is gone.

In the 14th century, 14 merchant families, or "tribes" as they were known, controlled Galway's commercial traffic, including the lucrative wine trade with Spain and France. These English families were constantly clashing with the local Irish. While the wall was built to "keep out the O's and the Macs," it didn't always work. A favorite prayer at the time was "From the fury of the O'Flaherty's, good Lord deliver us."

Galway's support of the English king helped it prosper. But with the rise of Oliver Cromwell, Galway paid a price. After sieges in 1651 by Cromwell and in 1691 by the Protestant King William, Galway declined. It wasn't until the last half of this century that it regained some of its importance and wealth.

Galway Legends

Because of the dearth of physical old stuff, the town milks its legends. Here are a few you'll encounter repeatedly:

In the 15th century, the mayor, one of the Lynch tribe, condemned his son to death for the murder of a Spaniard. When no one in town could be found to hang the popular boy, the dad—who loved justice more than his son—did it himself.

Columbus is said to have stopped in Galway in 1477. He may have been inspired by tales of the voyage of St. Brandon, the Irish monk who is thought by some (mostly Irish) to have beaten Columbus to the New World by nearly a thousand years.

On the main drag you'll find a pub called the King's Head. It was originally given to the man who chopped the head off of King Charles I in 1649. For his safety he settled in Galway, about as far from London as an Englishman could go back then.

Every sight in town finds a way to tell you the story about the Claddagh ring—so I won't.

Planning Your Time

Galway's sights are little more than pins on which to hang the old town. The joy of Galway is its street scene. You could see its "sights" in three hours but without an evening in town, you missed the best. Many spend three nights here with two days: one for the town and another for a side trip to Connemara, the Burren, or the Aran Islands.

Galway, Aran Islands, and County Clare

Orientation (tel. code: 091)

The center of Galway is Eyre Square. Within two blocks of the square you'll find the TI, Aran boat offices, bike rental shop, tour pickup point, the best place for cheap beds, and the train station. The train and bus station butt up against the Great Southern Hotel, a huge gray railroad hotel that overlooks and dominates Eyre Square. The lively old town lies between Eyre Square and the river. From Eyre Square, Williamsgate Street leads right through the old town (changing names several times) to Wolfe Tone Bridge. Nearly everything you'll see and do is within a few minutes' walk of this spine.

Tourist Information: The TI, just off the lower side of Eyre Square at the corner of Victoria Place and Merchants Road, is a big busy center with a bookshop and many booking services (daily 9:00–17:45, summer until 20:00, tel. 091/563-081). Pick up the TI's *Galway Magazine* (£1, includes three walking tours).

Helpful Hints

Crowd Control: Expect huge crowds during the Galway Arts festival (15 days in mid-July) and the Galway Races (late

July/early August, three days in mid-September, and three days in late October).

Bike Rental: Irish Cycle Hire is next to the Great Western Hotel opposite the station (tel. 091/561-498).

Laundry: Prospect Hill Laundrette (Monday–Saturday 8:30–18:00, closed Sunday, £4 self-serve, £7 drop off, 44 Prospect Hill, 100 meters from the town square, tel. 091/568-343).

Cyber Café: Internet Arcade in Fun World on Eyre Square rents internet access for £3 per hour (tel. 091/561-415).

Sights—Medieval Galway's "Latin Quarter"

From the top of Eyre Square, Williamsgate Street (named for the old main gate of the Norman town wall that once stood here) is the spine of medieval Galway, leading downhill straight to the Corrib River. While the road changes names several times (William, Shop, High, and Quay Streets), it leads generally downhill and straight past these sights:

Lynch's Castle (now a bank), Galway's best surviving 16th-century fortified townhouse, was the home of the Lynch family—the most powerful of the town's 14 tribes. More than 60 Lynch mayors ruled Galway in the 16th and 17th centuries.

St. Nicholas' Church (half a block off the main street, on the right) is the finest surviving medieval building in town (1320), dedicated to St. Nicholas of Myra, the patron saint of sailors. Columbus is said to have worshiped here (1477) while undoubtedly contemplating a scary voyage. Its interior is littered with obscure town history (£1 donation for admission). On Saturday morning a wonderful market surrounds the church.

Quais Pub and Restaurant, once owned by "Humanity Dick," an 18th-century member of Parliament who was the original animal-rights activist, is worth a peek inside for its lively interior. The lane just before it leads to the 100-seat Druid Theatre. Drop by to see if anything's playing tonight (£8 tickets for top-notch contemporary Irish theater).

Spanish Arch/City Museum, overlooking the Corrib River (on the left), is the best-surviving chunk of the old city wall. The Spanish Arch (1584), the place where Spanish ships would unload their cargo, is a reminder of the trading importance Galway once enjoyed. The tiny museum is really pretty weak—but if it's fragments of old Galway you're looking for, this is where they're kept (£1, daily 10:00–13:00 and 14:15–17:15 May–October, less off-season, tel. 091/567-641).

At the **Corrib River** you'll find a riverside park perfect for a picnic (although the town's best chippie, McDonagh's, is across the street). Over the river (southeast of the bridge) is the modern housing project that, in the 1930s, replaced the original **Claddagh**. The Claddagh was a picturesque Gaelic-speaking fishing village with a strong tradition of independence—and open sewers. This gaggle of thatched cottages actually functioned as an independent community with its own "king" until early in this century. Nothing survives today except for the tradition of the popular Claddagh ring—two hands holding a heart—which comes with a fascinating story.

Notice the monument (just before the bridge) given Galway by the people of Genoa celebrating Columbus' visit here in 1477. (That acknowledgment, from a town known in Italy for its stinginess, helps to substantiate the murky visit.) From the bridge look up the river. The green copper dome marks the new city cathedral. Down the river is a tiny harbor with a few of Galway's famous square-rigged "hooker" fishing ships tied up and on display. Beyond that a huge park of reclaimed land is popular with the local kids for Irish football and hurling. From there the promenade leads to the resort town of Salthill.

Sights—Galway

▲▲▲**Walking Tour**—Kay Davis enjoys taking small groups on intimate walks through old Galway. Starting at the TI, she covers Eyre Square, the cathedral, and the old town, then finishes up at the Spanish Arch. Her two-hour walks go daily except Sunday at 11:30 (£3.50, June–September, tickets at TI, Kay does private walks for £12, tel. 091/794-435). Western Heritage does a similar walk at 14:30 (same price and starting point, specifics at TI). While several bus companies do one-hour £5 Galway tours, Galway tours better on foot.

▲**Eyre Square**—In the Middle Ages this was a green just outside the town wall. The square is named for the mayor who, in 1710, gave the land to the city. While still called Eyre Square, it now contains John F. Kennedy Park—established in memory of the Irish-descended president's visit in 1963 a few months before he was assassinated. On a sunny day it's a popular grassy hangout. Walk to the rust-colored *Quincentennial Fountain* (built in 1984 to celebrate the 500th anniversary of the incorporation of the city). The sails represent Galway's "hooker" fishing ships and the trading vessels that made Galway a trading center so long ago. The Browne Doorway, from a 1627 fortified townhouse, is a reminder of the 14 family "tribes" that once ruled the town. Each had a town castle—much like the towers that characterize the towns of Tuscany with their feuding noble families. So little survives of medieval Galway that the town makes a huge deal of any surviving window or crest. The cannons are from the Crimean War (1854). The statue is of Patrick O'Connor, Galway's favorite Gaelic poet, who'd sit on a limestone wall, as sculpted, recording the local life.

The Eyre Square Shopping Center (arcaded entry from the square) leads to a surviving piece of the old town wall that

Galway

includes two reconstructed towers. Today it's a modern, people-filled shopping mall.

▲▲**Cathedral** (of our Lady Assumed into Heaven and Saint Nicholas)—Opened by American Cardinal Cushing in 1965, this is one of the last great stone churches built in Europe. The interior is a treat: mahogany pews set on green Connemara marble floors under a Canadian cedar ceiling. The acoustically correct cedar is good for the church's fine pipe organ. Two thousand worshipers sit in the round facing the central altar. A Dublin woman carved 14 larger-than-life stations of the cross. The carving above the chapel (left of entry) is from the old St. Nicholas church. Explore the modern stained glass. Find the Irish holy family—with Mary knitting and Jesus offering Joseph a cup of tea. The window depicting the Last Supper is particularly creative—find the 12 apostles. Church bulletins at the doorway tell of upcoming Masses and concerts.

Salmon Weir Bridge—This bridge was the local bridge of sighs. It led from the courthouse (opposite the church) to the prison (torn down to build the church—unlikely in the United States). Today the bridge provides a fun view of the fishing action. Salmon run up this river most of the summer (look for them). Fishermen, who wear waders and carry walking sticks to withstand the strong current, book long in advance to get half-day appointments for a casting spot. Canals multiplied in this city (sometimes called the Venice of Ireland) to power more water mills.

Sights—Outer Galway

▲**Galway Irish Crystal Heritage Center**—This is a grand-sounding name in a grand new building for a sight made-to-order for big bus groups. Still, this cheap and handy (for drivers) tour is the place to see the making of Irish crystal. Tours go every half-hour. After a 10-minute video subliminally sells you crystal while wowing you with Galway sights, you follow a rushed guided tour past craftsmen cutting crystal and then through a small museum. The museum, which is more interesting then Galway's City Museum, gives you a good rundown on the Claddagh Village and a chance to see a large "hooker" named *Fiona* (£1, daily 9:00–20:00, less on weekends and off-season, good cafeteria, five minutes out of Galway on the Dublin road N6, or take any bus—every 20 minutes—from Eyre Square to Merlin Park, tel. 091/757-311).

▲**Salthill**—This small resort packs pubs, discos, amusement centers, and a fairground up against a fine mile-long beach promenade. For sunny time on the beach, a relaxing sunset stroll, or late-night traditional music or later-night disco action, Salthill hops (bus #1 or #2 from Eyre Square).

Dog Racing—Join the locals and cheer on the greyhounds on Tuesday and Friday evenings from 8:15 to 22:00 (£3, 10-minute walk from Eyre Square to the stadium).

Entertainment

▲▲▲**Traditional Irish Music in Pubs**—Galway (like Dingle and Doolin) is a mecca for good Irish music (nightly 21:30–23:30).

Unlike Dingle and Doolin, this is a university town and the pubs are often overrun with noisy students. Still, the chances of landing a seat close to a churning band surrounded by new Irish friends are pretty good any evening of the year. Touristy and student pubs are found and filled around Eyre Square and along the main drag down to the Spanish Arch. Across the bridge along William Street West and Dominick Street Upper you will find Galway's classic old pubs, people, and great folk music that you can actually get close enough to hear. The **Crane Bar** is a local favorite hosting top-notch musicians. **Monreo's** is also very good and can get wild when fiddlers get into high gear. **Rushing Dove** is also worth a look. For a more cozy and quiet bar, try the snug **Taylor's**.

Pop into the **Cellar Bar**—there's music up and down stairs. If there's a cover for an Irish group, pay it and be thankful for the smaller, more serious audience (Eglinton Street a block below Eyre Square). Other pubs known for Irish music include **Taaffe's** (nightly music, Thursday, Friday, and Saturday at 17:00, Shop Street, across from St. Nicholas Church) and **The Quays** (very young scene, Quay Street). I like **The Lisheen** the best. There's generally no cover and beer is £2 a pint. Enjoy the painting of the firelit "crossroads dance," an event that still takes place (5 Bridge Street, tel. 091/563-804).

Sleeping in Galway
(£1 = about $1.50, tel. code: 091)
Sleep Code: **S** = Single, **D** = Double/Twin, **T** = Triple, **Q** = Quad, **b** = bathroom, **t** = toilet only, **s** = shower only, **CC** = Credit Card (**V**isa, **M**asterCard, **A**mex).

There are three price tiers for most beds in Galway: high season (Easter–October), off-season, and charge-what-you-like festival times (e.g., race weekends). I've listed high-season rates. B&Bs simply play the market. If you're on a tight budget, call a few and see what the prices do. All B&Bs include a full fried breakfast in their price.

Kinlay House is the no-nonsense place for budget train travelers to sleep. Just 100 yards from the train station, it's incredibly well-run with 150 beds (one to eight beds per room) in bare, clean, and simple rooms. Prices range from £8 for a bed in an eight-bed room to £30 for a double with bath (CC:VM; includes continental breakfast, elevator, self-service kitchen, Internet access, laundrette, luggage storage, and budget USIT travel agency downstairs; across the street from the TI on Merchants Road, tel. 091/565-244, fax 091/565-245). Easygoing people of any age will feel comfortable here. **Great Western House**, even closer to the station, is similar but bigger, scruffier, and a bit more expensive (Frenchville Lane, tel. 091/561-150, e-mail: shaungwh@id.ie).

Barnacle's Quay Street Hostel is a shiny new, well-run hostel right in the center of town (£9 dorm beds in four-bed rooms, with bath £12, breakfast included, 10 Quay Street, tel. 091/568-644).

Expensive B&Bs on College Road

Drivers, following city center signs into Galway, drive right by a string of B&Bs just after the Greyhound racing stadium. These are a five-minute walk from Eyre Square. The first two listed are the best values. Most are clever and scheming in the battle for the tourist punt. **Petra House**, a peaceful-feeling brick building renting seven rooms including one family room, is the best I found on the street (Sb-£30, Db-£45, CC:VM, second door from stadium on right at 29 College Road, tel. & fax 091/566-580, run by Joan and Frank Maher). **College Crest Guest House**, a more formal affair with 10 rooms, feels like a small hotel (Sb-£30, Db-£50, Tb-£60, CC:VM, almost smoke-free, closest to town at 5 College Road, tel. & fax 091/564-744, Marion Fitzgerald). **Balcony House B&B** rents nine rooms, all with private bathrooms (Db-£50, 27 College Road, tel. 091/563-438, Michael and Teresa Coyne). **The Graduate B&B** is an industrious place with 10 rooms, some of which are wonderful. The ones on the garden out back, however, are pretty small and cramped for the price (Db-£45, CC:VM, 26A College Road, tel. 091/569-534). **Copper Beech House B&B** rents five rooms a bit cheaper than its neighbors but with an absentee owner (Db-£32–45, CC:VM, 26 College Road, tel. 091/569-544).

Cheap B&Bs on Prospect Hill

Prospect Hill Road is lined with small rowhouses, many of which do B&B. These are very central, just two blocks off Eyre Square (from Richardson's Bar). **Mrs. Bridie Flanagan's B&B** is a humble, friendly old home with a welcoming living room and four rooms—two big and two cramped (fine Db-£32, tiny D-£30, 85 Prospect Hill, tel. 091/561-515).

Jurys Galway Inn offers all the American comforts in a 128-room modern hotel ideally located where the old town hits the river. Big bright rooms have two double beds and huge modern bathrooms (£65 for all rooms whether filled by a single, couple, three adults, or a family of four; £49 in the off-season, breakfast is extra, noisy elevators, lots of tour groups, parking-£5, CC:VMA, Quay Street, tel. 091/566-444, fax 091/568-415, U.S. tel. 800/ 843-3311).

Out of Town in Salthill

Carraig Beag B&B, the classiest, friendliest, and most peaceful of all, is a big brick home on a residential street a block off the beach just beyond the resort town of Salthill. Catherine Lydon, with the help of her newly retired husband Paddy, rents six big, bright, and

comfy rooms with a welcoming living room and a social breakfast
table (Sb-£30–35, Db-£36–40, family room-£50–60; eight-minute
drive from Galway: Follow the beach past Salthill, take second
right after golf course on Knocknacarra Road, and go two blocks
to 1 Burren View Heights; tel. 091/521696). The #2 bus (3/hrly,
60p) goes from Eyre Square to the Knocknacarra stop at the
B&B's doorstep.

Eating in Galway

Being a tourist and college town, the city is filled with colorful,
fun, and inexpensive eateries. People everywhere seem to be
enjoying their food. Two handy places to try (one at the top and
the other at the bottom of the old town):

McDonagh's Fish and Chips is everybody's favorite chippie.
They have a fast, cheap section and a classier restaurant. If you're
determined to try Galway oysters, remember that they're in season
September through April only. Other times you'll eat Pacific oysters—which doesn't make much sense to me (£3 cheap lunch, £10
in restaurant, nonsmoking, near the river at 22 Quay Street, tel.
091/565-01).

The Galway Bakery Company is a popular and basic place for
a quick Irish meal (£3–5 meals in the ground-floor cafeteria, more
pricey restaurant upstairs, 9 Williamsgate Street, near Eyre Square).

If you have a car, consider a **Dunguaire Medieval Castle
Banquet**, in Kinvarra, a 30-minute drive south of Galway (for
more information, see Kinvarra, near end of chapter). The 17:30
banquet can be done very efficiently as you're driving into or out
of Galway (B&Bs are accustomed to late arrivals if you call).

Transportation Connections—Galway

By train to: Dublin (4/day, 3 hrs). For **Limerick**, **Tralee**, and
Rosslare, you'll need to change in or near Dublin. Train info: tel.
091/564-222.

By bus to: Ennis (5/day, 1 hr), **Doolin/Cliffs** (3/day, 2.5
hrs), **Rosslare** (3/day, 6.5 hrs), **Dublin** (8/day, 4 hrs). Bus info: tel.
091/562-000. Nestor Travel runs a cheap and fast bus service from
Galway to Dublin and the Dublin airport (4/day, 3 hrs, tel. 091/
797-144 for specifics).

ARAN ISLANDS

The Arans are made up of three limestone islands: Inishmor,
Inishmaan, and Inisheer. The largest, Inishmor (eight miles by two
miles) is by far the most populated, interesting, and visited. The
landscape of all three islands is harsh—windswept, rocky fields
divided by stone walls and steep, rugged cliffs. During the winter
severe gales sweep the islands; because of this, most of the settlements on Inishmor are found on its more peaceful eastern side.

There's a stark beauty about these islands and the simple lives of its inhabitants. Precious little of the land is productive; in the past its people made a precarious living from fishing and farming. The layers of limestone rock meant that there was little natural soil. Farming soil has been built up by the islanders—the result of centuries of layering seaweed and sand together. The fields are small, divided by more than 800 miles of dry-stone wall. Most of these are built in the Aran "gap" style, where angled upright stones are filled with smaller stones. This allows a farmer who wants to move stock to dismantle and rebuild the walls easily. Nowadays tourism boosts the local economy.

The islands are a Gaeltacht area. While the islanders speak Irish among themselves, they happily speak English for their visitors. Many of them have direct or personal connections with America, and will ask you if you know their cousin Paddy in New York City.

Today the 900 people of Inishmor (literally, "the big island") greet as many as 2,000 visitors a day. The vast majority of these are day-trippers. They'll hop on a minibus at the dock for a 2.5-hour tour to the Dun Aengus fort and spend an hour or two browsing through the few shops or sitting at a picnic table outside a pub with their Guinness.

The other islands, Inishmaan and Inisheer, are smaller, much less populated and less touristed. While extremely quiet, they have B&Bs, daily flights, and ferry service. For most, the big island is quiet enough.

Kilronan, on Inishmor

By far the Aran Islands' largest town, Kilronan is still just a village. Groups of backpackers wash ashore with the landing of each ferry. Minibuses, bike shops, and a few old men in pony carts sop up the tourists. There are five or six shops and about as many pubs, restaurants, and B&Bs. All of Kilronan is within a few minutes' walk. The Heritage Center, post office, bank (open only on Wednesday and Thursday), and best folk-music pub are a few blocks inland. The huge SPAR supermarket, two blocks inland from the harbor, seems too big for the tiny community. Several huts rent bikes (about £3 for four hours to £6 for 24 hours).

Tourist Information: The TI is helpful (daily in summer 10:00–18:45, shorter hours March–October, closed in winter, faces the harbor, tel. 099/61263), but don't rely on them for accommodations. The only people who work with them are out of town and desperate.

Getting Around Inishmor

Just about anything rolling functions as a taxi. A trip from Kilronan to Dun Aengus costs about £2 in a shared minibus. Flag them down and don't hesitate to bargain. Pony carts cost about £20 per load for a trip to the west end of the island. Biking is great. Bikers take the high road over and the low road back—fewer hills, scenic shoreline, and at low tide, 50 seals sunbathing.

Sights—Inishmor

▲**Aran's Heritage Center**—This little museum, while nothing impressive, offers a worthwhile introduction to the island with displays covering the geology, its archeological wonders, and the traditional lifestyle (£2.50, daily 10:00–19:00, tel. 099/61355).

Man of Aran—The 1934 movie *Man of Aran*, giving a good look at traditional island life with an all-local cast, is shown at the Heritage Center (£3, six showings/day in summer, one hour). The movie features *currachs* (canoe-like boats) in a storm, fishing for sharks with handheld harpoons, how the fields were made from bare rock, and turn-of-the-century life when you couldn't rent bikes.

▲**Island Minibus Tours**—There couldn't be more than 100 vehicles on the island and the majority seem to be minibuses. A line of buses awaits the arrival of each ferry offering 2.5-hour, £5 island tours. Tourists complain that many "guides" don't say much. There's really not much to say. I learned that 900 islanders live in 14 villages with three elementary schools and three churches. Most own a small detached field where they keep a couple of cows (sheep are too much trouble). When pressured for more information, my guide explained that there are 400 different flowers and 19 different types of bees on the island. The tour is a convenient time-saver, zipping you to the end of the island for a quick stroll in the desolate fields, giving you 10 minutes to wander through the historic but visually unimpressive "seven churches," and then dropping you for 90 minutes at Dun Aengus (20 minutes to hike up, 30 minutes at the fort, 20 minutes back, 20 minutes in café or shops at drop-off point) before running you back to Kilronan. Ask your driver to take you back along the smaller coastal road (scenic beaches and sunbathing seals).

▲▲▲**Dun Aengus**—This is the island's blockbuster sight. The stone fortress hangs spectacularly and precariously on the edge of a cliff 300 feet above the Atlantic. The crashing waves seem to say, "You've come to the end of the world." Little is known about this 2,000-year-old Celtic fort. Its concentric walls are 13 feet thick and 10 feet high. As an added defense, the fort is ringed with a commotion of spiky stones sticking up like lances called a *chevaux de frise* (literally "Frisian horses," named for the Frisian soldiers who used pikes like these to stop a charging cavalry). Slowly, as the cliff erodes, hunks of the fort fall into the sea. Dun Aengus doesn't get crowded until after 11:00. I enjoyed half an hour completely alone at 10:00 in the tourist season. Be there early or late if you can (free, always open, 5.5 miles from Kilronan). A small museum displays findings from recent digs and tells the story of the fort.

Inishmor Island

Seven Churches (Na Seacht Teampaill)—Close to the western tip of the island, this gathering of ruined chapels, monastic houses, and fragments of a high cross date from the eighth to 11th centuries. The island is dotted with early Christian reminders of how, in the fifth century, Christianity was brought to the islands by St. Enda, who established a monastery on the island. Many great monks studied under Enda. Among these "Irish apostles"—who started Ireland's "Age of Saints and Scholars" (A.D. 500–900)—was Columba, who founded the monastery of Iona in Scotland.

Kilmurvey—The island's second village sits below Dun Aengus. With a gaggle of homes, a laid-back hostel (listed below), a B&B, a great sheltered beach, and a pub, this (except for the folk music in the pub) is the place for solitude.

Pub Music—Several pubs in Kilronan offer live music nearly nightly in summer. (Off-season you're likely to find music on Wednesday, Friday, and Saturday evenings.) Joe Watty's Pub, just past the post office, has reliably good Irish folk music and tons of tourists. Tigh Fitz, on the airport road, has a more local crowd and great folk music and dancing on Friday, Saturday, and Sunday.

Other pubs offer Irish tunes but with musical detours beyond the tin whistle. The town hall (Halla Ronain) becomes a dance hall on most Saturday and Sunday nights, when from midnight to 02:00 locals have a *ceilidh* (kay-lee), the Irish equivalent of a hoedown.

Sleeping in Kilronan, Inishmor
(£1 = about $1.50, tel. code: 099, mail: Kilronan, Aran Islands)

Remember, this is a poor island. Nearly all rooms are plain, with facilities down the hall. No one takes credit cards.

St. Brendon's B&B, the only place with real charm, is the best place in town. With a cozy living room behind ivy-covered walls and a breezy garden, Kathleen Tierney rents eight rooms (D-£26, Db-£30, about £5 less outside of summer, save £2 if you settle for a continental breakfast, tel. 099/61149).

Bayview House is the biggest place in town and overlooks the harbor (eight rooms, seven with harbor view, D-£34, Db-£40 in July and August, less otherwise, tel. & fax 099/61260).

Costello's B&B has four plain rooms in a plain home in a fine garden setting (D-£28, Db-£32, tel. 099/61241, Sally Costello).

Aran Islands Hostel, overlooking the harbor above the Joe Mac Pub, is cheap but noisy (beds around £9, four to six beds per room, self-service kitchen, laundry service, tel. 099/61255).

Dun Aengus Hostel is for those who really want to get away from things. It's located near Dun Aengus, five miles from Kilronan, and is surrounded by birds, stone walls, and vast views. It's also near a pub (with good music), a restaurant, and a fine beach (£7 per bed in two- and eight-bed rooms, communal kitchen, small shop, free pickup upon arrival if you call, tel. 099/61318, run by friendly manager, Janette). Another B&B nearby is the **Kilmurvey House** (tel. 099/61218).

While Kilronan is getting pretty touristy, you can get out into the Aran countryside and find true peace. The *Man of Aran* **B&B** is as classy as a thatched cottage can be. Rooms are quiet and rustic with fireplaces. The restaurant uses all organic and homegrown vegetables and herbs (£15 meals) and the setting is pristine (this is where the movie was filmed, D-£36, Db-£42, reserve well in advance, 100 meters past the Dun Aengus turnoff, four miles out of Kilronan, tel. 099/61301).

Eating in Kilronan
Kilronan's cafés dish up soup, soda bread, sandwiches, and tea. **Joe Watty's Bar** does good pub grub. Two restaurants do good dinners: the **Aran Fisherman** and the classier **Dun Aengus** (more expensive, tel. 099/61104). The **SPAR** supermarket has all the groceries you'll need.

Transportation Connections—Aran Islands
By ferry from Galway: O'Brien Shipping, with daily departures at 10:30 from Galway (the dock is a five-minute walk from TI) and 17:00 from Inishmor, offers a reliable and easy passage (90 minutes sailing time, £15 return, tel. 091/568-863).

By ferry from Rossaveal: Island Ferries is the most weather-resistant of the companies sailing from a port 20 miles west of Galway (3/day in summer, 2/day off-season, 35-minute crossing but allow two hours including bus connection from Galway, £19 round-trip including shuttle bus from and back to Galway). Shuttle buses depart from Galway 75 minutes before the boat sails. Summer schedule: from **Rossaveal** at 10:30, 13:30, and 18:30; from **Inishmor** at 9:00, 12:00, and 16:30. Island Ferries office is in an alley one block from the Galway TI (tel. 091/561-767).

By ferry from Doolin: This ferry is handy if you're in Doolin, but it's notorious for being canceled because of wind or tides (for specifics, see Doolin, below).

By plane: Aer Arann, a friendly and flexible little airline, flies three planes a day and stops at all three islands (£35 round trip). They fly their nine-seat planes from the Connemara Regional Airport, 20 miles west of Galway (not the Galway airport). A shuttle bus—£5 round-trip—runs from Galway for each flight. The Kilronan airport is small (baggage is transported from the plane to the "gate" in a shopping cart). A minibus shuttle to and from Kilronan costs £2 round-trip (two miles from the airport). For reservations and late seat availability, tel. 091/593-034, fax 091/593-238. Ask for a 10 percent discount—they have lots of coupons out.

COUNTY CLARE AND THE BURREN

Those connecting Dingle in the south with Galway, the urban center of the west, can entertain themselves along the way by skipping through the fascinating landscape and tidy villages of County Clare. Ennis, the major city of the county with a medieval history and a market bustle, is a workaday Irish town ideal for anyone tired of the tourist crowds that plague so many Irish stops these days. The Cliffs of Moher, a series of dramatic cliffs overlooking the Atlantic, offer tenderfeet a thrilling hike. The Burren is a unique, windblown, limestone wasteland that hides an abundance of flora, fauna, caves, and history. For your evening entertainment you can join a tour bus in a castle for a medieval banquet at Kinvarra or join traditional Irish music enthusiasts from around Europe at a tin whistler's mecca, Doolin.

Planning Your Time

By train and bus, Ennis is your gateway to the county.

By car the region can be an enjoyable daylong drive-through or a destination in itself. None of the sights have to take much time. But if you hike for an hour or three, both the Cliffs of Moher and the Burren are better experiences. If driving between Dingle/Tralee in the south and Galway/Aran Islands in the north, the following is a rushed and long day but much more interesting than the fast road via Limerick: north from Tralee to catch the

Tarbert–Killimer car ferry (avoiding the 80-mile drive around the Shannon estuary, see Route Tips in the Dingle chapter), then drive the scenic coastal route to the Cliffs of Moher for an hour break. The scenic drive through the Burren with a couple of stops and a tour of the caves takes about two hours. There's a 17:30 medieval banquet at the Dunguaire Castle near Kinvarra or you could head straight to Galway for a less touristic evening romp through its old town.

Sights—County Clare and the Burren

▲▲▲**Cliffs of Moher**—A visit to the Cliffs of Moher is one of Ireland's great natural thrills. For five miles the dramatic cliffs soar as high as 700 feet above the Atlantic. Drivers park at the visitors center (£1, TI office, shop, and cafeteria; three public buses stop here daily in the summer). From the center, walk 200 yards past harpists and accordion players along a low wall of the local Liscannor slate (notice the squiggles made by worms, eels, and snails a few years ago when the slate was still mud on the sea floor) to the cliff edge. O'Brien's Tower (1853) marks the highest point. The wonderful trail leads along the cliffs three miles south to Nag's Head.

For the best thrill, read the warning, consider the risk, then step over the slate barrier and down onto the stone platform. Here there are no crowds. If you're a risk-taking fool, gingerly belly out to look over the ledge and find yourself in a dramatic world where the only sounds are the waves, the wind, the gulls, and your stomach signaling frantically for help. There's a particularly peaceful corner of the platform over on the far right. In the distance, on windy days, the Aran Islands can be seen wearing their white necklace.

Doolin—This town is a strange phenomenon. Tourists go directly from Paris or Munich to Doolin. It's on the touristic map for its three pubs that feature nightly Irish folk music. A few years ago, this was a mecca. Irish musicians came together here to jam before a few lucky aficionados. But now the crowds and the foreigners are overwhelming the musicians, and the quality of music is not as reliable. Still, Irish as well as European music-lovers crowd the pubs and the bodhran beat goes on.

Doolin has plenty of accommodations (see Sleeping, below), several good restaurants, and a Greek island-without-the-sun ambience. Each pub serves decent dinners before the music starts. The "town" is hard to recognize as a town. It's strung out along a road from the tiny harbor for a couple of miles. Nearest the harbor, the Lower Village (Fisherstreet) has **O'Connor's Pub** (tel. 065/74168) and is the closest thing to a commercial center. A mile farther up the road, the Upper Village (Roadford) straddles a bridge with the other two destination pubs, **McGann's** (tel. 065/74133) and **McDermott's** (tel. 065/74328). Music starts around 21:30 and finishes around midnight. On my last trip I hit Doolin on a mediocre music night. The *craic* is fine regardless.

From Doolin you can hike or bike (rentals in town) up the Burren Way for three miles to the Cliffs of Moher. (Get advice locally on the trail condition and safety.)

The boats from Doolin to the Aran Islands can be handy but are often canceled. Even a balmy day can be too windy (or the tide can be too low) to allow for a sailing from Doolin's crude little port. If you are traveling by car and have time limits, don't risk sailing from Doolin. Without a car you can travel on from the Aran Islands by the bigger boats so Doolin might work for you (one-hour cruise, £20 return, tel. 065/74455 to see what's sailing).

Lisdoonvarna—This little town of 1,000 was known for centuries for its spa and its matchmakers. Today, except for a couple of weeks in September when it celebrates its Matchmaking Festival, it's pretty sleepy. (The bank is open one day a week.) Still, it's more of a town than Doolin and apart from festival time, less touristy. Lisdoonvarna is becoming known for reliably good traditional music in its pubs. I'd stay here rather than in Doolin (see Sleeping, below) and commute. Doolin is just a couple miles down the road.

▲▲**The Burren**—Literally the "rocky place," the Burren is just that. The 50-square-mile limestone plateau is so barren a disappointed Cromwell surveyor described it as "a savage land, yielding neither water enough to drown a man, nor a tree to hang him, nor soil enough to bury him." But he wasn't much of a botanist, because the Burren is a unique ecosystem with flora that has changed little since the last ice age 10,000 years ago. It's also rich in prehistoric and early Christian sights. The first human inhabitants of the Burren came about 6,000 years ago. Today this "Limestone Land" is littered with more than 2,000 historic sites, including about 500 Iron Age stone forts.

Botany of the Burren in Brief: The Burren supports the greatest diversity of plants in Ireland. Like nowhere else, Mediterranean and Arctic wildflowers bloom side by side in the Burren. It's an orgy of cross-pollination that attracts more insects than Doolin does music-lovers—even beetles help out. Limestone, created from layers of sea mud, is the basis of the Burren. (This same basic slab resurfaces 10 miles or so out to sea to form the Aran Islands.) The earth's crust heaved it up. The glaciers swept it bare, dropping boulders as they receded. Rain slowly drilled potholes into the surface. Rainwater cut through weak parts in the limestone, leaving crevices on the surface and Europe's most extensive system of caves below. These puddles grew algae, which dried into a powder. That, combined with bug parts and rabbit turds (Irish hares abound in the Burren), creates a very special soil. Plants and flowers fill the cracks in the limestone. Grasses and shrubs don't do well here, and wild goats eat down any trees that try to grow, giving tender little flowers a chance to enjoy the sun. Different flowers appear at different months, sharing space rather than competing. Flowers are best in June and July.

Sightseeing the Burren: The drive from Kilfenora to Bally-vaughan offers the best quick swing through the historic Burren.

Kilfenora (five miles southeast of Lisdoonvarna) is a good starting point. Its humble but hardworking community-run Burren Centre gives a quick tour of its one-room museum followed by an intense 12-minute video explaining the geology and botany of the region (£2.20, daily 9:30–18:00 in summer, tel. 065/88030). You'll see copies of a fine eighth-century golden collar and ninth-century silver brooch (now in Dublin's National Museum). The ruined church next door has a couple of 12th-century crosses but isn't much to see. Mass is still held in the church, which claims the Pope as its bishop. (In the 16th century, when the Anglican English were taking over Ireland, the Pope defended the town as best he could—by personally declaring himself its bishop.) The Burren Centre lunchroom is handy.

At the Leamaneh Castle, a ruined shell of a fortified 17th-century house not open to anyone these days, turn north on R480 (direction Ballyvaughan). After about five miles you'll hit the start of the real barren Burren and see a stone table a couple hundred yards off the road (to the east, toward an ugly gray metal barn building).

This is the **Portal Dolmen** (also called the Poulnabrone Dolmen—a stone table). Two hundred years ago, locals called this a "druid's altar." Four thousand years ago it was a grave. Wander over for a look. Wander farther afield for some quiet time with the wildflowers. (It's crowded in midday with tour buses, but it's all yours early or late.)

The **Cahercommann** ring fort (one of 500 or so in the area) can be seen on the crest of a hill just off the road about a half-mile south of the Portal Dolmen. (You can park at the intersection and walk up the gray farm's driveway and through the gate marked "stone fort" for a look, but there's really not a lot to see.) The stretch from the dolmen north to Ballyvaughan offers the starkest scenery.

The **Aillwee Caves** are touted as "Ireland's premier show-cave." I couldn't resist a look. While fairly touristy and not worth the time or money if you've seen a lot of caves, they are impressive and offer your easiest look at the massive system of caves that underlie the Burren. Your guide will walk you 300 yards into the plain but impressive cave giving you a serious 30-minute geology lesson. During the Ice Age underground rivers carved countless caves like these. Brown bears, which became extinct a thousand years ago, used this cave for hibernating. At a constant 50 degrees it may have been ideal for a sleeping bear, but I needed my sweater

Burren

(£4, £14 family deal, daily 10:00 to about 18:00; it's clearly sign-posted just south of Ballyvaughan, tel. 065/77036).

Kinvarra—This two-pub town, between Ballyvaughan and Galway (half an hour from each), is waiting for something to happen in its minuscule harbor. It faces the Dunguaire Castle, a four-story towerhouse from 1520 standing a few yards out in the bay. (For B&Bs, see Sleeping, below.)

The **Dunguaire Medieval Castle Banquet** is Kinvarra's most tourist-worthy sight. The 500-year-old Dunguaire Castle hosts a touristy but fun medieval banquet (17:30 and 20:00, tel. 091/637-108). The evening is as intimate as 70 tourists (two tour groups and a few travelers) gathered under one time-stained barrel vault can be. For £30 you get a mediocre three-course meal with wine served amid an entertaining evening of Irish tales and folk songs. It's a small and multitalented cast: one harpist and three singer/actors who serve the "lords and ladies" between tunes. The one-hour medieval stage show that comes with dessert is the highlight (but the Ruthin banquet in Wales is much better).

Ennis—This simple little market town, the main town of County Clare (15,000), provides those relying on public transit with a handy transportation hub (good connections to Limerick, Dublin, and Galway; see Transportation Connections, below) and a chance to wander around a workaday Irish town that is not reliant upon the tourist dollar.

The Franciscan monks arrived here in the 13th century. The town grew up around their friary. The **Ennis Friary**, from 1300,

with some fine limestone carvings in its ruined walls, is worth a look
(£1 includes a personalized tour, daily in summer 9:30–18:30). Ask
the guide to fully explain the crucifixion symbolism in the 15th-
century Ecce Homo carving. (Ennis regional TI tel. 065/28366.)

The town has its history, but apart from the friary, it's best simply wandered through. If you're spending the night (see Sleeping,
below) you'll find plenty of live music in the pubs. In fact, Ennis is
emerging as the next "Doolin" on the traditional music scene. **Kear-
ney's** is the most active pub in the traditional music scene with paid
musicians on Thursday, Friday, and Sunday nights and ad-lib music
on other nights (across the bridge from the Friary, 200 meters up
Newbridge Road, tel. 065/24888). In the next block is Kerins (music
on Fridays). **Quinn's** on Lower Merket Street and **Brogan's** on
O'Connell Street are also likely to have live music.

Sleeping in County Clare and the Burren
(£1 = about $1.50)

Sleeping in Doolin *(tel. code: 065)*
Harbour View B&B is a fine modern house a mile from the
Doolin' fiddles overlooking the valley. Mrs. Cullinan keeps the
fire on in the guests' living room (which is stocked with touring
books and games) and serves a classy breakfast (Sb-£21, Db-£34,
larger family room-£54, on the main road halfway between Lisdoonvarna and the Cliffs of Moher next to the Statoil gas station,
tel. 065/74154). **Doolin Hostel**, right in Doolin's Lower Village,
caters creatively to all the needs of backpackers there for the music
(£8 dorm beds, £18 private rooms, Lower Village, tel. 065/74006).

Sleeping in Lisdoonvarna *(tel. code: 065)*
Each of these three places is on the main "Galway" road near the
center square and church: **Marchmont B&B** rents two large
twin/family rooms and two small doubles in a fine old house (Db-
£32, just past the post office, tel. 065/74050, Eileen Barrett). **Banner County Lodge** (D-£30 and Db-also £30, tel. 065/74340) and
St. Genevieves B&B (D-£26, Db-£30, tel. 065/74074) are closer
to the square but bigger, scruffier, and less personal.

Sleeping in Kinvarra *(tel. code: 091)*
Cois Cuain B&B is a small but stately house with a garden overlooking the square and harbor of the most charming village setting
you'll find. Mary Walsh rents three super-homey rooms for nonsmokers (Db-£36, The Harbour, tel. 091/637-119).

Sleeping in Ennis *(tel. code: 065)*
These three places are clustered a block toward the town center
from the train/bus station: **Greenlea B&B** is a charming little

place with three spacious and comfy rooms run in a simple way by Mary Conway (S-£13.50, D-£27, £1.50 less per person with a continental breakfast instead of a full fry, Station Road, tel. 065/ 29049). **Grey Gables B&B**, just across the street, is a bit more upscale and has four rooms (two small D-£30, two large Db-£36, Station Road, tel. 065/24487, Mary Keane). **St. Judes B&B** rents three sleepable rooms in a bunker-like annex (Db-£32, twin room is much better than the cramped doubles, around the corner from Grey Gables, tel. 065/42383, Catherine Quinn).

The **Clare Hostel** is well-run with good dorm beds (£10, two blocks from the market up Summerhill at the N18, tel. 065/29370, e-mail: stay@clarehostel.ie).

Transportation Connections—Ennis

By train to: Limerick (6/day, 40 min), **Dublin** (7/day, 3 hrs). Train info: tel. 065/40444.

By bus to: Galway (6/day, 1 hr), **Dublin** (5/day, 4 hrs), **Rosslare** (2/day, 5 hrs), **Limerick** (4/day, 70 min), **Doolin/ Lisdoonvarna** (2/day), **Tralee** (5/day, 3 hrs). Bus info: tel. 065/24177.

NORTHERN IRELAND

Ireland was once part of Great Britain—a colony made more distant from London than its Celtic cousins, not so much by the Irish Sea as by its Catholicism. Protestant settlers from England and Scotland were "planted" in Ireland to help assimilate the island into the British economy, but the Catholic Irish held strong to their culture.

Over the centuries, British rule was never easy. But in the beginning of this century the sparse Protestant population could no longer control the entire island. Ireland won its independence but the northern six counties (the only ones with a Protestant majority) voted to stay with Britain.

With 94 percent of the Republic of Ireland Catholic and only 6 percent Protestant, there was no question who was dominant. But in the North, the Catholic minority was a sizable 35 percent that demanded attention. Discrimination was considered necessary to maintain the Protestant status quo in the North and that led to "The Troubles" that have filled headlines since the late 1960s. It is not a fight over Catholic and Protestant religious differences. It's whether Ireland will be free or part of Britain. And the indigenous Irish, who generally want a free, united, and independent Ireland, happen to be Catholic.

When Ireland won its independence (a 1921 treaty gave it dominion status within the British Commonwealth—like Canada) the issue of unity with the North had to be dealt with. It was uncertain what the final arrangement would be. In the North the long-established Orange Order and the newly mobilized Ulster Volunteer Force (UVF) worked to defend the union with Britain. The UVF became the military muscle of the "Unionists." This would be countered on the Catholic side by the Irish Republican

Army (IRA). With the Republic's neutrality and the North's enthusiastic support of the Allied cause in WWII, Ulster won a spot close to London's heart. After WWII the split seemed permanent, and Britain invested heavily in Northern Ireland to bring it solidly into the United Kingdom fold.

With the Civil Rights movement of the 1960s, Irish rights issues needed to be addressed. Extremists polarized things and demonstrations became violent. As Protestants and Catholics clashed in 1969, the British Army entered the fray. They've been there ever since. In 1972, a watershed year, combatants moved from petrol bombs to guns. A new, more violent IRA emerged. In the most recent 25-year chapter in the struggle for an independent and united Ireland, more than 3,000 people have been killed.

A 1985 agreement granted Dublin a consulting role in the Northern Ireland government. Unionists bucked this and violence escalated. In that same year, the Belfast City Hall draped a huge and defiant banner under its dome proclaiming "Belfast Says No."

In 1994 the banner came down. In the 1990s, with Ireland's membership in the European Union, the growth of its economy, and the weakening of the Catholic Church's influence, the consequences of a united Ireland are less threatening to the people of the north. A strong movement toward peace seems to be underway.

In 1994 the IRA declared a cease-fire. The Protestants followed suit and talks are underway. The Republicans want British troops out of Ireland and political prisoners released. The Unionists want the IRA to turn in its arms and figure their prisoners are terrorists and jail is where they belong. Optimists hail the signing of the Good Friday Accord in 1998. Major hurdles to a solid peace persist, but the downtown checkpoints are history, "bomb damage clearance sales" are over, and more tourists than ever are venturing to Belfast.

Terminology

Ulster consists of nine counties in the north part of the island of Ireland. Six of those make up Northern Ireland (three counties remain part of the Republic). *Unionists* want the North to remain with Britain. *Republicans* (and *Nationalists*) want a united and independent Ireland ruled by Dublin. *Sinn Fein* is the political wing of the Irish Republican Army (IRA). In 1996 Sinn Fein (whose leader is Gerry Adams) got its best election ever, with 15 percent of the vote in Northern Ireland. Orange, and the red, white, and blue of the Union Jack, are the favored colors of the Unionists. Green is the color of the Republicans.

Northern Ireland is a Different Country

When you leave the Republic of Ireland and enter Northern Ireland, you are crossing an international border. You change money, stamps, phone cards—and your Eurailpass is no longer valid. The

Irish punt (while worth nearly one British pound sterling) must be changed. Northern Ireland issues its own Ulster pound and also uses English pounds. Like the Scottish pound, Ulster pounds are interchangeable with English pounds. But it's best to change your Ulster pounds into English ones before returning to England (free at any bank in either region).

Safety

Tourists in Northern Ireland are no longer considered courageous (or reckless). Traveling there is as safe as traveling in England. You have to really look for trouble to find it here. Just don't seek out spit-and-sawdust pubs in working-class Protestant neighborhoods and sing Catholic songs. July 12 is Orange Day, the day Protestants parade and flex in favor of remaining separate from the Republic of Ireland. Catholics have their similar days in mid-August. Lie low if you stumble onto any big green or orange parades.

BELFAST

Seventeenth-century Belfast was only a village. With the resettle-ment, or "plantation," of Scottish and English settlers and the suc-cess of the local linen, rope-making, and shipbuilding industries, it boomed. The Industrial Revolution took root with a vengeance in Belfast. While the rest of Ireland remained rural and agricultural, Belfast earned its nickname "Old Smoke" and built many of the brick buildings you'll see today. In 1888 Queen Victoria gave city status to Belfast (which had a population of 300,000). Its citizens then built the town's centerpiece, City Hall.

Belfast is the birthplace of the *Titanic* (and many ships that didn't sink). The two huge, mustard-colored cranes (the biggest in the world, nicknamed Samson and Goliath) rise like skyscrapers above the harbor as a reminder of this town's shipbuilding might.

It feels like a new morning in Belfast. Security checks, once a tiresome daily routine, are now rare. What was the traffic-free security zone has shed its gray skin and is now a bright and bustling pedestrian zone. On my last visit, the children dancing in the street were both Catholics and Protestants. They were part of a community summer camp program giving kids from both com-munities reason to live together rather than apart.

Still, it's a fragile peace and a tenuous hope. The pointedly Protestant billboards and the helicopter that constantly hovers over the Catholic end of town remain reminders that the island is split, and about a million Protestants prefer it that way.

Planning Your Time

Big Belfast is thin on sights. For most, a day of sightseeing is plenty.

Day trip from Dublin: With the handy 130-minute Dublin–Belfast train (and its cheap £17 day-return tickets, £26 on

Friday or Sunday) you could make Belfast a day trip: 7:40—Catch the train from Dublin, 10:30—City hall tour, browse the pedestrian zone, lunch, ride a shared cab up Falls Road, 15:00—Ulster Folk and Transport Museum, Evening—Return to Dublin (last train 20:10).

Two days in Northern Ireland from Dublin: Take the train to Portrush for two nights and a day to tour the Causeway Coast (castle, whiskey, Giant's Causeway, resort fun), then follow the Belfast-in-a-day plan above.

Two days in Belfast: This allows time to splice in the Living History tour, a city walking tour, Ulster Museum, Botanic Gardens, and some low or high after-dark culture.

Orientation (tel. code: 01232)

For the first-time visitor in Belfast for a quick look, the town is pretty simple. There are three zones of interest: central (Donegall Square/City Hall/pedestrian shopping/TI), southern (Ulster Museum/Botanic Gardens/university/accommodations), and western (working-class sectarian neighborhoods beyond the freeway). Belfast's "Golden Mile"—stretching from the Europa Hotel to the university district—connects the central and southern zones with many of the best dinner and entertainment spots. To call Northern Ireland from the Republic of Ireland, dial 08, then the city code (for Belfast: 01232), then the local number.

Tourist Information: This modern TI has an enjoyable bookshop (Monday–Saturday 9:00–19:00, Sunday 12:00–16:00 in summer; closes at 17:15 and all day Sunday in winter; on the north edge of the city center at 59 North Street, tel. 01232/246-609). Get the fine free city map and the biweekly entertainment guide, *That's Entertainment*, which covers pub music, concerts, theater, movies, restaurants, and cultural news. Refer to this for your evening fun.

Arrival in Belfast: Arriving by fast train, you'll go direct to Central Station. Slower trains arc through Belfast, stopping at several downtown stations including Central Station, Great Victoria Station (most central, near Hotel Europa and Donegall Square), Botanic (close to the university and Botanic Gardens), and Adelaide (near several of my recommended accommodations).

Helpful Hints

Laundry: The Laundry Room at 37 Botanic Avenue (weekdays 8:00–21:00, Saturday 8:00–18:00, Sunday 12:00–18:00, self-serve £4.40, drop off £6).

Cyber Café: Revelations Internet Café at 27 Shaftsbury Square, near Belfast Hostel (£5/hour, tel. 01232/320-337).

Bike Rental: McConvey Cycles at 10 Pottingers Entry, near Cornmarket (tel. 01232/491-163).

Getting Around Belfast

If you line up your sightseeing logically, you can do most of the town on foot.

By Bus: Handy buses with friendly drivers go from Donegall Square East to Malone Road and all recommended accommodations (#70 and #71, 90p/ride, all-day £2.40 pass). A free Centerlink bus loops from Central Station to Donegall Square and to Shaftesbury Square, stopping near the TI on North Street (free with any new or old local train or bus ticket, 4/hrly, not Sunday).

By Taxi: Taxis are reasonable and should be considered. Rather than use their meters, which lots of locals don't trust, many cabs charge a flat £3 rate for any ride up to two miles. It's £1 per mile after that. Use a shared cab if you're going up Falls Road (explained below).

Tours of Belfast

▲**Walking Tour**—A 90-minute Town Walk introducing you to the historic core of town leaves from the TI (£4, Saturday at 14:00, call TI for additional times, tel. 01232/246-609).

▲**Bus Tours**—The "Belfast: A Living History" bus tour offers the best introduction to the city's recent and complicated political and social history. You'll cruise the Catholic and Protestant working-class neighborhoods with a commentary explaining the political murals and places of interest—mostly dealing with "The Troubles" of the last 25 years. You see things from the bus and get out only for a tea break (£8, Tuesday and Sunday at 13:00, 2.5 hours, from Castle Place, tel. 01232/458-484). Minibus tours leave from the hostel every morning. They cover the troubled areas in more depth and take time for photo stops (£7.50, two hours, book in advance, tel. 01232/324-733).

Sights—Belfast

▲▲**City Hall**—This grand structure, with its 173-foot-tall copper dome, dominates the town center. Built between 1889 and 1906, with its statue of Queen Victoria scowling down Belfast's main drag and the Union Jack flapping behind her, it's a stirring sight. In the garden you'll find memorials to the *Titanic* and the landing of the U.S. Expeditionary Force in 1942—their first stop en route to Berlin. Take the free, 45-minute tour (summer Monday–Friday usually at 10:30, 11:30 and 14:30, Saturday at 14:30, less off-season, call to check schedule and book, tel. 01232/320-202, ext. 2346). If you can't manage a tour, at least step into the interior with its marble swirl staircase. (Politely ask the receptionist for the free City Hall booklet and postcard that tour-takers get.)

The tour gives you a rundown on city government and an explanation of the decor that makes this an Ulster political hall of

Belfast

fame. Queen Victoria and King Edward VII look down on city council meetings. The 1613 original charter of Belfast granted by James I is on display. Its Great Hall—bombed by the Germans in 1941 and by the IRA in 1991—looks as great as the day it was made.

Across the street, the 200-year-old Linen Hall Library welcomes guests (17 Donegall Square North, tel. 01232/321-707). It has a fine hard-bound ambience, coffee shop, royal newspaper reading room, and a top floor of documents and posters documenting "The Troubles" (top floor by tour only—call for schedule).

Golden Mile—This is the overstated nickname of Belfast's liveliest dining and entertainment district, which stretches from the Opera House to the university district.

The **Grand Opera House**, originally built in 1891, bombed and rebuilt in 1991, and bombed and rebuilt again in 1993, is extravagantly Victorian and the place to take in a concert, play, or opera (closed to sightseers, for ticket information tel. 01232/241-919). **Europa Hotel**, next door, while considered the most bombed hotel in the world, feels pretty casual.

Across the street is the museum-like **Crown Liquor Saloon**. Built in 1850, it's now a part of the National Trust. A wander through its mahogany, glass, and marble interior is a trip back into the day of Queen Victoria (although the privacy provided by the snugs—private booths—allows for un-Victorian behavior; open 11:30–24:00).

Lagan Lookout Visitors Centre—This center shows off the fruits of the city's £750 million investment in its harbor. The tides of the River Lagan left the town with daily unsightly mud flats. The weir, built in 1994, controls the tides, stabilizing the depth of the harbor. It also doubles as a free pedestrian bridge over the river, affording walkers a fine view of the harbor area including the big cranes and the new convention center. The visitors center, while mildly entertaining and enthusiastically "interactive," is not really worth the £1.50 entry fee (Monday–Friday 11:00–17:00, Saturday 12:00–17:00, Sunday 14:00–17:00, a short walk from the TI, just past the Albert clock tower).

▲▲**Falls Road**—It will be a happy day when the sectarian neighborhoods of Belfast have nothing to be sectarian about. For a look at one of the original home bases of the "The Troubles," explore the working-class Catholic Falls Road neighborhood.

At the end of Castle Street you'll find a square filled with old black cabs—and the only Gaelic-language signs in downtown Belfast. These shared black cabs efficiently shuttle residents from outlying neighborhoods up and down Falls Road and to the city center. Any cab (except those in the "Whiterock" line) goes up Falls Road, past Sinn Fein headquarters and lots of murals, to the Milltown Cemetery (70p, sit in front and talk to the cabbie). Easy-to-flag-down cabs run every minute or so in each direction on Falls Road. They do one-hour tours for £12 (cheap for a small group of travelers).

At the Milltown Cemetery walk past all the Gaelic crosses down to the far right-hand corner (closest to the highway) where the IRA "Roll of Honor" is set apart from the thousands of other graves by little green railings. They are treated like fallen soldiers. Notice the memorial to Bobby Sands and the 11 other hunger strikers who starved in protest for a united Ireland in 1981.

The Sinn Fein headquarters is near where Divis Road becomes Falls Road (look for the protective boulders in the sidewalk and the

Irish Republic flag on the roof). The adjacent bookstore is worth a look. Page through books featuring color photos of the political murals that decorate the buildings. Money raised here supports families of imprisoned members of the IRA.

A sad corrugated wall called the "Peace Line" runs a block or so north of Falls Road, separating the Catholics from the Protestants in the Shankill Road area.

Sandy Row—While you can ride a shared black cab through the Protestant Shankill Road area, the easiest way to get a dose of the Unionist side is to walk Sandy Row. From the Europa Hotel, walk a block down Glengall Street then turn left and enjoy a 10-minute walk along a working-class Protestant street. A stop in one of the many cheap eateries here may give you an opportunity to talk to a local. You'll see a few murals filled with Unionist symbolism. The mural of William of Orange's victory over the Catholic King James II (Battle of the Boyne, 1690) stirs Unionist hearts. (From the south end of Sandy Row it's a 10-minute walk to the Ulster Museum.)

▲**Ulster Museum**—While mediocre by European standards, this is Belfast's one major museum. It's free and pretty painless: Ride the elevator to the top floor and follow the spiraling exhibits downhill with a cheery café halfway down. You'll find an interesting *Made in Belfast* exhibit just before an arch that proclaims "Trade is the golden girdle of the globe." The history section is given an interesting British slant (such as the implication that the famine was caused by the Irish population doubling in 40 years—without a mention of various English contributions). Top things off with soggy bits of gold, silver, leather, and wood salvaged from the Spanish Armada's shipwrecked *Girona* (lost off the Antrim Coast north of Belfast in 1588) and a pretty darn good mummy (free, Monday–Friday 10:00–17:00, Saturday 13:00–17:00, Sunday 14:00–17:00, tel. 01232/383-000).

▲**Botanic Gardens**—This is the backyard of Queen's University. On a sunny day, you couldn't imagine a more relaxing park setting. On a cold day, step into the Tropical Ravine for a jungle of heat and humidity. Take a quick walk through the Palm House, reminiscent of the Palm House in London's Kew Gardens, but smaller (free, Monday–Friday 10:00–12:00 and 13:00–17:00, weekends 14:00–17:00, tel. 01232/324-902).

Sights—Near Belfast

▲▲**Ulster Folk and Transport Museum**—This 60-acre two-museum complex straddles the road and rail at Cultra, midway between Bangor and Belfast (eight miles out of town).

The Folk Museum, an open-air collection of 30 reconstructed buildings from all over the nine counties of Ulster, is designed to showcase the region's traditional lifestyles. After wandering through the old town site (church, print shop, schoolhouse, humble Belfast rowhouse, cyber café, and so on), you'll head off into the country to nip into cottages, farmhouses, and mills. Each house is warmed by a wonderful peat fire and a friendly attendant. It can be dull or vibrant, depending upon your ability to chat with the attendants. Drop a peat brick on a fire.

The Transport Museum (downhill, over the road from the folk section) consists of three buildings. Start at the bottom and trace the evolution of transportion from 7,500 years ago—when people first decided to load an ox—to modern times. There are intriguing sections on the local Gypsy culture and the sinking of the Belfast-made *Titanic*. In the next two buildings you roll through the history of bikes, cars, and trains. The car section rumbles from the first car in Ireland (an 1898 Benz) through the "Cortina Culture" of the 1960s to the local adventures of John De Lorean with a 1981 model of his car. (£4, £9 for families, Monday–Saturday 10:30–18:00, Sunday 12:00–18:00 April–September; closes daily at 16:00 in winter; check schedule for any special events on the day of your visit, allow three hours minimum, tel. 01232/428-428.)

From Belfast reach Cultra by taxi (£8), bus #1 or #2 (2/hrly, 30 minutes from Oxford Street) or train (2/hrly, 15 minutes, from any Belfast train station or Bangor). Trains and buses stop right in the park. Public transport schedules get skimpy on Saturday and Sunday. There's a complete schedule on the wall at the bottom building in the Transport area. Drivers can drive from one section to the next.

Sleeping in Belfast
(£1 = about $1.70, tel. code: 01232; to call Belfast from the Republic of Ireland, dial 08-01232 before the local number)
Sleep Code: **S** = Single, **D** = Double/Twin, **T** = Triple, **Q** = Quad, **b** = bathroom, **t** = toilet only, **s** = shower only, **CC** = Credit Card (Visa, MasterCard, Amex).

Belfast's best budget beds cluster in a comfortable area just south of the Ulster Museum and the university. Two train stations (Botanic and Adelaide) are nearby, and buses zip down Malone Road every few minutes (#70 and #71). Any red-and-white bus on Malone Road goes to Donegall Square East. (For the first three places, get off the bus immediately after the green BP gas station or ride the train to Adelaide.) Taxis, cheap in Belfast, will take you downtown for £2.50 (your host can call one). Belfast is more of a business town than a tourist town, so business-class room rates are lower or soft on weekends.

Queen's Elms Halls of Residence is a big brick Queen's University dorm renting more than 300 rooms to travelers during summer break (mid-June–mid-September). While the rooms, all singles and twins, are indestructibly basic with showers down the hall, they come with a free laundry service and a self-serve kitchen

(S-£14, D-£22, cheaper for students, 78 Malone Road, tel. 01232/381-608, fax 01232/666-680).

Ulster People's College Residential Centre rents 30 beds in 10 cheery, non-dormish rooms year-round on a quiet street near the stop for the bus into town (S-£16, D-£32, £2-per-bed cheaper with a continental rather than Irish breakfast, free laundry, 30 Adelaide Park, tel. 01232/665-161, fax 01232/668-111).

Malone Lodge Hotel provides slick, modern, business-class comfort and professionalism in a charming environment on a quiet, leafy street. Its 33 bright rooms have a contemporary French feeling and are discounted on weekends. The lounge and dining room are sumptuous (Sb-£70 weekdays, £40 on Friday, Saturday, and Sunday, Db-£88/£56 on weekends, Tb-£96/£74, elevator, CC:VMA, 60 Eglantine Avenue, Belfast BT9 6DY, tel. 01232/382-409, fax 01232/382-706).

Camera House Guest House is newly renovated with large smoke-free rooms and an airy, hardwood feeling throughout (Sb-£35, Db-£45–52, CC:VM, 44 Wellington Park, Belfast BT9 6DP, tel. 01232/660-026, fax 01232/667-856, Paul Drumm).

Malone Guest House is a classy stand-alone Victorian house fronting the busy Malone Road. It's well-run by Mrs. Millar with two spacious singles and six large, pastel twins (Sb-£35, Db-£50, 79 Malone Road, Belfast BT9 6SH, tel. 01232/669-565).

Windermere House rents 11 rooms, including several small but pleasant singles, in a large Victorian house (S-£22, Sb-£30, very small D-£30, D-£44, Db-£46, T-£47, 60 Wellington Park, tel. 01232/662-693).

Liserin Guest House rents six new-feeling rooms (S-£20, Sb-£23, Db-£40, 7 Eglantine Avenue, tel. 01232/660-769, Sid and Ina Smith). **East Sheen Guest House** rents five basic rooms and includes a light supper at 22:00 (S-£19.50, D-£39, 81 Eglantine Avenue, tel. 01232/667-149, Mrs. Davidson). Nearby, on the same street, you'll find the **George B&B** (D-£35, Db-£42, 9 Eglantine Avenue, tel. 01232/683-212, Colette McGuinness) and the **Eglantine Guest House** (S-£20, D-£38, T-£54, 21 Eglantine Avenue, tel. 01232/667-585).

Belfast International City Hostel is big, basic, and creatively run with 40 twins and quads. It's located near the Botanic train station in the heart of the lively university district and close to the center. Features include free lockers, left luggage, self-serve £3 laundry, cheap cafeteria, elevator, and no curfew (S-£18, D-£26, beds in a quad-£11, includes breakfast, CC:VMA, 22 Donegall Road, tel. 01232/324-733, fax 01232/439-699, e-mail: info@hini.org.uk).

Jurys Inn, the latest in this popular chain, is a huge American-style place that rents its several hundred identical modern rooms for one simple price in downtown Belfast (up to three adults or two adults and two kids for about £65, two blocks from City Hall on Fisherwick Place, tel. 01232/533-500, fax 01232/533-511, e-mail: info@jurys.com).

Sleeping in Bangor
(£1 = about $1.70, tel. code: 01247, mail: Bangor, County Down)
To stay in a laid-back seaside hometown—and more comfort per pound—sleep half an hour south of Belfast in Bangor. Formerly a slick Belfast seaside escape, Bangor is now sleepy and almost residential-feeling. But with elegant old homes facing its newly spruced-up harbor, not a hint of big-city Belfast, and easy train connections to downtown Belfast (2/hrly, 30 min), Bangor appeals. The harbor is a five-minute walk from the train station. The first three listings face the sea a few blocks to the right. The last faces the harbor on the left.

Pierview House B&B is a chandeliered winner with three of its five spacious rooms overlooking the sea (D-£32, grand Db-£34, family room, CC:VM, 28 Seacliff Road, tel. 01247/463-381, Mr. and Mrs. Watts). **Sea Crest B&B** is homey and friendly with no lounge but four fine rooms (D-£32, CC:VM, 98 Seacliff Road, tel. 01247/461-935, Irene Marsden).

Battersea Guest House, one of a row of tall stately homes overlooking the yacht basin, rents four rooms (small D-£34, grand seaview double-£37, 47 Queen's Parade, tel. 01247/461-643, Rene and John Brann).

Royal Hotel is a fine old place right on the harbor with good weekend rates on its 34 rooms (Db-£70 weekdays, £50 on weekends, rooms with a view are pricier, CC:VMA, 26 Quay Street, BT20 5ED, tel. 01247/271-866, fax 01247/467-810).

Eating in Bangor
Your hosts can direct you to their favorite eatery. The bar at **Royal Hotel** (facing the harbor) serves great £6 dinners in a welcoming atmosphere. The **Steamer Bar** (next door, upstairs from the pub) is also good. **Dragon House** provides a tasty Chinese break from all the pub grub (76 High Street, tel. 01247/459-031).

Transportation Connections—Bangor
By train to Belfast: Trains go from Bangor station (the end of the line, don't use Bangor West) into Belfast via Cultra (Ulster Folk and Transport Museum). The journey (2/hr, 30 min) gives you a good close-up look at the giant Belfast harbor cranes. Belfast Central has a free Rail-Link shuttle bus to the town center (4/hrly, not Sunday). Stay on until the Botanic train station for the Ulster Museum, Golden Mile, and Sandy Row.

Transportation Connections—Belfast

By train to: Dublin (8/day, 2.25 hrs), **Larne** (hrly, 1 hr), **Portrush** (7/day, 2 hrs). Train info: tel. 01232/899-411.

By bus to: Portrush (6/day, 2 hrs), **Glasgow** (2/day, 6 hrs), **Edinburgh** (2/day, 8 hrs), **London** (2/day, 12 hrs). Ulsterbus tel. 01232/337-003.

By plane: British Air flies to **Glasgow** (3/day, 45 min, £62 one day in advance) and **London** (5/day, 1 hr, £77 one-way, but you can buy a £55 round-trip ticket and forget to return—it's allowed).

By ferry to: Liverpool via North Irish Ferries (tel. 01232/779-090) and **Stranraer, Scotland** (via *Sea Cat* catamaran, or Stena Line ferry—£25, tel. 01232/747-747). The *P&O Ferry* goes from Larne (20 miles north of Belfast) to **Cairnryan, Scotland** (tel. 0990-980-777).

ANTRIM COAST AND PORTRUSH

The Antrim Coast—the north of Northern Ireland—is one of the most interesting and scenic coastlines in Britain and Ireland. Within a few miles of the train terminal of Portrush, you can visit some evocative castle ruins, tour the oldest whiskey distillery, and hike along the famous Giant's Causeway—a World Heritage Site.

The homely seaside resort of Portrush used to be known as "The Brighton of the North." While it's seen its best days, it retains the atmosphere and buildings of a genteel, middle-class seaside resort. Portrush fills its peninsula with family-oriented amusements, fun eateries, and B&Bs. Summertime fun-seekers promenade along the toy harbor and tumble down to the sandy beaches, which extend in sweeping white crescents on either side.

Superficially, it has the appearance of any small British sea-side resort, but its history and high population of young people (students from the University of Coleraine) give Portrush a little more personality. There are the usual arcade amusements, but also nightclubs, restaurants, summer theater in the town hall, and convivial pubs that people from Belfast travel for. At the end of the train line and just a few miles from several important sights, it's an ideal base for exploring the highlights of the Antrim Coast.

Planning Your Time
You need a minimum of a full day to explore the Antrim Coast, so allow two nights in Portrush. An ideal day might be a bike tour lacing together Dunluce Castle, Old Bushmills Distillery, and Giant's Causeway followed by nine holes on the Portrush pitch-and-putt course. Consider this side trip north from Dublin:
Day 1: 11:00–16:00—Train to Portrush.

Day 2: All day for Antrim Coast sights and Portrush.
Day 3: 8:00–10:00—Train to Belfast, all day in Belfast; 19:00–21:00—Train back to Dublin.

Orientation (tel. code: 01265)

Portrush's pleasant and easily walkable town center features sea views in every direction. On one side is the harbor and restaurants, and on the other are Victorian townhouses. The tip of the peninsula is marked by a lighthouse and a park filled with tennis courts, lawn-bowling greens, and putting greens.

The city is busy with students during the school year. July and August is beach resort boom time. June and September it's laid-back and lazy. Families pack Portrush on Saturdays and revelers from Belfast pack its hotels on Saturday nights.

Tourist Information: The TI, more generous and helpful than those in the Republic, is in the big, modern Dunluce Centre (weekdays 9:00–17:00, weekends noon–17:00, until 20:00 mid-June–August, tel. 01265/823-333). Get their free driving map, the "Places to Visit" brochure, and a free Belfast map if you're Belfast-bound.

Arrival in Portrush: The train tracks stop at the base of the tiny peninsula that Portrush fills. (The small station has no bag check.) The TI is three long blocks from the train station (follow signs down Eglinton Street and turn left at the fire station). All listed B&Bs are within a five-minute walk of the train station (see Sleeping, below). The bus stop is two blocks up and to the right from the train station.

Getting Around the Antrim Coast

By Bus: In the summer open-top "Bushmills" buses connect Portrush, Dunluce Castle, Old Bushmills Distillery, and the Giant's Causeway every two hours (maybe hourly in summer, weather permitting). You could spend two hours at Bushmills and the Causeway, but you'd be bored at the castle (£3.20 round-trip, buy ticket from driver, pick up a schedule at the TI, tel. 01265/43334).

By Car: Distances are short and parking is easy. Don't miss the treacherously scenic coastal route down to the Glens of Antrim.

By Taxi: Groups go cheaper by taxi, which costs only £6 from Portrush to Giant's Causeway. (For £12 the cabbie may wait and bring you back.)

By Bike: Portrush's only bike rental place has closed. Ask around if anyone's renting bikes.

Sights—Portrush

Barry's Old Time Amusement Arcade—This is a fine chance to see Northern Ireland at play. Just below the train station on the harbor, it's filled with candy floss (cotton candy) and little kids

Portrush

learning the art of one-armed bandits—2p at a time. Get £1 worth of 2p coins from the machine and go wild.

Pitch-and-Putt at the Royal Portrush Golf Course—Irish courses, like those in Scotland, are highly sought after for their lush but dry greens in glorious settings. While serious golfers can get a tee time at the Royal Portrush, rookies can get a smaller dose of this wonderful golf setting at the same course's "Skerry 9 Hole Links" pitch-and-putt range. You get two clubs and balls for £4.50 and they don't care if you go around twice (daily 8:30–19:30 April–September, five-minute walk from the station, tel. 01265/823-335).

Sights—Antrim Coast

▲**Dunluce Castle**—The romantic ruins of Dunluce Castle, perched dramatically on the edge of a rocky headland, are a testimony to this region's turbulent past. During the Middle Ages it resisted several sieges. But on a stormy night in 1639 dinner was interrupted as half the kitchen fell into the sea, taking the servants with it. That was the last straw for the lady of the castle. The Countess of Antrim packed up and moved inland and the castle "began its slow submission to the forces of nature." While it's one of the largest castles in Northern Ireland and it's beautifully situated, there's precious little to see among its broken walls.

Expansion of the castle was financed by the salvaging of a shipwreck. In 1588 the Spanish Armada's *Girona*—returning home after an abortive English mission and laden with sailors and valuables of three abandoned sister ships—sank. More than 1,300 drowned and only five washed ashore. The shipwreck was excavated in 1967 and a bounty of golden odds and silver ends ended up in Belfast's Ulster Museum.

Castle admission includes a little impromptu guided tour of the ruins and a 15-minute video that's interesting for its effort to defend the notion of "Ulster, a place apart—facing Scotland, cut off from the rest of Ireland by dense forests and mountains . . . " (£1.50, daily 10:00–19:00 April–September, 10:00–15:30 in winter and shorter hours on Sunday, tel. 01265/731-938).

▲▲Old Bushmills Distillery—Bushmills claims to be the world's oldest distillery. While King James I (of Bible fame) granted their license to distill "Acqua Vitae" in 1608, whiskey has been made here since the 13th century. Distillery tours take you through the process, making it clear that Irish whiskey is triple-distilled while Scotch whiskey is only double-distilled. The 45-minute tour starts when the mash pit is filled with a porridge that eventually becomes whiskey. (The leftovers of that porridge are fed to the county's particularly happy cows.) You'll see thousands of oak casks—the kind used for Spanish sherry—filled with aging whiskey. Some of the casks are filled with a special "millennium whiskey" from 1975 that will age until the year 2000, when those who paid £4,000 for each will be delivered 250 very special bottles for their celebration. (In an uncharacteristically shrewd move, Goldie Hawn bought one before they sold out.) The finale, of course, is the tasting in the 1608 Bar—the former malt barn. When your guide asks for a tasting volunteer, go for it. Two volunteers per tour get to taste test eight different whiskeys (Irish vs. Scotch and bourbon). Everyone else gets a single glass of their choice. Non-whiskey enthusiasts might enjoy their special spicy (cinnamon and cloves) hot toddy. To see the distillery at its lively best, visit when the 100 workers are manning the machinery—Monday morning through Friday noon (weekend tours see a still still). Tours are limited to 25 and book up. In summer call in your name to get a tour time before you arrive (£2.50, daily March–October, tours depart on the half-hour starting at 9:30 with last tour at 16:30, closed winter week-

Northern Ireland's Antrim Coast

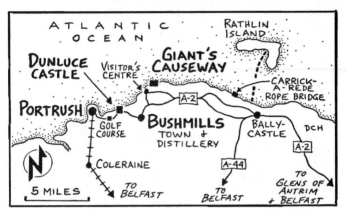

ends, tel. 01265/731-521). The distillery is a signposted quarter mile from Bushmills town center. (Valley View Farm B&B rents rooms at 6a Ballyclough Road, Bushmills, tel. 012657/41608).

▲▲▲**Giant's Causeway**—This four-mile-long stretch of coastline is famous for its bizarre basalt columns. The shore is covered with hexagonal pillars that stick up at various heights as if someone was offering God his choice of 37,000 six-sided cigarettes.

Geologists claim the Giant's Causeway was formed by volcanic eruptions 60 million years ago. As the lava surface cooled, it contracted and cracked into hexagonal shapes. As the layer of hardened but alligatored rock settled, it broke into its many stair steps.

In actuality, the Giant's Causeway was formed by an Ulster warrior giant named Finn MacCool who wanted to reach his love on the Scottish island of Staffa. The causeway once did stretch to Scotland, way back when the two lands were connected. Today, while settled, the formation still extends undersea to Staffa, just off the Scottish coast. Finn's causeway was ruined (into today's "remnant of chaos") by a rival giant. As the rival fled from ferocious Finn back to his Scottish homeland, he ripped up the causeway so Finn couldn't chase him.

For more information on Finn, as well as details on the ridiculous theories of modern geologists, start your visit in the Visitors Centre. The multimedia show is more relaxing than interesting (£1, 4/hrly, 12 min). The real information is on the walls of the exhibition. There are, of course, a gift shop and cafeteria standing by.

A minibus (60p each way, 4/hrly) zips lazy ones a half mile directly to the Grand Causeway, the highlight of the entire coast. But consider walking the mile along the cliff tops to the steep stairs down, and then back up to the Visitors Centre. Or you could walk the entire five-mile Giant's Causeway trail and see the entire honeycombed coastline. The most commanding view of the causeway is from a cliff-top perch called Hamilton's Seat (at the farthest point out on the tour). The 75p hiking guide points out the highlights named by 18th-century guides (Camel's Back, Giant's Eye, and so on). The causeway is always free and open (Visitors Centre open daily 10:00–17:00, until 19:00 in July and August, £2.50 to park, tel. 01265/731-855).

Causeway Coast Bike Ride—This tour requires a bike and, at last check, no one was renting them in Portrush—ask around. It's an eight-mile, one-hour pedal from Portrush past Dunluce Castle and Bushmills to the Giant's Causeway Visitors Centre. From Portrush to Dunluce Castle, allow 20 minutes: Bike along the Royal Portrush Golf Course and past some beautiful beach scenery (a bike-friendly sidewalk keeps timid riders away from traffic). It's another 20 minutes to Bushmills; the distillery is a quarter-mile detour inland from the town square. Bushmills is a good place for a lunch break; choose among the fancy Bushmills Inn, several pantries, and a happy chippie called Hip Chip. From Bushmill the Giant's Causeway is 20 minutes farther. The hills are gentle and traffic's not bad.

▲**Carrick-a-Rede Rope Bridge**—For 200 years fishermen have strung a narrow 80-foot-high bridge (planks strung between wires) across a 65-foot-wide chasm between the mainland and a tiny island. The bridge (not the original) still gives access to the salmon nets that are set during the summer months to catch the fish turning the coast's corner. The island affords fine views and, especially during nesting season, great chances to see seabirds (free, daily 12:00–18:00, strung April–September, 20-minute walk from the £2 car park).

▲**Antrim Mountains and Glens**—Not particularly high (never more than 1,500 feet), the Antrim Mountains are cut by a series of large glens running northeast to the sea. Glenariff, with its waterfalls, especially the "Mare's Tail," is the most beautiful of the nine glens.

Sleeping in Portrush
(£1 = about $1.70, tel. code: 01265, zip code: BT56 8DG)
Sleep Code: **S** = Single, **D** = Double/Twin, **T** = Triple, **Q** = Quad, **b** = bathroom, **t** = toilet only, **s** = shower only, **CC** = Credit Card (Visa, MasterCard, Amex).

Portrush's many B&Bs all seem well-worn. But small-town well-worn is better than big-town well-worn. August and Saturday nights can be tight. Otherwise it's a "you take a half a loaf when you can get it" town. Rates vary with the view and season—probe for softness. Each listing faces the sea, though sea views are worth paying for only if you get a bay window. Ask for a big room (some doubles can be very small; twins are bigger). Lounges are invariably grand with bay-window views. All places listed have lots of stairs but are perfectly central and within a few minutes' walk of the train station. Parking is easy.

A-Rest-A-While Guest House overlooks a seaside park with a grand strand view. Margaret and Ross Torrens keep their old (some say dumpy) 10-room house tidy and completely smoke-free. They promise to honor these prices throughout 1999 (two tiny view S-£15, D-£30, Db-£36, ask for one of their four huge seaview £26 doubles—a great value even with the plumbing down the hall, one huge view family room, 6 Bath Terrace, three blocks from the station on the quiet side of town, tel. 01265/822-827).

Ma Ring B&B rents 14 well-worn but decent rooms (S-£15, Sb-£20–25, D-£25–30, Db-£30–40, family room, self-service kitchen, CC:VMA, 17 Kerr Street, facing the harbor a block in front of the station, tel. & fax 01265/822-765 or tel. 01265/824-499). Call Jim or Eveline to get their best price; then ask for a 10-percent cash/direct booking discount for readers of this book.

West Strand Guest House, run by Muriel Robinson, has 15 tidy tree-house rooms, none with private bathrooms (S-£13–15, D-£26–30, fine view lounge, 18 Kerr Street, tel. 01265/822-270).

Bethel House B&B is a cozy, completely smoke- and alcohol-free Christian-run place overlooking the sea on the quiet side of town. Request the bigger or view rooms. Some doubles, especially on the top floor, are tiny, but all are nicely refurbished (S-£17, Sb-£20, D-£34, Db-£40–42, elevator, big homey lounge used nightly in the summer for a 30-minute hymn-singing fellowship, 7 Lansdowne Crescent, tel. 01265/822-354, Tom and Marie Graham).

MacCool's Portrush Youth Hostel is a friendly and laid-back place with 20 beds in four rooms (two, four, six, and eight beds each, £7 per bed, one tiny £14 double, one all-girls' room, lockers, guests' kitchen, game-stocked lounge, 5 Causeway View Terrace, halfway between the station and the tip of the peninsula in the center of Portrush, tel. 01265/824-845).

Eglinton Hotel, the only real big normal hotel in town, is central but noisy and impersonal. It's a dark place with small doubles and bigger twins (Db-£50–70 with demand, CC:VMA, 49 Eglinton Street, BT56 8DZ Portrush, across the street from the train station, tel. 01265/822-371, fax 01265/823-155).

Drivers may want to stay just out of town at Glenkeen Guest House (11 rooms, Sb-£25, Db-£38, some smoke-free rooms, CC:VM, 59 Coleraine Road, seven-minute walk from the station, tel. 01265/822-279, Mrs. Little) or **Summer Island House** (five rooms, Sb-£20, Db-£40, family room, 14 Coleraine Road, five-minute walk from station, tel. 01265/824-640, Mrs. Armstrong).

Eating in Portrush

Being a university town and a get-away-from-Belfast town, Portrush has more than chips joints. Eglinton Street is lined with cheap and cheery eateries. The great place for dinner is the **Ramore Wine Bar**. While the upstairs restaurant is exclusive and pricey, the much-loved bar below is bursting with happy eaters enjoying the most inviting menu I've seen in Ireland. Huge £7 meals range from steaks to vegetarian, and their good red wine (£1.50 glass) is a nice break after all the Guinness. Come early for a table or sit at the bar (£4.50 lunch specials, dinner 17:30–21:30, closed Sunday, tel. 01265/824-313).

Transportation Connections—Portrush

By train to: Coleraine (2/hrly, 12 min, sparse on Sunday morning), **Belfast** (7/day, connection in Coleraine, 4/Sunday, 2 hrs), **Dublin** (7/day, 1/Sunday, 5 hrs, several tight but easy connections, £21 one-way, £28 round-trip with Belfast stopover, buy ticket in Coleraine).

By bus to: Belfast (along scenic coast, 2/day, 3.5 hrs, £6).

APPENDIX

BRITAIN

Britain was created by force and held together by force. It's really a nation of the 19th century. Its traditional industry, buildings, and the popularity of the notion of "Great" Britain are a product of the wealth derived from the empire that was at its peak through the Victorian age . . . the 19th century. Generally, the nice and bad stories are not true and the boring ones are. To best understand the many fascinating guides you'll encounter in your travels, have a basic handle on the sweeping story of this land.

What's So Great About Britain?

Regardless of the revolution we had 200 years ago, many American travelers feel that they "go home" to Britain. This most popular tourist destination has a strange influence and power over us.

Britain is small (about the size of Uganda or Idaho)—600 miles long and 300 miles at its widest point. Its highest mountain is 4,400 feet, a foothill by our standards. The population is a quarter that of the United States. Politically and economically, Great Britain is closing out the 20th century only a weak shadow of the days when it boasted that "the sun never sets on the British Empire."

At one time Britain owned one-fifth of the world and accounted for more than half the planet's industrial output. Today the Empire is down to token and troublesome scraps such as the Falklands and Northern Ireland. Great Britain's industrial production is about 5 percent of the world's total, and Italy has a higher per-capita income.

Still, Britain is a world leader. Her heritage, her culture, and her people cannot be measured in traditional units of power. The United Kingdom is a union of four countries—England, Wales, Scotland, and Northern Ireland. Cynics call it an English Empire ruled by London, and there is some tension between the dominant Anglo-Saxon English (46 million) and their Celtic brothers and sisters (10 million).

In the Dark Ages the Angles moved into this region from Europe, pushing the Celtic inhabitants to the undesirable fringe of the islands. The Angles settled in Angle-land (England), while the Celts made do in Wales, Scotland, and Ireland.

Today Wales, with 2 million people, struggles with a terrible economy, dragged down by the depressed mining industry. A great deal of Welsh pride is apparent in the local music and the bilingual signs—some with the English spray-painted out. The Welsh language is alive and well.

Scotland is big, accounting for one-third of Great Britain's land area, but sparsely inhabited, with only 5 million people. Only about 80,000 speak Gaelic, but the Scots enjoy a large measure of autonomy with their separate Church of Scotland, their own legal system, and Scottish currency (interchangeable with the British). In a 1998 vote, Scotland has decided to "devolve" further. In 2000 it will pull its members of Parliament from Westminster and, for the first time in nearly 300 years, reestablish its own parliament. International affairs will still be decided in London, but Edinburgh will call most of the local shots.

Ireland is divided. Most of it is the completely independent Catholic Republic of Ireland. The top quarter is Northern Ireland, ruled from London. Long ago the Protestant English and Scots moved into the north—the Catholic, industrial heartland of Ireland—and told the Catholic Irish to "go to hell or go to Connemara." The Irish moved to the bleak and less productive parts of the island, like Connemara, and the seeds of today's "Troubles" were planted. There's no easy answer or easy blame, but the island has struggled—its population is only one-third (3 million) of what it used to be—and the battle continues. Recently the moderate center (which, in spite of the headlines, is the vast majority) has voted major concessions to each side. Protestants acknowledged Catholics have equal rights in the North and Catholics removed the lines refusing to recognize British rule in Ulster from the Republic's constitution.

Just as the United States Congress is dominated by Democrats and Republicans, two parties dominate Britain's Parliament: Labor and Conservatives. (Ronald Reagan would fit the Conservative Party and Bill Clinton the Labor Party like political gloves.) Today Britain's Labor Party, currently in charge, is shoring up a social service system undercut by years of Conservative rule (Thatcher, Major). While in charge, the Conservatives (who consider themselves proponents of Victorian values—community, family, hard work, thrift, and trickle-down economics) took a Reaganesque approach to Britain's serious problems.

This led to a huge Labor victory and the prime ministership of Tony Blair. He's the most popular PM in memory, and his party rules Parliament with a vast majority. Blair's Labor Party is "New Labor"—akin to Clinton's "New" Democrats, it's fiscally conservative but with a keen sense for the needs of the people. Conservative Party fears of old-fashioned big-spending bleeding heart Union-style liberalism have proven unfounded. The Liberal Parliament is more open to integration with Europe. The economy is booming with very low inflation, unemployment, and interest rates. Social programs such as health, education, and the minimum wage are being bolstered but in ways more measured than Conservatives predicted. It looks like Britain is in for a long period of Labor rule.

Basic British History for the Traveler

When Julius Caesar landed on the misty and mysterious isle of
Britain in 55 B.C., England entered the history books. The primi-
tive Celtic tribes he conquered were themselves invaders who had
earlier conquered the even more mysterious people who built
Stonehenge. The Romans built towns and roads and established
their capital at "Londinium." The Celtic natives, consisting of
Gaels, Picts, and Scots, were not subdued so easily in Scotland and
Wales. The Romans built Hadrian's Wall near the Scottish border
to consolidate their rule in the troublesome north. Even today, the
Celtic language and influence are strongest in these far reaches of
Britain.

As Rome fell, so fell Roman Britain, a victim of invaders and
internal troubles. Barbarian tribes from Germany and Denmark,
called Angles and Saxons, swept through the southern part of the
island, establishing Angle-land. These were the days of the real
King Arthur, possibly a Christianized Roman general fighting
valiantly, but in vain, against invading barbarians. The island was
plunged into 500 years of Dark Ages—wars, plagues, and
poverty—lit only by the dim candle of a few learned Christian
monks and missionaries trying to convert the barbarians. The
sightseer sees little from this Saxon period.

Modern England began with yet another invasion. William
the Conqueror and his Norman troops crossed the English Channel from France in 1066. William crowned himself king in Westminster Abbey (where all subsequent coronations would take
place) and began building the Tower of London. French-speaking
Norman kings ruled the country for two centuries. Then followed
two centuries of civil wars, with various noble families vying for
the crown. In one of the most bitter feuds, the York and Lancaster
families fought the War of the Roses, so-called because of the
white and red flowers the combatants chose as their symbols. Battles, intrigues, kings, nobles, and ladies imprisoned and executed in
the Tower—it's a wonder the country survived its rulers.

England was finally united by the "third-party" Tudor family.
Henry VIII, a Tudor, was England's Renaissance king. He was
handsome, athletic, highly sexed, a poet, a scholar, and a musician.
He was also arrogant, cruel, gluttonous, and paranoid. He went
through six wives in 40 years, divorcing, imprisoning, or behead-
ing them when they no longer suited his needs.

Henry also "divorced" England from the Catholic Church,
establishing the Protestant Church of England (the Anglican
Church) and setting in motion years of religious squabbles. He
also "dissolved" the monasteries (around 1540), leaving just the
shells of many formerly glorious abbeys dotting the countryside
and pocketing their land and wealth for the crown.

Henry's daughter, Queen Elizabeth I, who reigned for 45

years, made England a great trading and naval power (defeating the Spanish Armada) and presided over the Elizabethan era of great writers (such as Shakespeare) and scientists (Francis Bacon).

The long-standing quarrel between England's "divine right" kings and nobles in Parliament finally erupted into a civil war (1643). Parliament forces under the Protestant Puritan farmer Oliver Cromwell defeated—and beheaded—King Charles I. This civil war left its mark on much of what you'll see in England. Eventually, Parliament invited Charles' son to take the throne. This "restoration of the monarchy" was accompanied by a great colonial expansion and the rebuilding of London (including Christopher Wren's St. Paul's Cathedral), which had been devastated by the Great Fire of 1666.

Britain grew as a naval superpower, colonizing and trading with all parts of the globe. Her naval superiority ("Britannia rules the waves") was secured by Admiral Nelson's victory over Napoleon's fleet at the Battle of Trafalgar, while Lord Wellington stomped Napoleon on land at Waterloo. Nelson and Wellington—both buried in London's St. Paul's—are memorialized by many arches, columns, and squares throughout England.

Economically, Britain led the world into the industrial age with her mills, factories, coal mines, and trains. By the time of Queen Victoria's reign (1837–1901), Britain was at the zenith of power with a colonial empire that covered one-fifth of the world.

The 20th century has not been kind to Britain. Two world wars devastated the population. The Nazi blitzkrieg reduced much of London to rubble. The colonial empire has dwindled to almost nothing, and Britain is no longer an economic superpower. The "Irish Troubles" are constant as the Catholic inhabitants of British-ruled Northern Ireland fight for the independence their southern neighbors won decades ago. The war over the Falkland Islands in 1982 showed how little of the British Empire is left, but also how determined the British are to hang on to what remains.

But the tradition (if not the substance) of greatness continues, presided over by Queen Elizabeth II, her husband Prince Philip, and Prince Charles. With economic problems, the turmoil of Charles and the late Princess Diana, the Fergie fiasco, and a relentless popular press, the royal family is having a tough time. But the queen has stayed above it all and most British people still jump at an opportunity to see royalty. With the death of Princess Diana and the historic outpouring of grief, it's clear that the concept of royalty is alive and well as Britain enters the third millenium.

Britain's Royal Families

| 802–1066 | Saxon and Danish kings |
| 1066–1154 | Norman invasion, Norman kings (William the Conqueror) |

1154–1399	Plantagenet
1399–1461	Lancaster
1462–1485	York
1485–1603	Tudor (Henry VIII, Elizabeth I)
1603–1649	Stuart (with civil war and beheading of Charles I)
1649–1659	Commonwealth, Cromwell, no royal head of state
1660–1714	Stuart restoration of monarchy
1714–1901	Hanover (four Georges, Victoria)
1901–1910	Edward VII
1910–present	Windsor (George V, Edward VII, George VI, Elizabeth II)

Architecture in Britain

From Stonehenge to Big Ben, travelers are storming castle walls, climbing spiral staircases, and snapping the pictures of 5,000 years of architecture. Let's sort it out.

The oldest ruins—mysterious and prehistoric—date from before Roman times back to 3000 B.C. The earliest sites, such as Stonehenge and Avebury, were built during the Stone and Bronze Ages. The remains from this period are made of huge stones or mounds of earth, even manmade hills, and were created as celestial calendars and for worship or burial. Britain is crisscrossed with lines of these mysterious sights (ley lines). Iron Age people (600 B.C. to A.D. 50) left desolate stone forts. The Romans thrived in Britain from A.D. 50 to 400, building cities, walls, and roads. Evidence of Roman greatness can be seen in lavish villas with ornate mosaic floors, temples uncovered beneath great English churches, and Roman stones in medieval city walls. Roman roads sliced across the island in straight lines. Today, unusually straight rural roads are very likely laid directly on ancient Roman roads.

As Rome crumbled in the fifth century, so did Roman Britain. Little architecture survives from Dark Ages England, the Saxon period from 500 to 1000. Architecturally, the light was switched on with the Norman Conquest in 1066. As William earned his title "the Conqueror," his French architects built churches and castles in the European Romanesque style.

English Romanesque is called "Norman" (1066–1200). Norman churches had round arches, thick walls, and small windows; Durham Cathedral and the Chapel of St. John in the Tower of London are typical examples. The Tower of London, with its square keep, small windows, and spiral stone stairways, is a typical Norman castle. You'll see plenty of Norman castles—all built to secure the conquest of these invaders from Normandy.

Gothic architecture (1200–1600) replaced the heavy Norman style with light, vertical buildings, pointed arches, soaring spires, and bigger windows. English Gothic is divided into three stages. Early English (1200–1300) features tall, simple spires, beautifully carved capitals, and elaborate chapter houses (such as the Wells Cathedral). Decorated Gothic (1300–1400) gets fancier, with more elaborate tracery, bigger windows, and ornately carved pinnacles, as you'll see at Westminster Abbey. Finally, the Perpendicular style (1400–1600, also called "rectilinear") goes back to square towers and emphasizes straight, uninterrupted vertical lines from ceiling to floor with vast windows and exuberant decoration, including fan-vaulted ceilings (King's College Chapel at Cambridge).

Through this evolution, the structural ribs (arches meeting at the top of the ceilings) became more and more decorative and fanciful (the most fancy being the star vaulting and fan vaulting of the Perpendicular style).

As you tour the great medieval churches of England, remember that nearly everything is symbolic. For instance, on the tombs, if the figure has crossed legs, he was a Crusader. If his feet rest on a dog, he died at home; but if the legs rest on a lion, he died in battle. Local guides and books help us modern pilgrims understand at least a little of what we see.

Wales is particularly rich in English castles, which were needed to subdue the stubborn Welsh. Edward I built a ring of powerful castles in Wales, including Caernarfon and Conwy.

Gothic houses were a simple mix of woven strips of thin wood, rubble, and plaster called wattle and daub. The famous black-and-white Tudor, or half-timbered, look came simply from filling in heavy oak frames with wattle and daub.

The Tudor period (1485–1560) was a time of relative peace (the War of the Roses was finally over), prosperity, and renaissance. Henry VIII broke with the Catholic Church and "dissolved" (destroyed) the monasteries, leaving scores of England's greatest churches gutted shells. These hauntingly beautiful abbey ruins surrounded by lush lawns (Glastonbury, Tintern, Whitby) are now pleasant city parks.

Although few churches were built during the Tudor period, this was a time of house and mansion construction. Warmth was becoming popular and affordable, and Tudor buildings featured small square windows and many chimneys. In towns where land was scarce, many Tudor houses grew up and out, getting wider with each overhanging floor.

The Elizabethan and Jacobean periods (1560–1620) were followed by the English Renaissance style (1620–1720). English architects mixed Gothic and classical styles, then Baroque and classical styles. Although the ornate Baroque never really grabbed England, the classical style of the Italian architect Palladio did. Inigo Jones (1573–1652), Christopher Wren (1632–1723), and those they inspired plastered England with enough columns, domes, and symmetry to please a Caesar. The Great Fire of London (1666) cleared the way for an ambitious young Wren to put his mark on London forever with a grand rebuilding scheme, including the great St. Paul's and more than 50 other churches.

The celebrants of the Boston Tea Party remember England's Georgian period (1720–1840) for its lousy German kings. Georgian architecture was rich and showed off by being very classical. Grand ornamental doorways, fine cast-ironwork on balconies and railings, Chippendale furniture, and white-on-blue Wedgewood ceramics graced rich homes everywhere. John Wood, Jr. and Sr., led the way, giving the trend-setting city of Bath its crescents and circles of aristocratic Georgian rowhouses. "Georgian" is English for "neoclassical."

The Industrial Revolution shaped the Victorian period (1840–1890) with glass, steel, and iron. England had a huge new erector set (so did France's Mr. Eiffel). This was also a Romantic period, reviving the "more Christian" Gothic style. London's Houses of Parliament are neo-Gothic—just 100 years old but looking 700, except for the telltale modern precision and craftsmanship. Whereas Gothic was stone or concrete, neo-Gothic was often red brick. These were England's glory days, and there was more building in this period than in all previous ages combined.

The architecture of our century obeys the formula "form follows function"—it worries more about your needs than your eyes. England treasures its heritage and takes great pains to build tastefully in historic districts and to preserve its many "listed" buildings. With a booming tourist trade, these quaint reminders of its—and our—past are becoming a valuable part of the British economy.

British TV

British television is so good—and so British—that it deserves a mention as a sightseeing treat. After a hard day of castle-climbing, watch the telly over tea in the living room of your village B&B.

England has five channels. BBC-1 and BBC-2 are government regulated, commercial-free, and traditionally highbrow. Channels 3, 4, and 5 are private, a little more Yankee, and have commercials—but those commercials are clever and sophisticated and provide a fun look at England. Broadcasting is funded by an £80-per-year-per-household tax. Hmmm, 35 cents per day to escape commercials and public television pledge drives.

Britian is about to leap into the digital age ahead of the rest of the TV-watching world. In 1999 a new TV age will dawn in Britain. Ultimately every house will enjoy literally hundreds of high-definition channels with no need for cable or satellites.

Whereas California "accents" fill our airwaves 24 hours a day, homogenizing the way our country speaks, England protects and promotes its regional accents by its choice of TV and radio announcers. Commercial-free British TV, while looser than it used to be, is still careful about what it airs and when.

American shows (such as *Frazier* and *ER*) are very popular. The visiting viewer should be sure to tune their TV to a few typical English shows including a dose of English situation and political comedy fun, and the top-notch BBC evening news. Quiz shows are taken very seriously here. Micheal Parkinson is the Johnny Carson of Britain for late-night talk. For a tear-filled slice-of-life taste of British soap dealing in all the controversial issues, see the popular *Brookside*, *Coronation Street*, or *Eastenders*.

Benny Hill comedy has become politically incorrect but is rumored to be coming back. And if you like Monty Python–type comedy, you've come to the right place.

IRELAND

Irish History

One surprising aspect of Ireland is the richness of its history. While the island is not particularly well-endowed with historic monuments, it is soaked in history. Here's a thumbnail overview.

The story of Ireland can be broken into four sections:

500 B.C.–A.D. 500	Iron Age
500–900	"Age of Saints and Scholars"
900–1900	Age of invasions and colonization
20th century	Independence and the question of a united Ireland

The Celtic people left the countryside peppered with thousands of ancient sights from the Iron Age. While most of what you'll see are little more than rock piles and take a vigorous imagination to reconstruct (ring forts, wedge tombs, monumental stones, and so on), just standing next to a megalith that predates the pharaohs while surrounded by lush Ireland is evocative. The finest gold, bronze, and iron work of this period is in the National Museum in Dublin.

The Romans called Ireland Hibernia, or "Land of Winter"; it was apparently too cold and bleak to merit an attempt to take over and colonize. The biggest non-event in Irish history is that the Romans never invaded. While the mix of Celtic and Roman contributes to what makes the French French and the English English, the Irish are purely Celtic. If France is *boules* and England is cricket, then Ireland is hurling. This wild Irish national pastime (like airborne hockey with no injury timeouts) goes back to Celtic days, 2,000 years ago.

Celts worshipped the sun. Perhaps St. Patrick had an easy time converting the locals because they had so little sun to worship.

Whatever the case, a former Roman slave boy, Patrick, helped Christianize Ireland in the fifth century. From this period on, monks established monastic centers of learning that produced great Christian teachers and community builders. They traveled, establishing monastic communities all over Ireland, Britain, and Europe. One of the monks, St. Brandon, may have even sailed to America.

While the collapse of Rome left Europe a mess, it meant nothing to Ireland. Ireland was and remained a relatively cohesive society based on monastic settlements rather than cities. While Europe was rutting in the Dark Age mud, the light of civilization shone brightly in Ireland through a Golden Age lasting from the fifth through the ninth centuries. Irish monks—such as those imported by Charlemagne to help run his Frankish kingdom in A.D. 800—actually carried the torch of civilization back to Europe. Perhaps the greatest art of Dark Age Europe are the manuscripts (such as the ninth-century Book of Kells, which you'll see in Dublin) "illuminated," or richly illustrated, by Irish monks. Impressive round towers dot the Irish landscape—silent reminders of this impressive age.

Viking invasions of the ninth century wreaked repeated havoc on the monasteries and shook Irish civilization. Vikings established trading towns (such as Dublin) where before there were only Celtic settlements and monasteries.

The Normans, who invaded and conquered England after the Battle of Hastings (1066), were Ireland's next uninvited guests. In 1169, the Anglo-Normans invaded Ireland. These invaders, bigtime organizers, ushered in a new age in which society (government, cities, and religious organizations) was organized on a grander scale. Individual monastic settlements (the basis of Irish society in the Age of Saints and Scholars) were eclipsed by monastic orders just in from the Continent, such as the Franciscans, Augustinians, and Cistercians.

The English made a concentrated effort to colonize Ireland in the 17th century. Settlers were "planted" and Irish society was split between an English-speaking landed gentry and the local Irish-speaking landless or nearly landless peasantry.

During the 18th century Ireland thrived under the English. Dublin was Britain's second city. Over time, greed on the top and dissent on the bottom required colonial policies to become more repressive. The Enlightenment provided ideas of freedom and the Revolutionary Age emboldened the Irish masses. (Even the non-Catholic Dubliner, Jonathan Swift—dean of St. Patrick's cathedral in the early 18th century—declared "Burn all that's British, except its coal.")

To counter this Irish feistiness, English legislation became an out-and-out attack on the indigenous Gaelic culture. The harp, symbol of Irish culture, was outlawed. Written and unwritten laws made life for Catholics and Irish-speakers very difficult.

The potato famine of 1845–1849 was a pivotal event in Irish history. The stature of Ireland and its language never recovered. In a few years Ireland's population dropped from 8 million to 5 million (3 million either starved or emigrated). Ireland's population has not grown since. Britain's population, on the other hand, has grown from 12 million in 1845 to around 60 million today. (During this period, Ireland's population, as a percent of England's, has dropped from 65 percent to 8 percent.)

While the English are likely to blame the famine on overpopulation (Ireland's population doubled in the 40 years leading up to the famine), many Irish say there actually was no famine—just a calculated attempt to starve down the local population. In fact, there was plenty of food grown on the island for export. It was only the potato crop that failed . . . and that happened to be what the Irish subsisted on.

The average farmer grew fancier export products for his landlord and was paid in potatoes which, in good years, he grew on the side. (If this makes you mad at the English landlords, consider American ownership of land in Central America where the landlord takes things one step further by not growing the local staple at all. He devotes all the land to more profitable cash crops for export and leaves the landless farmer no alternative but to buy his food—imported from the United States—at plantation wages, in the landlord's grocery store.)

The famine was a turning point in Irish history. Before the famine, land was subdivided—all the boys got a piece of the family estate (which grew smaller and smaller with each generation). After the famine the oldest son got the estate and the younger siblings, with no way to stay in Ireland, emigrated to Britain, Australia, Canada, and the United States. Today there are 40 million Irish-Americans.

After the famine, Irish became the language of the peasant. English was for the upwardly mobile. Because of the huge immigration to the United States, Ireland began to face west, and American influence increased. (As negotiations between Northern Ireland and the Irish Republic continue, American involvement in the talks is welcomed and considered essential by nearly all parties.)

The tragedy of the famine inflamed the nationalist movement. Uprising after uprising made it clear that Ireland was ready to close this thousand-year chapter of invasions and colonialism. Finally, in 1919, Ireland declared its independence. While the northern six counties (the only ones without a Catholic majority) voted to stay with Britain, the independent Republic of Ireland was born. (For a review of the ongoing "Troubles" between the North and the Republic, see the Northern Ireland chapter.)

The Irish Pub

When you say "a beer, please" in an Irish pub, you'll get a pint of Guinness (the black beauty with a blonde head). If you want a small beer, ask for a half-pint. Never rush your bartender when he's pouring a Guinness. It takes time—almost sacred time. If you don't like Guinness, try it in Ireland. It doesn't travel well and is better in its homeland. Murphy's is a very good Guinness-like stout but a bit smoother and milder.

In an Irish pub you're a guest on your first night; after that you're a regular. Women traveling alone need not worry—you'll become part of the pub family in no time.

It's a tradition to buy your table a round and then for each person to reciprocate. If an Irishman buys you a drink, thank him by saying, "*Guh rev mah a gut.*" Offer him a toast in Irish—"*Slahn chuh!*" A good excuse for a conversation is to ask to be taught a few words of Gaelic.

Craic (crack), the art of conversation, is the sport that accompanies drinking in a pub. People are there to talk. If you feel a bit awkward, remind yourself of that.

Here's a goofy excuse for some *craic*: Ireland—small as it is—has many dialects. People from Cork are famous for talking very fast (and in a squeaky voice)—so fast that some even talk in letters alone. ABCD fish? (Anybody see the fish?) DR no fish. (There are no fish.) DR fish. (There are fish.) CDBD Is? (See the beady eyes?) OIBJ DR fish. (Oh aye, be Jeeze, there are fish.) For a possibly more appropriate spin, replace the fish with "bird" (girl). This is obscure but your pub neighbor may understand and enjoy hearing it. If nothing else, you won't seem so intimidating to him anymore.

You might ask if the people of one county are any smarter than the next. Kerry people are considered by some of their neighbors to be a bit out of it.

Traditional Irish Music

Traditional music is alive and popular in pubs throughout Ireland. "Sessions" (musical evenings) may be planned and advertised or impromptu. Traditionally, musicians just congregate and jam. There will generally be a fiddler, flute or tin whistle, guitar, bodhran (goatskin drum), and maybe an accordion. Things usually get going around 21:30 or 22:00. Last call for drinks is around 23:30.

The bodhran is played with a small two-headed club. The performer's hand stretches the skin to change the tone and pitch. The wind and string instruments embellish melody lines with lots of improvised ornamentation. Occasionally the fast-paced music will stop and one person will sing an a capella "lament." This is the one time when the entire pub will stop to listen as sad lyrics fill the smoke-stained room. Stories—ranging from struggles against English rule to love songs—are always heartfelt. Spend a lament enjoying the faces in the crowd. A *ceilidh* (kay-lee) is an evening of music and dance . . . an Irish hoedown.

The music comes in sets of three songs. Whoever happens to be leading determines the next song only as the song the group is playing is about to be finished. If he wants to pass on the decision, it's done with eye contact and a nod.

A session can be magic or lifeless. If the chemistry is right, it's one of the great Irish experiences. The music churns intensely while the group casually enjoys exploring each others' musical style. The drummer dodges the fiddler's playful bow with his cigarette sticking half-ash straight from the middle of his mouth. Sipping their pints, a faint but steady buzz is skillfully maintained. The floor on the musicians' platform is stomped paint-free and barmaids scurry artfully through the commotion gathering towers of empty cream-crusted glasses. With knees up and heads down, the music goes round and round.

Make yourself right at home, drumming the table or playing the ten-pence coins. Talk to your neighbor. Locals often have an almost evangelical interest in explaining the music.

Let's Talk Telephones

Here's a brief primer on making direct phone calls. For more information, see the Introduction: Telephones. *page 20.*

Dialing Direct

Calling Between Countries: First dial the international access code, then the country code, then the area code (if it starts with zero, drop the zero), and the local number.

Calling Long Distance Within a Country: First dial the area code (including its zero), then the local number.

Europe's Exceptions: France, Italy, Spain, Norway, and Denmark have dispensed with area codes entirely. To make an international call to these countries, dial the international access code (usually 00), the country code (see chart below), and then the local number in it entirety (okay, so there's one exception: for France, drop the initial zero of the local number). To make long-distance calls within any of these countries, simply dial the local number.

International Access Codes

When dialing direct, first dial the international access code of the country you're calling from. Most European countries use "00" as their international access code. Exceptions follow:

Estonia: 800
Finland: 990
Lithuania: 810
Russia: 810

Spain: 07
Sweden: 009
United States/Canada: 011

BRITIAN / (SCOTLAND IS "00"

Calling home

Country Codes

After you've dialed the international access code, dial the code of the country you're calling.

Austria: 43	Italy: 39
Belgium: 32	Latvia: 371
Britain: 44	Lithuania: 370
Czech Republic: 420	Netherlands: 31
Denmark: 45	Norway: 47
Estonia: 372	Portugal: 351
Finland: 358	Russia: 7
France: 33	Spain: 34
Germany: 49	Sweden: 46
Greece: 30	Switzerland: 41
Ireland: 353	United States/Canada: 1

Calling Card Operators

You can call direct more cheaply by using a British or Irish phone card from any phone booth, but if you'd prefer to use AT&T, MCI, or Sprint, these are the numbers that you'd use. (Note: Calling to hear an answering machine is a $5.50 mistake; you're billed a service charge plus $3 for the first minute even for a five-second call. Call home first with a 20-pence coin to see if anyone's home. Then call back.)

The following numbers are toll-free. You might need to use a coin or phone card to prompt a dial tone, but first try simply dialing these numbers.

	AT&T	**MCI**	**Sprint**
Britain	0800-89-00-11	0800-89-02-22	0800-89-08-77
Ireland	1800-55-00-00	1800-55-10-01	1800-55-20-01

Telephone Directory

For train info anywhere in Britain, dial 0345/484-950.

Britain	**Tourist Info**
Bath	01225/477-101
Blackpool	01253/478 222
Cambridge	01223/322-640
Cardiff	01222/227-281
Chipping Campden	01386/841-206
Coventry	01203/832-303
Durham	0191/384-3720
Edinburgh	0131/557-1700
Hadrian's Wall	01434/605-225
Inverness	01463/234-353
Ironbridge Gorge	01952/432-166

Keswick	017687/72645
London	0181/846-9000
Oban	01631/563-122
Ruthin, N. Wales	01824/703-992
Stow-on-the-Wold	01451/831-082
Stratford	01789/293-127
Wells	01749/672-552
Windermere	015394/46601
York	01904/621-756

Ireland	**Tourist Info**	**Train Info**
Dingle Town	066/51188	—
Dublin	1-850-230-230	01/836-6222
Galway	091/563-081	091/564-222
Kilronan, Inishmor	099/6126	—

Other Useful Numbers in Britain

Emergency (police and ambulance): 999
Operator Services: 100
Directory Assistance: 192 (free from phone booth,
    otherwise expensive)
International Info: 153 (80p)
International Assistance: 155
United States Embassy: 0171/499-9000
Eurostar (Chunnel Info): 0345/303-030
Train and Boats to Europe Info: 0990-848-848

*Note: Understand the various prefixes: Any prefix starting with 01 is a
normal long-distance call. 0891 numbers are telephone sex–type expensive.
Prefixes 0345 and 0845 are local calls nationwide. And 0800 numbers are
entirely toll-free. If you have questions about a prefix, call 100 for free help.*

London's Airports and Airlines

Heathrow
General Information: 0181/759-4321 (transfers to airport,
    arrivals, airline phone numbers, etc.)
Air Canada: 0181/745-6584
American: 0345/789-789
British Air: 0345/222-111 , 0181/759-5511
British Midlands: 0345/554-554, 01332/854-000
SAS: 0171/734-4020, 0181/750-7675
United Airlines: 0800-888-555, 0845/844-4777

Gatwick
General Information: 01293/535-353 for all airlines—
    except British Airways at 0990-444-000.

Climate

The chart below gives average daytime temperatures and average number of days with more than a trickle of rain.

	J	F	M	A	M	J	J	A	S	O	N	D
London	43°	44°	50°	56°	62°	69°	71°	71°	66°	58°	51°	45°
	15	13	11	12	11	11	12	11	13	14	15	15
S. Wales	45°	45°	50°	56°	61°	68°	69°	69°	65°	58°	51°	46°
	18	14	13	13	13	13	14	15	16	16	17	18
York	43°	44°	49°	55°	60°	67°	70°	70°	65°	57°	49°	45°
	17	15	13	13	13	14	15	14	14	15	17	17
Edinburgh	42°	43°	46°	51°	56°	62°	65°	64°	60°	54°	48°	44°
	17	15	15	14	14	15	17	16	16	17	17	18
Dublin	40°	41°	44°	47°	52°	57°	60°	59°	56°	50°	45°	42°
	13	10	10	11	10	11	13	12	12	11	12	14

Numbers and Stumblers

•Europeans write a few of their numbers differently than we do. 1 = 1 , 4 = 4 , 7= 7 . Learn the difference or miss your train.
•In Europe, dates appear as day/month/year, so Christmas is 25-12-99.
•Commas are decimal points and decimals commas. A dollar and a half is 1,50 and there are 5.280 feet in a mile.
•When pointing, use your whole hand, palm downward.
•When counting with fingers, start with your thumb. If you hold up your first finger to request one item, you'll probably get two.
•What we Americans call the second floor of a building is the first floor in Europe.
•Europeans keep the left "lane" open for passing on escalators and moving sidewalks. Keep to the right.
•And please . . . don't call your waist pack a "fanny pack."

Weights and Measures

1 British pint = 1.2 U.S. pints
1 imperial gallon = 1.2 U.S. gallons or about 5 liters
1 stone = 14 pounds (a 175-pound person weighs 12 stone)
28 degrees Centigrade = 82 degrees Fahrenheit
Shoe sizes = about .5 to 1.5 sizes smaller than in the United States

British-Yankee Vocabulary

advert advertisement

afters dessert

"A" levels advanced high school exams

anorak parka

anti-clockwise counterclockwise

aubergine eggplant

Balloons Belgians

banger sausage

bangers and mash sausage and mashed potatoes

bank holiday legal holiday

bap hamburger-type bun

ben Scottish for mountain

billion ten of our billions (a million million)

biro ballpoint pen

biscuit cookie

black pudding sausage made from dried blood

bloke man, guy

bobby policeman ("copper" is more common)

Bob's your uncle there you go (with a shoulder shrug), naturally

bomb success

bonnet car hood

boot car trunk

BR British Rail

braces suspenders

bridle way path for walkers, bikers, and horse riders

brilliant cool

BTA British Tourist Authority

bubble and squeak cold meat fried with cabbage and potatoes

bum bottom or "backside"

candy floss cotton candy

car boot sale temporary flea market with car trunk displays (a good place to buy your stolen goods back)

caravan trailer

cat's eyes reflectors on the road

ceilidh Scottish informal evening of song and folk fun (kay-lee)

cheap and nasty cheap and bad quality (pay monkeys, get peanuts)

cheeky (or saucy) smart alecky

cheerio goodbye

cheers thanks (also, a toast)

chemist pharmacist

chips french fries

chockablock jam-packed

cider alcoholic apple cider

clearway road where you can't stop

coach long-distance bus

concession discounted admission

cotton buds Q-tips

courgette zucchini

courier tour escort or guide

craic (crack) good conversation (Irish and spreading to England)

crisps potato chips

cuppa cup of tea

dear expensive

dicey iffy, risky

digestives round graham crackers

dinner lunch or dinner

diversion detour

donkey's years until the cows come home

draughts checkers

drawing pin thumbtack

dual carriageway divided highway (four lanes)

estate agent realtor

face flannel washcloth

fag cigarette

fagged exhausted
faggot meatball
fanny vagina
fell mountain, hill, or high plain
first floor second floor
flat apartment
football soccer
force waterfall (lake district)
fortnight two weeks
Frogs French people
Full Monty The whole sha-bang. Everything.
gallery balcony
gallon 1.2 American gallons
gangway aisle
gaol jail (same pronunciation)
garden yard
Geordie from northeast England (Durham): coal-mining culture/accent
give way yield
glen Scottish for narrow valley
goods wagon freight truck
grammar school high school
half eight 8:30 (not 7:30)
heath open land without trees
holiday vacation
homely likable or cozy
hoover vacuum cleaner
hundredweight 112 pounds
ice lolly popsicle
interval intermission at the theater
ironmonger hardware store
jelly jello
Joe Bloggs John Doe
jumble sale, rummage sale
jumper sweater
keep your pecker up be brave
kiosk booth
kipper smoked herring
knackered exhausted (Cockney: cream crackered)
knickers ladies' panties
knocking shop brothel

knock up wake up or visit
ladybird ladybug
lead leash
let rent
lip salve chapstick
loo toilet or bathroom
lorry truck
mac mackintosh coat, raincoat
mate buddy, friend (boy or girl)
mean stingy
mews courtyard stables, often used as cottages
minced meat hamburger meat
motorway highway
nappy diaper
natter talk and talk
neat a straight drink
neep Scottish for turnip
nosh food or eat
nought zero
noughts & crosses tic-tac-toe
off license liquor store or a place selling take-away liquor
take away to go
pasty crusted savory (usually meat) pie
pavement sidewalk
petrol gas
pissed (rude), paralytic, bevvied, sloshed, wellied, popped up, ratted, pissed as a newt drunk
pillar box postbox
pitch playing field
plaster Band-Aid
poppers (or press studs) snaps
pram baby carriage
publican person who runs a pub
public convenience public toilets
public school private "prep" school (Eton)
put a sock in it shut up

queue line
queue jump crowd in line
queue up line up
quid pound (money, worth about $1.60)
randy horny
redundant, made fired or laid off
Remembrance Day Veterans' Day
return ticket round-trip
ring up call (telephone)
rubber eraser
sanitary towel sanitary napkin/pad
sausage roll sausage wrapped in a flaky pastry
Scotch egg hard-boiled egg wrapped in sausage meat
self-catering accommodation with kitchen facilities, rented by the week
sellotape Scotch tape
serviette napkin
single ticket one-way ticket
sleeping policeman speed bumps
smalls underwear
snogging kissing and cuddling
solicitor lawyer
starkers buck naked
starters appetizers
stone 14 pounds (weight)
subway underground pedestrian passageway
surgical spirit rubbing alcohol
suss out figure out
swede rutabaga
sweet dessert
sweets candy
ta thank you
taxi rank taxi stand
tea towel dish towel
telly TV
theater live stage (not "cinema")
tick a check mark

tight as a fish's bum cheapskate (water-tight)
tights panty hose
tipper lorry dump truck
tin can
to let for rent
top hole first rate
topping excellent
top up refill a drink
torch flashlight
towpath path along a river or canal
tube subway
twee quaint, cute
underground subway
VAT value-added tax
verge grassy edge of road
verger church official
wellingtons, wellies rubber boots
wee urinate
whacked exhausted
witter on gab and gab
yob hooligan
zebra crossing crosswalk
zed the letter "z"

Road Scholar Feedback for
GREAT BRITAIN & IRELAND 1999

We're all in the same travelers' school of hard knocks. Your feedback helps us improve this guidebook for future travelers. Please fill this out (attach more info or any tips/favorite discoveries if you like) and send it to us. As thanks for your help, we'll send you our quarterly travel newsletter free for one year. Thanks! **Rick**

Of the recommended accommodations/restaurants used, which was:

Best _____

    Why? _____

Worst _____

    Why? _____

Of the sights/experiences/destinations recommended by this book, which was:

Most overrated _____

    Why? _____

Most underrated _____

    Why? _____

Best ways to improve this book:

_____

I'd like a free newsletter subscription:

___ Yes   ___ No   ___ Already on list

_____
Name

_____
Address

_____
City, State, Zip

_____
E-mail Address

Please send to: ETBD, Box 2009, Edmonds, WA 98020

Jubilee 2000—Let's Celebrate the Millennium by Forgiving Third World Debt

Let's ring in the millennium by convincing our government to for-give the debt owed to us by the world's poorest countries. Imagine spending over half your income on interest payments alone. You and I are creditors and poor countries owe us more than they can pay.

Jubilee 2000 is a worldwide movement of concerned people and groups—religious and secular—working to cancel the international debts of the poorest countries by the year 2000.

Debt ruins people: In the poorest countries, money needed for health care, education, and other vital services is diverted to interest payments.

Mozambique, with a per capita income of $90 and life expect-ancy of 40, spends over half its national income on interest. This poverty brings social unrest, civil war, and often costly humanitarian intervention by the U.S.A. To chase export dollars, desperate coun-tries ruin their environment. As deserts grow and rain forests shrink, the world suffers. Of course, the real suffering is among local people born long after some dictator borrowed (and squandered) that money. As interest is paid, entire populations go hungry.

Who owes what and why? Mozambique is one of 41 countries defined by the World Bank as "Heavily Indebted Poor Countries." In total, they owe $200 billion. Because these debts are unlikely to be paid, their market value is only a tenth of the face value (about $20 billion). The U.S.A.'s share is under $2 billion.

How can debt be canceled? This debt is owed mostly to the U.S.A., Japan, Germany, Britain, and France either directly or through the World Bank. We can forgive the debt owed directly to us and pay the market value (usually 10 percent) of the debts owed to the World Bank. We have the resources. (Norway, another wealthy creditor nation, just unilaterally forgave its Third World debt.) All America needs is the political will . . . people power.

While many of these poor nations are now democratic, corrup-tion is still a concern. A key to Jubilee 2000 is making certain that debt relief reduces poverty in a way that benefits ordinary people: women, farmers, children, and so on.

Let's celebrate the new millennium by giving poor countries a break. For the sake of peace, fragile young democracies, the environ-ment, and countless real people, forgiving this debt is the right thing for us in the rich world to do.

Tell Washington, DC.: If our government knows this is what we want, it can happen. Learn more, write letters, lobby legislators, or even start a local Jubilee 2000 campaign. For details, contact Jubilee 2000 (tel. 202/783-3566, www.j2000usa.org). For informa-tion on lobbying Congress on J2000, contact Bread for the World (tel. 800/82-BREAD, www.bread.org).

Faxing Your Hotel Reservation

Most hotel managers know basic "hotel English." Faxing is the preferred method for reserving a room. It's more accurate and cheaper than telephoning and much faster than writing a letter. Use this handy form for your fax. Photocopy and fax away.

One-Page Fax

To: _____ @ _____
       hotel   *fax*

From: _____ @ _____
         name   *fax*

Today's date: ___ /_____ /___
                  day *month* *year*

Dear Hotel _____,

Please make this reservation for me:

Name: _____

Total # of people: _____   # of rooms: _____   # of nights: _____

Arriving: ___ /_____ /___ My time of arrival (24-hr clock): _____
             day *month* *year* (I will telephone if I will be late)

Departing: ___ /_____ /___
                day *month* *year*

Room(s):   Single___   Double___   Twin___   Triple___   Quad___

With: Toilet___   Shower___   Bath___   Sink only___

Special needs: View___   Quiet___   Cheapest Room___

Credit card: Visa___   MasterCard___   American Express___

Card #: _____

Expiration Date:_____

Name on card: _____

You may charge me for the first night as a deposit. Please fax or mail me confirmation of my reservation, along with the type of room reserved, the price, and whether the price includes breakfast. Thank you.

_____
Signature

_____
Name

_____
Address

_____
City   *State*   *Zip Code*   *Country*

_____
E-mail Address

INDEX

Accommodations, 21–27
Airports: Dublin, 229; London, 82–83, 318
Avebury, 101, 107–108

Banking, 7
Bath, 89–110
Beatles, 158–159
Bed-and-breakfasts, 23–25
Beer, 28–29, 315
Blackpool, 153–159
Britain: background, 305–312; architecture, 309–311; history, 307–309; Royal Families, 308–309; TV, 312

Car, 18–20; rental, 17–18; vs. train, 13–15
Channel, London–Paris crossing, 84–85
Churchill, 41,47,59,119–120
Climate, 5, 319
Cook, Captain James, 192
Costs, trip, 2–4
Cotswolds, 111–130

Eating in Britain, 27–29
Edinburgh, 195–212; Edinburgh Festival, 205–206; Royal Mile, 200–203
England: Avebury stone circle,101, 107–108; Bamburgh, 194; Bath, 89–110; Beamish Open–Air Museum, 192; Beatrix Potter's Farm, 167; Bibury, 119; Blackpool, 153–159; Blenheim Palace, 119–120; Bourton–on–the–Water, 115; Broad Campden, 123–124; Broadway, 119; Cambridge, 86–88; Castle Howard, 183; Castlerigg Stone Circle, 165–166; Chipping Campden, 119, 122–123; Cirencester, 119; Cotswolds, 111–130; Coventry, 129; Derwentwater, 163–166; Wordsworth's Dove Cottage, 166; Durham, 184–194;

Glastonbury, 101, 103–104; Hadrian's Wall, 189–192; Hidcote Manor, 119; Holy Island, 194; Ironbridge Gorge, 131–137; Keswick, 162–163; Lake District, 160–172; Liverpool, 158–159; London, 32–88; Moreton–in–Marsh, 114, 115, 124; North York Moors, 182– 183; Staithes, 193; Stanton, 118; Stanway, 116–118; Stonehenge, 101, 108; Stow–on–the–Wold, 114, 121–122; Stratford–upon–Avon, 126–128; Ullswater, 167; Upper and Lower Slaughter, 116; Warwick Castle, 128–129; Wells, 101, 104–107; Whitby, 192–193; Windemere Lake District, 166–167; Woodstock, 120; Wookey Hole, 107; York, 173–183
Europe Through the Back Door, 11–12
Exchange rates, 4

Ferries; England–Ireland, 151–152, 219; Ireland–France, 241–242; Ireland–Scotland, 296
Flying to London, 82–83
Food, 27–29

Galway, 263–272
Glastonbury, 101, 103–104
Guidebooks, recommended, 11

Heart attack, on a plate, 27
Herriot, James, 183
Highlands, Scottish, 220–225
Hikes, Lake District, 163, 164–165, 166, 167, 168
Hostels, 26
Hotels, 21–27; reservation form, 325

Industrial Revolution, 132–134
Ireland, 226–304: Antrim Coast, 297–304; Aran Islands, 272–277;

Belfast, 287–296; Blasket Islands, 258–259; Burren, 277–283; Cliffs of Moher, 278–279; County Clare, 277–283; Dingle Peninsula, 245–262; Dingle Town, 248–253; Doolin, 278–279; Dublin, 226–244; Dun Aengus, 274; Ennis, 277, 281–283; Galway, 263–272; Glendalough, 242–244; Inishmor, 273–277; Kilronan, 273–277; Kinvarra, 281, 282; Lisdoonvarna, 279, 282; Minard Castle, 259; Tralee, 260–262; Wicklow Mountains, 242–244
Ironbridge Gorge, 131–137
Ireland, background, 312–316

Lake District, 160–172
London, 32–88; day trips, 67–68; theater, 65–67

Mail, 21
Maps, 12
Meals, 27–29

North Wales, 138–152
Northern Ireland, 284–304

Oban, 213–225

Philosophy, Back Door, 31
Potter, Beatrix, 167
Pubs, 28–29

Roman Britain: Cirencester, 119; Hadrian's Wall, 189–192
Royal Shakespeare Company, 66
Ruthin, 140–143; medieval banquet, 140–141

Scotland, 195–225; Ben Nevis, 222; Caledonian Canal, 222; Culloden Battlefield, 223; Edinburgh, 195–212; Glencoe, 220–222; Highlands, Scottish, 220–225; Inverness, 223–224; Iona, Island, 218–220; Mull, Isle of, 218, 220; Loch Ness,
222–223; Oban, 214–225; Pitlochry, 224
Shakespeare's birthplace, 126
Sightseeing priorities, 5–6
Slate mining, 150
Sleep code, 22
South Wales, 108–110
Stonehenge, 101, 108
Stow–in–the–Wold, 114, 121–122
Stratford–upon–Avon, 126–128

Tax, refunds, 6
Telephoning, 20–21, 316–318; directory, 317–318
Tourist information, 10–11, 34
Tours, 12–13
Transportation, 13–20; bus, 15, 17; car, 17–18; flights, 15–17; train, 13–18

Vocabulary, British–Yankee, 320–322

Wales, 108–110, 138–152; North Wales, 138–152: Beddgelert, 149; Betws–y–Coed, 148; Blaenau Ffestiniog, 150–151; Caernarfon Castle, 147–148; Conwy, 144–146; King Edward's Castles, 143–144; Llangollen, 143; Llechweld Slate Mine Tour, 150; Ruthin, 140–143; Snowdonia National Park, 148–150; Woolen Mills, Trefriw, 148–149; South Wales, 108–110: Caerphilly Castle, 109; Cardiff, 108; St. Briavals Castle, 110; Tintern Abbey ruins, 109–110; Welsh Folk Museum, 108–109; Wye River Valley, 110
Weather, 5, 319
Wells, 101, 104–107
Welsh language, 138
Wordsworth Country, 166–167

York, 173–183
Youth Hostels, 26

A new book from Rick!

1978   1998

Rick Steves' Postcards from Europe
25 Years of Travel Tales from America's Favorite Guidebook Writer

TRAVEL GURU RICK STEVES has been exploring Europe through the Back Door for 25 years, sharing his tricks and discoveries in guidebooks and on TV. Now, in *Rick Steves' Postcards from Europe*, Rick shares his favorite stories and his off-beat European friends.

Postcards takes you on the fantasy trip of a lifetime. While goofy and inspirational, it's informative, too—giving you a close-up look at contemporary Europeans.

You'll meet Marie-Alice, the Parisian restaurateur who sniffs a whiff of moldy cheese and says, "It smells like zee feet of angels." In an Alpine village, meet Olle, the schoolteacher who lets Rick pet his edelweiss, and Walter, the innkeeper who schemes with Rick to create a fake Swiss tradition. In Italy, cruise with Piero through his "alternative Venice" and learn why all Venetian men are mama's boys.

Postcards also tracks Rick's passion for wandering—from his first "Europe-through-the-gutter" trips, through his rocky early tours, to his career as a travel writer and host of a public television series.

These 272 pages of travel tales are told in that funny, down-to-earth style that makes Rick his Mom's favorite guidebook writer.

Rick Steves' Postcards from Europe is available at your local bookstore. To get Rick's free travel newsletter, call (425) 771-8303 or visit www.ricksteves.com. For a free catalog or to order any John Muir Publications book, call (800) 888-7504.